FISHER H

ORIENTATION – FISHER ROW 1578-1850

Agnas 1578

Loggan 1675

Hoggar 1850

UFR   Upper Fisher Row   MFR   Middle Fisher Row   LFR   Lower Fisher Row

Note: In the original maps by Agas and Loggan the south is to the top of the page (see pp. 3 and 30). Here they have been turned round to bring them into conformity with the modern convention.

FISHER ROW

Fishermen, Bargemen, and Canal
Boatmen in Oxford, 1500-1900

MARY PRIOR

Sometime Calouste Gulbenkian Research Fellow,
Lucy Cavendish College, Cambridge

PHILLIMORE

2011

Published by
PHILLIMORE & CO. LTD
Andover, Hampshire, England
www.phillimore.co.uk

Originally Published in the United States
By Oxford University Press, New York, 1982.

© Mary Prior 1982

ISBN   978-1-86077-652-6

Printed and bound in Great Britain

Manufacturing managed by
Jellyfish Print Solutions Ltd

In memory of
ARTHUR PRIOR
who preferred the Severn

Acknowledgements

This book has been written over a lengthy period and during this time I have received so much generous help from so large a number of people that it is not possible to name and thank them all individually; nor, indeed do I know their names in every case. It is painful to have to select, but this seems no reason for not trying to thank as many as I can within a reasonable space, and acknowledge with gratitude the help of many unnamed as well.

First I would like to thank all those who have shared their recollections with me of Fisher Row, of St Thomas's, of the River and the Canal: Mr H. Arnold of Willaston, Mr H. Ayres, Mr F. J. Beesley, Mr J. H. Beesley, Mrs I. Bostock, Miss May Buckle, Mrs Burden (née Kilby), Mr W. Cox, the late Mr L. Cox, Mr R. de la Mare, Mrs Dixey, Mr R. A. J. Earl, Mr W. Forman, Mr and Mrs H. Gardiner, Mr L. Gunter, Mrs A. Hall, the late Mr J. James, Mr and Mrs Jennings, Mr E. W. Jennings, Mr F. Lay, Mrs J. Lowe, Mrs M. Masserella (née Cox) of Weymouth, Mr W. C. A. Molyneaux, the late Mr and Mrs J. Skinner, Mr and Mrs A. Tustin, Mr H. L. Webb, Mrs D. Weller (née Tustin). Also several people whose names I never knew, but who have talked to me illuminatingly about the Row and parish at various times. I should also like to thank Mr Don Chapman('Anthony Wood' of the *Oxford Mail*) through whose good offices I met many of these people; also Messrs J. J. Tawney, and W. G. Bowen whose genealogical researches on forebears in the parish have been so generously laid open to me.

Secondly I would like to thank the two women's colleges which gave me the opportunity in mid-life to become a historian. The belief that education does not end at 21 or 25 receives fairly general lip-service nowadays, but not always much practical help. So I would thank St Hilda's College, Oxford, where I was a post-graduate student, and Lucy Cavendish College, Cambridge, where as a Calouste Gulbenkian Research Fellow this book took its final shape. Lucy Cavendish must also be thanked for a grant towards the preparation of the MS for publication. The Greening Lamborn Trust gave me a grant for travel expenses, and the William Abel Pantin Charitable Trust a grant towards the artwork. I would like to thank them both.

My thanks are due in no small measure to Canon John Lucas for arranging for me to have access to St Thomas's parish records. Oxford librarians and archivists have been unfailingly helpful, and I owe an especial debt to Dr D. M. Barratt and Mr David Vaisey of the Bodleian Library and to the staff of the Reserve Desk in Duke Humfrey; to Mr Malcolm Graham of the Local History Collections Library, The Oxfordshire County Library, and his staff, as well as to Miss Shirley Barnes of the Oxfordshire County Record Office and Mr John Wing of the Library at Christ Church. I owe a lesser but real debt to many other libraries and librarians: in Oxford to those of Lincoln College and New College; in Cambridge the University Library; in London to the Public Record Office, The British Library, the old British Transport Historical Records, and the Corporation of London Record Office (and Miss B. R. Masters); in the provinces, the County Record Offices of Berkshire, Gloucestershire, Staffordshire, Warwickshire, Wiltshire, and Worcestershire; the Coventry City Record Office, the Birmingham, Reading, and Swindon Public Libraries.

At the time this book was being written the Oxfordshire staff of the Victoria County History was at work on the volume on Oxford, and I am grateful for their generous help, notably to Mr Alan Crossley, Mr Christopher Day, and Dr Janet Cooper who discussed the topography of Oxford in great detail.

For practical and technical help of many varieties I would like to thank Prof. Peter Geach, Dr Anthony Kenny, and Dr Kit Fine; Mrs Danny Fine and Miss Gabriel Porter; Malcolm Chapman, Anthony Hyder, and my brother, Andrew Wilkinson; Martin Prior, my son, and Ann Prior, my daughter; my heroic typists, Mrs Pamela Street and Miss Eleanor Chance. Like so many scholars I remember with gratitude both the late Dr Richard Hunt and the late Mrs Kit Hunt. Many people have helped me with material on canals, and I would especially like to mention Messrs A. J. Lewery, Kingsley Belsten, Michael LeRoy and Harry Hansen, with whom I have discussed canal life at length. Dorothy McLaren and Barbara Todd have discussed earlier periods and many wider aspects of my subject; Hanni Bretscher, Jean Robin, Lawrence Chase, and Michael Bull have read drafts, and I have profited from their patient discussion, detailed criticism, and eye for errors. To all these I owe a deep debt of gratitude, and also to Raphael Samuel who has discussed, stimulated and encouraged this work over many years.

Finally and pre-eminently I would like to thank Dr Joan Thirsk who has read and discussed so many drafts, given me so much of her time, encouraged me over so many years, and forced me to generalize and think for myself in a field which is notoriously difficult.

My husband lived only long enough to see me embark on this project. His sense of the joy of intellectual labour, and its importance, was infectious, and has borne the book along to its conclusion.

Oxford, 1980   Mary Prior

PUBLISHER'S NOTE

The author is most grateful to the following bodies and individuals through whose kindness the photographs and prints in this book were made available. In particular she would like to thank for the pictures indicated: The Oxford University Press for Nos 1 and 2, from the *Oxford Almanack 1835* and *1837*; the *Oxford Mail and Times* for Nos. 3 and 8; The Bodleian Library for No. 7; The Oxfordshire County Libraries for No. 5 and the photograph on the dustjacket; Mr Anthony Hyder for No. 6, and Dr A. C. Wilkinson for No. 9.

She would also like to thank The British Association for the Advancement of Science for permission to reproduce the map 'The Geology of Oxford' from 'The Growth of the City of Oxford' in A. F. Martin and R. W. Steel (ed.), *The Oxford Region* (OUP, 1954); Dr R. J. Morris for permission to use Map I from 'The Friars and Paradise' (*Oxoniensia*, 1971, vol. 36, p. 74) as a basis for Fig. 1.3, 'The Bounds of the Parish of St Thomas'; and the General Editor of the Victoria History of the Counties of England, the Institute of Historical Research, the University of London, for permission to use their map of The Liberty, *The Victoria County History of Oxfordshire, IV, The City of Oxford*, as a basis for her map of The Free Waters.

She is also grateful to the following for permission to quote from manuscript material: to the Archivist, Christ Church, for Ch.Ch. Archives, MS estates 77, fos. 230-2; to the Controller of Public Relations and Publicity, British Railways Board, for RAIL 855/106; The Archivist, the City of Oxford for permission to quote F.5.4, fos. 252 and E.4.9, and The Archivist of the Oxfordshire County Record Office for permission to quote Wi/VII/18 18 and CH.N. III/ii/ 14; Mr H. L. Webb and Mrs M. Massarella for permission to quote from their letters.

I acknowledge with thanks permission granted by George Allen and Unwin (publishers) Ltd. to quote from *The Inland Waterways of Great Britain*, by L. T. C. Rolt.

Contents

List of Plates   XV

List of Tables   XVII

List of Family Trees   XIX

List of Figures and Maps   XXI

List of Abbreviations   XXIII

Key to Abbreviations used in Figures and Family Trees   XXIV

INTRODUCTION: *The Search for Fisher Row*   1
   i.   Its Situation   1
  ii.   Its Discovery   4
 iii.   Means and Methods   12
 iv.   The Lessons of the Row   19

I: FROM REFORMATION TO INDUSTRIAL REVOLUTION

1. *Parish, River, and Row*   29
   i.   Orientation: The Parish and its Bounds   29
  ii.   Secular and Religious Overlords   34
 iii.   The Castle Mill and Fisher Row   40
 iv.   Disputed Ground   43
  v.   The Dissolution of the Monasteries and the Row   51

2. *The Fishermen of Fisher Row*   55
   i.   The Market for Fish   55
  ii.   The Fishermen and the Free Waters   61
 iii.   Fishermen's Work   66
 iv.   Leases and Landlords   75
  v.   The Families of the Row   82

vi.	The Wodesons	83
vii.	The Hickses of the Second and Third Tenements, Lower Fisher Row	89
viii.	The Bonner alias Pittses and the Curtices of the First Tenement	97

3.	*The Bargemen of Fisher Row*	105
i.	The Medieval River	105
ii.	The Improvement of the River	112
iii.	Fisher Row and the Navigation	123
iv.	Bargemen's Work	129
v.	Barging Families and the Linear Community	136
vi.	The Tawneys and the Clarkes of Lower Fisher Row	139
vii.	The Gardners of Upper Fisher Row	153
viii.	Middle Fisher Row and the Crawfords	166
iv.	The Bargemen and the Community	170

II. FROM THE INDUSTRIAL REVOLUTION TO THE DISINTEGRATION OF THE COMMUNITY

4.	*Canal, River, and Row*	180
i.	Reorientation	180
ii.	Alternative Routes	183
iii.	Alternative Futures	195

5.	*The Canal Boatmen and the Row*	199
i.	A New Sort of Boatman	199
ii.	The Boatman and his Work	202
iii.	The Social Framework of Canal Life	206
iv.	The Formation of the Canal Community	218
v.	The Community of the Row, 1841-71	229
vi.	Stability and Continuity	233
vii.	Canal Boatmen and the Extended Family— Fishermen and the Nuclear Family	248
viii.	Kin and Community	253

6.	*The Decline of Fisher Row*	259
i.	The Timetable of Decline	259
ii.	Competition and Feud: The Bossoms and the Beesleys	261
iii.	The Fishermen and their Common Rights	270

iv.	Reform and Rights of Common	276
v.	The Beesleys v. the Reformed Council	286
vi.	The Beesleys v. the Thames Conservancy	292
vii.	Diversification and the dispersal of the Fishermen	298
viii.	Railways and the Canal	306
ix.	Measuring Decline	308
x.	The Church, the Boatmen, and the Funeral of Fanny Bossom	310
xi.	The Dark Years	313
xii.	From the World of the Row to the World of the Cut	316
7.	*History and Memory*	325
i.	Physical Destruction	325
ii.	The Living Memory	327
Appendices		347
I.	Building a Mill	347
II.	The Extent of the Free Waters	348
III.	The Leases of Upper Fisher Row	351
IV.	Calculations of the Cost of Bow-haling, *c*. 1770	364
V.	Upper Fisher Row: Census 1841-71	368
VI.	1841 Census, Middle Fisher Row	372
Bibliography		375
Indices		
1.	Index of Names	387
2.	General Index	399

List of Plates

(between pages 232-3)

1. The Castle Mill, *c*.1857, by J. H. Le Keux

2. Hythe Bridge, Wharf and Canal

3. Lower Fisher Row, 1951, showing The Lock

4. Middle Fisher Row and The Nag's Head, *c*.1909

5. Upper Fisher Row, *c*.1885

6. The Tawneys' House at the foot of Lower Fisher Row, 1972

7. The Floating Chapel, *c*.1860

8. Mrs Rose Skinner and Miss Jean Humphries emptying a boat at Juxon Street, 1956

9. The Tombstone of a Family of Boatmen, Oseney Cemetery

List of Tables

2.1. Archbishop Cranmer's Lenten Fare   58
2.2. Comparison of Average Annual Matriculands and
      Total Number of Fishermen's Apprentices per
      Decenium   72
3.1. Tenements of Upper Fisher Row   164
5.1. The Landlords of the Boatmen's Pubs of the Row
      c.1797-1903   210
5.2. Comparison of the Number of Boat and Bargemen
      in St Thomas's Baptismal Register, 1813-23   219
5.3. The Incidence of Canal Boatmen in the Parish of
      St Thomas according to the Baptismal Register   221
5.4. The Assimilation of Boatmen into Middle
      Fisher Row and Hythe Bridge Street   223
5.5. Immigration into St Thomas's Parish by
      Staffordshire and Warwickshire Boatmen   224
5.6. Distribution of Canal Boatmen in St Thomas's
      Parish according to the Censuses, 1841-1871   233
5.7. The Descendants of Thomas Beesley the elder,
      1841-1871   253
6.1. Decline of Fishermen in St Thomas's Parish,
      1813-1890   299
6.2. The Trade of the Oxford Canal   308
6.3. Marriages of Boatmen and Baptisms of their
      children by Decades, St Thomas's Parish   310
6.4. Intermarriages between Boatmen and
      the Daughters of Boatmen in St Thomas's Parish,
      1861-1920   319

List of Family Trees

2.1	The Wodeson Family	84
2.2	The Hickses of Lower Fisher Row	88
2.3	The Bonner alias Pittses and Curtices of Lower Fisher Row	96
3.1.	Henry Hicks's Connections with barging families along the River	137
3.2.	Tawney of Lower Fisher Row	142-3
3.3.	The Tomkins Family of Abingdon	150
3.4.	The Gardners of Upper Fisher Row	154-5
3.5.	The Crawfords of St Thomas's Parish and Northmoor	165
5.1.	The Beesley Family of St Thomas's, Part I	226-7
5.2.	The Howkins Family	237
5.3.	The Corbeys	244
5.4.	The Beesleys of St Thomas's, Part II	250-1
5.5.	The Common Descent of the Bossoms and the Beesleys from the Gardners	256
5.6.	The Beesleys of Upper Fisher Row: Contrasting Occupational Patterns	257
6.1.	The Bossoms (tentative)	262-3
6.2.	The Skinners	317
6.3.	The Gibbons	320

List of Figures and Maps

Frontis. Orientation – Fisher Row, 1578-1850

Intro. 1. Fisher Row, from David Loggan's Map of
Oxford, 1675   3

1.1. Fisher Row, from Ralph Agas's Map of Oxford,
1578, engraves by R. Whittlesey, 1728   30

1.2. The Geology of Oxford, from E. W. Gilbert,
'The Growth of the City of Oxford', in
Martin, A. F., and Steel, R. W., eds. *The
Oxford Region*   31

1.3. The Bounds of the Parish of St Thomas   32

1.4. The Basic Structure of Waterways Supplying
a Mill   41

1.5. The Evolution of Waterways West of Oxford,
1182-*c*.1578, resulting from the dispute
between Oseney and Oxford   45

2.1. The Castle and Warham Bank, engraved by
J. Skelton, *Oxonia Antiqua Restaurata* (1823),
from a drawing at Christ Church, before 1618   56

2.2 The Leases of Christ Church and the City in
Fisher Row and the Swans Nest Area   74

2.3. Tenants and Subtenants of Tenements 1-6
Lower Fisher Row   78-9

3.1. Map of the Thames   106

3.2. St Thomas's Parish, 1750. Detail from
John Taylor's Map of Oxford   156

3.3.   The Changing River: the Navigation Channel
            of the Thames and other Waterways in
            St Thomas's Parish   157

4.1.   St Thomas's Parish, 1850. Detail from
            Robert Hoggar's Map of Oxford   180

4.2.   The Sequence in which the Canals were
            Opened to Navigation   184

4.3.   Population of St Thomas's Parish, 1672-1841.
            Births and Deaths by Calendar Year   193

5.1.   Diagrammatic Plan of Middle Fisher Row
            and Hythe Bridge Street in 1829   212

5.2.   Descendants of the Gardner Family in
            Upper Fisher Row by Deceniums, from
            leases, 1671-1831, and from the Census,
            1841-71   254

7.1.   Marriages between Families of Canal Boat-
            men Listed by Mrs Burden   342

App. II.1. The Free Waters of the City of Oxford   349

App. III.1. Upper Fisher Row, Late 17th Century,
            based on Loggan's Map of 1675   352

App. III.2. Upper Fisher Row, Mid-18th Century,
            based on the Map of J. Taylor, published
            in 1750   353

List of Abbreviations

Athenae	Anthony Wood, *Athenae Oxonienses*, ed. P. Bliss (4 vols. 3rd ed., 1813-20)
BL	British Library
Ch. Ch.	Christ Church
City	Oxford City Archives
Council Acts	*Oxford Council Acts,* 1583-1801, ed H. E. Salter and M. G. Hobson (6 vols., OHS, 1928-62)
Hearne, Collections	*Remarks and Collections of Thomas Hearne*, ed. C. E. Doble and others (11 vols., OHS, 1928162)
JOJ	*Jackson's Oxford Journal*
LP Henry VIII	*Letters and Papers, Foreign and Domestic of the Reign of Henry VIII*
OCP	*Oxford City Properties*, ed. H. E. Salter (OHS, lxxxiii, 1926)
OED	*Oxford English Dictionary*
OHS	Oxford Historical Society
Oseney	*The Cartulary of Oseney Abbey*, ed. H. E. Salter (6 vols., OHS, 1929-36)
Oxon.	*Oxoniensia*
PP. Eng.	Parliamentary Papers
PRO	Public Record Office
RO	Record Office

Thacker, *Highway*	Fred. S. Thacker, *The Thames Highway* (2 vols., 1914-20, London and Kew, repr. 1968)
UBD	*The Universal British Directory of Trade, Commerce and Manufacture* (4 vols., London, 1790-7)
VCH	*Victoria County History*, followed by the appropriate abbreviations for counties
Wood, *City*	Anthony Wood, *History of the City of Oxford*, ed. Andrew Clark (3 vols., OHS, 1889-99)
Wood, *Life*	Anthony Wood, *The Life and Times of Anthony Wood*, ed. Andrew Clark (5 vols., OHS, 1891-1900)

Note: The name of the Library is given on the first citation of a class of material, except in the case of the Bodleian Library, Oxford.

Key to Abbreviations used in Figures and Family Trees

a.f.	admitted a freeman	St B	Barriabas' parish
ap.	apprentice	St E	Ebbes parish
B	canal boatman	St F	Frideswides parish
Bam	bargeman	St M.M.	St Mary Magdalen
BaM	bargemaster		parish
d.	died	St P. le B.	St Peter le Bailey
d/o	daughter of		parish
e.s.	eldest son	St P.	St Pauls
F	fisherman	wid.,	widow
F.T.	family tree	y.s.	youngest son
L.D.	Lady Day	1643	date of baptism
Mich.	Michaelmas	(1643)	date of marriage
n.k.	not known	=	married
s/o	son of	?	doubtful
St A.	Aldate's parish	+	died in infancy

Note: Baptisms, burials, and marriages are in the parish of St Thomas unless otherwise indicated. All dates are given New Style.

The Search for Fisher Row

I. ITS SITUATION

Fisher Row lies in the parish of St Thomas, which is, with the possible exception of St Ebbes, the seediest parish in Oxford at the present day. Once these parishes were beautiful places. In St Ebbes were the great houses of the Black and Grey Friars, whose fame was known throughout all Christendom, whilst in St Thomas's parish stood two abbeys. Nothing remains of the friaries, and little more of Rewley and Oseney Abbey. The traveller, alighting at the railway station, must traverse the larger part of St Thomas's before he reaches the city centre, but even the most determined sentimentalist is unlikely to be moved by its streets. As he follows the stream of traffic into the town he will see nothing to arouse his interest in the history of this ravaged parish. He will cross the Castle Mill Stream with scarcely a glance, and it is unlikely that he will notice Fisher Row itself, which lies on the western bank of the stream. Already the wall of Worcester College is in sight. He follows it gratefully, and leaves the parish behind him as he turns into Beaumont Street. Here at last is the Oxford he has come to see. Fisher Row is not, and never has been on the tourist map. Perhaps in the early 18th century some antiquary, on his way to view the ruins of Oseney, which still stood at that time, might have paused, remarking the contrast between the low line of hovels which fringed the water, and the great ruined tower of Oseney which arose beyond them; but it is unlikely, for men had yet to be taught to admire the picturesque.

Nevertheless he would have done well to look at Fisher Row more closely, for the history of the Row is even older than

that of Oseney itself. It stretches back into unrecorded time.
When Oseney was founded in 1129 by Robert d'Oili, the Keeper
of the Castle, it was given certain houses which stood on the
weir-ham (*supra waram*) of his mill as part of its original
endowment; but who built these houses, and when, we do not
know.[1] As for the name Fisher Row, that came much later.

Fisher Row was the home of the boat-people of Oxford for
many generations: fishermen, bargemen, and canal boatmen.
The oldest group was the fishermen. The first extant rental of
Oseney Abbey for the area, one for 1278, is very detailed, and
it shows three fishermen living there then.[2] Few rentals are
so careful, and it is therefore impossible to be sure whether
boatmen lived there continuously throughout the Middle Ages.
It seems almost certain that the bank of the mill-stream was
abandoned after the Black Death, but little else is clear, except
that from time to time, when the occupations of inhabitants
do happen to be given, sometimes fishermen appear. From
the 16th century records are abundant, and they show three
sorts of boatmen in the Row. From the 16th century until the
end of the 19th century fishermen lived there. Bargemen (that
is river boatmen) colonised the undeveloped part of the Row
in the 17th century, when the river navigation was improved;
canal boatmen married into the community after the Oxford
Canal was opened in 1790. At its greatest extent, between
1790 and the 1840s, it contained from 300 to 400 boat-people
– family included. Long before 1790 Fisher Row had become
a very tight-knit community of boat-people who were united
both by occupation and kinship. As well they married others
in the same occupation elsewhere on the river, for the Oxford
community formed a part of a larger community, a linear
community stretching the length of the Thames. Fisher Row
was by no means unique, such communities were found all
along the Thames. Alexander Pope, who lived at Twickenham,
noted their existence 'in ev'ry town where Thamis rolls
his tyde':

> At ev'ry door are sunburn matrons seen,
> Mending old nets to catch the scaly fry.

Yet until the middle of the 19th century the community in Fisher Row escaped description and comment.

---

[1] *Oseney*, I.1.   [2] *Oseney*, III. 117.

There is no hint of its existence in Anthony Wood: 'Fish Rew took its name from one Fish living there in King James' time.' Certainly there was a fishmonger, Thomas Fish, who gave evidence in a dispute about the land on which the Row stood in the reign of James I, but there is no evidence that he ever lived there.[3] It throws a revealing light on the mind of Anthony

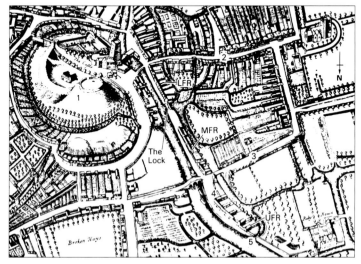

UFR = Upper Fisher Row   MFR = Middle Fisher Row   LFR = Lower Fisher Row
1. The Castle   2. St Thomas's High Street   3. Hythe Bridge Street   4. Wharf   5. The Lasher

Fig. Intro. 1. Fisher Row, from David Loggan's map of Oxford, 1675. Note: The 'upside-down' orientation of this map is out of line with the modern convention.

Wood that he should prefer such an explanation of the name, when in his day there were boats along the Row for all to see. David Loggan's map of Oxford, which was published in 1675, shows four boats moored there (see Fig. Intro. 1). It was perhaps too well known, too ordinary a feature of the town for description. Thomas Hearne, the 18th-century antiquary, certainly knew the place, for he refers to more than one of the boatmen by name; he probably employed boatmen from here for excursions on the river, as did Parson Woodforde the late 18th-century diarist.

[3] Wood, *City*, I. 314, n. 1; *Oseney*, III. 18.

The first explicit reference to the community is to be found in a sentimental Victorian guide-book, *The Book of the Thames*, by Mr and Mrs S. C. Hall, which appeared in 1859, when the community was already in decline. The Halls approached Oxford from upstream: '... as we near one of the most ancient of its bridges – Hithe, or Hythe, Bridge – we observe a small cluster of rude and primitive houses, the small dwellings of a race of fishermen, who have followed that calling from father to son, in unbroken succession, for several hundred years.[4] The description has an air of being mere sentimental embroidery, though the qualification 'several' might perhaps suggest otherwise. The book proceeds with a mixture of guide-book descriptions and anecdotage more appealing to Victorian than modern taste. Confidence is quickly lost.

In 1881 'a more explicit and trustworthy account of the community is to be found. The politics of Oxford were notoriously corrupt, and the second Select Committee in a quarter of a century was inquiring into the conduct of an election. There were altogether too many candidates' committee rooms, and the number of 'messengers' attached to these rooms, often drunk, usually poor, suggested corruption. An over-zealous agent was being forced to justify the existence of these rooms one by one: 'Q. 1802. What need was there for this establishment at Howkins, when you had a committee room at Hollybush Row, with 14 messengers?–...There is a peculiar population round Howkin's ... It would embrace Hythe Bridge Street and Upper and Lower Fisher Row, inhabited chiefly by fishermen and boatmen: and those men that were at that committee room were intimately acquainted with them.'[5]

II. ITS DISCOVERY

The fact that Fisher Row should have existed for so long unobserved, only to be described when it was in decline makes it abundantly clear how sketchy is our knowledge of working-class life in the past. A wall of silence divides us from the

---

[4] Mr and Mrs S. C. Hall, *The Book of the Thames* (London, 1859), 86.
[5] PP. Eng. 1881 /xliv (C-2856), *Report of the Commissioners into the Existence of Corrupt Practices in the City of Oxford*, 43.

world of ordinary men and women before about 1820, which it is difficult to penetrate. After this date there are descriptions by men of wide sympathies, letters, and even the diaries of working-class men, but before this date little is to be found. The story of how Fisher Row was discovered illustrates very well the problems to be encountered in breaking through this barrier.

Initially I had no interest in the study of Fisher Row or any other community: I was interested in the origins of canal-boat decoration. The first English canals were built in the second half of the 18th century, and the narrow boats which are peculiar to the canals of the Midlands were worked by a remarkable group of boat-people. They were described as sui generis, a race apart, as water gypsies. The sense of their being an alien group was increased by the distinctive style in which they decorated their boats. It was bold and colourful, and governed by a strong sense of tradition. Though there had been much speculation about it at the time there had been little attempt to discover its origin. I decided to look for an answer.

At first results came swiftly. An excellent description of canal boat decoration was written by John Hollingshead in 1858 – a description of a boat which was then in need of re-painting. It showed that at that time boats were decorated in exactly the same style as in the 20th century, with wreaths of flowers, castles, mountains, and lakes.[6] Yet though I read memoirs, books of travel, Parliamentary papers, newspapers, and the reports of missionary societies, I found no detailed description written at an earlier period. Only one other account, written by George Mogridge, described the appearance of the boats in any detail, and this was tantalising, for it suggested so much, and said so little:

The View from the Warwick Canal, as I passed was a busy scene ... and the loading of the boats at Pickfords all contributed to the general effect. The freighted vessels, their packages piled high, covered with tarpauling, and fancifully decorated in front by the spare rope in many a graceful fold, proceeded on their way ... At the next bridge was a flottilla of 19 boats; their cabins and helms ornamented profusely with

[6] 'On the Canal', *Household Words*, XVIII (1858), 322. The article is by John Hollings-head, and is to be found reprinted in his *Odd journeys, in and out of London* (London, 1860), 1-65.

vermilion and blue, undergoing a general purification. Here a woman was mopping the sides of the 'George', there a man brushing the helm of the 'Defiance' and yonder a boy scraping the cabin of the 'Regent'. Have you never, Mr Editor, stood to admire a boatman in his holiday hosen and best clothes? He is a picture rivalling that of the woodman a blue coat with ample buttons, fiery waistcoat, blue plush breeches, blue worsted hose, with red garters below the knees, a pair of inflexible shoes, hobnailed to the toes, and a straw hat ... These are every-day scenes; but they are our men, and as we have no castle cliff nor Alpine crag to gaze on, let us make the most of them.[7]

Earlier than this I found only the most perfunctory descriptions of boats and boatmen. Boat-painting may have existed: descriptions did not, or, if they did, to look for them was as hopeful a procedure as looking for needles in a haystack. Possibly the origins of boat-painting might emerge in a more broadly based study of boat-people, and this itself presented a challenge. However, Parliamentary papers and newspapers, directories, the minutes of canal companies, accounts, and letter books only provided meagre and episodic information about boatmen. They told more about running a canal carrying business than about boatmen, and what little they did tell was entirely from the point of view of the employer. Here was nothing of the life of the men themselves.

Although the Victorian period produced a large volume of writing about working-class life, the canal boatmen received little mention before 1858, when Hollingshead's account of a trip on the Grand Junction Canal appeared in *Household Words*, edited by Charles Dickens. Indeed Dickens had himself given one of the few accounts of canal boatmen in *The Old Curiosity Shop*, published in weekly parts in 1840-1; but an even fuller and earlier description appeared over the *nom de plume* M. D. Heavisides in 1823, at almost the same time that Mogridge had written his description of the canal boats in Birmingham.[8] Before this date it seemed as difficult to find

---

[7] 'Letter to the Editor, signed 'Jeremy Jaunt', *The Birmingham and Lichfield Chronicle*, 19 Dec. 1823. Quoted in Charles Williams, *George Mogridge: his Life, Character and Writings* (London, 1856), 165-6. Mogridge was the son of Mathias Mogridge a dealer in canal shares. He and his brother set up as japanners, and after the company became bankrupt he wrote tracts under the name 'Old Humphrey'. He was a friend of Edward Irving.

[8] M. D. Heavisides, 'The Staffordshire Collieries', *Knight's Quarterly Magazine*, I (1823), 298-9.

a serious and detailed description of the boatmen as to find one of their boats.

This was perhaps not surprising, for throughout the years of the wars with France, and for some time thereafter, the propertied classes had been gripped by the fear of revolution, and any expression of working-class aspiration was likely to be seen as confirming these fears. Little sympathy was shown even for material distress. The literature of the period was escapist: Gothic novels, romantic poetry, and the historical romance were popular. Realism was represented by the circumscribed world and the constricted sympathies of Jane Austen. Such was the literary diet of the middle and upper classes on the eve of Peterloo.

The description by the mysterious M. D. Heavisides of canal boatmen in 1823 represents then an early enlargement of the imaginative sympathy such as was to be found later in such writers as Dickens and Mayhew:

... I remember once mounting rather hastily the outside of a stage coach which was passing through the coal district, and setting myself down in the first place that offered itself, without taking time to reconnoitre. When I had opportunity for inspection, I found at my right an old man with a rope coiled round him like a belt, by which my practised eye at once recognised him for a canal boatman, carrying home his towing-line. On my left was a personage whose dress was not a little equivocal, consisting of a man's hat and coat, with something like petticoats below. The mysterious effect of this epicene costume was heightened by the wearer's complexion, which reminded the spectator of dirty wash-leather. A short pipe adorned the mouth, with which it seemed well acquainted; and the tout ensemble sat in deep silence ... .At length my fellow passengers began to converse, or rather, I suppose, to resume a conversation which I had interrupted. The lady I found was of the same profession as the gentleman on the other side – a conductor of boats. They appeared not to have had much, if any, previous acquaintance, but seemed drawn together by community of sentiment and pursuit. They were soon engaged in an occupation interesting alike to all ranks of society; namely, an inquiry into the characters of their common friends.

Lady. Dun yo know Soiden-mouth Tummy?

Gentleman. Ees: an', a 'neation good feller he is tew.

Lady. A desput quoiet mon! But he loves a sup o' drink. Dun yo know his woif?

Gentleman. Know her! Her's the very devil when her sperit's up.

Lady. Her is. Her uses that mon sheamful – her rags him every neet of her loif.

Gentleman. Her does. Oive known her come into the public, and call him all the nearnes her could lay her tongue tew afore all the company. Her oughts to stay till her's got him the boat, and then her mit say what her'd a moind. But her taks aiter her feyther.

Lady. Hew was her feyther?

Gentleman. Whoy, singing Jemmy.

Lady. Oi don't think as how Oi ever know'd singing Jemmy. Was he ode Soaker's brother?

Gentleman. Ees, he was. He lived a. top o' Hell Bonk. He was the wickedest, swearinst mon as ever I know'd. I should think as how he was the wickedest mon i' the wold, and say he had the rheumatiz so bad.

Who then was the author of this piece? M. D. Heavisides' was the pseudonym of Matthew Davenport Hill, brother of Rowland Hill, and later Recorder of Birmingham. In 1823, when this description appeared, he was a young Birmingham Radical, a barrister, who had lately defended the aged Major Cartwright, the champion of universal male suffrage, at his trial in Warwick. At this time the political aspirations of the Birmingham artisans and the middle class were united in the agitation for parliamentary representation for their city.[9] It is therefore not surprising that the only two known detailed descriptions of canal boatmen should come from this area. George Mogridge was also a Birmingham man, the son of a wharfinger and canal agent. These were men living in an unusual political climate. Their interest in working-class life was unusual at that period amongst literary men, and it was unlikely that the sources used so far could be made to yield further information.

To re-create the world of boatmen before 1820 I had to try new methods. A change of scale must be attempted, and closer, more intensive methods must be used. The tools of micro-history are essentially those of the historical demographer and the local historian. They can only be applied to groups of people who live in some particular geographic area, whose records can be studied intensively. They cannot be used to study a population which has no roots in any place at all.

In the popular imagination canal boatmen are often regarded as 'water gipsies', people totally divorced from the land. Yet

---

[9] Rosamund and Florence Davenport-Hill, *The Recorder of Birmingham: A Memoir of Matthew Davenport Hill* (London, 1878), 49-51, 69; E. P. Thompson, *The Making of the English Working Class* (London, 1963), 808-11.

this view is false.[10] Many boatmen lived together in small communities. In Hollingshead's article 'On the Canal' such a 'boatman's village' is described, a place 'where the people of the land seemed to belong to the people on the water; where everybody knew everybody, and seemed glad to see everybody'.[11] This village was on the Grand Junction Canal somewhere near Braunston. Accounts by canal missionaries of their labours seemed to suggest that there were concentrations of boat-people in other places and at these missions were established.

I examined the 1841 Census enumerators' books to identify such boatmen's villages. It seemed likely that these communities would be found at junctions between rivers and canals or between two canals, indeed, many of these places were known to be places where there had been missions to boatmen. Worcester, Gloucester, and Oxford were examples of the former, Preston Brook and Longford in the parish of Foleshill of the latter. Finally I chose Oxford. It was an excellent example of such a community, with good documentary records, and, not least important, I lived there.

The Census showed a sizeable community, and it also showed that the Row contained other sorts of boatmen besides canal boatmen. There was a sprinkling of fishermen and one or two river bargemen. At first I ignored these. Ultimately however, another question had to be asked: where did the canal boatmen come from? Who had lived in Fisher Row before the canal was cut?

T. S. Willan's *River Navigation in England, 1600-1760* provided a clue to the second question, for its footnotes contained a reference to H. E. Salter's *Cartulary of Oseney Abbey*, which summarised the leases of Middle and Lower Fisher Row.[12] These houses had belonged to Oseney Abbey before the Dissolution, and at the foundation of Christ Church Henry VIII had endowed the Dean and Chapter with them as well as most of the other lands of the abbey.[13]

These leases showed how old this community was, for here were leases to 16th-century fishermen, and 17th-century

---

[10] The view that they were gipsies was resented by boat people. One boatwoman, interviewed in 1969, refused to talk to me until assured that I did not hold this view.

[11] Hollingshead, 'On the Canal', 359.

[12] *Oseney*, II. 494-505. [13] *LP Henry VIII, XIII*, pt, ii,§§ 332 (26), 648 (25).

bargemen. There had been boat-people living there continuously from that time. I felt like an anthropologist who, after months of travel, at last parts the leaves and finds before him some unknown tribe. The only leaves that had been parted here though were the pages of books, and it had been an exploration into a different dimension from that of the anthropologist, an exploration in time rather than space. This unknown community lay between the Bodleian Library and the railway station. It seemed arbitrary now to limit the study to the canal age. The study had been contracted from one of canal boatmen in general to those of a particular place, now it expanded again, back into the more distant past.

Occupational communities were singled out by Gideon Sjoberg as one of the distinguishing features of the pre-industrial city, but such communities can be found in other types of city too. What, for instance is a university campus? Occupational communities can be used to study the social, economic, and family structure of our towns in the past.

So far the problems of dealing with urban populations have deterred historians from anything more than aggregative studies.[14] The problems of dealing with the populations of towns are, on the face of it, formidable. Numbers are large, occupations diverse, landlords many, and, to make matters worse, the town is divided into many close-packed parishes, so that migration from one to another is easy. Yet the problem is not beyond solution, for occupational communities provide suitable segments of population to handle. Charles Booth observed for instance that often migration was more apparent than real: 'In many districts the people are always on the move; they shift from one part of it to another like "fish in a river"...On the whole, however, the people usually do not go far, and often cling from generation to generation to one vicinity, almost as if the set of streets which lie there were an isolated country village.'[15] On the whole the anthropologists rather than the historians have recognised the possibilities of

[14] Such as, for example, Michael Anderson 'Household Structure and the Industrial Revolution; mid-19th Preston in comparative perspective', in Peter Laslett and Richard Wall, ed., *Household and Family in Past Time* (Cambridge, paperback edn., 1974), 215-35.

[15] Charles Booth, ed.,' *Labour and Life of the People*, I (2 vols., 2nd edn., London, 1889-93), 26-7.

identifying groups of a suitable size to study, ranging from Bethnal Green, where loyalties to individual streets are strong, to flats in South London, and from immigrant Italian restaurateurs to the occupational dynasties of Highgate.[16] Mr Laslett has observed that our folk-memory of craft and town is stronger than it is of the countryside. Yet we have failed to make use of one strand of this folk memory which might help us in dividing urban society into groups of manageable size. We all half know that in the past there were quarters in towns given over to different trades, places where shoe-makers made shoes, or parchment-makers made parchment, or candle-makers candles. John Stow himself tells us that this was indeed so, though these quarters or streets were not immutably dedicated to one craft. In his own day he noted how some were moving to new parts, whilst others remained in their traditional homes.

The goldsmiths of Gutheron's lane and Olde Exchange are now for the most part removed into the south side of West Cheape ... The drapers of Lombard street and of Corne hill are seated in Candlewick street and Watheling street; the skinners from St Marie Pellipers, or at the Axe, into Budge row and Wallbrooke ... the vintners from the Vinetree into divers places. But the brewers for the more part remain near to the friendly waters of Thames ... the founders remain by themselves in Lothberie; ... pater noster makers of old time, or bead-makers, and text-writers, are gone out of Pater noster row, and are called stationers of Paules churchyard; patten-makers, of St Margaret, Pattens' lane, clean worn out...[17]

So Stow wrote in the 16th century. Such differentiation certainly existed in the 13th century in Oxford, where the area in which the Bodleian Library now stands (where so much of the research for this book was done) was even then a bookish place. According to a modern scholar 'the odds are five to two that an inhabitant of Cat Street was in the book trade'.[18] This occupational differentiation of various regions of the town survived in London even after the

---

[16] M, Young and P. Willmott, *Family and Kinship in East London* (London, 1957); R. Firth, ed,. *Two Studies of Kinship in London* (London, 1956); Dorothy Crozier, 'Kinship and Occupational Succession', *The Sociological Review,* New Series XIII (1965), 15-43.

[17] John Stow, *The Survey Of London* (Everyman edn., repr. 1970), 74-5.

[18] Graham Pollard, 'William of Brailles', *Bodleian Library Record,* V (1954-6), 205-9.

invention of the bicycle. Charles Booth gives us a late 19th-century picture of the same sort of thing:

Thus it will be seen that Whitechapel is the dwelling place of the Jews – tailors, bootmakers and tobacco-workers – and the centre of trading both small and large; Stepney and St George's the district of ordinary labour; Shoreditch and Bethnal Green of the artizan; in Poplar sub-officials reach their maximum proportion, while Mile End, with a little of everything, very closely represents the average of the whole district...

Each district has its character – its peculiar flavour. One seems to be conscious of it in the streets. It may be in the faces of the people, or in what they carry – perhaps a reflection is thrown in this way from the prevailing trades...[19]

Fisher Row was just such an area, but it was an occupational enclave of a particularly strongly differentiated sort, almost an extreme case. Such cases demonstrate dramatically how characteristics of social and family structure vary with changing circumstance, and so help us to understand more clearly the structure of society as a whole.

III. MEANS AND METHODS

Many people have moved into history from other disciplines, bringing with them new approaches, or, when faced with new problems find inspiration in the way other disciplines solve them. It was my ambition to follow the lives of obscure men and women not merely as a group, but as individuals. I tended to think of the task as very like that of the birdwatcher with his files of bird-sightings, from which he builds up his histories of the lives of individual birds. Only my birds were not ringed. Nevertheless it still seems to me a good analogy, and it was one which, from the beginning, suggested methods of storing information, whilst the decision to concentrate on the community in Oxford opened up a splendid array of new sources. Reading such works as Dr E. A. Wrigley's *An Introduction to Historical Demography*, and especially his chapter on Family Reconstitution, taught me much about refining my own techniques, though as my aims were different, methods had to be adapted.

Recently Dr Alan Macfarlane has produced a fascinating account of a method of reconstructing a historical community

---

[19] Booth, op. cit. 65-6.

He formalises a method which others have used with less than his machine-like consistency and thoroughness. His programme is very labour-intensive, and we must await Dr Macfarlane's own final results – the actual reconstruction of a community – before passing judgement on it. The proof of the pudding is in the eating.

However, dealing with an occupational community poses its own problems, and methods had to be developed for handling them. Both Dr Wrigley and Dr Macfarlane treated the parish as their unit for study, and the parishes they have dealt with are rural. An occupational community is not co-extensive with a parish (unless one regards a village as an occupational community of agricultural workers); it is an urban rather than a rural phenomenon. In cities there is considerable occupational differentiation and this is one of the most important social differences between town and country. It is certainly central to this study.

Because parish and occupational community are not co-extensive it is necessary to identify what members of the parish (or parishes) are members of the occupational community being studied. This is one problem. Another is posed by the nature of many occupational groups. An occupational community need not be closely intermarried (nuns are not), but very often they are, and the occupation is inherited (again, not by nuns). Families engaged in a traditional occupation are likely to be conservative in other matters as well as choice of occupation: such as the naming of children. Therefore, in many communities such as Fisher Row, the number of Christian names and surnames is few, and the number of individuals who bear them is uncomfortably large. Amongst themselves they used nicknames and other methods of identifying each other as can be seen in the dialogue 'M. D. Heavisides' noted down, already quoted.[21] Unfortunately these 'aliases' are

---

[20] Alan Macfarlane, in collaboration with Sarah Harrison and Charles Jardine, Reconstructing Historical Communities (Cambridge, 1977), 81-112.

[21] The article goes on to describe how in the collieries in general nicknames had almost replaced baptismal names, which were half forgotten even by close friends and relatives:

Many anecdotes might be collected to shew the great difficulty of discovering a person in the Collieries without being in possession of his nickname. The following I received from a respectable attorney. During his clerkship he was sent to serve some legal process on a man

rarely given in official documents and the unambiguous identification of individuals presents difficulties which must be
surmounted. These are the problems I shall deal with briefly
here. Those who have no interest in such technicalities should
skip the rest of this section.

First, in a study in which occupation plays so important a
part, it is essential to examine every aspect of the craft or
trade in which the community is involved. This obvious fact
needs stressing, for it is curious how often it is passed over.
Most historians have learned at some time in their training a
great deal about common fields and the round of agricultural
labour, so it is not surprising that in studies of rural society
such basic knowledge is often assumed. In a town every one
of its many trades and crafts had its own particular regime
of work which must be understood. This background study
prevents the misinterpretation of data, provides new insights,
and frequently leads to the discovery of new sources. It is
also useful in establishing the social milieu of the community. In dealing with Fisher Row I visualised the round of
toil in which the members of the community were involved,
and listed the trades of the people whom the various sorts
of boatmen were likely to encounter at work. For a fisherman these associated trades included the following: millers,
keepers of locks and weirs, net and weel-makers, boat-builders,
basket-makers and osier-growers, hemp-dressers, fishmongers,
leech-gatherers and men fishing for pleasure. Bargemasters and
bargemen met roughly the same sort of people, though where

whose name and address were given to him with legal accuracy. He traversed the village to
which he had been directed from end to end without success; and after spending many hours
in the search, was about to abandon it in despair, when a young woman, who had witnessed
his labours, kindly under-took to make inquiries for him, and began to hail her friends for
that purpose.

Oi say, Bullyed, does thee know a mon neamed Adam Green?

The Bull-head was shaken in sign of ignorance.

Loy-a-bed, dost thee?

Lie-a-bed's opportunities of making acquaintance had been rather limited, and she could
not resolve the difficulty.

Stumpy (a man with a wooden leg), Cowskin, Spindleshanks, Cock-eye, Pigtail, and
Yellow-belly, were severally invoked, but in vain, and the querist fell into a brown study, in
which she remained for some time. At length, however, her eyes suddenly brightened, and
slapping one of her companions on the shoulder, she exclaimed, triumphantly, 'Dash my wig!
shoy he means moy feyther!' and then turning to the gentleman, she added, 'Yo should'n ax'd
for Ode Blackbird!'.

the bargemaster tended to meet his employer the bargeman was more likely to meet his man. The list for barge-people included millers and lock-keepers, carriers and carters, wharfingers and publicans, woodmongers and timber merchants, stone-masons, coopers, coal and corndealers, maltsters, brewers, horse-keepers and bow-halers; and in London, lightermen, watermen, coal-meters, and keelmen. For canal boatmen the list was shorter; though like the bargemen they encountered people all along the route, and at their destination. For canal boatmen this would be in the collieries and the manufacturing districts rather than London. Their list included coal- and corn-dealers and other merchants or their men, lock-keepers, lengthmen, boat-gaugers and other canal officials, wharfingers and other agents of individual carrying companies, victuallers licensed and unlicensed, boat-builders and horse-dealers. All these trades were associated in some way with boat-people. Sometimes they were rival groups and there proved to be no other social connection between the groups. This was in itself an interesting fact, but most could be classed as supporting trades. If boat-people moved up the social scale out of boating, it would usually be into one of these trades, or if a boatman married outside his own occupation group he most commonly married amongst the daughters of such tradesmen, who formed an important peripheral group which had to be watched all the time 'out of the corner of the eye'.

In collecting material to study an occupational group it is necessary to follow the advice to the cook, 'First catch your fish'. The members of the community had to be identified. Therefore material must be studied in a definite order. The golden rule is to deal with documents in which occupations are stated first of all, later moving on to those where occupation is not given, when the names of members of the community are known. Parish registers, for instance, usually amongst the first material to be handled, must be amongst the last. In dealing with Fisher Row, Freemen's Apprenticeship Enrolments, and Hanasters' (i.e. Freemen's) Enrolments proved the most useful source of occupations, as all fishermen and most bargemen were freemen. However, there are some towns where the occupations of freemen and their apprentices are not given. There can be no hard and fast rule about the

order in which particular classes of documents are dealt with
– and even if there were it would be unrealistic to counsel following it, as it often takes a very long time to locate all the
relevant material.

Once the names of the members of the community are familiar
the parish registers can be tackled, but actually reconstituting the families of the community down to the finest detail
should be left until further information has been assembled
from sources in which occupations are not given. In dealing
with this material we are often faced with the problem of trying to decide whether a man, say John Smith, is a member of
the community, or just part of the world's super-abundance of
John Smiths. If we know who some of his relatives were from
the parish register we may decide to include him tentatively in
our nominal file. It therefore helps, at this stage, to transcribe
the relevant material from the parish register and perhaps also
to reconstitute straightforward families. In dealing with registers I did not attempt to transcribe the whole register but
only the names of members of the community and the members of such associated trades as I could readily identify. If I
could identify them it was likely that they had some connection of some sort with the community, and if not, they were
unlikely to be of great importance. The boat-people made up
about a 10th of the population of the parish, and I transcribed
about one third of the register. If I were doing this work again
I would transcribe the whole marriage register, for the extra
work would not be great, and marriages are such a useful guide
to the structure of a parish.

It is important in this work however, to keep one's main end
in view all the time and not to be side-tracked into doing jobs
which serve other ends, over-impressed by a desire for com-
pleteness. It might be thought that instead of separating out
the members of the community at this stage it would be better to do a complete family reconstitution for the parish rather
than only for the occupational community. However, this is a
job in itself, and so large an undertaking that it would be like
climbing Everest as a training to climb Mont Blanc. When
Wrigley wrote his chapter on Family Reconstitution ten years
ago only one parish had been fully reconstituted, and even
now the number is small. What would be gained by a full

reconstitution? Ultimately the occupational community must be isolated for study.

The families of the community should be reconstituted as fully as possible only when all the documents relevant to the community have been transcribed or extracted and filed. At the same time it is helpful to relate the families to the houses which they occupied, for where there are problems of building a family tree, or sorting out a sequence of leases each process casts light on the other. My method of reconstituting families was adapted from Dr Wrigley's, though methods had to be devised for unambiguously identifying individuals. Help in doing this was obtained from the nominal file in which all information about each individual member of the community was stored. All the entries for a given surname in this file were shuffled into strict chronological order, and then copied out onto A4 sheets of paper so that a large number of events could be scanned at a time. These sheets were used in conjunction with the parish register slips to reduce ambiguities, and then the nominal file was resorted to for reconstituting individual life-histories. At this stage many cards made out from sources which did not give occupations had to be abandoned as it could not be established for certain whether they referred to a member of the community or only someone bearing the same name. The nominal file is however often of considerable value in settling difficulties. A break in the run of births to a certain Thomas Beesley was explained on referring to the nominal file by evidence of his having been sentenced to transportation, and having later returned. Together they cleared up the confusion as to which of three Thomas Beesleys was which. Only by a great deal of patient work involving the nominal file and the parish register can such ambiguities be resolved, and even then some ambiguities will remain. These must be indicated on the family tree.

At the time of writing his seminal chapter, 'Family Reconstitution', Wrigley stated that in work on mortality rates the use of supporting documentary material in conjunction with parish registers was 'slight as yet', and involved difficulties of principle, hard to overcome; 'for example, if the effect of the use of one class of record were to increase the proportion of full reconstitutions of a single social type, it would bias the

sample of families used in calculating demographic rates'.[22]
This was not a problem which affected my work as my aims
were different.

A stage had now been reached where it was at last possible to gain a picture of the structure of the families, and
so to begin to generalise about the community. At the same
time lacunae in the family trees were now obvious, and this
was therefore the time to examine the registers of neighbouring parishes to attempt to fill these gaps. The two processes
continued side by side. From the family trees it was now
possible to establish whether an occupation was inherited,
and how many sons followed the occupation of the father;
how closely the families married within their own occupation group, and whether when they married outside it they
married into associated occupation groups. They also showed
what alternative occupations were adopted by men who did
not follow the family occupation, and whether there were preferred alternatives. When the houses in which the families
lived were identified, further patterns emerged, showing the
social structure of the community. Whenever these could be
related to Census-type listings or the Census itself, the internal structure of households could be examined. In Fisher Row
no Census-type listings existed which were full enough for an
analysis of household structure before the Census; but it was
found useful to compare the households in the Censuses of
1841-71 (the only four yet available). These gave details of the
occupants of each household.

The sources for each period between 1500 and 1900 had
their own strengths and weaknesses. Wills for instance,
were far fuller, and far commoner in the 17th century than
in the 19th, whilst establishing men's occupations was
often difficult until the 19th century, when parish registers and the Census automatically give such details. The
great strength of 19th-century material, however, lay in the
number of reliable listings of persons which were available
or could be constructed. This made it possible to 'ask the
material questions' which could seldom be asked in earlier
periods. It was possible for instance to take nominal index

[22] E. A. Wrigley, 'Family Reconstitution' in E. A. Wrigley, ed., *An Introduction to English Historical Demography* (London, 1966), 152.

cards for two listings and mesh them together to answer such questions as which families were living in Middle Fisher Row in 1802 were still living there in 1829? The process of meshing together two such listings was easy enough, but the formulating of precise questions which could be answered by this method was often surprisingly difficult. However, it illustrated very well that in this type of work the imagination should be given freest rein in the formulation of questions, not of answers.

IV. THE LESSONS OF THE ROW

This method of reconstituting an occupational community is time-consuming, and results in a fine-grained and very detailed study of a very tiny segment of the population of Oxford. What can it teach us about the social, economic, and even political position of men and women in the past which justifies this effort? An occupational community is, after all, a small, probably specialised group, and, in the case of Fisher Row, the occupations in which its members were involved are now obsolete. River fish are no longer sold commercially, and goods are no longer sent by river or canal. We cannot claim that we are studying the origins of a group of workers engaged in an occupation which still plays an important part in the life of the country, like the brewing industry or coal or steel.

Certainly it is true that the community in Fisher Row is all but forgotten, but from the 16th century to the 19th century it was a community of economic and social importance. In the 16th and 17th century, in particular, its fishermen provided the city with fresh fish for its fast days, for these remained in force long after the Reformation; whilst its bargemen and canal boatmen played a major part in the provisioning of the city. Within the city too they had a definite standing, for all the fishermen, and most of the bargemen were freemen. They were men who not only had a voice in local government, but they had the vote. Oxford was a town with a wide franchise. As a group they were rumbustious and had a reputation for a sort of cheerful violence. They were to the fore in town and gown affrays and formed an identifiable portion of the mobs at election time. They were working-class voters when few men, let alone working men, had the vote.

It may also be said to have a more general interest, for in Fisher Row we have a community whose whole life-span can be studied from birth to death. We can see how it adapted itself – or failed to adapt – to changing conditions during the 400 years of its existence. We can trace it from its beginnings in the 16th century, when the community consisted of only a handful of boatmen who supplied the town and the university with fish, especially at times of fast, at a time when roads were bad and the river obstructed, and towns were victualled as much as possible from the immediate neighbourhood. As Oxford grew in size, improved communications were necessary, and with river improvement bargemen moved into the Row, and fishermen also turned to the trade, for fasting was declining. The opening of canals brought new trade and new competition to which the community adapted as best it could. It had grown with the improvement of transport, and risen to the challenge of competition, changing in response to change from without; but railway transport brought a challenge which no amount of adjustment within the Row could meet, and so the community declined and dispersed.

We might see it perhaps as a microcosm in which the great social and economic events of the nation are mirrored. However, as a microcosm Fisher Row presents at times a very weird reflection. This is perhaps the most interesting thing about the Row, but there are some ways in which, particularly in economic history it presents a simple and uncomplicated reflection of economic conditions. Transport workers' lives are sensitive to the fluctuations of trade, and here the condition of the Row can fill in, if only circumstantially, some gaps in our knowledge. In economic history there are many blanks on the map, and the internal trade of England is a notorious case. It lacks adequate documentation. There are no sources to compare with the Port Books which cover the coastal trade, and statistics are few. Nevertheless, denied the luxury of extensive statistics, we may yet gain some impression of the trade of the river by examining the condition of the families employed in it.

If the economic historian would see depression or boom exemplified, he may see it here: the first is revealed in leases unrenewed, and rents unpaid, in bargemasters reduced to bargemen who apprentice their sons outside the trade; or in the prosecution of adult bargemen for attempting to take up other trades than those for which they were apprenticed; at such times men's horizons became narrow and opportunity failed, whilst in times of prosperity things were contrariwise.

The history of the Row can also cast light on how trade was organised at a time when carrying companies did not exist, and we have no business records. We can see from the marriages of bargemasters and their families to others of their kind along the river, and to men in associated trades, that the trade of the river lay very much in the hands of related families all along the banks of the river. For the Oxford bargemaster 'our man in Abingdon' – or Lechlade or London – was likely to be a brother or brother-in-law. Trade and family ran together; indeed, amongst boat-people we shall find over and over again that family ties, family welfare, and family honour dominated the life of the Row.

The study of a community over such a long period makes it possible to observe long term changes in the status of the members of the community. In the 16th and early 17th centuries the status of at least some of the fishermen was fairly high. Men held their property on leases of years, they married their children to men of some standing in the city, and their wills and inventories show them to have been mildly prosperous, with modest but comfortable houses. In many ways we know more about these 16th- and 17th-century men than we do about almost any others, even in the recent past, for in later times few members of the community made wills, and in the 19th century only two wills are found. Inventories are not found after 1732. This marks a change in probate administration and not one in the standing of the inhabitants of the Row, but the decline in will-making does seem to mark such a change. Wills are only made when there is an estate to be disposed of. They are not made gratuitously. By the 19th century most of the property in the Row had become investment property, which was mainly in the hands of the large breweries in the parish, and the inhabitants rented their houses without any security of tenure, probably on a weekly basis. Their leaseholds had been an investment to hand down within the family; few had them now.

Few of the inhabitants of the Row ever became really wealthy; apart from one family who had prospered in the river trade in the 17th century and then moved out into brewing in the 18th. On the whole the gap between the barge-masters and the bargemen widened. When the river first opened, small boats rather than barges were used, and the boats tended to be crewed by members of the family, much as canal boats were in later times – though on the river women never formed part of the crew of the boat. Later on, as the navigation was improved, larger boats were used and more men were employed with less prospect of rising to become bargemasters. The position of labouring men in society as a whole seems to have been falling. More classes were inter-posed in the social scale, whilst in the south of England in the 19th century unemployment was increasing as the economic initiative moved to the north.

We have left the most important feature of the life of the Row to the last. This was the importance of family. The Row was a highly traditional society in which sons followed the occupation of their fathers from generation to generation. Men learned their trade from their fathers, worked with them, lived in the same street as they did, and often married the daughters of other fishermen or bargemen.

Yet it would be wrong to think that the three occupation groups which lived in the Row all shared the same charac-teristic family structure. They did not. Amongst the various types of boat-people there were different patterns of work which favoured diversity. Extended families, for instance, are found very commonly amongst canal boatmen in the 19th century, but not among fishermen. The number of sons who could follow their fathers' occupations also differed from group to group and from time to time. Here economic climate as well as the nature of the job seems to have been an important factor.

Fisher Row contained three sorts of boatman, and each developed characteristic patterns of family life. These are displayed first in family trees. All the families were much intermarried, and in all three occupation groups sons followed in their father's footsteps. The occupation was inherited. Amongst fishermen usually one son followed in his father's footsteps, for a fishery on a river was a limited resource, and the number of mouths it could support was limited. In this it was probably more like farming than deep-sea-fishing. Only in a period of serious depression did many fishermen's sons follow their father's trade, when there were no alternative opportunities of employment. This led to feuding. In the barge trade, on the other hand, many sons followed their father's trade, to the general benefit of the family – at least in good times – for bargemen provided a service, and the larger the numbers involved the more successful it was likely to be. In the canal carrying business there was no limit to the number of sons who could be involved in the business. Boats were small and did not require a crew of strong men. Women and children could help to work the boats, though often the wife and younger children remained ashore if the family was prosperous.

Amongst fishermen, as amongst the English rural population, one finds nuclear, patriarchal families of the sort which we have been taught to expect in north-western Europe. This can be seen in the census, but we do not know the structure of the river bargeman's household, for by the 1841 census the barge trade was all but extinct. However, we know that in 1772 when a survey listed the heads of households, Upper and Middle Fisher Row were inhabited by closely related families, so that the area had become a sort of large household under many adjacent roof-trees. It is perhaps a matter of definition whether such families are counted as extended families or not. We do know that the households of canal boatmen were often extended, and that the women in the absence of their menfolk seem to have drawn together for mutual support. In the 19th century it is clear that in the Row, as in industrial Preston, the extended family flourished.[23]

It thus provides another counter-example defying that modern mystical dogma that the nuclear family has always prevailed in England. In Fisher Row it prevailed in one occupation group, but not in another. It is also obvious why one group should have one family structure and the other an entirely different one: it depended on the demands occupation made upon the families. Occupation has seldom been given

[23] Anderson, op. cit.

serious consideration in studies in social history, and it is here that this study breaks new ground. All three types of boatman were dominated by the importance of family. Feuds do not break out in families without sense of family solidarity. We cannot say that the feud between the Bossoms and the Beesleys achieved the ferocity of a blood feud, but it kept the families in the news for the best part of 100 years. In earlier centuries we have no such clear proof of family solidarity, but the closeness of the families and the advantages of family continuity are evident in the family trees. Occupations were inherited and the benefits of being a freeman fell to the sons of freemen, as men became freemen by their father's copy. Freemen had the right to fish the free waters: therefore it was unthinkable that any fisherman should not be a freeman. The dynasties of fishermen were supported by the very structure of the town's government.

The importance of family piety amongst the Establishment – and particularly the 18th-century Establishment – is well known. Eighteenth-century values made the promotion of 'casa nostra' a sacred duty, and it would be surprising if such values were not to be found elsewhere in English society. There is a mafia-like strain which runs throughout English politics, but the luxuriant thickets, plotted by Namier, of families which fixed the election of their kin to parliament, were only equalled by the luxuriant thickets of family among the bribable electorate: to bribe sufficiently was to gain the allegiance of a clan. Through the 18th and 19th century the records bear witness from time to time to the support of the Whigs by the bargemen and fishermen of the Row. In the eminently bribable borough of Harwich the government was able to reward its supporters with minor posts in connection with the port. Here too the list of the persons who must be fixed consisted largely of boatmen, and even the most cursory inspection shows some of them to have been relations.[24] The bribed and the bribers understood each other very well. Harwich and Fisher Row were the soft underbelly of politics in Namier's century.

The industrial revolution did not necessarily affect the pattern of family life; it might or it might not, according to the

---

[24] Lewis Namier, *The Structure of Politics at the Accession of George III* (2nd edn. repr. 1975), 358-89.

nature of men's work, but it brought new sets of values, or, rather, gave a new authority to an alternative set based not on an ethic of family loyalties and privileges, but on merit: ability, responsibility, and hard work in the political sphere, professional expertise and experience in specialised work outweighed, at least in theory, the claims of family and friendship to special consideration in the filling of jobs. Even in the church itself the rites of baptism and marriage ceased to be the almost automatic right of the parishioner. A changing society strained the parish system, and as the state assumed more of the secular functions of the church, the church was free to demand higher spiritual qualifications of its flock. It was such shifts in attitudes and values rather than any immediate and direct effect on the structure of the family which was brought by the industrial revolution. But a loosening of the sense of family obligation must have an effect in the long run. It provided industry with emotionally unattached workers who could be more readily moved around according to its dictates. The old Fisher Row had not gained wealth from the traditional system, but it had gained tangible benefits. In the 19th century it found itself at odds with a changing world, which it took on in a doomed last-ditch struggle.

The world which the Row championed consisted of nuclear and extended families, of small and large households, but whatever they were, it was a world which thought in terms of family duties, family alliances, of inheritance, of favour and privilege. Fisher Row was a place in which such attitudes found expression. Here we can see one of the great differences between the past and the present.

Part I

FROM REFORMATION
TO INDUSTRIAL REVOLUTION

CHAPTER 1

Parish, River, and Row

I. ORIENTATION: THE PARISH AND ITS BOUNDS

The geography of any area dictates its character, and this is forcefully illustrated by the parish of St Thomas. It is a riverside parish, and, until present times, its people lived by, with, and on the water. Its politics were as much concerned with power as they are in other places, but they were the politics of water and water-power. In the battles to gain control of the water supply the land was cut and channelled and cut again, and in this process Fisher Row was created.

As its name suggests Oxford is situated by a river crossing. It stands just above the meeting of the Thames and the Cherwell. Here the Thames is still a comparatively small river, and the Cherwell a largish tributary. Moreover, just above this confluence the Thames is divided into several streams, which made it even easier for the founders of the town to establish a route across the river. The Saxon town of Oxford stood in Mercia at the gateway to Wessex, and the Thames was the boundary. Much ingenuity has been spent on arguing whether the route to Abingdon which crosses the river south of the town was on the original 'Ox Ford', or the route to Abingdon west of the town, by Ferry Hinksey. Whichever it was, the town stood at an important river crossing.

The walled town itself stood high over these river flats with their many water courses, on the tip of a long, gravel terrace thrown up between the Thames and Cherwell (see Fig. 1.2). On this desirable, well-drained site the colleges of the university were built, and here lived those of the tradesmen and citizentry whose trades did not involve a heavy reliance on water and the river. As the town grew more populous the haves

29

slowly pushed the have-nots off the well-drained land on to the heavy, cold, ill-drained river-plain.

St Thomas's lay low, outside the walled city, intersected by the Thames itself, and fretted by many smaller streams. It was an extensive parish, sprawling along the west side of Oxford,

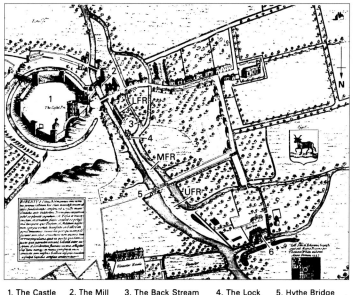

1. The Castle   2. The Mill   3. The Back Stream   4. The Lock   5. Hythe Bridge
6. Rewley Abbey

Fig. 1.1. Fisher Row, from Ralph Agas's Map of Oxford, 1578.
Note: The 'upside-down' orientation of this map is again out of line with modern convention.

with four parishes bordering it on its eastern townward side (see Fig. 1.3). The parish of St Mary Magdalen was situated outside the North Gate of the town, and St Giles lay even further north. Both ran along the gravel shelf. South of these St Thomas's was bordered by the parish of St Peter le Bailey which stood high, within the city wall. When the bounds were beaten in the 17th century the inhabitants of St Peter le Bailey and St Thomas fought over the question as to whether the boundary lay along the top of the outer ramparts, or at their foot, in the moat. To the south of St Peter le Bailey, outside the wall, lay the parish of St Ebbe. Like St Thomas's, St Ebbe's lay on the river plain.

In the Middle Ages St Thomas's was a rag-bag of a parish, containing an unexpected variety of buildings and institutions: Oxford Castle, the Castle Mill, and the Abbeys of Rewley and

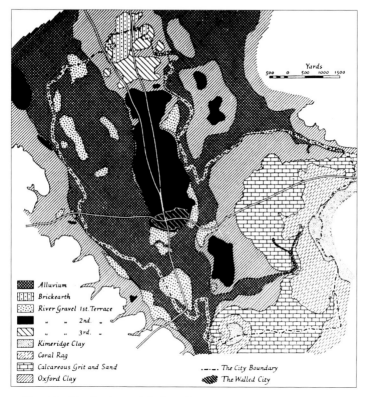

Fig. 1.2. The Geology of Oxford, from E. W. Gilbert, 'The Growth of the City of Oxford', in A. F. Martin and R. W. Steel, eds., *The Oxford Region*.

Oseney (with its Mills). The church of St George in the Castle and a house of the Benedictines, Gloucester College, on the site of Worcester College also lay within its perimeter. The houses of the inhabitants lay huddled between them in a small built-up area which stretched from the castle and Oseney on the south to Rewley and Gloucester College on the north. This however was but a small part of the whole parish, which included much pasture even beyond the walls of the two abbeys. The parish stretched west as far as the furthest steam of the Thames by Botley Mill, and from the Thames on the south to Port Meadow, the common land of the freemen of Oxford on the north. Its area is now much reduced, for as the population

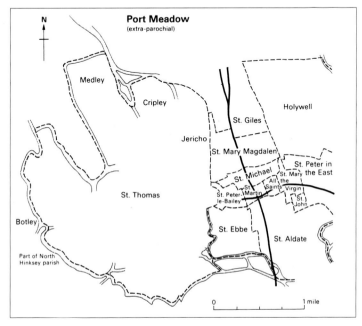

Fig. 1.3. The Bounds of the Parish of St Thomas.

of the parish increased in the 19th century, new parishes were carved out of the old. On the north-east St Paul's and St Barnabas' were formed to cater for the population which had grown up in the suburb of Jericho, whilst in the west Between the railway and Botley now lies the parish of St Frideswide on land which was only enclosed last century. Today the parish of St Thomas takes in little more than the land which has been settled ever since the 13th century. The inhabitants of the parish have not lost their fighting spirit, and have been as happy to defend new boundaries as old, within living memory. According to an interview in the *Oxford Mail*: 'If we weren't charging the Friars (St Abbess),' recalls Mrs Ashmall with a chuckle 'we were charging Oseney Town.'[1]

The fierce independence and even, some would say, lawless character of the area was in part due to the fact that it was a parish itself on a boundary, for on the west its boundary was also the boundary between Oxfordshire and Berkshire, and to the south, the county boundary lay very near, just beyond the main stream of the Thames. The map shows the woods of Bagley and Wytham clothe the hills just over the boundary on the west, and the acres of riverside pasture provided an ever present temptation to poachers. The case of escape out of the jurisdiction of the county encouraged them further. Like so many inhabitants of other places on boundaries the inhabitants of St Thomas's sat lightly to the law.

It was, however, the river above all else which determined the character of the parish, for it attracted industry. Here the river was exploited in every conceivable way. Its streams powered mills to grind corn and full cloth. Brewers, tanners, and dyers utilised its waters, and the town's laundresses washed their clothes here. Oxford was a consumer society, and St Thomas's was its most industrialised parish. Here the products of the countryside were gathered in and processed to supply the demands of town and university.

Because the parish was industrial it required transport, and St Thomas's always was and still is concerned with transport. Goods came in by land and water, by pannier, pack, cart, punt, and barge. In the late 18th century the Oxford Canal opened up a new trade route to the Midlands. In the 19th century two railway stations were built here, competing with older forms of transport, while in the present century car parks abound and the bus station, Gloucester Green, lies just outside the border of the parish.

Where there is transport there are travellers, and therefore by its nature the parish engendered two types of population, one stable, one highly mobile. The moving population included carters, drovers, and seasonal workers who were catered for by cheap lodgings in the parish. This accommodation also catered for an even more transient population on their way through

---

[1] *Oxford Mail*, 28 Nov. 1974.

the countryside: travelling soldiers, migrants moving London-wards, beggars attracted by the easy generosity of students (and earlier by the hospitality of the abbeys), women and children, the purpose of whose travels are not known. From time to time the casual tragedies of this moving population are noted in the parish registers, and most clearly in the careful register of Edward King, parish clerk from 1670 to 1719.[2]

22 April [1684] Evan Jones Amongomery shiere man.

29 November [1691] The wife and child of Henry Weston a stranger
11 January [1692] Richard Orpham a souldier
19 February [1708] Hannah Somewhich Shipson upon Stower 6 March [1709] Thomas Goodale, Brightwell poor.
23 August [1712] Elizabeth Thom a child of a travelling woman, buried from the holybush [an inn].

Not every year, but sometimes more than once a year, and especially in the winter, the most vulnerable of those on the move appeared in the burial register. At other times the registers were less explicit, but the itinerants continued. They were probably most numerous in the 16th century, when contemporaries complained most of sturdy vagabond. Those places where great abbeys were, observed the 17th-century historian, Thomas Fuller, 'swarm most with poor people at this day'.

If it had been possible to find two census-type listings of the parish such as Peter Laslett was able to analyse for Clayworth, St Thomas's would have given an impression of high mobility. This impression would be misleading. It had a stable core. The mobility of a parish does not depend on how many people leave a parish, but who they are. If there is a high turnover of newcomers while a substantial group of native families continues, the effect will not be serious, but if over the years it is the oldest established families which are emigrating, the structure of the parish will cease to be stable. In St Thomas's the older families continued, and amongst the most stable were those of the bargemen and fishermen.

II. SECULAR AND RELIGIOUS OVERLORDS

Open parishes, which had no resident lord of the manor were usually built on poor, marginal land. The inhabitants were as

---

[2] St Thomas's parish records have been deposited in the Bodleian Library since this was written, and await cataloguing.

poor as the land itself, and they also had a reputation for being freebooting, tough, and enterprising as the inhabitants of St Thomas's itself. It might well be thought that St Thomas's was just such a place; but this was far from being so. The parish had too many overlords. In the Middle Ages Oseney Abbey was lord of the manor of South Oseney, Rewley Abbey of North Oseney, and each held their own courts. As well the city had its jurisdiction in the parish, and the Castle Mill, from whose profits part of the fee-farm of the town was paid, also had its own court. The parish suffered from government from all directions. In the upshot this seems to have amounted to very little government indeed.

If this was true of the parish in general, it was particularly pronounced in the case of Fisher Row, for it lay like a bone between three dogs, an area of disputed jurisdiction. The his-tory of the Row before the 16th century is known largely from the chronicle of the disputes between three institutions, Oseney, Rewley, and the town of Oxford. The two abbeys represented spiritual authority, and they tended to act in alliance against the third, the town, the secular authority; and perhaps their quarrels were the more bitter for that. Not for nothing had the church which Oseney built for the inhabitants of the area been called after St Thomas Becket. This confrontation was further embittered by the frustration of the town in its long drawn out struggle with the university, a struggle in which it seemed permanently cast as the loser. Under Henry VIII the church became St Nicholas, and most of the lands of the two abbeys passed to Christ Church, but the old quarrel continued unabated until well into the 17th century. These battles were intimately connected with the Row, but before we trace their history let us consider the protagonists.

We shall take the town first. Oxford had been a major town in Saxon times. According to Domesday its burgesses had common pasture outside the wall of the town even then. This common, Port Meadow, still exists. The town's early commercial importance may be seen by the fact that Saxon Oxford had its own mint; as well there was some trade on the river, at least as far downstream as Abingdon. The town suffered at the Conquest, but the 12th century saw further growth, and the town gained its fee-farm, usually taken as the criterion of municipal freedom, in 1199. The early 13th century probably saw the peak of its commercial prosperity: it had a thriving cloth industry, a large colony of Jews, and the river had been opened from Oxford to London. Merton, the first of the Oxford Colleges, was founded in 1264.

Even before the Black Death, however, Oxford was showing some economic decline. The decline of the cloth industry in the towns was a feature of the 13th and 14th centuries, and Oxford was no exception. Indeed before the end of the 13th century the industry was moving out into the country to avoid guild regulation. In 1290 the Jews were expelled, and by the early 14th century the river was so obstructed by mills and fish weirs that no more is heard of the trade from Oxford to London by river until the 16th century.

As the town declined the university grew, and as rents decayed property fell empty and the university moved in. Yet the greatness of the town was by no means a thing of the past. In 1334 it ranked eighth in wealth amongst provincial towns according to Prof. Hoskins's calculations.[3] The middle years of the 14th century were a time of distress and financial disaster for the town. It suffered heavily from a visitation of plague in 1349, and in 1354 the notorious St Scholastica Day disturbances occurred, when the town and gown rioted and forty students and 23 townsmen were massacred. On its anniversary, for five centuries, the town was forced to humiliate itself before the University in one way or another, and it is not surprising that relations between the two remained strained: new grievances arose, and the fires of contention were kept well stoked. The fortunes of the town fluctuated but never recovered, and by the early 16th century its comparative standing was low. Hoskins's calculations, based on the lay subsidies of 1523-7, show that the town now stood 27th among provincial towns.[4] Such calculations may be at best a rough-and-ready guide, but the signs of diminished prosperity cannot be gainsaid. In its dealings with the two abbeys it had all the touchiness of a power struggling to maintain its dignity. It had an air of justified paranoia.

[3] W. G. Hoskins, *Local History in England* (2nd edn., London, 1972), 238.
[4] Ibid.

The occasion for most of the town's struggles with the two abbeys was the infringement of the rights of the Castle Mill. The Castle Mill stood hard against the west wall of the Castle where the gravel shelf most closely approached the river-plain, and its mill-stream ran close to the walls of the Castle. Behind it rose the tower of the garrison church, St George in the Castle. The Castle has now been replaced by the County Gaol and the tower of the church is generally called the Castle. The mill itself was pulled down between the wars, and only its sluices mark the position of its water-wheels.

The Mill is thought to be Saxon. It is usually identified with the mill mentioned in Domesday Book for which in the times of King Edward the town paid £20 a year to the King and six sextars of honey and to Algar, Earl of Mercia, £10. After the Conquest the Mill was held by the Keeper of the Castle, but later it reverted to the King. A moiety of the Castle Mill was granted to the town in 1199 when it gained its fee-farm, and from then on it was a trump card in any appeal the town might make against the infringement of the rights of the mill, for any loss in the profits of the mill would affect the ability of the town to pay their fee-farm to the King. The King retained the other moiety of the mill in his own hands, granting it from time to time to various persons who seem to have had no interest in it beyond the rent. These tenants seem to have sub-let it to the City, for there is no evidence of its being in other hands for any practical purpose.[5]

One of the feudal dues exacted by an overlord was soke of mill, the obligation to grind corn at the lord's mill. No doubt it was exacted by Saxon and Norman lords of the Castle Mill, and it was not abandoned by the town when it gained possession of the mill, for all freemen were compelled to grind their corn there. Possibly grinding corn at the mill now seemed less onerous than when it was in other hands, but the requirement was stringently enforced. The town had, however, no power to force those of its inhabitants who were servants of the University to grind at their mill, even if they were bakers, and the town resented the competition provided by other mills in the neighbourhood.

[5] *OCP* 200; H. E. Salter, ed., *Munimenta Civitatis Oxonie* (OHS lxxi, 1920), pp. xxxvi-xxxix; Wood, City, I. 404.

Freemen who failed to grind their corn at the Castle Mill
were amerced before the Court of the Castle Mill, a body of
which we first learn from its proceedings in 1337.[6] It also had
power to try those who obstructed the water supply, and men
from as far upstream as Binsey and Wolvercote were haled
before it. The mill was in the hands of millmasters in the 16th
and early 17th centuries, but when it was decided to lease the
mill out in 1623 these officials were no longer appointed, The
first lease in the City Ledger Books, one of 27 September
1623, shows that the right to hold courts was granted to the
lessee, for it was leased with 'All manner of Liberties Royal-
ties Courts ffines forfeitures priviledges and customes to the
said mills used or belongenge.'[7] The ensuing leases continued
to mention the court for about another century. The lease of
1763 was the first to omit any mention of it.[8] By then it had
probably been defunct for some time. Leases are often strangely
conservative documents.

So much for the secular power. Let us now turn to the
abbeys. The Augustinian abbey of Oseney was the older foundation, and we shall deal with it first. It was founded by Robert d'Oili II, the Keeper of the Castle, in 1129, and it lay in the
southern part of the Isle of Oseney to the east of the present
main stream of the Thames, amongst the river meadows, on
a site 'though low ... yet very pleasant both in respect of the
chinking rivuletts running out it, as also for the shady groves
and walks...'[9] It received some land in the parish as well as
much else, and it added to this as opportunity offered. About
1140 Robert d'Oili renounced his manorial rights over Oseney
and its tenants. The abbey prospered, and from being a priory it became an abbey in 1154. It acquired a mill by 1182-9,
which we shall hear much more of later, and by 1279 it was
the largest landlord in the parish. It owned 69 out of about
200 tenements listed in the Hundred Rolls in that year.[10] Most

[6] H. E. Salter, ed., *Snappe's Formulary and other Records* (OHS lxxx, 1923), 220-1, 260-2.

[7] City, D.5.5, fo. 395.

[8] City, D.5.12, fo. 159. For some inexplicable reason H. E. Salter in his work on city
leases omits all the leases before 1763, saying 'the city retained the Mill in its own hands'
(*OCP* 200).

[9] Wood, *City*, II. 195.

[10] Rose Graham 'Description of Oxford from the Hundred Rolls of Oxfordshire, A.D.
1279', *Collectanea, 4th series* (OHS xlvii, 1905), 62-3; Janet Cooper, 'The Hundred Rolls of
the Parish of St Thomas, Oxford', *Oxon.* XXXVII (1972), 165-76.

of these were situated in its own manor of South Oseney, This lay almost entirely south of St Thomas's High Street. A few tenements were in the manor of North Oseney, and others on the east bank of the Castle Mill Stream lay within the jurisdiction of the city. The site of Fisher Row lay on the boundary of the two jurisdictions. Within their liberties Oseney claimed to administer their own justice in minor cases, and freedom from many of the taxes levied on the town. Such rival jurisdictions have always provided a place where a town's regulations could be flouted. A town's authorities looked bleakly on such a place where their writ did not run.[11]

As a landlord Oseney was energetic and quick to improve its rents by increasing the industrial capacity of its property in the parish, and it built and maintained roads and bridges. Even within its own gates there seems to have been a certain amount of industrial activity. The place was busy and populous, so much so that Wood who described it as if he had seen it himself, tells us it was 'called oftentimes "villa de Ousney"' – the town of Oseney.[12] How true Wood's picture was we have no means of knowing, for even the foundations of Oseney have been obliterated. An outhouse and an arch are all that remain. We are not, however, concerned here with the activities of Oseney's tanners, wax-chandlers, luminours, tailors, brewers, and parchment-makers of whom Wood speaks, but rather with Oseney mill, and other lesser mills which Oseney erected on the streams of the Thames, and with the Abbey's attempts to wrest power from the Castle Mill to serve them.

Rewley was founded by Cistercians in 1281, much later than Oseney. The Earl of Cornwall was the second largest landowner in 1279, according to the Hundred Rolls. The Manor of North Oseney formed part of the Honour of St Walery of which he was the lord. In all he had 27 tenements there and these were used to endow Rewley. The abbey itself lay on a particularly low, moated site just west of the northern section of Fisher Row. Its watergate and part of its wall can still be seen from the top of Fisher Row.

The returns for the parish appeared partly under the North-West Ward and partly under the South-West.

[11] Joyce Youings, *The Dissolution of the Monasteries* (London, 1971), 84.
[12] Wood, *City*, II. 208-9.

As befitted a house of a contemplative order it took no such energetic interest in developing its property as the more wordly Augustinian canons of Oseney. It owned no mills or other industrial property so far as we know. Its entire property seems to have been in houses and meadows. They were affected by the way the Castle Mill was managed. As their land was as low-lying as any in the parish, and lay next to the Castle Mill Stream, if the miller at the Castle Mill held up the stream to a very high level then the site flooded. Most of their interventions in the battle for the control of water were aimed at preventing this.

III. THE CASTLE MILL AND FISHER ROW

Fisher Row stands on an island. This is not immediately obvious at present for high walls and buildings obstruct the view. The island is known as Warham Bank. It is the weir-ham of the mill, and forms an integral part of the structure of the mill, just as much as the mill stones. The structure of a water mill consists not only of its machinery but also of the channels and sluices or weirs which supplied and regulated the water which powered it, and this concerns us.

The siting of a mill was all important because on this depended the power that could be generated to turn the wheel. A place was chosen where there was a change in level in the ground so that the water fell from one level to the other at the point where the mill-wheel was placed. The position of the site might be nowhere near the water. Mills were built on dry land and the water was then brought to them, whether the site was beside a river or at a distance. It was easier to bring the water to the mill than build one in running water. Often an existing stream could be made use of for part of the mill-stream, but digging channels was labour-intensive – it required only primitive technology.

Every mill consists of two streams: one, the mill-stream, feeds the mill-wheel, and the other diverts water from it (See Fig. 1.4). The quantity of water to the mill can be regulated by opening or shutting up the appropriate channel by means of sluices. In the mill-stream, just above the wheel, sluices were built. When they were shut, no water passed to the wheel at all. A channel was dug from the mill-stream to carry off surplus

water and prevent flooding.[13] This was also controlled by a
sluice, which is essentially a small weir. The arrangement
of these two streams varies according to the terrain of each
Mill.[14] The Castle Mill Stream had this overspill channel cut
in its west bank. It was known as the Back Stream, a common
name for such a channel. It carried the surplus water some
distance before rejoining the Mill Stream. This was essential,
as otherwise the water could 'back up', and interfere with the

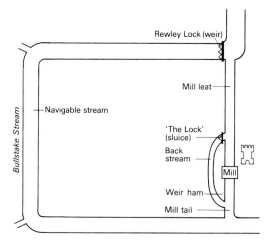

Fig. 1.4. The Basic Structure of Waterways Supplying a Mill.

turning of the mill-wheel. Between the two streams lay an
artificial island. However much it may be adapted to local
conditions, this is the underlying structure of the channels of
a simple watermill like the Castle Mill. This can be seen very
clearly on Agas's Map (see Fig. 1.1). Though the structures were
similar, names varied; though so far as the appurtenances of
the Castle Mill go, they show little imagination. The artificial island between the two streams was called Warham Bank
– the weir-ham, whilst the sluice was called 'Le Lok' in some
old documents, and we shall refer to it as The Lock. In the
late 16th century a second sluice was cut in the west bank
of the Castle Mill Stream, and its channel ran into the Back

---

[13] See Appendix I for a description of the siting of a mill and digging its channels.
[14] John Vince, *Discovering Watermills* (Tring, 1970), 10-12.

Stream, so that the length of the weir-ham was extended, and it came to consist of two long narrow islands, divided from each other by The Lock, and with a second sluice, known as The Lasher, at the north end of the Bank. This can be seen in the 17th-century map of David Loggan (Fig. Intro. I). The southern island was divided into two parts by a road, St Thomas's High Street, which ran from Quaking Bridge, just above the mill to the parish church, crossing the Back Stream by means of a small bridge called Bookbinders Bridge. It is the oldest street in the parish, and the most twisted. On the south side of this road between the two streams, lies a triangular piece of land, The Swan's Nest. Fisher Row runs north from St Thomas's High Street along Warham Bank. At first there were no houses north of The Lock. It was waste land until the 17th century. This northern part of the Bank is now crossed by two roads, one medieval, one built in the 18th century. The former is Hythe Bridge Street. It spans the two streams by means of two bridges, Hythe Bridge, and Little Hythe Bridge. It is moderately straight. The latter, the New Road is the straightest of all (Fig. 4.1). It leaps across the whole Row by the means of a single span, Pacey's Bridge, and immediately changes its name to Park End Street. It then rushes straight out of town to Botley and the west. The three roads divide the Row into three parts, which have not been called by the same names consistently over the whole period, but which we shall call by their modern names, Upper, Middle, and Lower Fisher Row. The most northern is Upper Fisher Row, and the oldest and most southern, Lower Fisher Row.

We have strayed a little from describing the structure of the channels and sluices or weirs of the Castle Mill, for we have not yet done. There was yet a third control of the water supply besides the two sluices in Fisher Row, and it also played an important part in the development of the Row. This was a large weir known as Rewley Lock built across the mainstream of the Thames. It diverted water from the mainstream of the Thames to the Castle Mill. The purpose of the two smaller sluices was to prevent the Castle Mill receiving too much water; this served to see it received enough.

Although they differed in size, The Lock, The Lasher, and Rewley Lock were all varieties of weir. Weirs came in different shapes and sizes and served many purposes on a river. A weir could be an impervious barrier in a river, such as a bank, or a structure to allow boats or water to pass. It could be a barrier of brushwood or osiers; an adjunct of a mill or a fishery or both. It could act as a door, a bridge, or an impervious barrier. One might pass over it, up or down stream, pass water through it, dam it up, or traverse it from side to side. The word could give rise to confusion, for it meant so many things, and served so many purposes.

IV. DISPUTED GROUND

We do not know when the fishermen first moved onto Warham Bank. Where there was a mill there were usually fishermen, for, as we shall see more fully later, mills provided ideal conditions for fish. Perhaps Vluuius the fisherman mentioned in Domesday lived there, and, if he did, very likely he was not the first. We do not know: there are no records, and it is therefore a matter of prehistory, and belongs to a world of which the historian's methods can tell us nothing.

The history of the Row begins when there were already houses on the bank. It began on that day in about 1130 when Robert d'Oili II, Keeper of Oxford Castle, and Editha, his wife, confirmed their gift of extensive estates to their newly-founded priory of Oseney.[15] In this grant Robert d'Oili named first those lands which lay closest to hand, lands which he possessed in the Isle of Oseney and the houses on the *wara* of his mill next the Castle of Oxford *cum omnibus mansuris quas habui supra waram que est de molendinis.* Oseney prospered and increased its estates. It acquired its own mill, and some time about 1182-9 Bernard de St Valery granted the abbey a lock or weir and the stream which ran to the mill (see Fig. 1.5. i). The name of this lock is not mentioned, and the commonsense assumption would be that it was the weir which diverted water from the mainstream of the Thames to Oseney Mill. The deed was endorsed *Carta ... de gurgite iuxta Osen' quie uocatur Lok*, which makes this seem likely, but H. E. Salter the great authority on the topography of Oxford has taken it to refer to Rewley Lock.[16] If it did Oseney got little benefit from owning it, as we shall see.

---

[15] *Oseney*, I.1.   [16] *Oseney*, II. 462-3.

So far Oseney owned a mill, and the town of Oxford did not. The position was soon to be rectified, for in 1199 Oxford was granted half of the Castle Mill, and became, to all intents and purposes, the owners of the other part also. The stage was now set for the long struggle between the town and the two abbeys, a struggle which affected the Row profoundly.

The struggle was inevitable, because the Castle Mill was so placed that it could divert as much water as it pleased from the river, and Oseney was powerless to stop it. All the water which passed down the Castle Mill Stream was lost to Oseney.

There were three ways in which Oseney could attempt to improve its situation. First, it could attempt to control the amount of water which was diverted to the Castle Mill by Rewley Lock (Fig. 1.5.i). Second, it could attempt to obtain water from The Lock, either to turn a mill or mills nearby (Fig. 1.5.ii), or, thirdly, and more ambitiously, it might seek to divert the water from The Lock across to Oseney Mill through new channels (Fig. 1.5.iii). Finally, it could cut an entirely new sluice in the bank of the Castle Mill Stream (Fig. 1.5.iv). All these methods were tried in turn, and in the process law-cases were fought, channels dug, and the geography of the entire area was altered. Yet though the quarrel recurs from time to time throughout the next two and a half centuries, this is probably only the tip of the iceberg, for men do not go to court over every minor check and irritation. Strife was built into the very geography of the parish.

A satisfactory agreement over the amount of water which each mill might have received from Rewley Lock would have eased the situation, but Oseney does not appear to have been in a strong bargaining position, for in 1315, when some form of rationing was imposed by the decision of a jury of Northgate Hundred, it was Oseney rather than the town which suffered. Normally Rewley Lock was held up to two and a half feet in height, and Oseney received the overplus, but in time of drought it was now agreed that the level of the lock should be raised to three feet, and Oseney should receive only as much water as flowed through three holes, each of four inches diameter.[17]

Oseney was therefore driven to try the second means of obtaining control of the water, by gaining control of The Lock.

[17] Ibid. 463-4.

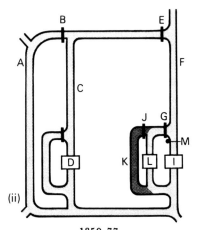

1182-9
i. *The grounds of dispute established.*
1199, Castle Mill granted to the town;
1286, Petition by Rewley.

1350-77
ii. *Water diverted to turn a mill on the Back Stream.* Cases against Oseney, 1350; Thos. Whiteley and Oseney, 1373; decision on Oseney's jurisdiction, 1377.

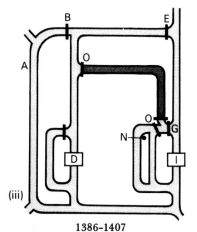

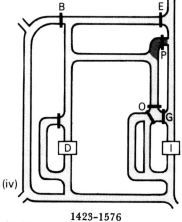

1386-1407
iii. *Oseney gains a lease of the Castle Mill*, and a lateral cut is made.

1423-1576
iv. *The Lasher cut,* filled in and cut again.

A = Bullstake Stream
B = Lock granted Oseney 1182 – 9
C = Oseney Mill Stream
D = Oseney Mill
E = Rewley Lock
F = Castle Mill Stream
G = 'The Lock'
H = The Back Stream
I = The Castle Mill

J = Kyndelweir
K = The back stream of the
      Back Stream
L = Mill erected by Oseney
M = Thos. Whiteley's house
N = Horsemill
O = 'the mills of Rewley'
P = The Lasher
▬ = New cuts

Fig. 1.5. The Evolution of the Waterways West of Oxford 1182-*c*.1578,
resulting from the dispute between Oseney and Oxford.

It was not, however, first in the field here, for in 1286, soon after its foundation, Rewley Abbey had petitioned that it be granted the *wara* of the Castle Mill from the mill itself upwards. The decision reached then showed very clearly the importance that the Castle Mill placed on The Lock, and Oseney's efforts must be seen against the background of this case.[18]

When Rewley petitioned the King for the grant of the Bank an *inquisitio quod damnum* was set up to consider the matter, and the jury pronounced that the bank was appurtenant to the King's Mill at the Castle. At that time, half was held by the Queen Mother and half by the burgesses of Oxford towards the payment of their fee-farm. The part to the north of Hythe Bridge was said to have no value except inasmuch as it contributed to the preservation of the *wara—quam sustenatio warre reprendit* – or, one might say, its importance lay in its being there. If it were breached it would cause £20 worth of damage to the King, because it would draw off water from the King's Mill. It must be kept intact. On this condition it could be granted to Rewley. The portion south of the bridge was worth 10s., and must not be granted to Rewley, for it was necessary that the *wara* should be opened or shut according to the state of the river, and if it could not be adjusted by the custodian of the mill it would cause considerable flooding and damage; indeed they said, it could cause flooding up river as far as Cricklade to the tune of £300 and more a year.

The case was no doubt watched with interest by Oseney, whom one half suspects of having aided and abetted Rewley, for the two abbeys tended to act together against the town. It must also have been watched with equal interest by the inhabitants of the Bank itself. We know from rentals of Oseney's tenants that three fishermen were living on the bank in 1285, and that they had been there some time, for they were living there at the time of the earliest known rental of the vicinity, some seven or eight years earlier.[19]

Here is a list of the tenants of the bank in 1285 – the year Rewley made its petition:

Cotagium primum super waram per Lucam piscatorem.
Cotagium secundum per Tropinel.

---

[18] Ibid. 470-3. [19] *Oseney*, III. 117, 127.

Cotaguim tercium per Matildam Mareys.
Cotagium quartum per Hankynun.
Domus Roland.
Domus [Ricardi le] Lingedraper.
Domus angularis cum duabus proximis.
Domus Nicholai piscatoris.
Domus Galfridi piscatoris.

It is interesting to notice that the tenant of the northernmost house – *primum cotagium super waram* – the house beside The Lock was occupied by a fisherman. From 1573 to 1829 the leases of this property show that it always had fishermen's families as tenants or subtenants.[20] In the same way the tenement next to The Lasher also attracted fishermen. Sites by sluices were attractive because a sluice provided an ideal place for setting up weels, that is a type of fish-trap favoured on the Thames. Once fixed in position in the mouth of the sluice these weels sieved out all the fish which came through with the sluice in a very efficient manner. The house by The Lock had ready access to it and there must have been a strong temptation for the fishermen to tamper with the sluices, and we find such interference expressly forbidden in a lease to a fisherman of lands on either side of The Lasher in 1852: '...it is hereby declared and agreed ... that the said Lasher called Ruley Lasher is not included in this demise and that the said Thomas Beesley ... shall not draw the sluices thereof or meddle with or use the same in any way whatever...'[21]

Now these fishermen who lived beside The Lock were ten-ants of Oseney. Was it possible that Oseney made use of its power over them to gain control of The Lock? We do not know, but it seems likely enough, and one tenant of this particular house by The Lock certainly got into trouble for diverting water from the Castle Mill Stream, at a time when the Abbot of Oseney was charged with a similar offence.

This case came up before John Froyle, Escheator of Oxfordshire in 1373.[22] The first case was brought against Thomas Whiteley. Surviving rentals show he was the tenant of the

---

[20] *Oseney*, II. 494-5; Ch. Ch., Deed Box St Thomas's, Fish Row, Tenement 1.

[21] City, E.5.2, fo., 139.

[22] C. T Flower, ed., *Public Works in Medieval Law*, II (Selden Society, x1, 1923), pp.117-22; *Oseney*, II. 464. The date given by Salter is 1371, but the opening of the roll (Oseney Roll, 91) was illegible, and the date is a conjecture.

cotaqium primum super waram in 1387 and 1389, and probably he lived there in 1373 also.[23]

Thomas Whiteley was accused of drawing off a large volume of water from the Castle Mill Stream by means of a certain gutter over the past seven years, whilst the Abbot of Oseney was accused of drawing off half the volume of water from the Castle Mill Stream over a period of 20 years, and obstructing the stream called Bakwater with two mills as his weir called Kindelweir. These mills on the Back Stream must have been small, and may therefore have been fulling mills. Rivalry in the cloth trade may have fuelled the town's wrath. The case against the abbot was not settled, for he died at this juncture, and the affair dragged on and grew as time passed.

By 1376 the case had become very involved. It had become one of principle, revolving around the jurisdiction of town and abbey. The town, no doubt angry about the theft of water, and also about the industrial activities in 'the villa de Ousney' which rivalled its own, claimed that its jurisdiction ran west as far as the ford from which Oxford took its name, which the town identified as the one on the western route to Abingdon by Ferry Hinksey, on the south-west boundary of St Thomas's parish. This included Oseney.[24] Oseney for its part held that its jurisdiction stretched east as far as the Castle Mill Stream, and included Warham Bank as well as the houses on it. Within its jurisdiction it claimed view of frankpledge, chattels of fugitives and felons, sok, sak tol, tem, and infangthef, and exemption from shires, wards, danegeld, and so on. A judgement was given by the Bishop of Lincoln in the following year, 1377. It confirmed to Oseney all the rights it claimed in its manor, but did not allow that the jurisdiction of the abbey extended to and included the houses on the *wara*, even though they actually belonged to Oseney. The stream which ran under Bookbinders (the Back Stream) was the limit of its jurisdiction, and no mills were to be placed upon it.[25] The mills on the Back Stream were removed and replaced by a horse mill.[26] Today Morrell's Brewery stands beside the Back Stream, and the remains of a

[23] *Oseney*, III. 180, 186.

[24] H. E. Salter, editor, *Mediaeval Archives of the University of Oxford*, I (OHS 1 xx, 1917), 192-201; *Oseney*, II. 161; R. H. C. Davis, 'The Ford, the River and the City', *Oxon.* XXXVIII (1973), 258-62.

[25] Oseney, II. 477-9.   [26] Ibid. 392-3

small Victorian water-wheel can be seen beside it. Old ideas have a habit of recurring.

This case had resulted from the activities of the abbey under one abbot, and they were concluded by his successor. John Bokelonde, who became abbot in 1373 attempted a new policy, and his achievements were summarised, a little misleadingly by an early chronicler of the abbey: *Io. Bokelonde [1373-1403] cuius tempore adepti sumus le Newinn, molendina Castri et kingsmede Duo placita; contra burgenses Oxon' pro fran-shesiis & alterum contra nativum monasterii; edificavit le locke iuxta Regalem Locum & compositio facta est inter nos & Regalem Locum.* [27]

Quite a large part of his career had clearly been given over to the relations of town and abbey and the politics of water-power. At the opening of his period of office he had been involved in the case with the city about the extent of Oseney's jurisdiction, and had been also involved in another with his tenants – perhaps they found the jurisdiction of the abbey oner-ous, or objected to such pressures as may have been placed on Thomas Whiteley. There may well have been other causes of friction. We do not know. It was a period of some unrest anyway, for the Peasants' Revolt occurred in the period of Abbot Bokelonde's rule.

However, it was during this abbot's rule that the King granted to Oseney the lease of the half of the Castle Mill which he retained in his own hands. In 1286 it had been granted to the Queen Mother. It was granted to the Abbey in 1386, exactly a hundred years later.[28] Though the Abbey, like all other lessees sublet its share to the town, this grant must have identified the interests of town and abbey to some extent, improved its bargaining position also, and made it possible to adopt a well-planned and rational scheme for increasing the flow of water to Oseney. So far the water which Oseney had wrested from the Castle Mill had been used to power a nearby mill; now it was possible to think of a more ambitious scheme, to move it by means of new channels to power the wheels of Oseney Mill itself. Under Bokeland, apparently, a new lock was built near Rewley, by agreement with Rewley (see Fig. 1.5.iii), and the water diverted along a lateral cut to Oseney

[27] *Oseney*, I.xv.   [28] *Calendar of Patent Rolls*, 1385-9, 214.

Mill through the lands of Rewley. A reference to this name-
less lock or lockes 'of Rewley' in a lease of Rewley Abbey in
1555 puzzled H. E. Salter, who knew that it was not a reference to Rewley Lock, and thought it must refer to The Lock.[29]
In a 16th-century deed of Oseney Mill it was leased 'together
with the streame and watercourse of Rewley nigh Oseney *for
the aid of the mills of Oseney*'.[30] Part of this stream can be
seen on Agas's 16th-century map (see Fig. 1.1) and also that
of Loggan (see Fig. Intro. 1), made 100 years later.

The 14th century had been a disastrous one for Oxford in many
ways, with drought and famine in 1315-16, and visitations of the
Black Death later in the century. The prosperous cloth industry
of the 13th century had declined, but by the late 14th century
things were improving, and the mills which Oseney was struggling to power were probably fulling mills. In the 15th century
their number increased, and with it Oseney's demands for water.
In 1412 Oseney was presented at the town's View of Frankpledge
for taking water which ought to pass to the Castle Mill from
Rewley Lock to serve four new-raised mills.[31]

Whether this finally ended the truce between town and abbey
we do not know, but attempts to establish a new sluice commenced about a decade later. Rewley again was first to enter
the lists. In 1423 the abbot of Rewley was amerced for diverting
water from the Castle Mill through a sluice in the bank of the
Castle Mill Stream.[32] This was an attempt to reduce the flow of
the water to the Castle Mill by making a new cut, a fore-runner
to The Lasher (Fig. 1.5.iv). The purpose of this cut would be
to reduce flooding. Whether Oseney was to benefit by turning
this water into their own mill stream is not known. If Rewley
had been successful in keeping its cut open, it seems likely that
Oseney would have made use of it. This was not to be. The cut
was blocked up.

Between them Oseney and Rewley had sought by four different methods to divert water from the Castle Mill: by means of
Rewley Lock and The Lock, by building new locks at Rewley
and by means of The Lasher. They had had no success, and the
two abbeys were not to see it done before they were dissolved.

[29] *Oseney*, III. 101. [30] *Oseney*, III. 97.
[31] *Oseney*, II. 470.
[32] H.E. Salter, *Medieval Oxford* (OHS, c, 1936), p.148.

V. THE DISSOLUTION OF THE MONASTERIES AND THE ROW

For St Thomas's parish the uncertainty and upheavals of the Dissolution spanned a decade, from 1536 to 1546. Rewley surrendered first, as one of the smaller monasteries in 1536. Oseney was one of the greater houses, and these had a brief respite. Oseney surrendered to the commissioners at the end of 1539. Oseney was chosen as the seat of one of Henry VIII's six new dioceses, and the new see of Oxford was established with the abbey church at Oseney as its cathedral in 1542. This scheme did not last long, however, for Henry decided to merge it with the College of King Henry VIII (formerly Wolsey's Cardinal College) which was situated nearer the heart of the town, on the site of the Saxon Monastery of St Frideswide, which had been suppressed by Wolsey to found his college. The new Bishopric of Oxford was founded again, with the monastic church of St Frideswide as its cathedral. The new Dean and Chapter presided both over it and the metamorphosed College, together forming that strange amalgam, Christ Church. The endowments it received included the manor of South Oseney, the site of the abbey and Oseney mill, and the site of Rewley, which had passed in the first place to Dr George Owen, one of the King's physicians.[33] The Bishop of Oxford was granted the half of the Castle Mill which Oseney had held, and this was later leased to the town, or, as we should now say, the City.[34] With the establishment of the cathedral in Oxford the town's status was raised, and Oxford became a city.

The centuries-old dispute between the two mills continued under the new dispensation, and even increased as energetic methods were introduced to solve the economic problems the changes in the parish had produced. Unemployment was rife, and made more distressing by the inflation of the period. Vacant houses and arrears of rent bear witness, to the difficulties of the times. The problem was one which assailed other towns where great religious houses had been destroyed. As they travelled from one such place to another the commissioners

---

[33] *LP Henry VIII*, pt. ii, §§ 332(26), 648 (25).
[34] Ibid. 476 (9); *OCP* 200.

exercised themselves with the problem of the employment of the poor of these places. Cloth-making was the favourite scheme, and it was noted with approval or recommended to be undertaken at such places as Stamford, Abingdon, Oxford and Gloucester.[35]

At Oxford it was decided that Oseney should be leased to a clothier to establish cloth-making there. Perhaps it was due to John Leland, who had been a fellow of King Henry VIII College, and had written of William Stumpe's work at Malmesbury, that Christ Church decided to refurbish the mill and let it to the great clothier. He was to be prepared to set 2,000 people to work: 'Thyrdly, he must bynd hymself to fynd worke for ij M persons from tyme to tyme, if they may be gotten, that will do their work well contynually in clothemaking, for the succour of the Cytye of Oxenford and the contrey about yt, for which intent the mylles were made.'[36]

The venture did not go right. Almost immediately Stumpe assigned the lease to another clothier, James Atwood or at Wood, and the old antagonism of town and abbey was reactivated between the city and Christ Church when he set his wheel to work. The result may be seen in a letter of which a draft still remains in the archives of Christ Church. It was addressed to Sir John Williams JP.[37] Having recited the grant of the site of Oseney and of the mill and of the water course from the Thames through Oseney Lock for 'the succour and manteyning and setting a worke of the same citie' the Dean and Chapter related how they had erected a fulling mill and assigned it and the site to William Stumpe who in turn had assigned it to at Wood the clothier on 22 March 1547:

... though the mills bring great wealth to the City, and have always been enjoyed by the Dean and Chapter, and though the inhabitants of Binsey have time out of mind used the water course for conveying their corpses for burial, yet, not withstanding, one [Peirs] of Hinksey in Berks, being

---

[35] *LP Henry VIII*, pt ii, 613; ibid., pt. i, §§ 332, 1342; BL Cotton MS. Cleop. E. IV, fo. 251 (quoted in youings, *Dissolution*, pp. 178-9).

[36] MS Top. Oxon. c.22 (formally Gough MSS *Oxon*. 70), fos. 42,69-72.

[37] Ch. Ch. MS estate book 77, fo. 230-2. 'A Calendar of Estate Papers at Christ Church', VIII. 97. The suggestion that the farmer of Oxford [Mill] cut off the water supply appears in the transcript accompanying the original document in the estate book. At this time the miller at the Castle Mill was one Peirs, according to 'The Book of Evidences', 1, 223 (Ch. Ch. MS 1.c.2), which gives a synopsis of the affair.

farmer of Oxford Castle, by the abetting and stirring of the mayor and aldermen of Oxford ... [mutilated, but apparently he has cut off the water supply to the mill] ... The Mayor and aldermen have also grievously taxed and fined Wood, having procured judgment against him in their own courts where they acted as judges, and have caused diverse actions to be commenced against him in the courts within the liberties, by reason whereof Wood and his servants dare not come into the said liberties about their necessary affairs. On 13 August [1552] Walter Pytts, Harry Target, Edmund Robyrtson, Denys Hyck and Thomas Towseye of the parish of St Nicholas, and divers other 'misruled persons' to the number of eight or nine persons came in a riotous manner with pikes and staves and entered the freehold of the Dean and Chapter and apprehended one [blank], servant to Wood and took him by force out of the liberties and peaceable franchises of the Dean and Chapter.

This fracas at Oseney has particular interest for us, for some of the men involved were inhabitants of the Bank,–Pitts, Hicks, and Robinson - and two of these bear fishermen's names, Pitts and Hicks, which we shall meet again. Their first leases date from 1573,[38] but this case suggests that they were already living there, and were already fishermen in 1552. The complaint is that the miller of the Castle Mill has cut off the miller of Oseney's water supply, but the anger of the miller at the Castle Mill had surely been roused by the newly refurbished mill at Oseney depriving the Castle Mill of water. If this water was diverted through Rewley Lock this would affect fishermen in the Row who placed fishtraps in the waters of The Lock, and would make them willing tools of the miller at the Castle Mill, for their livelihood would be affected as much as his.

The quarrels over the Bank continued. The Bank did not cease to be disputed ground when it passed into the hands of Christ Church. The Atwoods continued at Oseney, but a new scheme was sought to set the poor to work. In July 1555 a lease was granted by the Dean and Chapter of the Bank from The Lock to Rewley wall for the erection of a fulling-mill to set the poor on work. The lessee was given leave to enclose this void ground with doors at either end, and to make a lock near Rewley wall, that is on the site of The Lasher. The scheme came to nothing, possibly because of the hostility of the city, perhaps even through a second riot, but the reference is obscure. [39]

---

[38] *Oseney*, II. 494-6. They were tenants of the first three tenements south of The Lock.

[39] *Oseney*, III. 99; Turner, *Records*, 224, City, C.13.I^q.

If a sluice was cut at this time it was filled in soon after, and it was not until 1576 that The Lasher was finally established probably to improve the drainage of the site of Rewley (see Fig. 1.5.iv).[40] It does not appear on Agas's map of 1578, which must have been surveyed before the cut was made (see Fig.1.1).[41]

The Lasher contravened the agreement of 1286 to keep the northern part of the bank intact. Perhaps because of this the city managed to gain control of the northern part of the bank by an exchange of property with the tenant sometime before 1583, an arrangement Christ Church apparently accepted.[42] With the building of The Lasher a second, northern weir-ham was carved out of the matrix of the bank, and on the long strip of land between two streams the Fisher Row and its community of boat-people developed.

---

[40] Turner, *Records*, 383-7.

[41] The engraving of Agas's map does not show the Bullstake Stream. Whether this is because Agas omitted it by mistake, or it was dried up in 1578, or this portion of the map was already illegible to the engraver, as it now is, is not known.

[42] 'Book of Evidence', I. 82.

CHAPTER 2

The Fishermen of Fisher Row

I. THE MARKET FOR FISH

Fishing and hunting are amongst the most primitive activities of man, and the tools of the early fisherman resembled those of the hunter. Both used the net and the trap. The fishermen of the Thames were therefore the inheritors of a tradition which goes back to prehistoric times. We can say exactly when the barging trade started in Oxford, but we cannot say when men started to fish in the Thames.

The importance of the harvest of river fish in times past is easy to overlook for at the present day fish from our rivers plays a negligible part in the diet of most English people. Few have ever eaten pike, perch, or even eels, for though angling is a popular sport, the fish are normally returned to the river at the end of the day rather than eaten. Yet, before the advent of the railways, locally-caught fish formed an important part of the diet, especially when fast-days were still observed. Under Henry VIII a victualling officer might count on supplying fish on three days out of every seven, and fasting did not end at the Reformation. Indeed, under Elizabeth the number of fast-days was increased for a period, so that one writer computed that there were as many fish days as flesh days in the calendar.[1] Though Protestants regarded fasting as superstitious, abstinence from flesh was enjoined for sound economic reasons. It acted as a form of rationing, husbanding the supplies of both cattle and corn, for man and beast must share alike the hard-won harvest. To winter a beast only to slaughter it in early spring, rather than breed from it, would be a great waste. If Lent had not existed it would have been necessary to invent it.

---

[1] *LP Henry VIII*, III, pt ii, § 2774; Thomas Cogan, *the Haven of Health* (London, 1584), 139.

Many fish were therefore required to victual a town the size of Oxford, and many fishermen must have been employed in

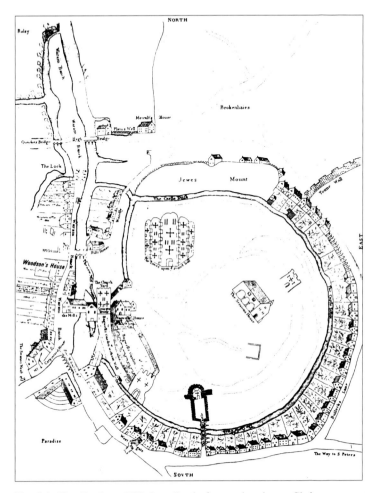

Fig. 2.1. The Castle and Warham Bank, from a drawing at Christ
    Church, before 1618.

supplying its needs. Yet, in the 16th century, before 1556, though 12 fishmongers took apprentices, no fishermen did so until January 1556. After this the position was reversed; there were many fishermen's apprentices and hardly any fishmongers'.

Clearly something odd was going on, some sort of power struggle or battle for the market, and we would do well therefore to investigate the state of the market and the emergence of the fishermen; for that there were fishermen, however obscure their situation, we may be as sure as there were fish in the Thames.

What sort of fish was available in Oxford in the 16th century? We have an excellent source in the accounts which the city bailiffs rendered for their expenses in maintaining Thomas Cranmer during his imprisonment in Oxford before his martyrdom.[2] Cranmer was in prison during Lent, and the bailiffs set out his daily fare as if it were a menu. The amounts were for four persons. At the onset of Lent, meat, cheese, butter, and eggs were withdrawn. Dried fruit, almonds, bread, ale, wine, and fish made up his diet. For dinner on most days he was presented with eel broth, herring, ling, and often oysters. A 'dish of the day' introduced variety. For supper a lighter meal was prepared, though dishes of perch and roach, or dace and roach (costing 6d.) were often provided, and occasionally mussel broth at 3d. A table analysing fish supplied for dinner is given in Table 2.1.

From this list we can see what a wide variety of fish was available in an inland town like Oxford during Lent to the wealthy – for even in prison a prince of the church was not treated as a poor man. Indeed the variety is puzzling. Part of the period would fall in the Fence Months, yet much freshwater fish is listed.

The fish may be divided into preserved (salt or dried), and fresh (salt-water and freshwater); into local and imported; into cultured and uncultured. The most important division however for our purposes is the division between imported and local. The first was the preserve of the fishmonger and the second might lie within his sphere also, or the fisherman himself might sell directly to the customer. Where both fisherman and fish-monger were in competition prices would naturally fall. As the mid-16th century was a period of serious inflation we may expect consumer resistance to high prices, and a conflict between the fisherman and the middleman would tend to arise.

[2] Turner, *Records*, 234-40. This is condensed without notice from Corpus Christi College Library, Cambridge, MS 128, 265-405.

The obscurity of early fishermen may reflect the paramountcy of the fishmongers in this conflict of interest between the two groups.

Table 2.1. Archbishop Cranmer's Lenten Fare. Dinners for 31 days and suppers for 19 days from 19 February to 20 March 1555/6.

Fish	Approx. Price	No. of Dinners	No. of Suppers	Total
Herring	3d.	30	19	49
Ling	7d.	27	19	46
Eel Broth	3d.	27	0	27
Oysters	3d.	19	0	19
Roach	6d.	3	16	19
Perch	6d.	0	16	16
Pickerell	12d.	14	0	14
Salt Salmon	9d.	7	7	14
Stockfish	5d.	6	1	7
Eels	6d.	6	0	6
Fresh Salmon	8d.	6	0	6
Thornback	8d.	2	3	5
Mussels in Broth	3d.	0	3	3
Dace	6d.	0	2	2
Gurnard	9d.	1	0	1

The fishmonger was a substantial merchant with wide interests. The trade in fish was a complex matter and capital was needed, both to survive the vicissitudes of the trade and to organise it, for fish had to be imported from London or other coastal towns. Sometimes they may have supplied river fish to London also, for it is unlikely that they travelled with empty panniers in one direction. An Oxford fishmonger had to have contacts in London, and it seems likely that trading links were developed between families in the two towns. Configurations of names can sometimes be discerned in this trade even where no details can be worked out, and no records of the trade exist. The will of the well-to-do London fishmonger Robert Yonge provides an example worth examination. His will was proved in 1576. He lived in the parish of St Mary at Hill in a corner tenement over against Billingsgate, which he had bought of John Smyth esq., and, amongst other property, he owned a tenement let to John Astill, tallowchandler. Besides a son, Thomas, he had two married children, one being Katharine Wilkinson, his daughter. If his family predeceased him, money was to be laid out to endow two scholarships at Oxford and one at Cambridge.[3] At Oxford, in about 1530/1, a Richard Yonge had appeared in the records as a rippier, in an incident to which we shall soon return. In 1542 a Thomas Younge of London sold his property in Oxford, and it included a house between one of Richard Gunter and one of John Pye.[4] Both these men were fishmongers, and both were mayors on more than one occasion. John Pye took as an apprentice fishmonger one William Wilkinson in 1536. Nor is this the end of this association of Oxford – London fishmongers' names. In 1599 Miles Astell was the occupant of the room under the Guildhall known as the Lower Guildhall. This lay immediately behind the fishmongers' stalls. In the next lease it was taken over by Michael Younge, yeoman.[5] The configuration of the names Younge, Astill, and Wilkinson in both places in an area given over to fishmongers is suggestive, even though the relationships of the families cannot be charted, and they occur over nearly 80 years.

The fish which the fishmongers imported fell into two classes: preserved and fresh. Preserved fish was eaten in large quantities and was relatively cheap. Its price reflected the fact that, though it might be brought considerable distances, its carriage created none of the problems which the carriage of fresh fish posed, for fresh fish was highly perishable. Dried fish seems indeed to have been almost indestructible, for it required one hour's beating and two of soaking before it was cooked. Such fish could be entrusted to anyone. Indeed, this, for the fishmonger must have been something of a problem, for not only could anyone carry it, but very often they did. The local carrier could bring it. Merchants carried it as back-loading, returning from the coast. Large institutions like Oseney Abbey and Christ Church bought their own supplies once a year, Oseney at Stourbridge Fair, Christ Church at London, and both bypassed the local fishmongers.[6]

---

[3] PRO PROB 11/58/39 (Robert Yonge).
[4] Turner, *Records*, 166-7.
[5] *OCP* 148-9.
[6] *Oseney*,VI, 283; *LP Henry VIII*, IV, pt. iii,§ 6788.

The market in fresh sea fish was a very different matter. It called for specialists, but it was a risky business. The market was affected by glut, dearth, war, and weather. A man needed a long purse to survive its vicissitudes, but if he did so the profits were great. Dealing in fish had something of the risks and rewards nowadays associated with playing the stock exchange.

The supply of fresh sea-fish to an inland town required speed in transit, and speed at a period when the roads were very poor indeed. In the 19th century, when a coach took six hours to make the journey from London to Oxford, the coachman Bayzand used to buy fish at five in the morning at Billingsgate market and transport it in a cradle slung on the axle-tree of the coach and had it in Oxford with his load of passengers and all their baggage by the evening.[7] In the 16th century there were no regular rapid coaches. Fresh fish was carried by 'rippiers'. These fish-carriers travelled fast, and organisation was required for speed. The rippiers who operated between Rye and Hastings and London, for instance, are known to have changed horses at Chipstead (near Sevenoaks), whilst those who brought 'south sea-fish' to Worcester and Gloucester ob-served some sort of time-table: 'A Common Inne in this village [Nimesfeild] addes fame thereto, by the constant customary baytes of the Ryppiers and their horses, each Thursday in the yeare, at fower of the clocke in the afternoone, for one hour only ...'[8] The fast-riding rippier, his cloak cast over each shoulder, his legs enveloped in boots made of ropes of hay belongs to one of those obsolete occupations which have left little trace. There is only one mention of them in the Oxford city archives, but presumably they worked to Oxford as regularly as to Worcester or Gloucester.

The incident involving a rippier at Oxford is, however, an interesting one, for it shows evidence of consumer resistance to the prices charged for fresh sea-fish. The University was incensed by the prices charged by the fishmongers, who would

[7] [William Bayzand], 'Coaching in and out of Oxford, 1820-40' in *Collectanea IV*, 269.

[8] John Smyth of Nibley, *The Lives of the Berkeleys Lords of the Honour, Castle and Manor of Berkeley in the County of Gloucester from 1066 to 1618. With a Description of the Hundred of Berkeley and its inhabitants*, ed. Sir John Maclean (3 vols., Gloucester, 1885), III. 302; *OED*, entry for 'rippier'.

not allow the rippiers to sell fish directly to the public. Instead, the fishmongers bought from the rippiers and then resold at a very high price indeed. The Commissary and the Proctors of the University had therefore seized the fish from the rippier, Richard Yong, and also from two fishmongers who had already bought their supply from him. The fish had then been sold by the University bedells and their wives at what the University officials considered a fair price.[9]

As well as sea-fish the fishmonger might sell freshwater fish. We have no means of knowing whether Cranmer was supplied with his pike, perch, roach, and eels by fishmongers or by fishermen. Possibly the Bailiff, Thomas Winkle, who had a tenement in St Thomas's, near Fisher Row about this period, arranged to be supplied by the local fishermen. On the other hand, a fishmonger may have supplied all that was required. The price of sea-fish could not be held up too far above that of local fish, and the wide waters of the Thames were both a threat and a challenge to the fishmongers of Oxford.

II. THE FISHERMEN AND THE FREE WATERS

The Free Waters of the city of Oxford were extensive, and though they are not mentioned in Domesday were probably as ancient as Port Meadow, the common land of the city. The waters stretched from Magdalen Bridge on the east side of Oxford, to Godstow on the west, well upstream from the medieval town. They took in most of the minor streams of the area, and have been estimated to have extended to seven miles of water.[10] In the 16th and 17th centuries the city also claimed jurisdiction over the 'Foreign Waters'. These seem to have stretched from Prynses Weres' to 'Scissiter' [Cirencester] and Cherwell, though the site of Prynses Weres is not known. Both the Free Waters and the Foreign Waters were under the control of the water-bayliff, an office which, like so many offices in the 16th and 17th centuries, was let out, the perquisites of office and the fines being profitable. In March 1556 the water-bayliff paid 20s. to the chamberlain for the Foreign Waters, and 6s. 8d. to the bailiffs for the Free Waters. As well, 26s. 8d. was also paid to the High

---

[9] Turner, *Records*, 79-80, 87-8.   [10] See Appendix II.

Waterbayliff. He was probably the Water-bayliff for the whole of the Thames, an official appointed by the King, who presumably sublet portions of his jurisdiction. A conflict of jurisdiction between this official and the city of Oxford arose in 1620, and nothing is heard of the foreign waters after this date.[11]

All freemen had the right to fish in the free waters, whether they were tanners or cordwainers, brewers or bakers, fishmongers or fishermen. They were therefore a great boon to the poorer freemen who could not afford to pay for fish from the fishmonger. The price of even the cheapest fish on Cranmer's menu amount to 3d., and at that time the daily wage of the unskilled labourer was about 6d.[12]

It is easy to see that freemen who were also fishmongers and fishermen would be able to exploit their position if they were powerful enough. Hence towns which had valuable commons in land and water tended to frown on men in high office holding more than one victualling trade, or indeed holding any during their period of office.'[13]

Fishmongers were men of substance in Oxford in the mid-16th century. Between 1530 and 1570 three of them were mayor: John Pye, Richard Gunter, and Ralph Flaxney. Between them they held office for nine years of this 40-year period: 1532/4, 1545/8, 1551/3, 1562/3, and 1567/8. Two of them, moreover, held two victualling trades. Richard Gunter was a fishmonger and brewer, and Ralph Flaxney a fishmonger and chandler.[14]

They were therefore in a position to attempt some sort of control of the waters and of the sale of fish outside the market. Two methods were open to them: they could prevent fishermen becoming freemen, or they could prevent freemen fishing the Free Waters. Our evidence for their preventing fishermen becoming freemen is entirely circumstantial. There are no statements of their policy, or acts of council to which we can

---

[11] City, A.4.1, fo. 50; ibid., F.5.2, fo. 28-9.

[12] E. H. Phelps-Brown and Sheila V. Hopkins, 'Seven Centuries of Building Wages', in E. M. Carus-Wilson, ed., *Essays in Economic History*, II (London, 1962), 168-78.

[13] Turner, *Records*, 139, 150-1.

[14] City, A.5.3., 'Enrolments of Hanasters & Apprentices to 1590'. Gunter took two apprentices 'in fishmongers and brewers craft' on 6 Mar. 1544, and Ralph Flaxney one as fishmonger and chandler on 26 Apr. 1552. The volume is not pagi-nated or in chronological order. A note in the front says 'This book seems to have been composed of detached portions of books and to have been bound up by a person unable to read dates'.

point. A man could become a freeman in three main ways: by serving an apprenticeship to a freeman, by buying his freedom, or 'by his father's copy', that is, the son of a freeman had a right to become a freeman. At this period there is little evidence of men becoming freemen by patrimony, and presumably, if they did, there was no way the fishmongers could have stopped them. Before 1560 fishermen were only admitted by purchase or enrolled as apprentices when other men who were not fishmongers were in office. On 6 September 1550 John Clark of Garford, Berkshire enrolled as an apprentice to Dionysius Hycks of Oxford, 'fysher, weler and netknytter', but, it was noted, in the margin, the apprenticeship fell through, as the necessary fees were not paid. This was not a common occurrence, but it could nevertheless have been entirely fortuitous. No further attempt was made to enrol any further fishermen's apprentices for nearly a decade, nor is it possible to tell from the evidence of the admission of freemen how many were fishermen, for their occupations were not stated. But other sources provide some evidence, and shed oblique light on the matter. In the late 1540s and 1550s several men who had a strong interest in fish were admitted as freemen perhaps by purchase under mayors who were not fishmongers. Two such men were John Owen and Nicholas Day.[15] John Owen was from Sandford, down river from Oxford, where a John Owen kept a weir – probably a fish weir – in 1585. Nicholas Day was a miller, who kept a mill at Wolvercote above Oxford, and later two mills below Oxford. His son Thomas became a fisherman. Whilst they were admitted without any apparent difficulty, when they attempted to fish the Free Waters during the mayoralty of the fishmonger Ralph Flexney they were arrested by the bailiffs.

John Owen of Sanford, in com. Oxon, and Richard Day of Long Witnam, in com. Berks, deposed before me, Tho. Owen, ... that in the last yere of King Edward vj[th], after the exaltacion of the crosse, xiiij[th], of September, what certayne day they remembered not, they went in fysshing in the common waters behind Friswythes, adjoining to Cowmede, together also wth one Nicholas Day of Wulvercotte, and that John Wayte and Thomas Cogan, then Bailyes of Oxford, came unto them wth a poer of men, and entred into their botes and tooke awaye their nette and fisshe, and took with them the said Nicholas Day and John Owen, and when

[15] Turner, *Records*, 174, 200.

they came to Karfoks, Alderman Irish there then sitting and espying them coming, askid what the matter was; quoth the said Wayte and Cogan, We have taken foryners in fishing in or common waters. Then quoth Alderman Irish, As for one of them, John Owen, I know he is free, for he was made fre in myne yere, and I will be suerty for him. Then quoth Nicholas Day, What say ye then to me, am not I also a freeman? Whereto Alderman Irish answered y^t he cowld say little for him, and the said Bailies said farder that he was no freeman … and therewth tooke away from him both his nett and his fissh; they then had him also to Bocardo, and did sette him in the stocke howse otherwize then freemen are wont to be used. Alderman Flaxon being then Mayor, which being complained unto refused to do him justice therein. Tho. Owen, Roger Hyrne, James Saddock.[16]

So far as John Owen was concerned the case misfired, for it came up before Alderman Irish, during whose mayoralty he had become a freeman. Nicholas Day, however, suffered the ignominy of being treated as if had never been admitted, and the Mayor, Ralph Flaxney refused his appeal – as might be expected.

The second method of control, by denying the freemen the use of the Free Waters, was achieved by leasing them out. If the waters were leased out to private individuals, in severalty, then even if they were not leased to fishmongers, it would mean that the fishing was in fewer hands, and therefore could be more easily controlled. On 24 March 1556, a few days after Cranmer's death, the Free Waters were thus leased out. Unless a few small streams escaped them, all were leased out, save for a minor concession to the Freemen. John Perse was to have the fishing from the High bridge [Hythe Bridge] to Godstow, saving to all men from Walton to Godstow and the other part to Angle only' and the town was to have one day to take fish 'as the custom hath been heretofore'. Bartholomew Lant was to have the water from the tail of the Castle Mill Stream to Oseney Mead. Four others were jointly to have the waters and all creeks from South Bridge [Folly Bridge] to Magdalen College, and Rychard Williams and Richard Flaxney were to have the waters from South Bridge to the ferry. Williams and Flaxney were also to have the Waterbaileyship, paying 20s. a year to the chamberlains for the Foreign Waters, 6s. 8d. to

[16] Turner, *Records*, 215. The original is lost. The Bodleian shelf-mark given by Turner is a nonsense. I am grateful to Dr Barratt, Mr Vaisey and the late Dr Hunt for instituting a search.

the bailiffs for the Free Waters and 26s. 8d. to the High Water-bailiffs. These sums were for the jurisdiction of these waters. The leases to the waters, themselves were for sums between £3 and 13s. 4d., and all ran for 21 years. Richard Flaxney who was one of the lessors of the waters, and jointly water-bailiff of the city was a chandler and a fishmonger, and brother to Ralph Flaxney.[17]

The leasing of the waters in this wholesale fashion however, seems to have caused an outcry amongst the freemen, and in May 1558 a decision to call in the leases to the Free Waters was embodied in an agreement between the mayor, aldermen, bailiffs, citizens, and common council. It was not just a decision of the inner Council but of the wider body.[18] This was not to be the end of leasing out the waters. From time to time more or less of the waters were leased out, but never again in this wholesale way.

The tide was turning for the fishermen, and fishermen and their apprentices began to be admitted freely. Denis or Dionysius Hicks took an apprentice on 20 January 1560, this time successfully, and others followed. Swithin Broadwater took an apprentice in the same year, having been recently admitted himself; Thomas Day was admitted in 1564 and John Wodeson and Thomas Angell in 1566, and all these in their turn took apprentices.

Matters were improving for the fishermen, but they were not yet entirely plain sailing. In 1577, for instance, the water-bayleyship was renewed, this time to Richard Williams and Alderman Williams. Perhaps as a result of some agreement made then the Council decided in the following year that no further fishermen's apprentices should be taken.[19] The letter of the law was obeyed. Until 1598 roughly during the 21 years of the lease, no boys were apprenticed as fishermen, but this did not prevent the fishermen taking apprentices; they were simply described as weelers and net-knitters.[20]

[17] City, A.4.1, A, fo. 50; Turner, *Records*, 134-5; City, A.5.3, 7 May 1541 and Sept. 1543 (Flaxney); ibid., 6 Mar. 1544 (Gunter).

[18] Turner, *Records*, 269.

[19] City, A.4.1, fo. 68; City, A.5.5, fo. 212.

[20] To Day: City A.5.3, 15 Mar. 1579 (Hunt) and 10 Dec. 1582 (Smythe). To Angell: City, A.S.3, 3 Mar. 1581 (Griffin); City, L.5.1, 15 Mar. 1592 (Nycolls) and 6 Apr. 1594 (Tawney).

As the numbers of fishermen increased the numbers of fish-mongers fell. There were no more fishmonger mayors, and the trade in preserved fish passed to the chandlers, who took over the fishmongers' stalls in the market.[21] The battle the fishmongers had fought had been lost, and those that remained specialised entirely in the luxury end of the market. This can be seen very clearly in the inventory of Nicholas Orum, who died in debt during a cold spell in January 1669. Letters of administration were granted to a creditor, who was anxious to realise what he could from Orum's assets. These consisted almost entirely of his stock-in-trade, which, because of the weather, seems to have kept well. It was worth £47 3s. 9d., and the perishables consisted of high-class goods. There was no stockfish, such as the chandlers sold, but whiting, rabbits, neats' tongues, four sturgeon, oysters, lobsters, and 'orringes and lemons being frost bitten'. He had come down in the world, and his house-hold goods were only worth £2 0s. 0d., yet they gave evidence of a more prosperous past, for they included pictures and 'a little howse for children to play with'.[22]

III. FISHERMEN'S WORK

So far we have been watching a struggle in which only one side has been visible, and the important one, so far as we are concerned, has been hidden from view. Now the fishermen are beginning to emerge, and it is time we considered them and the work they did, for the nature of their work had a profound effect upon the men and their families.

If fishmongers resembled corn-dealers or badgers in many ways, fishermen resembled farmers, though the acres they har-vested were acres of water rather than land. Like farmers their acres were limited in extent. A fisherman could not fish where he pleased. An Oxford fisherman might fish the Free Waters, but their extent was limited, and if he overfished them out-rageously he could expect to be unpopular with his fellow freemen. No fisherman could expect to make a good living from this source alone. The fishermen seem to have leased waters beyond the bounds of the Free Waters, though as these

[21] *OCP* 150.

[22] MS Wills Oxon. 171/2/5 (Nicholas Orum); E. Thurlow Leeds, 'Oxford Trades-men'sTokens', in H. E. Salter, ed., *Surveys and Tokens* (OHS, lxx 1920), 425-7.

fisheries were in the possession of many private persons, and many were not indentured, very few leases have been found, and even fewer for the fishermen who lived in Fisher Row. It is known, however that Walter Bonner alias Pitts of the first tenement, the one near the Lock, leased a fishery at Kennington, down the river from Oxford, in 1649, from the feoffees of the church of St Michael at the North Gate, Oxford.[23] Thomas Spindlove of North Hinksey, whose family later moved to Fisher Row leased the same fishery in 1733. In the 19th century the Beesley family is said to have leased Wolvercote Lake and Red House Lake, excavated to provide gravel when the railways were built, whilst in a guide for anglers to waters accessible from the Great Western Railway in 1869 it was said that at Radley, just downstream from Kennington the Beesleys 'go halves with the farmer and present lessee, who holds the power to net it'.[24] Some of the fisheries of the Oxford fishermen lay quite far afield, and the distinction between the city's freemen and the 'foreign' freemen may have been quite difficult to draw at times. Of course, some fishermen, like farm-labourers, were employees and not their own masters. Magnates who owned great estates along the river often had their own fishermen. During the time of the ascendancy of the fishmongers this must have been the position of most Oxford fishermen. Nevertheless those who were freemen were men who were normally self-employed.

The fisheries attached to mills were amongst the best, and were often sublet by the millers. The fishing of the locks, sluices, or weirs of a mill called for co-operation between miller and fisherman if the grinding power of the mill was not to be reduced, and often, where the mill was small, miller and fisherman were one. As mills grew larger, their productivity multiplied, as did the wealth of the miller. There was no similar potential for increased productivity and prosperity in fishing. In the 16th century the miller seems to have been poised between two worlds. The miller of Botley apprenticed his son to a fishermen in 1582; the occupational name Molineux is

[23]   Berks. RO D/EX. 75. T 15 (4, 5).

[24]   Interview with Messrs. F. J. and J. H. Beesley, watermen, St Edwards School, 20 May 1975; Greville F. Barnes, *The Rail and the Rod, or, Tourist Anglers' Guide to Waters and Quarters around London, II: Great Western Railway* (London, 1869), 60.

found in a family of fishermen at Wolvercote, relatives of Nicholas Day whose misadventure in fishing the Free Waters has already been discussed.[25] Nicholas Day himself was a miller whose son was a fisherman. Millers' sons were swept into the expanding education system of the 16th and early 17th century. In 1546 a Thomas Percye held Langford Mill and two locks [*lez gittes*] in South Hinksey; and it was from this hamlet that John Piers or Peirse, 'born of humble parent-age' went to Magdalen College in 1542, the first step in a career which ultimately led to the Archbishopric of York.[26] John Piers may not have been the son of Thomas Percye the miller, but it strains credulity to believe that in such a small place there were two unrelated families of that name. The horizons of the fishermen grew narrower as those of the miller enlarged.

Wherever he fished, the tools of the fisherman were the net and the fish-trap. Fish-traps were of two sorts, bucks and weels, sometimes called grig-weels, as they were mainly used to catch grigs, that is, eels. The weel was along vase-shaped structure, made of osiers, with a flared mouth, leading into an inner, baited chamber. The wide mouth was made of a cone of osier twigs which came together, but were not secured at the apex. The eel, nosing his way towards the bait, brushed through the yielding twigs which closed behind him, penning him in as effectively as a ring of retroverted teeth. The entrance was, in effect a primitive valve. The fish were removed through a plug-hole at the other end, which also served for the insertion of bait. Weels could be sunk in a row across a river or attached to weirs or to a sluice, such as the one at The Lock or The Lasher in Fisher Row. Bucks were large, permanent, standing frames to which mammoth weels were attached, which could be raised or lowered into the stream.

The nets used by Thames fishermen have not been as carefully described as weels and bucks or even the nets of deep-sea fishermen. In the past most treatises on fishing have been written by sporting gentlemen, and when they are not entirely

[25] City A.5.3, 10 Dec. 1582 (Smythe to Day); MS Wills Oxon. 43/1/65 and 43/1/62; Oxford University Archives, G.G.5, fo. 233.

[26] *LP Henry VIII*, XXI, pt.ii § 332 (26); DNB, John Piers.

[27] C. J. Cornish, *The Naturalist on the Thames* (London, 1902), 102-5 and plate opposite 146; H. R. Robinson, 'Life on the Upper Thames', *Art Journal*, New Series, XII (1873), 141-2.

devoted to angling, deal with nets yielding sport. The fishermen's nets on the other hand aimed at eliminating all elements
of sport or chance. In a fishermen's agreement of 1623 the use
of pitch-nets and flew-nets was regulated, whilst in 1620 the
Thames Waterbayliff demanded that the Oxford millers and
fishermen should bring all their 'Tramills, castingnetts, flag-
netts, trollnetts, shownetts, and all other nets and gynes' to
be measured according to the standard.[28] Whatever all these
nets were is not clear, but it seems clear that amongst nets,
flew- or draft-nets were much favoured.

Nets were made of hemp and steeped in preservative. In
his *Gentlemen's Recreation* Richard Blome suggested that
they be taken to the tanner or dyer.[29] For the Oxford fisherman, tanners, hemp-dressers, and dyers were to hand, for they
shared the river banks with such industries.

Fishermen were subject to certain bye-laws in fishing, in
the interests of preserving the stock of fish. The size of mesh
of nets was regulated. Presumably this was what the Water
Bailiff's 'standard' measured. As well, fence months were
observed when the river was 'put in defence', and fishing was
for-bidden. The length of the fence months differed from time
to time. In 1623 they stretched from the last day of February
to the first of June. Regulations governing the fence months
also varied.[30]

Fishermen needed bye-employments during the fence months
to tide them over the lean period. This would be the time

---

[28] *Council Acts*, 1583-1626, 314-15; City, F.5.2, fo. 28. Many of these names of nets are obsolete and perhaps some names even had different meanings in different localities. Descriptions
of various nets which were either used on the Thames or probably resembled those so used are
to be found in the following works: On draft, drag-, flew-, or seine-nets: F. M. Davis, *An Account
of the Fishing Gear of England and Wales*, V (Revised ed., 1927), but it deals mainly with sea-
fisheries; J. Geraint Jenkins, *Nets and Coracles* (Newton Abbot, 1974), 223-62 deals with Welsh
and west country rivers in the main, but has an extensive section on seine fishing, some of which
was probably applicable to the Thames. On casting nets see H. Cholmondeley-Pennell, *Fishing:
Pike and other Coarse Fish* (London, 1886), 47-9. Flag-nets were probably stake-nets or kyddels.
See Thacker, *Highway*, I. 23-4; Jenkins, *Nets and Coracles*, 41-3. For trammells see OED: Davis,
ibid. 219-21. For hoop-nets see Robinson, 'Upper Thames' *Art Journal* XIII (1874), 1412. For an
angler's view of nets and fish-traps generally see *Francis Francis, The Practical Management of
Fisheries* (London, 1883), 100-1.

[29] Richard Blome, *The gentlemans recreation* (London, 1686), pt. ii, 194-5.

[30] As for example *Council Acts, 1583-1626*, 314-15; *Bye Laws and Rules for the Regulation
and Preservation of the City of Oxford Fisheries* (Oxford, 1847), 5-6.

for refurbishing old equipment and for making new nets and weels for their own use and for sale. Some fishermen had osier hams attached to their fisheries, and these supplied withies or 'rods' for making weels and baskets. In 1626 in a terrier made of Egrove Water, a private fishery on the stream which leaves the Thames at the boundary of the Free Waters below Oxford, the hams and waters were listed and also 'the three kinds of radds of which baskets are made':

yewster radds: yellowe of colour.

Hormer radds: Redde

witam radds: yewster radde alias browne of colour ...[31]

The swift-growing crop of osiers was put to more uses then than now. In the Middle Ages for instance, platforms on scaffolding were made of basketwork.

Wild-fowling on the river flats where snipe were plentiful was probably not limited to Port Meadow, for the woods were near, and the county boundary made escape fairly easy, as we have seen. The fisherman in fact exploited all the resources of the riverside that lay to hand, and their diversity gave him security. He might not grow rich, but he would never starve.

The fisherman's work was not to be learned from books, but by example and practice. He must know the habits and movements of fish, and how weather and seasons affected them. He must know every deep and shallow of his water, and be sensitive to the changes which the action of flood or drought brought. Sons learned from their fathers, with whom they worked, or where there was no son the seven years of apprenticeship was passed in learning to exploit every contour of the fisheries. Students at the University spent less time acquiring their skills.

A fishery, like a farm, was a thing of value to be passed down from generation to generation, though son did not necessarily follow father. In a time of high mortality the father might outlive his sons, and the tradition be continued by a son-in-law or a grandson. The disappearance of a surname from a series

---

[31] New College Archives, No. 12527, Terrier of Egrove Water made by Arthur and Hugh Broadwater. Hormer rods would be named after Hormer Hundred, in which Egrove Water stood; and 'Witam' rods after the villages of Witham, north of Botley.

of leases to a fisherman's house or waters may mean no more than that the succession has passed through the female line, but it has still passed by inheritance.

A fishery was also like a farm in being a limited resource. The number of people it could support was finite, and a man must have extensive fisheries if more than one of his descendants were to follow in his footsteps. Usually a younger son must marry a fisherman's daughter and take over her father's fishery if he wished to be a fisherman too. Hence fishermen's children often intermarried, and in Fisher Row, where they lived close together, propinquity also played its part.

Alternative employment for fishermen's younger sons must often be found. Net-making and weel-making were used to some extent, and so was hemp-dressing. John Collins suggested it as an employment for sea-fishermen outside the fishing season, and here in Oxford it seems to have been a natural trade for men to follow who had been brought up amongst boats.[32]

The trade of the barber, or barber-surgeon, may seem a far cry from that of the fisherman, yet Richard Blome, in talking of nets in the late 17th century remarked 'The charge and difficulty of making them is easy, for almost every Barber is a proficient therein.[33] We shall see that three fishermen's sons from Fisher Row became barbers. Perhaps net-making learnt in childhood made such men deft in the making of hair-nets and wigs; perhaps the collecting of leeches also brought the two groups together. In Cambridge the inventories of privileged persons proved in the Vice-chancellor's Court included one of John Paske, surgeon, who owned a boat; another, John Thomas, owned nets.[34] The trade of the barber-surgeon is now obsolete, and its ramifications clearly included aspects of which we know nothing, which link it more closely to the trades than to the professions. Like the miller's trade, his was one whose status was raised over the centuries by knowledge and improved technology.

---

[32] John Collins, *A Plea for the Bringing in of Irish Cattle and Keeping out of Fish* (London, 1680), 17-18, 28-32.

[33] R. Blome, op. cit. 195.

[34] Cambridge University Archives, Vice-Chancellor's Court; Register 2, f0. 102 (Will of John Thomas, appraised 28 Oct. 1545). I am grateful to Miss Mary Siraut for this information.

Table 2.2. Comparison of average annual matriculands and total number of fisherman's apprentices per decenium.

Date	Estimated annual admissions of students*	Total apprenticeships per decade
1560-9	231	5
1570-9	413	4
1580-9	445	2
1590-9	358	3
1600-9	374	1
1610-9	363	3
1620-9	400	7
1630-9	530	0†
1640-9	219	2
1650-9	438	6
1660-9	458	4
1670-9	400	2
1680-9	321	1+1 'foreign freeman'‡
1690-9	303	1+1 ,, ,,
1700-9	316	2
1710-9	321	4+1 'foreign freeman'
1720-9	303	1+1 ,, ,,
1730-9	271	0
1740-9	221	1+2 'foreign freemen'
1750-9	182	0+3 ,, ,,
1760-9	205	1
1770-9	235	1
1780-9	254	1
1790-9	245	0

* Statistics for student admissions are from Lawrence Stone, 'The Size and Composition of the Oxford Student Body', in Lawrence Stone, ed., *The University in Society*, I (London, 1975), 91.

† Navigation open to London, 1635.

‡ Foreign freemen lived outside Oxford. How far they supplied the Oxford Market is not known. Like other freemen they had the right to vote in the parliamentary elections for the representation of the city, and were often brought in by the candidates of their parties to vote.

The number of fishermen working in Oxford depended both on their prosperity and the amount of fresh fish eaten per head of population, and on the total size of that population. The population of Oxford in turn depended to a large extent on numbers at the university (see Table 2.2). In the period of education expansion before the Civil War, a period when fasting was still observed, the apprentices of fishermen were more numerous that any other time. But after a brief resurgence at the end of the Civil War the numbers of students and fishermen fell away.[35] The decline in fasting as well as the development of the Thames for navigation in the 17th century also reduced their number. Not until the 19th century when unemployment was rife after the Napoleonic War were fishermen's numbers to show a significant increase again, and then their circumstances were very different from those of the period before 1800.

Between their emergence in the latter part of the 16th century and the end of the 19th century the Oxford fishermen were men with an independent position in society. Though they were in an occupation which was declining slowly from the middle of the 17th century, yet because of their variety of bye-employments they had a good measure of security. We have no contemporary descriptions of any of the fishermen of the Row in this period, but we have a vivid little vignette of a fisherman from Burcot, near Dorchester, below Oxford. It is by Thomas Hearne, who, though a crusty pedant and a bigot, had been born of poor parents, and worked as a day labourer himself before being educated by a patron. He had an ability to describe working men which is unusual in the early 18th century.

Yesterday as I came from Sandford, at Iffley I met with one Robert Day, a man of 66 years of age as he told me ... He lives at Burcot near Dorchester, with his wife by whom he has had (as I was told at Iffley) ten fine children, several of which are now living. He is a man who brings fish often to Oxford, and is a basketmaker by trade. He pretends too much sanctity and Religion, and great skill in the scriptures. But I was well informed that he is a Presbyterian, and often preaches ... to those demure people.[36]

Though Robert Day called himself a basket-maker to Hearne, and also when he made his will in 1728, his friends called him a fisherman when they made his inventory.[37] He came from a

[35] Stone, 'The Size and Composition of the Oxford Student Body, 1580-1619', 91.
[36] Hearne, *Collections*, VIII, 403-4.
[37] MS Wills Peculiars 67/2/35 (Robert Day).

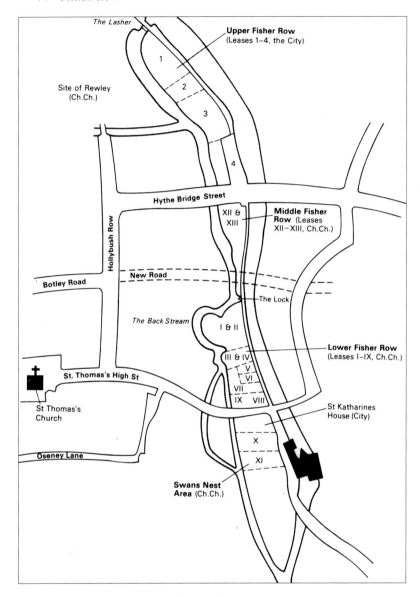

Fig. 2.2. The leases of Christ Church and the City in Fisher Row and the Swans Nest area.

dynasty of fishermen in the Dorchester area stretching from the 16th to the 18th century. The only other account of an Oxfordshire fisherman is very recent. William Beckley came of a line of fishermen who fished the Cherwell from the 17th century until about 1900. He lived at Islip where Robert Graves got to know him in the years after the first world war. Robert Graves described him in *Goodbye to All That*, a sturdy, fiercely independent rural socialist. It is interesting to find the same type of man in both descriptions two centuries apart. Though we shall find a similar spirit – carried to the point of bloody-mindedness – in the fishermen of the Row in the 19th century, our material on those of the 16th and 17th centuries tells us nothing of their attitudes. Nevertheless the position of the fishermen seems to have been remarkably independent, somewhat like that of the miller, a man who was frequently non-conformist and notoriously litigious. Such attitudes seem to have been engendered by their position in society and the nature of their work.

IV. LEASES AND LANDLORDS

The fishermen of St Thomas's parish come to light in the documents about the middle of the 16th century. It was a time of ends and beginnings, in the parish, for the two abbeys had been dissolved. It is often difficult to compare the state of the parish before and after this upheaval. We have one source however, which will serve this purpose fairly well in tax lists – the lay subsidies of 1523 and 1524 and that of 1544.[38] Though the assessments are not entirely comparable, they show that the parish was in a very unsettled state. In one case assessment was by goods or wages; in the second by property and household stuff. As well, the earlier returns were by parishes; the later one by wards. St Thomas's lay at least partly in the north-west ward, but possibly also partly in the south-west ward. Clearly no over-all comparison of the parish is possible at the two different periods. We can however see how many men paying tax in the earlier period survived into the latter. Of course many must have died in this time, whilst others will have fallen into poverty and senility in old age. In 1523 there

[38] PRO E 179/161/198, E 179/161/174, E 179/162/229.

were 52 assessable persons. In 1544 four survivors from this listing were found in the north-west ward, and three in the south-west ward – 13.5 per cent of the total listing at most. It is instructive to make a similar comparison in the 17th century, using the lay subsidy of 1648 and the poll tax of 1667.[39] By this time Oxford was more prosperous, and more settled. In the 1648 assessment 35 out of 76 individuals can be identified by Christian name and surname or, in one case, by title (Alderman) and surname. Of these 35 names 12 are still found in the assessment of 19 years later, or 34.28 per cent. The second assessment contains more names than the first list, and perhaps more who had become old and poverty-stricken were counted in the second 17th-century list than in the 16th-century one, but nevertheless the difference is considerable. The parish was more stable in the 17th century that in the 16th century. This is confirmed by the structure of the families of fishermen. By the 17th century they were beginning to form the dynasties which were characteristic of this occupation group. In the mid-16th century there is no sign of long generations in these families.

If we look closely into Agas's map of Oxford of 1578 we can see it shows the small terrace of houses in Fisher Row, just south of The Lock (see Fig. 1.1). Leases for the year 1573 show that three families with fishermen's names were living there and since these are the first leases of these properties, and great changes had affected the parish earlier in the century, we might well expect them to be newcomers in newly-built properties. In fact, however, two of these families had been in the parish in the 1540s. Denis Hicks (we shall dispense with exotic variations of spelling) was listed in the Subsidy for 1544 in the north-west ward, whilst Walter Pitts appeared in a list of arrears of rent for properties of the Dean and Chapter of the short-lived Cathedral Church of St Mary at Oseney for 1546-7.[40] Denis Hicks and 'Water boner' appear in a rental of Christ Church properties for 1549.[41] Though this does not necessarily show that they were then living on the bank, the

[39] E 179/164/499; City, P.5.7.
[40] *Oseney*, III. 290.
[41] Ch. Ch. MS xxix. b. 2.

fracas at Oseney in 1547, which involved both Walter Pitts and Denis Hicks, suggests that these 'misruled persons' were already there.

The fact that there were no earlier leases is not a matter of great importance as evidence of their occupation of property on the bank, for very few properties in the parish were leasehold before 1573. Until the 1570s most household tenements in the parish were probably copyhold, but in the 1570s legislation was passed regulating the management of college estates.[42] The Act of 1572 dealt particularly with their property in towns. Under this Act property could be leased at not less than the customary rent for not more than forty years, and could not be alienated unless by exchange for property of equal value, and repairs became the responsibility of the tenant. The aim of such legislation seems to have been to make it impossible for an irresponsible generation of fellows to live well at the expense of future generations. Leases of the small tenements of the parish began to appear, therefore, in the following years: four on 1 October 1573, seven on 1 October 1574, and further leases followed.

There is much to be learnt by studying the leases of the fishermen's tenements, so, before we turn to examine the individual families let us turn aside to study the framework of tenancy agreements. Understanding them will provide us with greater insight into the economic standing of the fishermen over the years (see Fig. 2.3).

The property was leased for forty years initially, and after this it reverted to the lessor unless in the meantime the lease had been renewed. By regular renewal security of tenure was achieved. The annual rent charged in the lease never varied, and rising costs were dealt with by changes in the entry fine which was payable when a lease was renewed. This fine which was at first arbitrary settled down to between one and a half times to twice the rack-rent (current commercial rent) of the property, if renewal was made at the normal time. In St Thomas's renewals were made every 14 years. If renewal was delayed more was normally charged. In the 19th century and perhaps earlier too, if property had been rebuilt or improved by the tenant it was the custom of Christ Church

---

[42] 13 Eliz. I c. 10; 14 Eliz. I c. 11; 18 Eliz. I c. 6.

Fig. 2.3. Tenants and subtenants of Tenements 1-6 Lower Fisher Row.

FIRST	SECOND	THIRD	FOURTH	FIFTH	SIXTH
1573 Richard Wilson [Joan Pitts alias Bonner]	n.k. Francis Robinson plumber & son Robert	1573 Denis Hicks fisherman	1573	Richard Wilson with first Tenement	[John Backester, labourer]
1574 Joan Pitts alias Bonner			1574	John Backester	John Backester
	1612 Thomas Hicks fisherman	1601 Thomas Hicks fisherman	1601	Robert Backester, fisherman	1601 Robert Cooke, fisherman & Phillip Dodwell of 7th Ten. granted portions on leases of years by R.B.]
1606 Walter Bonner alias Pitts, fisherman	1625 John Wright tailor	1619 Thomas Hicks fisherman	1604		Robert Backester, fisherman
1616 do. (Id.)			1633	do.	do.
1628 do. (Id.)	1650 John & Margaret Wright (d/o T.H.)	1650 John & Margaret Wright (d/o T.H.)			
	1658 2–5 leased to Ann Broad wid. (formerly 2nd wife of J.W.) 2nd sublet with 5th [Wm Tirrell S in L to R.B.]; 3 [Robert Carter]; 4 [John Carter]				1658 John Clarke waterman
1644 do. (Id.)	2 and 5 let together	3 and 4 let together		let with 2nd tenement	
1653 do. (Id.)	1681 William Gardner waterman	1670 Thos. Bowell, maltster, and Ann hwf. (formerly Wright then Broad) [Thos. Wilkinson] [Thos. Flight]			1681 John Clarke waterman [1670 Francis Rose, fisherman]
1669 John Curtice fisherman (DS)	1699 do.	1673 Ann Bowell wid. assigns to Thos. Reeve pipemaker			1699 John Applebee, tailor
1713 do. (Id.)	1719 Thos. Gardner bargeman (S)	1700 Francis Loader, brewer [John Lapworth & another]			1714 Richard Tawney I boatman [Rd. Tawney I] [Eliz. Clarke his M]
1727 do. (S)	1749 Richard Gardner boatman (S)				

Fig. 2. 3. (contd.)

2 and 5 let together	3 and 4 let together	let with 2nd tenement
1743 Jeremiah Bishop	1729 Thos. Loader, brewer (S)	1728 Richard Tawney I Binsey, boatmaster [Rd. Tawney I] [Mile Cook]
1784 Thos. Spindlove fisherman (6 tens.) assigned to	1743 Deborah Loader wid. [formerly Rd. Tawney]	1743 Richard Tawney I, brewer [Rd. Tawney I]
1788 Thos. Spindlove fisherman [P. Payne, fisherman]	1757 John Treacher, alderman & Mary hwf. (D) [Ed. Spindlowe]	1758 Eliz. Tawney, wid. of R.T. I
1802 do.	1771 do.	1772 Ed. Tawney mealman (S)
1809 Daniel Taunton gent.	1785 Rev. Thos. Treacher, (S?)	1786 Ed. Tawney, alderman (Id.)
1814 Daniel Taunton, 1, 2, and 5 let together	1799 Sir John Treacher, Kt.	1796 Fee simple sold to Ed. Tawney (Id.) [Ed. Grant]
1828 John Ingram Lockart M.P. 8 tenements	1829 Trustees of William Hall, brewer. Ann White, John Evetts & Thos. Duffield	

Key: Subtenants given in brackets
S = son of previous tenant
D = daughter of previous tenant

hwf. = his wife
Id. = identical with previous tenant
M = mother

S in L = son-in-law
ten. = tenement

Largely based on *Oseney II*, 494-9.

to waive any revaluation of the property for 28 years, charging meantime the fine at the old rate. This information comes from the evidence of the Chapter Clerk of Christ Church, Mr Baker Morrell before the Select Committee on Church Leases in 1837/8. Unfortunately we have no evidence of what was the custom when tenants died. It seems, though, that the tenure was disposed of by will, for we have wills for almost every leaseholder of the Row. When a widow inherited she seems to have entered her tenancy without paying any fine. Thus when Walter Bonner, alias Pitts, of the first tenement died about the end of 1663, he held a lease at 10s. a year, last renewed in December 1653. The entry fine was probably £10, as this amount was paid subsequently for some time. The rack-rent value of the property was therefore about £6 or £7, the lease had four years to run, and the lease was valued at £21, calculated on the value of the rack-rent. When his wife died four years later, in 1667, her lease was valued at £120.[43] There is no extant renewal of the lease, and probably never was one, the renewal being automatic and without fine. However, perhaps we are putting too much weight on the absence of a lease.

Over the years the terms of the leases became more stringent. The duties of tenants increased, and were made more explicit. How far these changes represented actual change and how much the codification of actual practice it is difficult to say. In some cases it is more one of power than economic gain. Yet, over-all, the leases bore more heavily on the tenant as time passed. At first as much as ten weeks' grace was allowed in the payment of rent, but later this was reduced to 28 or 30 days. Again, though repairs fell on the tenant, at first stone and 'great tymber' was supplied. Later no materials were mentioned. Doing service at the Courts of Rewley and Oseney was explicitly added to the conditions of the leases of the second, third, fourth, fifth, sixth, and tenth tenements between 1601 and 1658, but this may merely have codified existing requirements. Clauses requiring permission to sublet were included early in the 16th century, and licences to do so were granted for a fee later, and bonds for

---

[43] MS Wills Oxon. 6/2/19 (Walter Bonner alias Pitts); MS Wills Oxon. 6/3/21 (Elizabeth Bonner alias Pitts); *Oseney*, II. 495.

the execution of covenants were established.[44] With every lease obligations of tenants increased, and those of the land-lord decreased. The leases of the fourth, later the third and fourth, tenements provide a good example. Consider the following sequence of deeds: (1) 1 October 1574; (2) 18 December 1604; (3) 1 March 1633; (4) 16 April 1658. In (1) timber and great stone would be supplied for repairs. In (1) and (2) ten weeks' grace was allowed in paying rent. In (2) and (3) per-mission must be sought to sublet. In (4) a licence was necessary. In (3) and (4) the tenant was required to repair the pitching in front of his house. In (4) the tenant must do service at the Courts of Rewley and Oseney.

In these changes the tenants of the first tenement suffered least and latest of all. From at least 1616 they had permission to sublet, without further permission for as much as 20 years, and it was not until 1727 that they were brought into line with other tenants, but they were never required to do service at the manor courts. Their position next to The Lock which controlled the Castle Mill Stream gave them a position of strength. The city would have been unlikely to countenance the occupant of this house being under the jurisdiction of the Manor Court with which it competed for the water supply.

At first glance, the growing regularity with which leases were renewed might suggest that the inhabitants of Fisher Row were becoming more prosperous in the 18th century, but this was not so. The property was becoming investment property. The annual 'rent' paid by the lessee was considerably less than the rack-rent, so an investor could make a profit by subletting college property. The small tenant-occupier was not in such a position. He was simply a man seeking a roof over his head. Though the fines were not high, and the annual rent was very low, the cost of repairs (a euphemistic term which covered re-building), taken with the recurrent fine, bore heavily on men with few resources save their own labour. Sooner or later these expenses would coincide with slack trade, ill health, or old age. One way of overcoming the difficulty was by subdividing when rebuilding and then subletting, so turning part of the property

---

[44] Ch. Ch. Deed Boxes, St Thomas' Parish, Fish Row, tenements 2-6, 10; Ch. Ch., 'The Book of Evidences', I. 61-5, 69.

into an investment. The other recourse was to the money-lender. The fortunate might borrow from a relative, but this was the exception. One way and another the houses of the poorer tenants multiplied. As the conditions of leases grew more stringent too, tenants' difficulties increased. The economic stagnation of the mid-18th century did not reverse the trend. The process continued throughout our period, and by 1800 most of the Christ Church property in the Row was sublet.

V. THE FAMILIES OF THE ROW

Agas's map shows a small terrace of tenements just south of The Lock in 1578. At that time it was occupied by four families. First came the Bonner alias Pitts, next to The Lock, in the medieval 'cotaigium primum super waram'. They were fishermen. Next, in the second tenement, came the Robinsons, plumbers. By 1612 they had been replaced by the Hicks, who were fishermen, and who also leased the third tenement. At the end of this small terrace was the Backester's house (see Fig. 2.3). This family's occupation was sometimes said to be fishing, sometimes boating, and sometimes they were described as labourers. They had a large piece of land which they sub-divided. In 1575 their subtenant was Robert Cooke, a fisherman. Later it was subdivided on a permanent basis, and its tenants included families who were interested in barging.

We have, therefore a graded involvement in fishing in the Row, from The Lock southwards, starting with the family of the first tenement, occupying the most advantageous site and always fishermen, to the second and third tenements where men were frequently involved in fishing, down to the fourth tenement, where families were only slightly involved and living in an area which was only partially developed in the 16th century. By the time one reaches the houses at the foot of the Row, facing on to St Thomas's High Street, their occupants looked to the parish rather than the river. Finally the house in the Swans Nest area, which lay close to the mill, had its own fishery. This was a large house, only sometimes occupied by a fisherman. The fisherman here was clearly not interested in the Lock. To give some idea of the social and economic condition of the fishing families from the 16th to the 18th century, we shall take them in turn, starting with the Wodesons.

VI. THE WODESONS

The founder of this family, Nicholas Wodeson was the builder of the wharf at the top of the Row. The house which his son, John, occupied by the Swans Nest area was the largest house on Warham Bank, St Katharine's house. It stood on the corner of St Thomas's High Street, opposite the foot of Fisher Row. As this house suggests, the Wodesons were a family of some standing.

The words 'poor' and 'fishermen' tend to go together in our cliché-ridden minds, but it would be a mistake to regard the 16th- and 17th-century fishermen as amongst the poorer members of the community. It is true that none ever rose to great prominence in the affairs of the city, but they could be well connected. This, however, means something very different in the fluid and socially mobile society of 16th- and early 17th-century Oxford from what it would mean in the 18th century.

The mobility of this age depended very much on education. The changes of religious allegiance of successive reigns had depleted the clergy, so that by Elizabeth's reign there was an acute shortage. Many had to be educated to fill the vacancies, and the universities expanded to meet the demand.

John Wodeson, the fisherman, was son of Nicholas Wodeson, wharf-owner, and Superior Bedell of Theology, farmer and occupier of Rewley Abbey. He himself was a fisherman and Inferior Bedell of Arts. His stepmother married the sixth President of St John's. One of his sisters married the seventh President, and the other a substantial plumber. He was uncle to a bishop, father both to a fisherman and also to another Inferior Bedell of Arts.

The world presented to us by the Wodesons and their kin is one which is remarkably varied. A fisherman who was also an Inferior Bedell of the university seems to us an unlikely figure. In later times bedells were normally men of learning. Thomas Hearne was very briefly a bedell, yet in a university which was expanding so rapidly the number of well-qualified men must fall short of demand. What is remarkable is not so

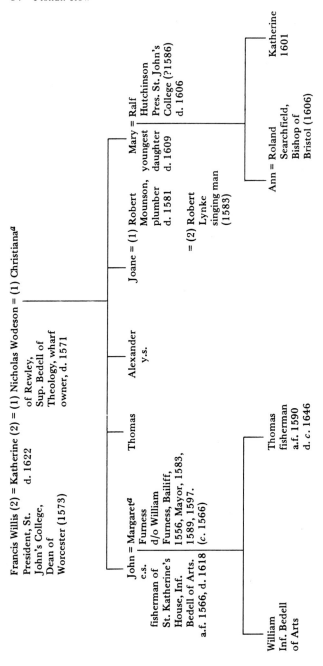

Family Tree 2.1.   The Wodeson Family.

a Order of children's births not known

much the worlds the Wodesons spanned as the remarkable achievements of the society which encompassed them.

Nicholas Wodeson, the head of this variegated family probably moved into the parish in the early 1540s. He was the lessee of Rewley Abbey when it was granted to Christ Church in 1546, and with the abbey went certain lands, pools, and fishings. He also became a Superior Bedell of Theology in 1559 in the place of Leonard Belsyre, the brother of the first President of St John.[45] He had three sons. Little is known of Thomas and Alexander. John, however, married Margaret, the daughter of a prominent baker, William Furness, some time before 1556. In that year John Wodeson became a freeman by purchase, paying a low fee because of the services rendered to the city by his father-in-law, then a chamberlain.[46] Perhaps it was about this time that his own father, Nicholas, acquired the lease of the land near Hythe Bridge where he built the wharf. This is about the earliest date he could have done so, for in July 1555 the land by the river from Rewley to the Lock had been leased out by Christ Church for an ill fated experiment in building a fulling-mill.[47] On 5 August 1569 John Wodeson took the son of a weeler as an apprentice. He probably worked to some extent in partnership with his brother-in-law, Robert Mounson, the plumber, who seems to have been as much involved in fishing as in his work as a plumber. Robert Mounson was one of a succession of three well-to-do plumbers who occupied tenements near the foot of Fisher Row from 1459 for over a century. He was an enterprising, grasping man, and had managed, by methods which were less than scrupulous, to lay his hands on most of the lands and tenements his predecessor had leased from Oseney as long leases just before its dissolution.[48] He was a prosperous, pushing man, and his interest in fish seems to have been as strong as his interest in plumbing.[49] Our evidence is here, as so often, scrappy and

---

[45] *LP Henry VIII*, XXI, pt. ii, § 648 (25); Andrew Clark, ed., *Register of the University of Oxford*, II (OHS x, 1887), 257.

[46] City, A.5.5, fo. 107.   [47] See above, p. 53.

[48] PRO C 3/177/30; C 3/182/18; *Oseney*, II. 501-2; *Oseney*, III. 96-7.

[49] In this William Thomas alias Plummer may have resembled him. He may also have had a connection with fishmongers, though the evidence is circumstantial. According to the Book of Evidences after his death the 11th Tenement, which he held before Mounson, passed to William Coppinger, and by his will to his daughter,

trivial, yet illuminating. In 1566 he provided pike for a feast for Queen Elizabeth; in 1577 along with his brother-in-law John Wodeson and two of the other fishermen, Thomas Angell and Denis Hicks, he was involved in overseeing the cleansing of the city waters. When he died his inventory showed him possessed of two boats. He also owned a pair of virginals, which suggests something of the varied world in which he lived.[50]

Nicholas Wodeson died of a summer fever in the room over the porch in his mansion house at Rewley in July 1571. He had made his will the previous April, perhaps at the time he married his second wife Katharine, and it was clear, even before his death that the will was going to cause difficulty between his son and his wife, to whom he had granted a wide discretion. His two elder sons, John and Thomas, only received gowns, while Alexander, the youngest son was given the meads and pastures of one of the leases of Rewley land. At the time of his death his daughter Joane seems to have been affianced to Robert Mounson. Robert had already been promised the wharf – perhaps as a marriage portion. This did not appear in his will. The two daughters were treated more equitably, each receiving £10 at 23 years or at marriage. Friends received handsome bequests as well, but the mansion house, its orchards

who sold it to Robert Mounson. William Coppinger is an uncommon name, but a William Coppinger was a mayor of London and a wealthy fishmonger, who died in 1513. Perhaps this later William Coppinger was a descendant. William Thomas's will also showed that he owed £10 a year to one John Austen of London. Possibly this was the John Austen, a former mayor of Oxford, and Water bailiff in 1532, who later moved to London. He had been a close associate of John Pye, mayor and fishmonger of Oxford. The name John Austen recurs in Oxford in the 17th century as one of its fishmongers, by then a rare breed. William Thomas alias Plummer also guaranteed the debt of Walter Pitts, in the Oseney list of arrears of rent of the year 1546. The Pitts family were to be the most important family of fishermen in the Row, and it is at least as likely that this Walter Pitts was working for Thomas as a fisherman as a plumber. As well, like Mounson, Thomas owned boats. If both these men had a strong interest in fishing, was it only because of the situation of their houses and the ownership of a fishery, or perhaps also because there was some economically advantageous way in which the two occupations could be run in double harness?

(William Herbert, *History of the 12 Great Livery Companies of London* (2 vols., 1834-6), II. 43; Turner, *Records*, 43-6, 108, 117, 156; MS Wills Oxon. 113/1/31 (John Austen); *Oseney*, III. 290; MS Wills Oxon. 300/3/2 (William Thomas alias Plummer).

[50] Turner, *Records*, 314, 392-2; Oxford University Archives, Chancellor's Court, Willis, Hyp/B/30, M-N (Robert Mounson).

and fishing went unconditionally to his widow, Katharine, his executrix and residual legatee.

After Nicholas's death, John and Thomas contested the will, and John maintained that he had been promised he should have the mansion house as a marriage portion. This had been before his father had remarried. His father had willed away what he had no power to will. Katharine emerges in the case as an able and determined woman, though whether grasping or as much concerned for the welfare of the younger children as herself is not clear.[51] Before the conclusion of the case she remarried. She married Francis Willis, bringing him the Rewley leases. In 1577 he became president of St John's.[52]

As for the wharf, Robert Mounson kept it for five or six years, and then assigned it to the City, on condition that they made him a lease of a property near the Castle Mill. So the land on which the wharf was built passed out of the hands of Christ Church to the City.[53] We shall not pursue the history of the wharf here, for its further history is bound up with the barge trade.

After Nicholas Wodeson's death John was granted a lease of St Katharine's house in 1576, and the fishery in the Back Stream which went with it, and in 1580 he was appointed an Inferior Bedell in Arts in succession to Thomas Hutchinson. He had two sons, each following a different aspect of his career. One son became a fisherman, one succeeded him as Inferior Bedell of Arts in 1618, John died, aged 82, still known as a fisherman. As for his sister, Mary, she lived with her stepmother at St John's for some time, and married Ralph Hutchinson about 1586. He succeeded Francis Willis as President of St John's.[54]

Although the Wodesons were in many ways very different from the fishermen of later centuries, the world they inhabited had characteristics which were perpetuated: the practice of patronage, of inheritance of occupation, and of the 'canny' marriage.

---

[51] OU Archs., Hyp/B/I, fos. 70-80.

[52] W. H. Stevenson and H. E. Salter, *The Early History of St John's College, Oxford* (OHS, New Series, i, 1939), 206-7.

[53] 'Book of Evidences', I. 82; City, A.5.5, fo. 206.

[54] Turner, *Records*, 381-2; *OCP* 193-5; *Council Arts*, *1583-1626*, 55; Clark, *Register*, II. 259; Stevenson and Salter, op. cit. 343.

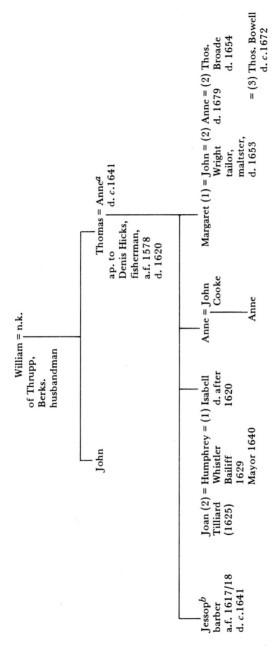

Family Tree 2.2.   The Hickses of Lower Fisher Row.

The men of Fisher Row in later times did not have the same well-placed friends to lead them to social success, and yet the notion of patronage persisted. The notion that special consideration was due to a man because of who he was rather than what he was formed part of the ethical system of the Row. The belief that the interests of kin were overriding was deeply entrenched and in the 19th century added a positively Balkan flavour to its affairs.

VII. THE HICKSES OF THE SECOND AND THIRD TENEMENTS, LOWER FISHER ROW

There is no evidence that the Wodesons were related to the other fishermen of the Row. Their houses stood apart, as if signifying they were not. Although the parish registers of St Thomas's do not start until 1667, we have strong circumstantial evidence that the two main fishing families of Lower Fisher Row, the Hickses and the Bonner alias Pittses were related, and the Hickses were also perhaps related to their neighbours the Robinsons. The families clustering near the Lock seem to have formed a tight little group.[55]

The oldest of these families was probably the Hickses of the second and third tenements. At the town's View of Frankpledge in 1423 the jury of the north-west ward presented that the Prior of the Preachers Brothers had taken 'sprittis and welys' in John Hickis water.[56] If this were an ancestor of Denis Hicks of Lower Fisher Row, then perhaps they were the oldest of the fishermen's families.

We have already encountered a few scattered references to Denis, or Dionysius Hicks who leased the third tenement in Fisher Row in 1573. In 1544 he had paid 2d. lay subsidy; in 1549 he was a tenant of Christ Church, and in 1552 had been involved in the Oseney fracas. He had also, we know, taken apprentices: he tried unsuccessfully to take one in 1550, and had gone on to take four others between 1560 and 1578. The records show that he was also involved in carrying from time to time, for in 1583 he was paid 6s. 8d. by Christ Church for carrying 13 loads of gravel for them. From 1582 also he kept an alehouse. However, few 16th-century Oxfordshire

---

[55] *Oseney*, II. 495-8 summarises the leases of these tenements.
[56] Salter, *Medieval Oxford*, 149.

wills have survived, and therefore despite all this information
we know little of his domestic circle, and he therefore remains
a somewhat shadowy figure.[57]
He must have been dead before 1601, for in that year his tenement was leased to the fisherman, Thomas Hicks, who was
not his son, but his last apprentice.[58] Thomas Hicks was the
son of William Hicks, a husbandman of Thrupp in Berkshire.
This particular Thrupp was almost certainly the Thrupp on
the banks of the Thames between Radley and Abingdon. Perhaps he was a relative. This adoption of a successor who was
not a son, but who bore the same surname and was probably a
relative, recurs in a period when mortality was high, and sons
might well predecease their fathers.[59]

Thomas Hicks's life was uneventful so far as can be made
out from contemporary records. In 1612 he acquired the second tenement in Fisher Row, adjoining the one he had taken
over from Denis Hicks. It had belonged to Francis Robinson,
the plumber, and his son. Thomas had become an alehouse-
keeper by 1596, probably in succession to his former master.
He took an apprentice in September, 1619, renewed his lease to
the third tenement in December and was dead by the following June, when his will was proved. Because both he and his
wife Ann left wills, and inventories were made of their goods,
we have a very full picture of this fisherman and his family.

Thomas Hicks's goods had been valued at £81 6s. 1d.,[60] and
he seems to have lived in modest comfort, perhaps in the Robinsons' tenement. When Francis Robinson had died, and an
inventory was made of his goods in 1609, he had had lights of
glass in the hall worth 2s. 6d., and in Thomas Hicks's inventory there were a dozen panes of glass. Glass windows were
still something of a luxury – the sort of thing a plumber would
install in his own house, being in that line of business, rather
ahead of his neighbours. No doubt Thomas Hicks was glad
to acquire a house with such a modern amenity, for as late as

---

[57] Ch. Ch. MS xii.b. 25, fo. 51; City N.4.1, Alehouse Recognizances, 1578-1653 (unpagi-
nated).

[58] City, A.5.3, 30 May 1578 (Thomas to Denis Hicks).

[59] Cf. Peter Clark's discussion on 'betterment migration' in 'The Migrant in Kentish
Towns 1580-1640', in Peter Clark and Paul Slack, editors, *Crisis and Order in English Towns
1500-1700* (London, 1972), 134-9.

[60] MS Wills Oxon. 30/3/50 (Thomas Hicks).

1607 glass was a movable fitting worthy of mention in one of the most prosperous houses in that prosperous little town of Burford. The house itself was two-storeyed, with parlour, buttery, hall, and little chamber downstairs, and a chamber over the buttery and another over the hall. A really well-to-do Oxford citizen, like the chandler Richard Goode, might own 50 pairs of sheets, but this fisherman had 20 pairs, outdoing most modern families. Though his will was only signed with a mark, he owned a Bible.[61]

Thomas Hicks had invested in property, and his tenements accounted for £40 of his whole estate. Besides his two houses in Fisher Row he had another tenement. This was a property in Dutton's Holdings, a group of 20 tenements across the Back Stream westwards, once owned by Rewley. They had passed to the Duttons of Sherborne in Gloucestershire, and some of these tenements were leased for 1,000 years in 1606.[62]

They formed a small pocket of near-freehold property amongst the holdings of Christ Church and the city of which the parish was otherwise almost entirely composed. Such land provided an attractive proposition to a man with a modest amount of money to invest, and one in which Thomas Hicks's neighbours the Bonner alias Pitts family also had an interest. As well he leased a ham called Little Cripley from the city. Cripley lay south of Port Meadow and bordered the river. Perhaps it had a fishery attached, for when its letting was considered in 1556 it was settled that no lease should be granted 'wythout the concent of the Councell of thys Cytye; and also for certen persons beyng fysshers'. Thomas Hicks's lease of Little Cripley was perhaps a subtenancy as no lease to him in traceable. Cripley was divided into two parts, and the smaller, known as Nether Cripley, may have been Thomas Hicks's 'Little Cripley'. It was leased by the city to Richard Robinson from 1607 to 1655, and to William Wright (who became Recorder of Oxford) and later members of his family from 1664 to 1799.[63] Thomas

[61] MS Wills Oxon. 85/2/6 (Robinson); Michael Laithwaite, 'The Buildings of Burford', in Alan Everitt, ed., *Perspectives in English Urban History* (London, 1973), 69-70; MS Wills Oxon. 25/3/19 (Goode).

[62] *Cal. Pat. Rolls, 1572-5*, 343; Blacker Morgan, *Historical and Genealogical Memoirs of the Dutton Family of Sherborne in Gloucestershire* (privately printed, 1899), 41-3, 213, 237; MS DD Pprs. Halls Breweries c. 33.

[63] Turner, *Records*, 256; *OCP* 191-3.

Hicks may well have been a subtenant of Richard Robinson. If so, we have the sequence of names, Robinson, Hicks, and Wright, repeated both in the leases of Cripley and the second tenement in Fisher Row. Here Thomas Hicks succeeded the Robinsons, and he himself was succeeded in Fisher Row by his son-in-law John Wright. This suggests that the Robinsons were related to the Hickses too (see Fig. 2.2).

Finally, as well as household goods and leases Thomas Hicks owned three fishing-boats, one 'carring bote' – perhaps inherited from Denis Hicks – and two flew-nets with other fishing 'gyns' worth five pounds. He also had three milch beasts and two pigs. Like Denis Hicks, he kept an alehouse, and after his death it was kept up by his widow. Both Denis and Thomas Hicks were clearly not dependent on fishing alone for their living. They acted as carriers by water, when required, and, though the alehouse may have consisted of little more than a group of neighbours drinking together, it was by a combination of bye-employments that the Hickses had attained their mod-est comforts. Thomas's milch beasts and pigs show him half a countryman, and Oxford still a countrified town.

By his will Thomas Hicks had made careful provision for his children and wife, which was respected. Anne Hicks survived her husband by some 20 years, dying about the end of 1641. She never remarried, and her estate was valued at £33 13s. 6d. The leases, except that of Little Cripley, had passed out of her hands, but otherwise the inventory was almost a carbon copy of her husband's, as far as possessions went.[64] Five sheets had vanished in the two decades, but the Bible was still there, and the goods in the kitchen were more particularly described. Even if she no longer held the lease of the two tenements in Fisher Row, she still seemed to be in occupation. In Thomas Hicks's inventory goods were mentioned as being in a small tenement in the Row, perhaps the small second tenement. In Anne's inventory there were goods in 'the low Room in the new house', and in 'the New house Chamber'. Some rebuilding must have taken place. What is most interesting, and suggestive of prosperity about the inventory, is the way Anne Hicks had been able to keep her home together.

---

[64] MS Wills Oxon. 201/121 (will); MS Wills Oxon. 298/2/10 (inventory).

Thomas and Anne Hicks had four children, a son. Jessopp, and three daughters, Anne, Margaret, and Isabell. Jessopp was apparently the son of an earlier marriage, for in her will Anne, the widow of Thomas called him her 'son-in-law'. He was the only son, but he did not follow his father's occupation. He became a barber.[65] If the apprentice whom Thomas Hicks took in the last year of his life was intended to provide him with a successor, he had left it too late. Yet possibly his chosen succession was too young to serve an apprenticeship then. On 25 April 1627 Thomas's neighbour Walter Bonner alias Pitts took as his apprentice one Henry Hicks son of Thomas Hicks, weaver of Witney. This may have been the intended successor. Yet oddly this young apprentice was, as we shall see, almost certainly a relative of the Bonner alias Pitts family, but we know nothing of how or even whether he was related to Thomas Hicks.

Anne Hicks, the daughter, married John Cooke, after her father's death. Two Cookes are known to have been fishermen in the parish, and she may have married into their family. One was a John Cooke who gave evidence in a law case about the extent of Warham Bank in 1617. He was 82 at the time and an unlikely spouse himself. The other was Robert Cooke, sub-tenant to Robert Backester.[66] Anne Cooke had a daughter who was named after her, but otherwise, apart from the fact that she herself died before her mother, we know nothing of her.

The two other daughters married into rising Oxford families. Isabell married Humphrey Whistler. He was a baker and twice mayor of the city, and acted as a Barge Commissioner. According to his apprenticeship his father was Ralph Whistler of Radley, yeoman, but Anthony Wood tells us he was 'of the same family as those of Whitchurch'. In 1585 the Whistlers had kept two weirs between Whitchurch and Goring. Isabell had died young, and her husband remarried, but according to Wood when he died in 1660 he was buried in St Thomas's parish by the side of his first wife Isabell, and their three children who had died in infancy.[67]

[65] City, L.5.2, 13 May 1619.
[66] *Oseney*, III. 19. Ch. Ch. Deed Box, Fish Row, Tenement 4.
[67] Wood. *Life*, I. 332; Lansdowne 30, fo. 49; *Council Acts 1626-65*, 139; City, L.5.l., 26 July 1606 (Whistler to Pool).

Margaret, a third daughter, married John Wright after her father's death. She was not mentioned in her mother's will. Humphrey Whistler received a piece of gold for a ring, the poor of the parish 20 shillings, and John Wright the residue of her estate. John Wright and his wife had held the leases to both the Fisher Row properties for some time: the second tenement was leased in their name in 1625, and the third in 1635.[68] It seems to have been a case of an unofficial family mortgage, the widow parting with the lease, but living on in the house she was used to. Quite often one suspects, this was the first step in the transition from owner-occupation to investment in property.

The Wright family, who came to lease Nether Cripley, were one of the most important families in Oxford in the 17th century, providing mayors on five occasions between 1614 and 1667, and also Barge Commissioners. John was a tailor and later a maltster. How he was related is not clear, and he does not seem to have been particularly prominent. He was a member of the Common Council, and in 1640 a chamberlaine, but his only action noted in the Council Acts was the leasing of Shire Lake, the stretch of water from Botley Mill to Hinksey ferry, one of the city's several fisheries, in 1650.[69] Links between the august Wrights and Fisher Row became attenuated with time. In 1656 a John Cooke, perhaps Anne Hicks's husband, was servant to the Mayor, Martin Wright, and in 1711 a Mary Hicks witnessed Martin Wright's will.

John Wright's will was made in March, 1653, and proved in May.[70] Anne, his 'now wife', survived him, and had a life interest in his estate. Anne Wright now married Thomas Broade, the son of an apothecary of the same name. He died very soon after, in 1654, and, after paying various bequests, his wife inherited the residue.[71]

By 1658 Anne Broade had come into possession not only of the second and the third tenements, but also a large part of the fourth tenement as well, and major changes in the Row now took place. The fourth tenement was subdivided, into three parts, which came to be known as the fourth, fifth and

---

[68] *Oseney*, II. 496: Ch. Ch. Deed Box, Fish Row, Tenements 2 and 3, 17 Dec. 1635.
[69] *Council Acts 1626-65*, 169.
[70] PROB 11/229/256 (John Wright).   [71] PROB 11/234/70 (Thomas Broade).

sixth tenements in the Christ Church Lease Books. The fourth and the fifth tenements went to Anne Broade, and the sixth to a boatman called John Clarke, of whom we shall hear more later.[72]

In 1658 the subtenant and occupant of the second tenement was William Terrill, who is known from other sources to have been a fisherman. He was probably the grandson or son-in-law of Robert Backester, the previous owner of the fourth tenement. When Robert Backester died he had made provision for his daughter, Jone Terrill, and her children, John, William, Henry, and Mairie, but there is no mention of her husband. She was his only daughter and was to be his sole executor.[73] It looks as if some sort of deal had taken place, perhaps after her death, in which William Terrill relinquished the lease of the large fourth tenement which had been mortgaged during Robert Backester's life, and he was granted the subtenancy of the second. It was smaller, but it seems to have been better placed for a fisherman than the fourth tenement. Perhaps money also changed hands or it was in repayment of a debt, we do not know. The lease had still many years to run. By this arrangement another fisherman came to occupy the second tenement. How long the Terrills kept it is unclear, for the Terrills were only subtenants. Anne Broade did not renew her lease of the second tenement, and in 1681 it passed into the hands of William Gardner, a waterman, who already held a lease in Upper Fisher Row, and at his death his daughter Elizabeth Stevens was living there (see next chapter, Section VII, The Gardners of Upper Fisher Row). By 1788 it was again leased to a fisherman, Thomas Spindelow, who also held the first tenement, and it was occupied by the fisherman William Payne.

As for the third tenement it was to have little more to do with fishermen for some time. Anne Broade married again, her new husband being a maltster, Thomas Bowell. After his death the lease passed to a tobacco-pipe-maker and then into the hands of a family of brewers. It was not until 1757 that this tenement was again sublet to a fisherman, Edward Spindelow, who was the father of the fisherman, Thomas Spindelow, who was lessee of the first and second tenements.

[72] *Oseney*, II 496-8.
[73] City L.5.3, 1652-3 (Terrill); MS Wills Oxon. 115/3/22 (Robert Backester).

Family Tree 2.3.   The Bonner alias Pittses and Curtises of Lower Fisher Row.

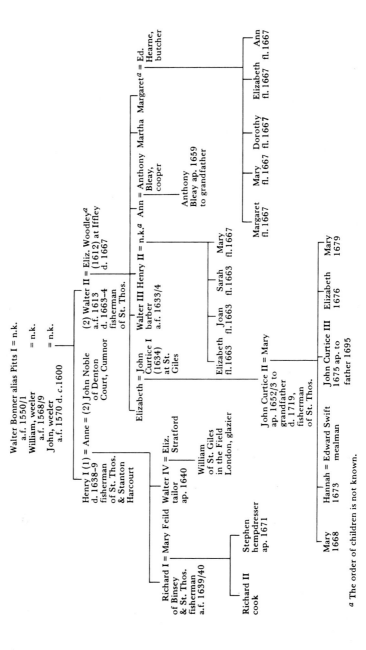

a The order of children is not known.

III. THE BONNER ALIAS PITTSES AND THE CURTICES OF THE FIRST TENEMENT[74]

The Bonner alias Pitts family occupied the prime position beside The Lock, one which attracted fishermen as a candle attracts moths. Fishermen were found in the first tenement more commonly than in any other on the Bank in the medieval period, and they lived there continuously in the modern period at least until 1829. The Bonner alias Pitts family held it from the 16th century until 1743, when it passed to a fisherman from outside Oxford, whose family has not been fully traced. In the first lease of this tenement from 1 October 1573 Joan Pitts alias Bonner was merely a sub-tenant unlike Dionysius Hicks who took out a lease on the same day further down the Row. A year later, on 1 October 1574, she became full tenant. She was a widow, and there is no indication of her husband's occupation.

The name Pitts had been known in the parish for some time. Walter Pitts was listed in arrears of rent in 1546, 'respondit magistro Plomer'. 'Magistro Plomer' would be William Thomas alias Plummer, a powerful man in the parish with many interests.[75] As he was responsible for Walter Bonner alias Pitts's debt it seems likely that it was because he was employing him, though whether as a fisherman or in connection with other interests we do not know. Nor do we know what occupation Walter Bonner alias Pitts was following when he bought his freedom in 1550-1, or even whether it was the same man.

The double-barrelled surname Bonner alias Pitts appeared first in the mid-16th century, and continued in use until about the end of the 17th century. It suggests a certain

---

[74] *Oseney*, II. 494-5 summarise the leases of this property.

[75] 'Book of Evidences', I. 68-70; Oseney, III. 289-90. He was a plumber like Robert Mounson, who took over many of his interests. He held the 8th, 10th, and 11th Tenements of Fisher Row on 99-year leases, and had interests in a small flock of 50 sheep, and owned a brewhouse and three boats. His leases were taken out just before the Dissolution. Many heads of religious houses disposed of property on long leases when they saw the dissolution as inevitable, and frequently these leases went to relations. In St Thomas's the recipients of these long leases seem to have been Welshmen: William Thomas and Will Ellis. After the Dissolution grants of land also went to Edmond Powell and Dr George Owen. The last Abbot of Oseney and first Bishop of Oxford, was Robert King, who was related to Sir John Williams, Secretary to the Court of Augmentations. Here the Welsh invasion of the Tudor period can be seen exhibiting strong nepotistic tendencies.

pride in family which invites exploration. The Pittses of Iffley are a family who immediately spring to mind as putative
relatives, for they owned a mill. They were very minor gentry.
Connections between millers and fishermen have already been
established elsewhere, and the coincidence of the name Pitts
among fishermen in Fisher Row and as lessees of Iffley mill
suggests that this family conformed to the pattern.

The Pittses of Iffley were an able and interesting family.
Arthur Pitts, formerly registrar of the Diocese of Oxford, leased
the manor with its water-mill from Lincoln College in 1558,
and in 1567 he also held the living from the Archdeacon of
Oxford. He died in 1579. His widow, Margaret, listed in 1585
as holding Iffley mill was also a recusant, and so were two
sons. One, Arthur, educated at Brasenose and Douai, became
Chancellor to the Cardinal of Lorraine. He was a friend of
Edmund Campion, and spent his last years as chaplain to the
Stonor family. The mill itself was in the hands of Phillip, a
son who conformed. No direct link between the Iffley family
of Pitts and the Bonner alias Pitts family is known, though a
Walter Bonner alias Pitts married at Iffley in 1612, and millers
and fishermen's names are linked again in Iffley itself: John
Broadwater was a later lessee of an estate which the Pitts held
at Iffley, and there was also an Iffley dynasty of fishermen
called Broadwater.[76]

The first clear connection of the Bonner alias Pitts family with fishing is found in 1568-9, when William Bonner
alias Pitts, a weeler became a freeman.[77] In Fisher Row Walter Bonner alias Pitts II, fisherman, succeeded Joan Pitts alias
Bonner in 1606. How they were related to her or to William
is not known. He and his brother, Henry I, who was also a
fisherman, were the sons of John Bonner alias Pitts, weelmaker. Henry took up his freedom in 1600 after his father's
death. Walter was not admitted until 1613.[78] Walter and Henry

---

[76] VCH Oxon., V. 193-6; Edward Marshall, *An Account of the Township of Iffley* (Oxford, 1870), 62-8; Lincoln College Deed Box, 'Ancient Documents', *Lincoln College v. William Stonor*, interrogatory of Ann Pitts; Dom Hugh Bowdler, ed., *Recusant Rolls 3 and 4, an Abstract in English* (Catholic Record Society, lxi,1970), 201-2; Thacker, *Highway*, I. 56; City, A.5.3, 25 Apr. 1560 (Gerringe to Broadwater); City, L.5.2, 12 Nov. 1624 (Franklyn to Broadwater); City, L.5.4, 2 Mar. 1674 (Broadwater to Tustian); City, L.5.5, 1783-4 (Joseph son of Richard Broadwater).   [77] City, A.5.3, 23 Jan. 1560 (S. Broadwater).

[78] Turner, *Records*, 332; *Council Acts, 1583-1626*. 134, 226.

lived across the Back Stream from each other. Henry, like Thomas Hicks, leased one of the tenements in Dutton's Holdings.

We shall only deal with Henry's family briefly, for he never lived in Fisher Row. Henry Bonner alias Pitts I took two apprentices, one in 1615, one in 1626. He had two sons, Walter IV a tailor, and Richard I who succeeded him as a fisherman.[79] He seems to have been quite well off. He died at Stanton Harcourt. His will was witnessed by the minister, and his inventory was appraised by William Wright, Esquire, probably a relative of the Hicks family, and Thomas Wodeson the fisherman. They valued the estate at £53. It included boats, nets, and fish. He left 20 shillings to the poor of St Thomas's, and everything else to his wife Anne for life, and after her death, to their sons.[80] Anne later married John Noble of Denton Court, and in 1654 assigned the property in Dutton's Holdings to her son Walter IV, having already made over the lease of a tenement in Stanton Harcourt to Richard together with 'severall Nettes Bottes Guines and Cattle'.[81]

Richard I married Mary, daughter of Thomas Feild of Medley, a yeoman, who owned boats, and had served an apprenticeship as a boat man.[82] One son became a cook, another, Stephen, was apprenticed to a hempdresser – the occupation suggested by John Collins as a bye-employment for sea fishermen. Several sons of rivermen were apprenticed to his master, Thomas Widdowes, who ran quite an extensive enterprise.[83]

Let us return to Walter Bonner alias Pitts II and Fisher Row. Walter Bonner alias Pitts married the recently widowed Elizabeth Woodley at Iffley in 1612, and took up his freedom by his father's copy in the same year.[84] This was more than a decade after Henry I, and well after he himself had leased the

[79] City, L.5.2, 26 Apr. 1615 (Cox to H. Bonner); ibid., 28 Mar. 1626 (Ford to H. Bonner); L.5.3, 17 Mar. 1641 (W. Bonnerto Dawson); ibid., 1648-9 (W. Bonner); ibid., 1639-40 (R. Bonner).

[80] MS Wills Oxon. 115/2/43 (Henry Bonner alias Pitts).

[81] Oxon. RO, MS D.D. Pprs. Halls Breweries c. 33.

[82] MS Wills Oxon. 23/2/8 (Feild); City L.5.2, 1624-5 (Feild).

[83] City, L.5.4, 18 Aug. 1671 (Stephen Bonner alias Pitts).

[84] MS Wills Oxon. 69/5/16 (Woodlief). William Woodlief or Woodley, gent. of St Thomas's occupied a house across the Mill Stream from Fisher Row. He died in August 1612 and his widow married Walter Bonner alias Pitts in September at Iffley (Iffley Parish Register, 24 Sept. 1612).

first tenement. He had two sons, but he took two apprentices before 1630, and two much later. One of the first of these was Henry Hicks.

Henry Hicks, the son of Thomas Hicks, weaver of Witney, was apprenticed to Walter Bonner alias Pitts in 1627. He was clearly regarded with affection by the family, for in 1666 when Walter's widow made her will she left to her 'kinsman' Henry Hicks, waterman of Abingdon, fifty shillings. Just what his relationship was to the Bonner alias Pitts family, or to the Hickses is not clear. Again, in a will of 1647 the widow Katharine Hicks of Witham left bequests to her daughter Mary Bonner and her grandchild Mary Bonner alias Pitts, but even this does not help to link Henry with the Hickses of Fisher Row.[85] Some time after serving his apprenticeship, Henry left Oxford. He could not expect to succeed to his master's fishing, for Walter had two sons approaching manhood. Henry settled in Abingdon and became a waterman. We shall consider his position in the barging community there later.

Walter's own son, Henry II became a freeman by his father's copy in 1633, and presumably followed his father's trade. A second son, Walter III became a barber, like Jessopp Hicks, being apprenticed in 1635 under the University's authority, for eight years to Thomas Collins, barber. Henry II died leaving four daughters and no sons – or at least, none which survived their grandparents. Perhaps it was Henry's death which led Walter III to take up his freedom by his father's copy in 1645/6. He predeceased his father also, and so left old Walter II without a son to succeed him.[86] In this he was like Denis and Thomas Hicks. For his next two apprentices he turned to the next generation and took two of his daughters' sons. John Curtice was apprenticed to him in 1653. He was the son of Walter's daughter Elizabeth and her husband John Curtice I.[87] Walter's wife left £5 to John Curtice, of the City of Oxford, fisherman, her grandchild, whilst Walter's will left legacies to John Curtice of Berkshire, fellmonger, and 'his son who now lives with me'. John Curtice II completed his apprenticeship

[85] City, L.5.2, 2 June 1627 (H. Hicks); MS Wills Oxon. 6/3/21 (Elizabeth Bonner alias Pitts); MS Wills Berks. 80/40 (Katharine Hicks).

[86] Clark, *Register*, 344; *Oseney*, II. 524; MS Wills Oxon. 6/2/19 (Walter Bonner alias Pitts).

[87] City, L.5.3, 7 Feb. 1653; St Giles Parish Register, Marriages, 14 July 1634.

in 1659-60, and almost simultaneously Walter took his last apprentice, Anthony Bley.[88] Anthony did not complete his apprenticeship before his grandfather's death.

Walter Bonner alias Pitts was the only member of his family to play any part in local politics, and that was slight. In 1662 with seven others he was elected to the Common Council, and the Mayor Roger Griffin nominated him his chamberlain. In October 1663 he was fined £1 with eight others who had neglected attending Council or had failed to pay towards the city lectures.[89] In Walter's case it was perhaps illness rather than apathy which caused his absence, for he was dead by February, when his will was proved.

The inventory of his goods gives some idea of his home. It was small, consisting of a hall chamber, an entry chamber, and a kitchen. No rooms are mentioned as being over each other, so it was probably only one storey high. A feather bed stood in the hall chamber, and an old bedstead and truckle-bed with flock mattresses in the entry. The furnishings were simple, even sparse, but not inadequate. There was no silver, almost no pewter or brass, no books or carved wooden chests, but there were 12 pairs of hempen sheets. A well-stocked linen chest suggests a carefully managed household.

His stock-in-trade consisted of three boats, two being very old, and the lot was worth only £1 10s. There were nets, and a roll of netting to make a flew-net worth £2 10s., and a pitch-net worth 10s. It was supposed there were about 600 fish in his pool worth 10s., and his total estate was valued at £47 6s.[90] He was old, and perhaps therefore not as well off as he had been once. His widow, who received the residue of his estate and the lease of their house, continued to live there until her death.

Walter Bonner alias Pitts died 'weak in body and very aged'. He had lived from the reign of Elizabeth into the reign of Charles II. He had outlived his neighbours: Thomas Hicks had died forty years earlier, when trade was still good; Robert Backester and his own brother Henry had died 20 odd years before, on the eve of the civil war, when trade was declining.

[88]   City, L.S.3, 16 July 1659 (Bley).
[89]   *Council Acts 1626-65*, 298-9, 314.
[90]   MS Wins Oxon. 6/2/19 (Walter Bonner alias Pitts).

Now, after the years of turmoil, the prospects of the industry were picking up – or so it must have appeared. The obligation of fasting had been proclaimed again in 1660, and further proclamations were to follow; the town was thriving, and trade was good; apprentices were coming forward.

John Curtice II, Walter's grandson and former apprentice, now took over the first tenement. He was a man of enterprise, but despite a promising start, his energy did not make him a markedly successful man. The times were against him. Fishing was no longer prosperous, for after the restoration fasting was less commonly observed, so that by the 1720s Alexander Pope, a Catholic, could mock the comfortable life of the country parson fasting only 'if he will'. Numbers at the university were also falling, and the town grew less prosperous in the 18th century.

John Curtice took four apprentices during his life, including his son John Curtice III, who was to succeed him. Two of these apprentices posed no problems of rivalry, for they came from the country, and, having served their time and taken out their freedoms, returned to the country, where they established dynasties of 'foreign freemen' who kept fisheries and fish-weirs and often kept alehouses nearby. The first of these was Thomas, son of Richard Rudge, labourer of Northmoor, apprenticed to him in 1666. The Rudge or Ridge family continued in the Northmoor region as fishermen and ferrymen until the 19th century.[91] The second was William, son of William Beckley, yeoman of Beckley, whose descendant, another William Beckley, was described by Robert Graves in a passage that has already been quoted.[92] The dynasties of fishermen outside Oxford were often longer than those in Oxford.

The value of The Lock was threatened by the cutting of The Lasher, which provided a rival sluice. Whilst this may not have affected the fishermen of Lower Fisher Row at first, once the land adjacent to The Lasher was leased to a fisherman it affected them adversely. In 1623 the site of The Lasher, tenement 1, Upper Fisher Row, was leased to the boatman, Thomas Pemerton, and from his inventory it is obvious that

[91] City, L.5.4, 29 Oct. 1666 (Rudge to Curtice); Thacker, *Highway*, II. 79-83.
[92] City, L.5.4, 30 Nov. 1678 (Beckley to Curtice); *VCH Oxon* VI. 206.

he was as much a fisherman as a boatman.[93] The situation must have seemed intolerable to the fishermen of Lower Fisher Row. The opportunity to get hold of the lease of tenement 1 came in 1682, and John Curtice seized it. It was the first in a series of investments which he made in property in the next few years, but he overstretched his resources, and by 1699 was forced to give up the lease of the house by the Lasher, retaining only the house he occupied in Lower Fisher Row.[94]

John Curtice died in 1719, and John III succeeded him. He was a shadowy and hapless man. He took no apprentices, but this is not surprising. Few apprentices were coming forward (see Table II). In 1728 another fisherman, Richard Sockwell was indicted for stealing his fish at the City Quarter Sessions, and the following year he was in Bocardo, the city gaol, for debt.[95] The lease of the first tenement passed in 1743 to Jeremiah Bishop, a Godstow fisherman. Whether he occupied the tenement is not known.

Towards the end of the 17th century the control of both the sluices came into the hands of a single family once again, when the Spindelow family held both the first tenement in Lower Fisher Row, and tenement 1 in Upper Fisher Row. Richard Spindelow, cook, held tenement 1 from 1763, and Thomas Spindelow, fisherman, the first tenement in 1784. By then Richard was dead, and the next lease was taken out by his trustee, Charles Curtis.[96] Whether this recurrence of the name connected with John Curtice II's former property has any significance is not known.

So long as only one of the tenements by the sluices was occupied by a fisherman all was well, or if both were controlled by the same family of fishermen. Problems were likely to arise where the tenements by the sluices were occupied by rival fishermen. This seems to have happened when Curtice held one and Pemerton the other, and the situation recurred in the 19th century, when it caused much friction.

---

[93] For Leases of tenement 1, Upper Fisher Row see Appendix III; MS Wills Oxon. 299/5/29 (Thomas Pemerton).

[94] *Oseney*, II. 519-20; MS D.D. Pprs. Hall's Breweries c. 33; Ch. Ch. Deed Box, 'The Timber Yard'.

[95] City, O.2.6, fos. 44, 66.

[96] Appendix III; PROB 11/961/378 (Richard Spindelowe).

We have traced the history of the fishermen of the Row from a period when river fish was a highly valued commodity, when fasting was strictly observed, and town and gown were expanding and flourishing. The vicissitudes of the 17th century, and the intellectual and economic torpor of 18th-century Oxford are all mirrored in the fortunes of the fishermen of the Row.

Our view of these early families of fishermen is both strangely intimate, and strangely impersonal. It has been limited by the documents available. We have penetrated into their homes, and we know the contents of their cupboards, the number of their pots and pans, the quality of their sheets. Yet is our knowledge of these people any more profound than that of the burglar who ransacks a house whilst the family are away? Can we look at the family portraits with more comprehension than he? What indeed do we know of their hopes and fears, loves and griefs? Must this world remain for ever hidden?

And yet is the situation entirely hopeless? Does not the very shape of their family trees show something of the forces which moulded their lives, and of how they reacted to them? Can we not learn from them something of their fears, something of their hopes? When we compare the structure of the families of these early fishermen with those of bargemen, canal boatmen, and even with those of later fishermen we shall see that there are significant differences in family structure, which will provide us with clues to a deeper understanding.

CHAPTER 3

The Bargemen of Fisher Row

1. THE MEDIEVAL RIVER

Even if we do not know when the first fisherman plied his trade in Oxford we can point to an actual date on which the first boatman was admitted a freeman of the city of Oxford: 14 August 1583. From this date the families of boat-people in the parish developed into a tight little community which also included fishermen, and which spread the length of the Bank from The Lasher to the foot of Fisher Row.

Whilst the initial existence of a small colony of fishermen in St Thomas's parish is easily enough explained, it seems, on the face of it, strange that the main community of bargemen should develop here too, on a side-stream of the river on the west side of Oxford, for the official wharf of the navigation was situated a mile downstream at Folly Bridge, on the south side of the town, beside the busy main road between Southampton and the North. Here the barges from London had their natural terminus, whilst Hythe Bridge was best placed to cater for the traffic from the small towns of the Upper Thames, places like Eynsham, Bampton and Radcot, and Lechlade. Nor were the boats that could use the upper river as large as those of the lower river. Folly Bridge was typically the home of barge-masters, Fisher Row of boatmasters.[1]

The community which developed at Folly Bridge was very different from that in Fisher Row. Folly Bridge had a small community with big boats, Fisher Row a large community with small boats. The families seldom intermarried except indirectly.

---

[1] On the Thames the word 'barge' was reserved for a large boat of about 70 or more tons. Smaller craft were 'boats'. We shall adopt this usage, and also the associated distinctions between boatman and bargeman. We shall treat 'bargeman' as the generic term. The word 'boat-people' is used more generically still, to include all sorts of men who use boats.

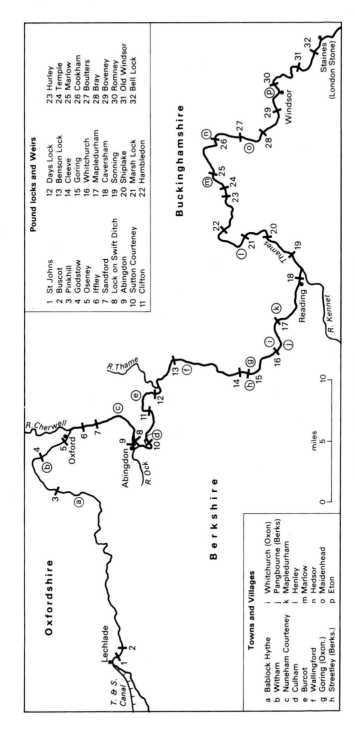

Fig. 3.1. Map of the Thames, c.1790-1800.

Pound locks and Weirs

1 St Johns	12 Days Lock	23 Hurley
2 Buscot	13 Benson Lock	24 Temple
3 Pinkhill	14 Cleeve	25 Marlow
4 Godstow	15 Goring	26 Cookham
5 Oseney	16 Whitchurch	27 Boulters
6 Iffley	17 Mapledurham	28 Bray
7 Sandford	18 Caversham	29 Boveney
8 Lock on Swift Ditch	19 Sonning	30 Romney
9 Abingdon	20 Shiplake	31 Old Windsor
10 Sutton Courteney	21 Marsh Lock	32 Bell Lock
11 Clifton	22 Hambledon	

Towns and Villages

a Bablock Hythe	i Whitchurch (Oxon)
b Witham	j Pangbourne (Berks)
c Nuneham Courteney	k Mapledurham
d Culham	l Henley
e Burcot	m Marlow
f Wallingford	n Hedsor
g Goring (Oxon.)	o Maidenhead
h Streetley (Berks.)	p Eton

They might be related through common relatives elsewhere along the banks of the Thames, perhaps at Abingdon or Lechlade. As well, though the two communities lay almost equidistant from the centre of the town (Oxford is a town which has a centre at a crossroads, Carfax – its 'quatre voies'), one lay within the county boundary, the other without, even though both lay within the boundaries of the town. The community at Folly Bridge was largely concentrated in an area called Grandpont which lay between a stream called Shire Lake, which was the county boundary, and Folly Bridge. The third arch from the south end of the bridge marked the boundary of the town. It was, in its own way built on a borderland, just like Fisher Row, but it was not an area which engendered conflict, for there was no built-up land to the south of it. This part of the town, Grandpont, lay in Berkshire, and until 1836 it even lay in a different diocese, that of Salisbury. Fisher Row's boatmen and boatmasters, like its fishermen, were freemen of Oxford. Only a few Folly Bridge bargemasters took out their freedom at all, and fewer still took apprentices or served apprenticeships. The boatmasters of the Row required small crews, and their boats were crewed by sons and apprentices. The barges of Folly Bridge might be captained by sons, but they were often crewed by employees. At Folly Bridge the bargemasters lived, half-foreigners, in their big houses at the foot of St Aldate Street.

The reason for the development of the larger community in Fisher Row in the first place must be sought in the structure of the river, which governed its use and therefore its history.

Oxford is situated at the point which marks a change in the river. Above Oxford the Thames is slow and sluggish with a very slight gradient, but down river the gradient is sharper. Above Oxford the tributaries of the Thames run briskly down the sides of the vale of the upper Thames into the slow-moving river, rather like the drainage from a corrugated iron roof into a gutter, which has itself only the slightest incline. If the Upper Thames was like a gutter, the Thames from Oxford downstream was more like the drainpipe into which the gutter debouched.[2] The gradient affected the distribution of mills,

---

[2] For a geological description of this terrain see A. F. Martin and R. W. Steel, ed., *The Oxford Region* (London, 1954), 1-36.

as mills can only work where there is an appreciable gradient. Therefore, above Oxford, mills were associated with the tributaries of the Thames rather than the mainstream, whilst from Wolvercote, on the outskirts of Oxford, and through Oxford downstream to London mills were also associated with the main river. Mill weirs like Rewley Lock were built across the river as mills proliferated between Oxford and London, but not on the river above Oxford. Fishermen might build their weirs on the upper river, but these were not so high as those downstream, and were not necessarily built right across the river. The upper river was more nearly in a state of nature, and though it was winding and silted up in places, this presented more difficulties to large than small craft. The difference in the nature of the river above and below Oxford therefore affected its navigation.

The history of the navigation of the Thames at Oxford stretches back to Saxon times when the river was navigable at least to Abingdon from Oxford. (For places on the river see Fig. 3.1.) About 1052 it was important enough for the Abbot of Abingdon Monastery to divert the river into a new course in response to a petition from the citizens of Oxford. A toll was exacted, and was still being paid after the Conquest.[3] By the 13th century the river was open from Oxford to London. In 1205 Letters Patent were granted to William, son of Andrew, to have one ship going and returning upon the Thames between Oxford and London, and the Governors of Wallingford and other riverports were to give him free passage.[4] This suggests a thriving and organised trade with tolls levied along the route. So does the mandate issued by the King in 1234 when he was building a hospital at Oxford to all whose lands would be traversed by the men bringing the timber by the Thames from Reading to facilitate their passage.[5] Boats were being towed upstream. We cannot even guess the volume of such trade, but in the 13th century Oxford flourished, and no doubt drew its provisions from a wide area.

The open navigation was always threatened by the weirs raised by millers and fishermen, and protests that they

---

[3] Joseph Stevenson, ed., *Chronichon Monasterii de Abingdon* (2 vols., Rolls series, 1858), I. 480-1; II. 119.

[4] T. D. Hardy, ed., *Rotuli Literararium Patentium* (London, 1835), I, pt. i. 38, 52.

[5] *Cal. Pat. Rolls, 1232-37*, 51.

obstructed the navigation occur from time to time. So long as these protests were accompanied by contemporary evidence of boats actually working on the river, transporting goods or even sinking in it, in the process of doing so, things were perhaps not too badly amiss. This seems to have been the position in the 13th century, and perhaps as late as about the time of Edward I or II when the merchants who frequented [*hauntent*] the water between Oxford and London complained that their common passage for ships of merchandise was obstructed.[6] However, in the 14th century the petitions and complaints continued, but without evidence of the river's actual use: the complaints seem to emanate from merchants who hoped to use the river rather than from actual users, and the time to which they referred when they spoke of its actual use is vague – 'in former times'. A statute of 1350 was enacted to facilitate the removal of obstructions raised since the time of Edward I, when presumably the river was passable, and under this there were prosecutions from time to time, as for instance those of the reign of Richard II against 15 lock-keepers between Reading and Wallingford.[7] Such a drive might well suggest that a serious attempt was being made to clear the river; whilst an indictment of about the same period against William Drayton of Rotherfield Peppard is so full of details about the locks of the time that it is hard to believe that the river was not in active use shortly before the prosecution: William Drayton and his ancestors had a lock and a winch by Meedmelle so that boats coming from London to Oxford with victuals, wine, and other merchandise might be drawn along by ropes since the river was too shallow at midstream for the boats to operate without this engine; the lock was in disrepair, the winch removed, and he ought to maintain them – but it does not say as he had formerly done, but as *his ancestors had done*.[8]

Thorold Rogers approaching the question of water-carriage from another angle – from the evidence of its cost – came to the conclusion that in the 14th century Henley must

---

[6] Lucy Toulmin Smith, ed., 'Parliamentary Petitions Relating to Oxford' in *Collectanea, IIIrd Series* (OHS xxxii, 1896), 109.

[7] Flower, ed., *Public Works*, II. 124-7.   [8] Ibid. II. 125, 127.

have been the head of navigation, as there was no evidence of payments for transport by water above this point in Oxford accounts. Thacker attacked this hypothesis, but by way of evidence produced material indiscriminately from any century, and whilst it is not strictly true, as R. H. C. Davis has said, that 'all Thacker's evidence was early, and all Roger's late',yet it is all unsatisfactory.[9] By the mid-14th century and perhaps much earlier the navigation can have had no real economic importance between Oxford and London.

We know almost nothing of any hythe, or landing-place, in Oxford for the London trade, but there was a hythe on the Cherwell, probably above Magdalen Bridge, for a dispute Between Magdalen and St Frideswides Priory in 1496 spoke of a fishery from the East Bridge to a place called Le Hytte, and reserved a right of free passage by water to Magdalen College.[10] It seems more likely though that the main medieval wharf was always by Folly Bridge. This place was known as Lambards Land in the Middle Ages, a name in itself redolent of commerce, and though he adduces no evidence H. E. Salter suggests that it was a bribe.[11]

We know more of the wharf by Hythe Bridge. It is first mentioned in a deed of 1.282, and the bridge was referred to as Hythe Bridge in that *inquisitio quod damnum* of 1286 in which Rewley gained the land to the north of the bridge, which was then said to be worth nothing.[12] Probably the wharf was on the townward side of the stream at that time, for a wharf is not without value. Though the wharf is not mentioned at the View of Eyre in 1285, complaint was made that Rewley had built a 'cameram forinsecam' (a gazebo?) over the water, 12 feet by six feet, which impeded the boats (*batelli*) carrying victuals and other necessities to the town of Oxford.[13] In 1299 stone was brought from Eynsham to La Huye for Merton and

---

[9]   J. E. Thorold Rogers, *A History of Agriculture and Prices in England* (8 Vols., Oxford, 1966-1902), V. 758; Thacker, *Highway*, I. 268-73; Davis, 'Ford, River, City', 264-5.

[10]   S. R. Wigram, ed., *The Cartulary of the Monastry of St Frideswide at Oxford*, I (OHS xxviii, 1894), 268.

[11]   H. E. Salter, *Survey of Oxford*, I, ed. W. A. Plantin (OHS, New Series, xiv, 1960), 242.

[12]   *Oseney*, II. 349-50.

[13]   J. E. Thorold Rogers, ed., *Oxford City Documents* (OHS xviii, 1891), 206-7.

again in 1331.[14] This was reloaded at the wharf and carted
to Merton. We have no evidence of any boat passing along
Bullstake Stream from above Oxford in the medieval period,
and the existence of the ford there would make it difficult
for anything larger than punts to pass. Therefore it seems
likely the traffic to Hythe Bridge came from the river above
Oxford alone.

The trade upstream drew on a prosperous and fertile area.
In 1334 the Oxford region was the wealthiest in England, and
Bampton Hundred which bordered the river yielded the highest
tax of all.[15] The hundred included as well as the wealthy town
of Burford with its quarries of Cotswold stone, rich agricultural
centres such as Bampton, Aston, and Radcot. Radcot stood on
the Thames and its inhabitants are thought to have prospered
by the trade of the river, for while they had little land they were
relatively prosperous. Their trade was probably with Oxford, like
that of the neighbouring town of Bampton. One of the services
of the yardlanders of Bampton was the carrying of the lord's
corn to Oxford.[16] In 1271 we have a vivid glimpse of the trade
at Radcot. Mathias de Beziles, King's yeoman, was granted
the boat wherein Gilbert son of Walter le Messer had been
lately drowned in the Thames in Mathias's liberty of Radcot,
together with its contents: 5½ quarters of wheat, an iron chain,
a lock, and 11 sacks, all of which were the King's deodands.[17]

While there are constant petitions from the towns below
Oxford for river improvement, the men of these towns of the
Upper Thames did not enter any such complaints. Such evidence as we have of trade on the Upper river deals with actual
trade, rather than the complaints of merchants who found the
river obstructed. Nevertheless even here there is nothing definite to show trade down to Oxford from Radcot and Bampton
in the late 14th century, but the obstruction of the river was
not likely to involve such large and solid structures as the mill
weirs of the Lower River, and would pose fewer problems to
the later improvers of the navigation.

---

[14] J. R. L. Highfield, ed., *The Early Rolls of Merton College* (OHS, New Series, xviii,
1963), 353.

[15] W. G. Hoskins, 'The Medieval Period' in Martin and Steel, op. cit., 109-11.

[16] E. Stone, ed., *Bampton Hundred Rolls* (Oxfordshire Record Society, xlvi, 1968), 13,
77, n. 3.   [17] *Cal. Pat. Rolls, 1266-72*, 610.

II. THE IMPROVEMENT OF THE RIVER

It is not surprising, therefore, in view of the structure of the river and its history during the medieval period, that when the river was reopened in the 16th and 17th century, it was open to navigation above Oxford before the through route to London was re-established. The community in Fisher Row was older than that at Folly Bridge by a full half-century.

In the improvement of the river one finds three strands: a generalised intellectual and theoretic interest in the improvement of rivers, stimulated from abroad by continental achievement; practical pressures for overall improvement, and also local pressure. Improvement seems to have received its first impulse under Henry VIII, perhaps under the influence of the engineers of the Italian Renaissance. The most eminent of these, though far from the first, was Leonardo da Vinci, who, after long experience of Italian canal-building and river improvement, discussed with Francis I of France, the patron of his old age, the building of a canal between the Atlantic and the Mediterranean – 'entre les deux mers'. This was later built and known as the Canal du Midi.[18] Leonardo died in 1519, and perhaps it was of canals as well as other matters that the two kings spoke on the Cloth of Gold. However this may be, Henry's contribution does not appear, on the face of it, to have been large. A campaign against unlawful weirs was mounted in 1535-6, when some were removed, but a bill for the same purpose in 1536 seems to have got no further than the drafting stage.[19]

The middle period of the 16th century was a period of innovation – the time when projects planned by such men as Sir Thomas Smith and Lord Cecil were first undertaken.[20] It is in this climate that the first river and canal improvements were made, though there seems to be no heralding literature. In the 1560s the Exeter Canal was built, employing a modern pound lock, and in the next decade another modern lock was built on the Lea at Waltham. It seems to have been a scheme

---

[18] A. W. Skempton, 'Canals and River Navigations before 1750' in Charles Singer and others, ed., *A History of Technology*, III (Oxford, 1957), 444-9, 459-60; A. F. Sieveking 'The Origin and Early History of Locks', Field, 10 Apr. 1915.

[19] *L P Henry VIII*, IX, § § 393, 519.

[20] Joan Thirsk, *Economic Policy and Projects* (Oxford, 1978), 9-17.

in which Cecil himself took a strong interest.[21] All who had schemes at this time turned naturally to Cecil, and we shall see it was to 'Sir William Burleigh' that a far-reaching proposal for improvement of the Thames was to be addressed in 1580.

Meantime river improvement was progressing: the Thames which had only been open to Henley in 1541, according to Thorold Rogers, had been opened as far as Culham by 1562. In that year Abingdon Corporation paid 4s. 8d. for the carriage of a hogshead of wine 'from London to Culneham in ye barge'.[22] In the late 1560s Thomas West, a Wallingford merchant, corn-dealer and woodmonger had an extensive trade from London upwards, trans-shipping goods at Sutton Courtenay and Burcot as well as Culham, sending iron for smiths even beyond Oxford, to Wolvercote and Commission.[23] The state of the navigation however, still left much to be desired. It was certainly not up to the best medieval standards, for winches were not established along the route where the passage was difficult, and Thomas West could not move far without his own portable winch, as the following entry from his accounts shows:

Itm I find that robart Woolly the second decemb[e]r caryd away my brok winch at cassame lok w[th] his barge called the hary and left it at my fathers and there my barge was fayne to ly ther all thester haffidayes and I was faigne to cary my winch from wallingford to cassome [Caversham] in cart cost iis.vjd. and I lost by the meanes 24 of March 1567 – vs.ob. [i.e. 5s. 0½d.][24]

Despite such difficulties he was a well-established man, for he supplied wood to the Court, and a surprisingly wide range of other goods along the river, from 'holy meditacions' and 'primarellis' to lace and cinnamon. At Burcot his agent for coal was one Davies. Perhaps he was the John Davies to whom the City of Oxford paid 2d. for 'coles' for a feast in honour of Lord Williams of Thame as early as 1556.[25] If this were so, then the river may even have been open to Burcot by then.

[21] Skempton, op. cit. 451,456; D. O. Pam, *Tudor Enfield: The Maltmen and the Lea Navigation* Edmonton Hundred Historical Society, Occasional Paper, New Series, xviii, n.d.), 7-10; J. G. Burriby and M. Parker, *The Navigation of the River Lee, 1190-1790* (Edmonton Hund. Hist. Soc., Occ. ppr., New Series xxxvi), 5-8.

[22] A. E. Preston, *The Church and Parish of St Nicholas, Abingdon* (OHS, xcix, 1935), 307.

[23] MS Wills Berks. 220 (inventory and account of Thomas West).

[24] Ibid., fo. 12.

[25] Turner, *Records*, 259.

West's trade was certainly well established when he died
about 1571.[26] In Oxford the new interest in river improvement seems to
have been felt first in the 1560s, at a time when an element
always present in the life of Oxford became more pronounced
with the secularisation of the university. It was typified by
the man of affairs who had some connection both with the
town and the university; who had interests in commerce and
the trade of the town. Such men were few, at a time when
fellows could not marry. They were limited almost entirely to
administrators: heads of colleges, manciples, bedells, butlers –
often family men who often required to augment their college
stipends, and who, by their gifts and opportunities were well-
placed to do so. Thus one finds them farming on the outskirts
of the city; Leonard Belsyre, Esquire Bedell of Theology, and
brother to Alexander Belsyre, President of St John's, was at
Kennington;[27] Griffith Lloyd, the second Principal of Jesus,
was at Oseney as a subtenant, Nicholas Wodeson, Esquire
Bedell of Theology, was at Rewley.[28] Licences to brew in the
city of Oxford were granted by the university, and university
families often had a connection with brewing at this time. The
Willis family of North Hinksey who claimed a connection
with Francis Willis of St Johns, and who were certainly related
to Bishop Fell, had connections with brewing. John Willis,
chapter clerk of Christ Church and his brother, the physician
Thomas Willis, were members of this family.[29] The Blagraves,
who came to own property at the south end of Fisher Row, were
a family boasting an ale-brewer and an esquire bedell. They
married into the Dodwell family, early 17th-century dyers,
and were related to the family of Robert Beesley, chaplain
of Mention.[30] As we have seen, the Wodesons too were

[26] West probably founded a dynasty of woodmongers which included Sir Thomas West,
Purveyor of Fuel to the King (PROB 11/84/60); *Calendar of the Committee for Compounding
etc., 1643-60*, pt. ii, 1038.

[27] PROB 11/42/55 (Leonard Belsyre); Clark, *Register*, 257.

[28] OU Archs., W. P. α 34 (1, 2); *Alumni*, Griffith Lloyd.

[29] William Bradbrooke, 'North Hinksey and the Willis Family', *North Oxfordshire
Archaeological Society*, LXXXI (1935), 63-73; DNB, Thomas Willis; Hearne, *Collections*,
VI. 201; *Athenae*, III. 1048-53.

[30] OU Archs., Hyp/B/21 (A-BE), (Beesley); ibid., Hyp/B/22 (BE-BU) (Blagrave); MS
Wills Oxon. 17/4/5 (Dodwell); *Oseney*, II. 499; *Council Acts, 1583-1626*, 104.

linked by marriage with two town families, and there were others of their kind. On the river some of the wealth that supported such activities was made, and here too perhaps some of their enterprise and intellectual curiosity found a practical outlet.

Probably we should see Nicholas Wodeson as falling into this class, as the Willis family certainly did; but we know nothing of what motivated him in building his wharf. Was he simply building a landing place for his son John's fishing boats or was he interested in inland navigation and in exploiting the river above Oxford? The question is, however not entirely simple, for before the improvement of rivers was being widely discussed no men called themselves boatmen in Oxford, and yet a certain amount of carrying by water was being done by men like Denis Hicks, who always called himself a fisherman. It was then but one of a fisherman's many bye-employments. The fisherman at that time might be regarded as a proto-boatman, an unspecialised ancestor. To supply a wharf was perhaps only to encourage that aspect of a fisherman's work, but need not be innovatory. On the other hand the period when it was built was one when the improvement of rivers and the building of canals was being undertaken at last, and Wodeson moved, though perhaps only on the edge, of a group we might expect to be receptive to such ideas, which were both intellectually exciting and practically profitable. Further Wodeson gave the wharf to his son-in-law, Robert Mounson, rather than his son, the fisherman John Wodeson, and this may suggest that he felt its future was more secure in the hands of that pushing plumber.

How Mounson put the wharf to use we do not know. After about six years, perhaps in 1578, he exchanged the lease for another city property, a tenement near the Castle Mill.[31]

With the wharf now in the hands of the town, we find signs of its use in the early 1580s in the accounts of St John's College, where the President was now Francis Willis, Katharine Wodeson's new husband. This traffic was concentrated on the river above Oxford, which was apparently then open at least

---

[31] 'Book of Evidences', 1. 82; City, A.5.5, fo. 206. Wood tells us (*City*, 1. 4356) that it was taxed in 1572, but this is a mistake. The passage he cites is 1582/3, and is printed in Turner, *Records*, 433-4). See below.

11 miles upstream. In June 1581 the college paid for the carriage of five loads of timber from Eaton, 'IIs. VIIId. the load to high bridge by water', and in 1581/2 they paid 5s. 6d. for two boatloads of wood 'from Bablock hyve to Hye bridge'. Below Oxford the river was still no better than when Thomas West had traded on it, for in March 1583 Christ Church paid for the carriage of two hundred of ling 'by barge from London to Burcot.[32]

The town's quickening interest in navigation can be seen in the enrolment of the first freeman, and the regulation of the wharf. John Howse, 'boteman' was admitted as a freeman on 20 June 1583, by Council Act, paying 40s. and the usual fees,[33] and on 14 August 1583, the tolls at Nicholas Wodesons's former wharf were regulated by the City:

Hit is agreed at this Counsell that frome henceforthe everie freeman that shall have any carriage by water to be unloded at Highe Bridge, shall paye unto this Cytie for everie bote lode of haye, woode, stone, slate, or other carriage whatsoever, one halpennye, and everie forriner j[d]., towards the mayntenaunce of the baricks and scowringe of the ryver theare, w[ch] by suche carriage and unlodinge theare is fflowndered. And that no person shall passe under the said bridge w[the] any kynde of lodinge, uppon payne of iij[s] iij[d] for everie suche carriage, to be payed by the bringer, and not by the owner of the said carriage.[34]

The improvement of the river below Oxford was now being given more serious consideration, and, as so often with projects and innovations, William Cecil, Lord Burghley, was the first person to be approached. In September 1580 John Bishop submitted to him a survey of the condition of the locks and weirs between Maidenhead (three miles above Windsor) and Abingdon, and the owners of the locks were listed.[35] Perhaps as a result orders were issued in 1584 for the conservation of the Thames, though it was only required that 'the faire wave be kept as depe and lardg as heretofore it hath bane'.[36] In 1585 John Bishop complained again of the hazards of the weirs and, in a poem directed to the Queen, described the sufferings

[32] Stevenson and Salter, *St John's*, 230, 236; Ch. Ch. MS xii. b. 25, fo. 45.
[33] City, A.5.5, fo. 257.
[34] City, A.5.5, fo. 260; quoted in Turner, *Records*, 433-4.
[35] Landsdowne 30, fos. 41-2.
[36] Lansdowne, 41, fo. 43; quoted in Thacker, *Highway*, I. 52. Thacker gives no sources, so vitiating much pioneer research.

of the bargemen and their families in a stumbling, lengthy, but moving poem.

> Mylls weares and locks men do them call
> that doe annoy that worthy streame
> Against the laws they doe stande all
> but still the [*sic*] drownde those symple men.[37]

As well he listed the locks and weirs, their owners and keepers, proceeding upstream to Iffley, the last lock below Oxford. The Oxford interest in navigation was therefore part of a wider interest.

As the river above Burcot was to be improved later, it is perhaps worth reproducing Bishop's list of the weirs between Burcot and Oxford.

32. Two locks and one myll kept by Richard Elstone & Richard Justice. In Sutton.
33. Abingdon Lock kepte by Thomas Tysdale.
34. Three Locks at Newham kept by John Mollyners. All in said parish.
35. Samfords Lock kept by John Ovens. The locke in the parish of Kennington.
36. Ifle Lock kept by one Mrs Parts.[38]

Some of these names are already familiar in connection with fishermen. Active interest in transport by river seems to have continued intermittently, for though there is no further evidence from pamphlet literature or other literary sources, Oxford was evidently attempting to establish its right to sell merchandise in London free of toll. This may well have been a preliminary step to opening the navigation and expanding trade. Oxford based its claim on its charters. On 14 November 1589 'Mr Rowe' was appointed to put forward Oxford's claim, and on 25 November the Court of Aldermen in London set up a committee to consider it.[39] The case continued into the following year. On 4 May 1590 the Oxford Council agreed that 'the Sherriffs or Waterbayliffs of London shalbe sued for taking tole, custome or warphage of the cytizens of this cytie', whilst in September in London a case was depending in the

---

[37] Lansdowne 44, fos. 117-18; Thacker, op. cit. 1. 52.
[38] Lansdowne 30, fo. 50; Thacker, op. cit. 1. 56.
[39] *Council Acts 1583-1626*, 52; Records Office, The Guildhall, London, Repertory 22, fos. 118, 126.

Court of Common Pleas between that city and the burgesses of Exeter and Oxford touching the non-payment of tolls.[40] The matter continued to concern the City of Oxford. In February 1603 Thomas Stone, mercer and bailiff, and Thomas Harris, mayor in the municipal year 1603/4, undertook a similar mission.[41] The Act for 'Clearing the Passage by Water from London to and beyond the Citye of Oxford', 3 Jac. I c.20, was passed in 1606, and on 21 March 1607 a commission was established to implement it with 18 members: four from each of the counties bordering the Upper Thames, and one each from the City and University respectively.[42] The Commission had power to clear the stream, and make cuts in adjacent land to improve the passage. As well, they had power to raise a levy on all persons in the four counties benefiting by the navigation, and to deal with defaulters. Four representatives from the city and four from the University of Oxford were to deal with matters relating to wharfage in the city. In its composition and in the method of levying tax from the county the Commission closely resembled a commission of sewers.

A meeting was held on 7 July 1607, and it was decided to inspect the river from Clifton [Hampden] to Cricklade, in three sections between 20 July and the end of the month, taking Jonius Stone and James 'Jesse' or Jessoppe to advise them throughout.[43]

James Jessoppe was an interesting man. He was probably the son of Thomas Jessoppe, miller of Oseney and the subtenant of Dr Griffith Lloyd. A James Jessoppe was servant

[40] *Council Acts 1583-1626*, 54; Records Office, Guildhall, Repertory 22, fo. 213.

[41] *Council Acts 1583-1626*, 150. Much later, in the 1680s, when the river traf-fic was booming, the matter came up again (*Council Acts 1666-1701*, 133-4; R., O., The Guildhall, Repertory 86, fo. 62; 87, fos. 21, 36; 88, fos. 5, 67, 127). That it was a matter of great concern to river transport is made very clear in 1687: 'The mayor informs the house that several actions have been brought by the City of London, or one of their officers, against several of the City boatmen for the toll of freemen of the City which was never used to be paid and from which we are exempt' (*Council Acts 1666-1701*, 192, 195).

[42] OU Archs., S.E.P. G2. The Commissioners were the following: Sir G. Hyde, Sir William Spencer, Sir John Hungerford, Sir F. Popharn, Sir Edmund Fettiplace, Sir William Greene, Sir M. Dormer, Sir Henry Stonor, John Dooley, William Dutton, Edmund Dunche, Anth. Hungerford, P. Gracye, Tho... John Ayliffe, William Stonehouse, and, *ex officio*, the Mayor of Oxford, and the Vice-Chancellor of the University.

[43] Thacker, *Highway*, I. 63-4.   [44] OU Archs., W.P. α 34 (1).

to Dr Lloyd's widow, Ann, and on this account was listed in 1589 as a privileged person. In 1592 he became a freeman, and took six apprentices in his trade as a millwright between 1589 and 1610. He lived in St Thomas's, next to the smith Thomas Winkle. This trade was one of the first in which engineering skills were developed, and no doubt his proximity to a smith was no accident. He seems to have been the Admirable Crichton of the Oxford Council, and his activities suggest that he may have seen service in the Low Countries, and learnt from Dutch examples. In 1596 he was drilling the city's troops, and he was also leased land to erect a windmill, for which the city provided old stones from the Castle Mill at a reduced price. Then, when river improvement was undertaken, the city turned to him again.[45]

The activities of the Commission are not recorded. By March 1609 James Jessoppe was ill, and the city made a payment to him 'towards his great extremitie of sickness having spent much in travaile about the navigation and being now in need and necessitie'. Similar payments were made the following January and September. Thereafter silence fell upon Jessoppe and the completion of the navigation.[46]

Nearly 200 years later another Jessoppe, William Jessopp, was to be consulted about the navigation. Perhaps when the fortunes of tradesmen have been studied with the assiduity now reserved for the nobility we shall be able to trace a connection between this son of the Oseney miller, James Jessoppe, in James I's reign, and the civil engineer, William Jessop, son of Smeaton's resident engineer for the building of the Eddystone Lighthouse. If there are dynasties of fishermen continuing for generations in the same occupations surely we may expect to find dynasties of engineers, stretching back to smiths, millers, and millwrights?

The achievement of the Act to improve the Thames navigation has been underrated, because it did not open the navigation to London, but this had not been its sole aim, and the

[45] Clark, *Register*, 396; City, L.5.1, 13 May 1598-12 Dec. 1610 *Oseney*, II. 533; *Council Acts, 1583-1626*, 98, 100-1. His experiments with a windmill are interesting. Was Jessoppe considering the replacement of water powered mills by windmills on the river? On the Wye such an experiment was tried around 1640, but the lie of the land was unsuitable. BL Add. MS 11,052, fo. 100.

[46] *Council Acts 1583-1626*, 190, 196, 202.

fact that it cleared the river west of Oxford so that no further legislation was required for its improvement has escaped remark. Yet the preamble to the next act, that for 1623/4, stated that the river 'for many miles beyond the Citie of Oxford Westward, is already navigable and passable for Boates of good Burthens and Contentes, and likewise is alreadie navigable for Barges from London to the Village of Bercott ...' Thorold Rogers found an entry for as early as 1609 for the carriage of three tons of stone from Radcot Bridge, 24 miles above Hythe Bridge, to Oxford. This was the usual embarkation point for Burford and Taynton stone in the latter part of the century. Whether the last seven miles up to Lechlade were open by then we do not know, but T. S. Willan's much-reproduced map of the Navigable Rivers of England 1600-60 needs revision here, for it shows Oxford as the head of navigation.[47]

Only a small reach of the river remained to be opened, about 12 miles, from Oxford to Burcot, below Abingdon, but though attempts were made to procure a bill as early as 1614, it was not passed until nearly ten years later.[48] The new Act (21 Jac. I c.32) dealt exclusively with this part of the river. Under it eight Barge Commissioners were appointed, four representing the town and four the gown. They were to scour the river, make all weirs and turnpikes (locks) fit for passage, open up any streams which would aid in making the river navigable, and erect wharves, turnpikes, or locks, and form pens for water as necessary. No land required for the navigation must be 'meddled' with before a satisfactory agreement had been reached with the owner or, if there was difficulty, before a settlement had been made by three impartial justices of Peace of the county. Towing-paths were to be established throughout the length of the route, and none were to impede the passage of the halers. The cost of improvement was to be borne by the city and the university equally. The Barge Commissioners were to regulate and control the navigation and its tolls. On 19 July 1624 the first Commissioners for the city were elected by the whole commons assembled together.[49]

---

[47] T. S. Willam, *River Navigation in England 1600-1750* (Oxford, 1936, repr. 1964), frontispiece.

[48] *Council Acts 1583-1626*, 241; OU Archs., W.P.P. 514.

[49] *Council Acts 1583-1626*, 325.

On the face of it, it seems strange that Abingdon, which also lay on the unrestored portion of the river, should not be involved in this scheme, yet an attempt to involve the town seems to have been repelled according to a letter from the town's authorities written to Secretary Dorchester in October 1631. They understood that in the business of clearing a passage for barges to Oxford, His Majesty had given a charge that their town should not be neglected. They acknowledged themselves much bound to His Majesty, but pointed out that the river had been open to Abingdon for barges for four years, but added that they would aid their neighbour town and University in all friendly offices.[50] They neither suggested nor took any further steps that can be discovered. The town of Abingdon may well have felt itself threatened by the improvement of the river. It had built bridges over the Thames which had given it communications superior to any that Oxford enjoyed, standing not only like Oxford on the road to Southampton, but on an excellent east-west route also, far superior to that at Oxford, which was no more than a packhorse road. They had two grounds for concern: they felt their position as an entrepôt threatened by an improvement in the river west of Oxford, which could rival their own overland route, and as well the navigation channel of the Oxford-Burcot Commission bypassed Abingdon, and diverted water which served the Abbey Mill and then ran past the town's wharves. Ultimately Abingdon gained by the navigation, becoming a major inland port, where goods were trans-shipped from boat to barge, or barge to boat, for it was the last point to which barges of great burden could come at all times. The improvement of the river did not so much pose a threat to the interests of Abingdon merchants as an opportunity. It was to be seized by the Abingdon rivermen who, when the river was opened to Oxford, played a significant part in the colonisation of the Folly Bridge area. This community was to have close links with Abingdon through trade and kinship.

No doubt the city of Oxford had hoped for co-operation from Abingdon in paying for the costs of river improvement, but for the university, which was the wealthier party, finance does not seem to have presented serious problems. For the

[50] *Calendar of State Papers Domestic*, XXVIII. 163.

City the matter was more difficult, and austerity was demanded. Heavy local taxation was introduced from 1629.[51] Onerous levies were laid on all city dignitaries on assuming office and a weekly tax on all inhabitants. This taxation fell at a time when the City was hard-pressed in other respects and it reached a crescendo in the '30s. The river in the environs of Oxford itself was 'floundered up', and labour or money had to be provided for its cleansing. There were other taxes to be paid. In 1634 there was a tax to provide gunpowder, and in 1634 and 1635 Ship Money was levied.[52] The rate of tax was too high. In 1631 one member of Common Council refused to pay towards the Navigation and was dismissed, but in 1633 and 1634 even newly-elected mayors and bailiffs were refusing office and payment, and extraordinary scenes accompanied the proceedings. After this, taxation was abandoned, and the town resorted to borrowing.[53]

Despite all its difficulties at length the navigation was opened, and on 31 August 1635 the first barge reached Oxford from London, and in 1638 the wharf-house and the 'turnpikes' (poundlocks) of the Oxford-Burcot Commission were leased out.[54] The river was now a going concern. At Folly Bridge a new, second community of bargemen was to grow up, with its sights set on the London trade.

It is not our purpose now to carry further the detailed history of the navigation. For this, despite an entire lack of footnotes, Fred S. Thacker's *Thames Highway* remains, so far, unsurpassed. Nevertheless we shall sketch here in outline the major legislation affecting the river before the building of canals altered the geography of water transport at the end of the 18th century.

Though the river was now open, many problems were unresolved which reduced the efficiency of the navigation. The Act of 1623/4 covered only a small stretch of the river. No overall authority controlled the whole river and dealt with the problems of financing, maintaining, and improving it, or even regulating the tolls taken by lock-keepers along its length.

---

[51] Wood, *Life*, IV, 51; *Council Acts*, 1626-65, 19-20, 60, 80.

[52] *Council Acts 1626-65*, xviii, 354-5, 357, 358-9, 361-2, 418.

[53] Ibid., 37, 47, 55-6, 59, 60.

[54] *The Diary of Thomas Crosfield*, ed. F. S. Boas (London, 1935) 80; OU Archs., S.E.P., G. 3b.

Repairs were left to local initiative, and were even financed by levies on passing bargemasters.[55] Under such management, or lack of it, the river could only deteriorate.

Attempts to deal with these problems were made from time to time by new legislation. Tolls were the subject of temporary acts in 1694 (6 & 7 Gul. and Mar. c.16) and in 1729 (3 Geo.II c.11). Tolls were also dealt with in a more far-reaching Act in 1751 (24 Geo.II c.8), which also attempted to deal with the oversight of the whole river, and established a permanent body of Commissioners. Improvements were to be financed by tolls rather than by levies, but remained essentially ad hoc. No planned improvement was possible. Under an Act of 1771 (11 Geo.III c.45) finance by loan made planning and overall improvement at last possible, and pound-locks such as had been installed by the Oxford-Burcot Commission were slowly installed in the river up to Oxford, and the Oxford-Burcot Commission sold its turnpikes, but not its wharf to them.

III. FISHER ROW AND THE NAVIGATION

How did the opening of the navigation affect St Thomas's parish and its boat-people? Once the river was open to London families of boat and bargemen from St Thomas's might have been expected to emigrate to St Aldates, but this did not happen. The community in St Thomas's was already over 50 years old when the wharf at Folly Bridge opened, and the earliest family of boatmen was now in its third generation. After fifty years it had become large enough and cohesive enough for its individuals to resist any temptation to move elsewhere.

What then was happening in St Thomas's in that period between 1583, the year tolls were established at the wharf in Upper Fisher Row and John Howse took out his freedom, and the opening of the navigation to London in 1635? If the behaviour of the rivermen of St Thomas's is anything to go by it would seem that river improvement was confidently expected in the 1580s, even though no parliamentary discussion and agitation is known. Between 1596 and the passing of the Acts in 1606 two men bought their freedom, one as a waterman and one as a boatman; two fishermen styled themselves boatmen

[55] PRO PC 2/47, 67.

and took apprentice-boatmen; John Howse's son, William, took up his freedom and followed in his fathers's footsteps.

The boatmen formed a cluster in Lower Fisher Row around the Fourth Tenement. This was quite a large messuage, and it tended to be subdivided. John Backester, labourer, had subdivided it as early as 1575, when his tenant was the fisherman, Robert Cook John's son Robert Backester bought his freedom in 1596/7 as a waterman, and succeeded to his father's tenement by 1601. His neighbour was John Howse – very likely the boatman.[56] The other aspiring boatman who took out his freedom was James Feild who bought his freedom in 1601/2. He probably had connections with fishermen and Fisher Row too, for when William Feild, fisherman, apprenticed his son in 1606 he was said to be *'nuper* Cook' – formerly Cook. Later James's daughter married Richard Bonner alias Pitts, and Thomas Hicks's daughter Anne married a Cook. Fishing and boating were intimately connected in this period.

This connection is also seen in the case of the two fishermen who took apprentice-boatmen, in anticipation of the improvement of the navigation. Thomas Smythe took Thomas Pemerton, son of Walter Pemerton, labourer of Oseney, as his apprentice in 1599 and Nicholas Strange took John Walter of Fifield as an apprentice just about the time the first act was passed.[57]

The river trade naturally attracted men from the low, riverside parishes west of Oxford, and from the hills of Wytham and Cumnor. John Howse, the first boatman, probably came originally from Wytham, for in the early 16th century a miller, Adam Howse, and a fisherman, William Howse, are to be found there.[58] James Feild himself had relatives at Binsey and Medley, Thomas Pemerton came from Oseney, and Nicholas Strange's apprentice, John Walter, came from Fifield, on the heights above the Hinkseys.

The low-lying land which formed the largest part of the parish of St Thomas's stretched to the Berkshire boundary, and together with adjacent small hamlets, formed a wild,

[56] Ch. Ch. Deed B ox, Fish Row, Ten. 4.

[57] City, L.5.1, 1601-2 (feild); ibid., 27 Apr. 1599 (Pemerton to Smith); ibid., 12 Jan. 1606 (Walter to Strange); ibid. 1599-1600 (William Howse).

[58] *LP Henry, VIII* XV, § 436(25); PRO Req. 2/7/109.

amphibious region, where a boat was an important piece of equipment. Indeed, for the farmer of Binsey, who had rights of inter-commonage on Port Meadow, a boat must have been a necessity to ferry his animals across the mainstream of the Thames. In this low-lying land, cut by many streams, which were sometimes only bridged temporarily at the hay-harvest, a boat was probably more use than a cart. Few wills survive of the husbandmen and yeomen who farmed this area below Wytham and Cumnor, and even fewer inventories. However, that of Thomas Banks, labourer of Botley, of 1636, and Thomas Feild of Medley, made in 1670, both show boats.[59] Thomas Banks was only worth £11 11s. 6d., and his main assets were two cows, a calf, and a boat worth £2. Thomas Feild was a man of some substance, and he owned two boats. It is easy to see that rumours of the improvement of the navigation would attract young and energetic men who were used to handling boats from these waterlogged acres.

In this period of anticipation, before the navigation to London was open, boatmen settled near the wharf. Robert Backester and John Howse were, as we have seen, living side by side in Lower Fisher Row in 1601. Deeds show four others settled nearby between 1616 and 1619, though in some cases they may have been there even earlier. William Howse, probably the son of John Howse, the first boatman, leased a propriety from the city across the Castle Mill Stream from the wharf in 1616; we know that one of the Pemertons was living in a tenement by the Castle Mill in 1617, and that in 1619 a Thomas Smith was the subtenant of the house next to John Wodeson's former home and Nicholas Strange was living nearby. We know too from a lease of a neighbouring property that William Tawney was living in a tenement on the east side of the Castle Mill Stream in 1626, more or less opposite the Lock, but how long he had already been there we do not know.[60]

Although the boatmen clustered round the wharf area, until the 1620s no houses were built there. Middle and Upper Fisher Row, where most of the bargemen were to live later, was still void and empty. The situation can be seen very clearly in an

---

[59] MS Wills Berks. 177 (Banks); MS Wills Oxon. 23/2/8 (Feild).
[60] City D.5.5, fo. 308 (Howse); *Oseney*, III. 19 (Pemerton); *Oseney*, II. 502 (Smith); ibid. 521 (Strange); ibid. 373 (Tawney).

undated early 17th-century map made not later than 1618 (see Fig. 2.1). The reason it should have been left undeveloped at a period when the town was expanding rapidly, when even the Castle moat had been filled in and built over, must have been uncertainty about the legal ownership of the area. As we have seen the place had been a no man's land, fought over by the town and Oseney before the Dissolution. Only when its position was clearly defined could it be leased and built up. The question of the actual ownership of the land north of The Lock was brought up in a very complex case between Christ Church and the city which lasted from 1615 to about 1621. The matter was raised somewhat obliquely, turning on the extent of Warham Bank. Christ Church held that it owned all houses on the bank, and claimed that the bank stretched from The Lasher by Rewley wall to the Swans Nest. The City held that the Bank stretched only from the house of Painter, the fellmonger at the foot of Fisher Row, to The Lock. The matter was put to many of the older people of the parish, including John Wodeson, now 82, to William Farr, the fisherman, once his apprentice; to Nicholas Painter, the fellmonger, and Roger Moore the painter, to Thomas Fishe, the fishmonger, John Cook, the fisher, and others. All but Wodeson were agreed that the Bank extended only from The Lock to Painter's house, and Painter himself remarked that he had been of the homage (of the court of the manor of Oseney) and when the matter was raised on two or three occasions and they had been pressed to find the extent of the bank, they had always found it to be from The Lock to Painter's house. The upshot of this seems to have been a compromise, for we find that while the City were landlords of Upper Fisher Row, that is, the land from The Lasher by Rewley wall to Hythe Bridge, Christ Church became landlords of Middle Fisher Row – the land from Hythe Bridge to The Lock. In June 1621 Christ Church leased out void land in Middle Fisher Row to William Pemerton, boat-man, and on 8 September 1623 the town leased out land at the north end of the 'Timber Wharf' to Thomas Pemerton, boatman (see Appendix III for leases of Upper Fisher Row).[61]

[61] *Oseney*, II, 503-5; III. 16-20; City, C.13.1*q*. C.13 1*bb*, C.13 2*k*.

The interest in the navigation was not limited to the boatmen of the parish at this time. It was also felt by its main landlord, Christ Church. Robert Burton, the chaplain of St Thomas's and a canon of Christ Church, was himself to write of the value of inland navigation in his *Anatomy of Melancholy* which came out in 1621, not long before the new act was passed,[62] whilst in the verse of another Christ Church man we find a description of the barges on the river during the bitter winter of 1634 which preceded and delayed the opening of the river to London:

> Our Rivers nowe are Cristal, shoars are fit
> Mirrours, being now not like to glass but it;
> Our ships stand all as planted, we may swear
> They are not born up only but grow there:
> Whilst waters thus are pavements, firm as stone,
> And without faith are each day walked upon.[63]

If, after the river was opened in 1635, there was no mass movement to Folly Bridge by the boatmen, neither was the land by the wharf in Upper Fisher Row taken up rapidly and built over, for the settled conditions necessary for the development of the trade did not last long. In October 1642, after Edgehill, Charles and his court entered Oxford, and the City found itself at the centre of events. The Civil War did not destroy the traffic of the river, but it interfered with it, for the boatmen were employed in various ways by the King's Commissioners." In his interesting article on the navigation during the Civil War, Mr I. G. Philip claimed the river between Oxford and Reading to have been of 'supreme importance'. However, his evidence suggests that while the river at Reading was busy, there was not 'fairly consistent traffic by *river* from Oxford to Reading'.[65] It may have reached Reading by water, but it seldom left Oxford in this way. However, the river does seem to have been used locally for the carriage of raw materials and for the construction of the fortifications,[66] but the newly opened navigation was scarcely past its teething troubles, and

---

[62] Robert Burton, *The Anatomy of Melancholy* (Oxford, 1621), Introduction, 53-4.

[63] William Cartwright 'On a Great Frost, 1634', in William Hicks, ed., *Oxford Drollery* (Oxford, 1671), 166.

[64] Add. D. 114, fos. 13, 14, 25, 26.

[65] I. G. Philip, 'River Navagation at Oxford during the Civil War and the Commonwealth', *Oxon.* 11 (1937), 156-7. Italics not in the original.

[66] Add. D. 114, fo. 103.

seems to have fallen into disrepair quite soon. In 1644 Alderman Potter, the tenant of the wharf, was granted a levy of five shillings on boat-loads of timber and other goods, as the wharf was in decay 'by reason of unloading of faggots and other materials there'. Only after the navigation was repaired in 1647 was it able to expand and develop.[67] In June 1649 two more tenements were leased out in Upper Fisher Row.

The fortunes of the navigation fluctuated considerably in the years which followed. Despite *ad hoc* methods of supervision and control, it flourished in the years after the Civil War, and the bargemen of St Thomas's prospered. A considerable traffic in corn, stone, and timber passed down river, whilst the requirements for coal increased in Oxford with the demand for comfort. London was expanding rapidly in the late 17th century, and, with rebuilding after the Great Fire, and the expansion of naval building, trade on the river grew brisk. In 1667/8, and again in 1681/2, the Oxford-Burcot Commissioners were able to repay part of loans from the City and University.[68] This was the zenith of their achievement, though trade remained good for some time into the 18th century. In 1707 a property of Lincoln College next to the wharf was leased, and the wharf and its facilities were extended.[69]

The period is not well documented, but from the diaries of Hearne a hint of its fortunes can be gained. In 1708 paper for his book was sent him by barge; in July 1711 he mentioned a trunk sent by barge, and in August some ale. In 1712 his friend Allen entrusted him with a complicated arrangement: he wished the furniture of his chamber and study to be sent to him in Kent by water. The bargeman on arrival in London was to deliver the goods to Mr Tappenden, Hoyman, at the Sign of the Hoy, Bear Key, near Billingsgate. The Tappendens were a substantial family of hoymen, later bankers. The furniture was not sent and in 1721 Allen wrote to Hearne from Murston in Kent: 'I designed the furniture of my room at Oxford for one of my rooms here, but Mr Bateman has never yet found an opportunity to send it me; last year he could not send it for lack of water in the River, and now he says the College are

[67] *Council Acts, 1626-65*, 120, 147, 149.
[68] Oxon. RO, CH. N. IX/i, fos. 67, 69; *Council Acts, 1666-1701*, 333, 338.
[69] Lincoln College Archives, St Aldate's Deeds.

not willing that he should doe it.[70] From then until 1751, apart from the births and deaths of bargemen and their families, the record of the river is almost silent.

Although the new legislation of 1751 and 1771 brought new trade and some improvement to the river as a whole, it did little for the trade above Oxford, and the Fisher Row community did not share in the improvement to any marked extent. On the whole Oxford was in a sluggish and depressed condition until near the end of the 18th century, whilst Abingdon was relatively prosperous, perhaps to some extent at Oxford's expense. On the whole Fisher Row fared better in the early 18th century, and Folly Bridge in the later part of the century.

IV. BARGEMEN'S WORK

Fisher Row was destined to be a larger community of boatmen and fishermen than that at Folly Bridge. It was established first, but the Folly Bridge wharf was the busier, and ties must be strong to hold the community together despite this. These must be sought in the nature of the bargemen's work which tended to develop a strong sense of solidarity between members of the community, based partly on the shared experience of working together, partly on the strong family ties which it developed. Family played an important part in the very organisation of the trade, and the families along the river were closely related.

Just as the work of the fishermen affected the very pattern of their family life, so also we find the bargemen's work affected theirs. The barging trade differed from fishing in a fundamental way. Fishing exploited a limited resource, whilst barging was a service industry which, whilst trade was buoyant, might well seem almost limitless. If fishing was like farming, barging was more like running a chain of stores like Mothercare or C. & A. Modes. Wherever there was a town of a suitable size and position, there was a demand to be met. In each generation only one of a fisherman's sons could normally expect to become a fisherman, and inherit his father's watery

---

[70] Hearne, *Collections*, II. 159; ibid. III. 200, 325; Denis Baker, 'The Marketing of corn in the first half of the 18th century: North East Kent', *Agricultural History Review*, XVIII, 1970, 134-5; Hearne, *Collections*, VII. 224.

acres.[71] The successful bargemaster, however, could provide openings for all his sons.

Barging was very much a family affair. The ambitious young bargeman might start by working one of his father's boats. After his father's death he might work the boat in partnership with a brother or his widowed mother.[72] As he prospered he might own a boat or a barge of his own, and he might take an apprentice. The number of hands he would require would depend on the size of his boat. A barge of 100 tons burthen, the largest size owned at Folly Bridge, might require five or more men, but a boat of sixty tons or less such as Fisher Row masters owned, might be worked by three men and a boy. As our bargemaster's sons grew up they would replace apprentices and hired bargemen, and as they reached maturity and the father extended his business they came at last to captain boats themselves, and the cycle was completed. Where trade was slack, of course, men might never come to manage boats of their own but manage a single boat within the family.

The larger the number of boats and barges a bargemaster might have, the better and more far-reaching the service he could offer. Thus a man who had only barges could not trade above Oxford; the man who had only boats was not well equipped for the trade downstream, for his overheads were higher than for a barge. Goods were often trans-shipped from boats to barges or vice versa at Oxford or Abingdon.

Not only was it necessary to crew boats, boats needed to be able to call on supporting services along the banks of the river. Agents were needed at wharves to handle goods, taking in consignments and storing them for forwarding, collection, or trans-shipment. A case which is found in Exchequer Depositions provides an example of the complexity of internal trade. In 1699 a miller of Upper Heyford, in Oxfordshire, ground five loads of wheat for a Chipping Norton corn-factor at his mill at Standlake, which is near the Upper Thames wharf at Newbridge. At Newbridge the meal was loaded onto a boat and carried 20 odd miles down river to Abingdon, where

---

[71] Compare the fishermen's position with that of the Irish peasants described in C. M. Arensberg and S. T. Kimball, *Family and Community in Ireland* (London, 1940).

[72] See for example, MS Wills Oxon. 57/4/7 (William Pemerton and 57/1/1 (John Rounsival).

it was trans-shipped. Two Abingdon bargemasters, William and John Ayris, carried it to London for delivery to a Piccadilly baker.[73]

This case is known because something went wrong with the transaction, but many others were handled smoothly. Stone from near Burford in Oxfordshire for instance, was carted to Radcot Bridge and carried to London for the building of St Paul's in London.[74] Such a load required much the same sort of handling, though its organisation was simpler, as Christopher Wren's master-mason Christopher Kempster was the owner of the quarry from which the stone came. These two cases illustrate very nicely the value of keeping transactions within as small a circle of persons as possible, in a world where communications were primitive.

At a wharf one must find all the services which any modern airport terminal supplies: access for freight, storage facilities, food and drink, a place for the leaving and transmitting of communications, forwarding agents, and so forth. Translated into 17th- and 18th-century terms, the services needed were wharves, warehouses, and wharfingers, alehouse-keepers, and carters. As well, clustered round the wharves there would be the yards of businesses dependent on water transport for their raw materials and finished products: timber and stone yards, breweries, malt-houses. The men who worked at such places and came in contact with the bargemen and the bargemasters had a strong interest in the fortunes of the navigation, and often had family connections with its workers. The aspiring bargemaster was fortunate if he could also call on relatives in towns along the route to smooth the way when complicated transactions required a man on the spot.

The nature of their work on the river threw the bargemen together and they depended on each other and their kind in the towns along the way, rather than on the wider community. The trip could be lengthy: to London and back could be done in less than a fortnight, but it might take four times as long, for there were many sources of delay. The river itself was always changing. Drought and flood, frost and wind acted on it continually, building up gulls, scouring out new channels;

[73] PRO, E 13418 Anne/Easter 14.

[74] W. J. Arkell, *Oxford Stone* (London, 1947, repr. 1970), 68-9.

sometimes impeding the bargeman through lack of water, sometimes by the force of the stream. Moving the long, clumsy, unpowered craft along the river required an enormous co-operative effort. Men worked together, relying for their lives on the strength of the ropes, and the presence of mind of their fellows, their sinews and their sureness of foot, as they heaved, sweated, plunged through the water or shouldered the winch.

Bridges and weirs, with their flash-locks, provided the main hazards. In going through bridges the stream was constricted and it tended to pile up, so that the boat met unusual resistance. As an amateur observed: 'It is very difficult going uphill through Bridges'.[75] Extra men or horses were needed as many bridges had no tow-paths through their arches, and as the tow-line must pass through the bridge, and not over it, skill and teamwork were required to avoid loss of control.

The weirs of fishermen and millers posed further problems. Mills were built at points where they took advantage of a change of gradient, and their weirs provided a method of checking and controlling the stream and moving from one level to another. The device used to effect this transition was originally the flash-lock. It was essentially a gate in a weir formed of a series of movable timbers or paddles.[76] Removing and replacing paddles required strength and judgement. Once the paddles were removed the levels above and below the weir equalised. Going downstream was rather like shooting the rapids, for the water flowed very rapidly though the narrow gap, whilst moving upstream required many halers, as did moving through a narrow bridge. The passage was helped by the use of a winch usually fixed to the bank.

The passing of boats through a flash-lock used vast amounts of water in equalising levels, as pounds between locks could be miles long. Often the upper pound was denuded and rendered impassable for hours, or even days in times of drought. For this reason boats congregated above flash-locks and were passed through in convoy. When the river was well organised flashes were run twice a week, passing each lock at a stated time, and the boats were carried along from lock to lock. To miss a flash then could mean days of delay.

[75] A. M. W. Stirling, *William de Morgan and his Wife* (London, 1922), 124.

[76] H. R. Robinson, *Art Journal*, New Series, xii (1973), 74.

To the miller the navigation represented a rival for water just as much as a second mill, and relations between millers along the river and bargemen were about as cordial as those between the rival millers of Oseney and the Castle Mill. As the millers controlled the flash-locks (which were appurtenant to their mills) the bargemen were in the miller's hands. This was the position below Oxford. Above, the weirs were kept by fishermen who, like millers, benefited from the obstructed stream. Their attitude to water was, however, less jealous, and relations were easier.

The introduction of pound locks reduced the amount of water required to pass from one level of the river to the next, for instead of equalising two very long pounds, by the interposition of a second gate a boat's length behind the first, the amount of water requiring to be equalised was reduced. Nevertheless in summer, or when the river was low or silted up, it was often necessary to 'buy a flash' to help the boats along.

These long periods of delay when the bargemen were congregated in one place, waiting for the regular flash controlled by the authorities, or for the miller to spare enough water from grinding corn to carry the barges on their way, threw the bargemen on their own company. Their life on the river was, and remains, something unknown to the men ashore, something hidden, and no doubt governed by its own customs, as the life of all-male groups is elsewhere.

The cost of a trip could not be budgeted for with any certainty. It consisted in part of routine payments, such as those for tolls and the horsing of the boats, and in part of payments for unforeseeable incidental expenses caused by delay. As there was no centralised system of management or accounting, all payments tended to be by cash rather than credit, and money had to be carried for all eventualities. The captain of the boat was entrusted therefore with sizeable sums of money, and the name by which the captain of Thames barges was known – the cost-bearer – is appropriate. The cost-bearer must be someone totally reliable. The small bargemaster with only one boat had no problems here, for he was his own cost-bearer, and it is not surprising that when a man had several boats he often had but one cost-bearer between them, and ran them in convoy. If he

could not go himself, a bargemaster's cost-bearers were likely
to be members of his family.

Despite all precautions the cost-bearer might run through the
sum of money which he carried, and here the bargemaster must
be able to count on obtaining credit from men along the bank
whom he knew, and who trusted him. It is not surprising that
in such a world, dependent on mutual trust and co-operation,
business ties and family ties reinforced each other. The bargemaster was dependent on the goodwill of his agents and relatives,
the wharfingers and pub-keepers, and on the corn- and timber-
dealers, maltsters and brewers whose goods he carried, and
amongst whose ranks the children of successful bargemasters
often found marriage partners.

The supporting services which the bargemaster required in
finance, handling, or warehousing were most necessary at points
of trans-shipment or at the end of the trip, and the barging families of St Thomas's had connections with families in Lechlade,
at the head of the navigation, and Abingdon. It is not known
what sort of connections they had with London families, with
barging interests. It is difficult to locate and identify such connections in large centres of population. Connections between
Folly Bridge families and London ones certainly existed, but
still require further investigation.

As well as the supporting services we have already described,
the barging trade required help in towing the boats upstream.
Towing was done by teams of horses when there were towing-
paths, and by gangs of men when there were none. The
introduction of towing-paths along the length of the Thames
was an achievement of the Thames Commission after 1770;
they were by no means common before that and on the Severn
were not introduced until much later. Towing, or bow-haling
as it was more commonly called, was extremely heavy work,
and involved very large teams of men or horses. Two detailed
calculations of the cost of navigating the unimproved and
improved river are to be found in the Oxford Record Office.[77]
One, covering the distance from London to Reading gave prices
for August 1770, the second, from Mapledurham to Oxford,
is undated. Taken together, they cover the whole line from
London to Oxford, and therefore it seems likely that they

[77] Appendix IV.

were made at the same time, when the act of 1771 was being contemplated. The costs and numbers of men and horses used on the unimproved river may be rather high, as men promoting new works tend to over-emphasise the failings of the prevailing system, but the estimates cannot be totally unrealistic, or contemporaries would not have accepted them.

Between London and Reading the requirements of a 200 ton barge with a crew of seven were computed. Between Windsor and Sonning, for instance, 45 men were required for haling, and the expense of three nights' lodging was included. They were augmented from time to time by additional men or horses: by eight horses from Boveney to Water Oakley; by 12 men at Hedsor, eight men going up Marlow Bucks, and so on.

Between Mapledurham and Oxford the expenses were calculated on the sort of boats usually navigated from Oxford to London at the time, a barge of 110 tons and a 'lighter' of 50 tons working together. Six 'service men' were required to work the boat up and down stream; but as well, going up from Mapledurham to Days Lock, a distance of 173/4 miles, 40 'hirelings' were required to tow, and they were paid for two days' work. From Culham to Oxford – one day's work – 40 men and six horses were needed. On the improved river the work would be easier and it was calculated that only four service men would be needed on the boat, whilst 10 horses replaced the 40 men. Haling was grinding, hard work, and progress on the unimproved river must have been slow. How long per day the men worked is unknown, so the speed the barge made cannot be computed. Barges may have travelled as much as two miles an hour, but there would be delays at the flash-locks, or when the path changed from one bank to the other. How did the gangs co-ordinate their activity? Was it by singing shanties such as sailors used? When such a question is raised it is brought home how sparse are first-hand accounts of men at work before the 19th century.

The only account of boat-halers that is known comes from the Richmond area where there was no horse-path until about 1800 and even this was incomplete.[71] It was written in 1866, but seems to be based on memory or first-hand information.

---

[78] Thacker, *Highway*, II. 485-6; Richard Crisp, *Richmond and its Inhabitants from the Olden Times* (London, 1866), 327-8.

The reader will probably be surprised to learn that all this heavy work which has been now for many years done by horses, was then exclusively done by men, hence the term 'Bargemen'. They were harnessed, if the expression be allowed, seven or eight in number, by means of broad leathern straps, which rested on and around the shoulders of each man; each of these straps being attached to the long rope or tow-line fixed to the barge, they thus hauled the same along the 'Silent Highway'. They worked, as it has been shown, by stages, not very long ones, and thus the loaded vessel by very slow degrees reached its destination. The price paid to the men for this description of work was at per ton, and it has been said that it was very remunerative work to those who were thus employed.

They were compelled to live as much together as possible in one particular locality in each place, which would be naturally near to the river bank; in Richmond the chosen and favourite spot was Water Lane, and when the traffic on this side of the river required, as it frequently did in the night, additional or extra assistance, those who sought it would proceed up that neighbourhood with a loud cry or call of 'Man to horse, Man to horse', an expression certainly difficult to reconcile with a strictly correct meaning; but upon hearing the well-known sound, the bargemen would in a few minutes have risen, and be ready to proceed with the vessel and its freight on the opposite shore to the spot appointed for a fresh relay to take it in charge.

Places like Water Lane would exist according to the dictates of the river. In difficult stretches, like Hedsor or Marlow, or where towpaths were bad or non-existent, men were needed as halers. They worked from their base upstream. Halers from Culham would therefore be known in Oxford, those from Oxford would be known on the upper river. As the boats above Oxford were smaller in size and fewer in number than downstream, the number of halers required in Oxford would not be large. Men were probably recruited amongst unemployed bargemen as the occupation 'haler' or 'hireling' is not found in Oxford records.

V. THE BARGING FAMILY AND
THE LINEAR COMMUNITY

Two distinct types of supporting services were therefore supplied from the shore: one connected with the trade of the river, one with the movement of the boats. Both played an important part in the linear village which stretched the length of the river, to which the boat-people belonged. Bargemen and fishermen married both within their own communities of boat-people and also elsewhere amongst men and women along the river

Family Tree 3.1.   Henry Hicks's connections with barging families along the river.[79]

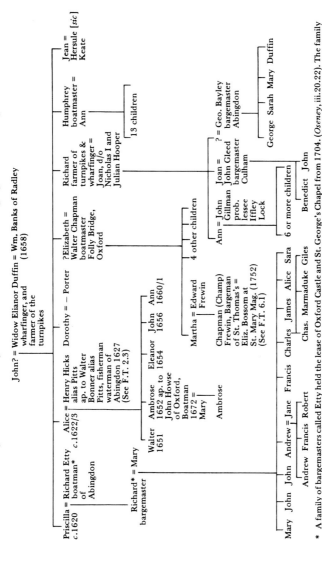

* A family of bargemasters called Etty held the lease of Oxford Castle and St. George's Chapel from 1704. (*Oseney*, iii.20.22). The family tree as reconstructed from the registers of St. Helens gives an incomplete picture of this family.

79 The information on which this genealogy is based comes from the parish register of St. Nicholas's, Abingdon, the Oxford Burcot Navigation Book (Oxon RO, CH. N. IX/i); *OCP* 104-5, and the following wills: MS Wills Berks. 47/19 (Eleanor Banks); PROB 11/404/65 (Walter Chapman); MS Wills Berks. 73/42 (William Giles), MS Wills Berks. 18/150 (Richard Duffin).

who were better known to them than the ordinary citizens of the towns and villages from which they came.

In dealing with Fisher Row we shall be concerned in the main with its dominant families. We shall note from time to time that men and women from families connected with the river elsewhere married into these major families, but we shall not be concerned with those from the Row who married out of this community into others. Yet it was this process of inter-marriage with others along the bank which fused the community into a larger unit. It is salutary to remember that the small, apparently insignificant family may be but the local represent-ative of some larger family along the river or that the member of a local family who disappears from the records of Fisher Row may turn up in some other riverside parish, having mar-ried into another riparian community.

Let us consider one such case, that of Henry Hicks, who served an apprenticeship as a fisherman to his kinsman Wal-ter Bonner alias Pitts in 1627 and who was mentioned in the will of Walter's widow as a waterman in Abingdon (see Family Tree 3.1).[80] He married a daughter of Widow Elianor Duffin, a wharfinger and farmer of the turnpikes of the Oxford-Burcot Commission from at least 1650 until she remarried in 1658. Her daughter Alice married Henry Hicks some time before 1651, and five of their children were baptised in St Nicholas Church, Abingdon. When the first three were baptised their parents called themselves Henry and Alice Pitts alias Hicks, and they called their eldest son Walter, presumably after Hen-ry's old master, and their eldest daughter Elianor, presumably after Alice's mother. Another son was called Ambrose.

As befitted the children of a woman who farmed turnpikes between Oxford and Abingdon, Elianor Duffin's seven known children married people from both places. We do not know the occupations of the husbands of two of the daughters, but Priscilla married an Abingdon boatman, Richard Etty, and another daughter a Folly Bridge boatmaster, Walter Chapman. The two sons were also involved in the river trade. Humphrey became a boatman, and Richard, like his mother became a wharfinger and farmer of turnpikes.[81] The relationship between

[80]   See also Family Tree 2.3, The Bonner alias Pitts Family.
[81]   St Nicholas's Church, Abingdon, Churchwardens' Accounts, 1694.

Folly Bridge and Abingdon continued. Richard married Joane Hooper, daughter of Nicholas Hooper I, fisherman and farmer of the Culham turnpike, while Joane's brother Nicholas Hooper II emigrated to the Oxford community at Folly Bridge, perhaps at the time he married Mary Giles, daughter of William Giles, boatman and landlord of The Anchor. This alehouse stood on the west side of Folly Bridge, across the road from the wharf.[82]

The dominant families of the river were of two sorts: the rich and the powerful on one hand, and the numerous on the other. Families in which some members married out of the Fisher Row community into those who provided supporting services connected with trade along the banks tended to grow rich and powerful; those who simply married into local families of bargemen might increase in number, but not in wealth. The first group were able to diversify in hard times and move out, the second might prosper when trade was buoyant, but when trade was depressed they all suffered, and, as depression decreased opportunity, and they were unable to move out, they grew poorer as they grew more numerous. The first group climbed socially, the second sank. We shall examine two connected families of each type: the Tawneys and the Clarkes, and the Gardners and the Crawfords.

VI. THE TAWNEYS AND THE CLARKES OF LOWER FISHER ROW

The Tawney family belonged to the first type. They were one of the oldest barging families in the community, and became over the generations the most powerful and successful. The family started humbly enough, with William Tawney, the son of John Tawney, an Oxford currier, who was apprenticed to Thomas Angell in 1594. Thomas Angell usually called himself a fisherman, sometimes a weelmaker, or a boatman. William was apprenticed to him as a weelmaker. Both of William Tawney's sons William II and Nicholas became boatmasters (see Family Tree 3.2).[83]

---

[82] *OCP* 104-5.

[83] City, L.5.1, 6 Apr. 1594 (Tawney to Angell). In the Hanaster enrolments Nicholas Tawney is said to be the second son of Nicholas, not William (City, L.5.3, 1654-5) but as there is no earlier Nicholas in the enrolments this is a mistake. Nicholas took up his freedom by his father's copy in 1654-5,

William Tawney I or II was living across the Mill Stream from Fisher Row in 1626. According to the Poll Tax of 1667 his descendants moved to Upper Fisher Row. In 1667 Nicholas and his family lived on one side of the boatman, Richard Shotterill, and his son, Edward on the other.[84] Richard Shotterill had leased tenement 3 in Upper Fisher Row in 1649. There were many connections between the Shotterills and the Tawneys, but there is no firm evidence of intermarriage.

Until 1667 we are handicapped in working out family relationships by the lack of parish registers for St Thomas's; before this date we are largely dependent on apprenticeship enrolments in building family trees. Trees built on such a basis present a very male-oriented family, as wives and sisters are not found in such material.

From 1667 registers and apprenticeships together show that in the second half of the century the Tawneys were closely connected with the local barging community, though we know more of the women's marriages than of the men's. These Tawney women do not appear on the family tree however, as we do not know whose daughters they were. In 1668 Joan Tawney married Richard Brookings (once Richard Shotterill's apprentice), and from 1699 to 1744 the name Richard Brookings was connected with tenement I, Upper Fisher Row. In 1670 Grace Tawney married a millwright, William Hands, and their son, William, was apprenticed to Richard Brookings in 1691.[85] From 1732 a William Hands leased part of Richard Shotterill's tenement, tenement 3 Upper Fisher Row. On the distaff side the Tawneys were making their presence felt in Upper Fisher Row. The Hands and the Brookings were to continue on the river after the Tawneys left it, the Brookings becoming established at Northmoor as alehouse-keepers, fishermen, and bargemasters.[86]

---

as a younger son, paying 9s. 6d. and his motive is clear, for in 1655 his own son, Edward, was apprenticed to him (City, L.5.3, 17 Sept. 1655). A son born before his father became a freeman could not be made free by his father's copy. He could however be taken as an apprentice.

[84] H. E. Salter, ed., *Surveys and Tokens* (OHS lxxv, 1920), 244. This is a transcript of City, P.5.7. Names which were scratched out were almost always omitted without indication by Salter. It is therefore not a satisfactory transcript.

[85] City, L.5.3, 7 Feb. 1662 (Brookings to Shotterill); City, L.5.4, 25 Feb. 1691 (Hands to Brookings).

[86] Appendix III, Tens. 1 A, 3 and 3C.

The apprentices of the Tawney men suggest that until almost the end of the 17th century their trade was still fairly local, being connected with the river above Oxford. Edward Tawney and his wife Elizabeth may have lived at Lechlade for some time, for in February 1665 John, son of Edward and Elizabeth Tawney was baptised there. Nothing more is known of John, but other sons were born to Edward Tawney, the bargemaster, and Elizabeth, his wife, in St Thomas's Oxford in subsequent years, and Edward took two apprentices from Lechlade, while his brother, William took one from Clanfield, near Radcot, in 1682. In 1691 Elizabeth Tawney, perhaps their sister or niece married one John Hart in St Thomas's, and in 1748 Joseph, the son of John Hart, fisherman of Fifield was apprenticed to a Tawney.[87]

Edward Tawney died in 1690 and it was through the marriage of his widow, Elizabeth that the Tawneys gained a footing in Lower Fisher Row. Elizabeth Tawney married John Clarke, boatman, member of a family with connections with the barge trade on the river between Oxford and London. John Clarke, the boatman lived in the sixth tenement in Lower Fisher Row from 1658.[55] He was probably the son of his neighbour a dyer of the same name. John Clarke, the dyer, held extensive holdings in and near Lower Fisher Row in the mid-17th century, but John Clarke, the dyer left no will, and we have no direct evidence, though we do know that John Clarke, the dyer was related to bargemen elsewhere on the river, and this makes the relationship more likely.

These relationships can be established through the will of his mother, Emme Clarke who died in 1635.[89] Emme Clarke was a widow with four sons John, William, Thomas, Stephen. Perhaps Richard, her executor, whose relationship was not given in the will was a fifth. She also had two married daughters, one being variously called Hellen, Ellen, or Elianor May. Elianor was perhaps even then a widow, and in 1639 she married Thomas Chappell at St Peter in the East, Oxford. After his death Christ Church granted her a lease in 1656 of waste land

[87] City L.5.4, 21 Apr. 1679 (Davis to Edward Tawney); ibid., 8 Dec. 1684 (Mathews to Edward Tawney); ibid., 12 Jun. 1682 (Goodenough to William Tawney); City, L.5.5, 29 July 1748 (Hart to Robert Tawney).

[88] *Oseney*, II. 498.

[89] MS Wills Oxon. 12/4/39 (Emme Clarke).

Family Tree 3.2. Tawney of Lower Fisher Row

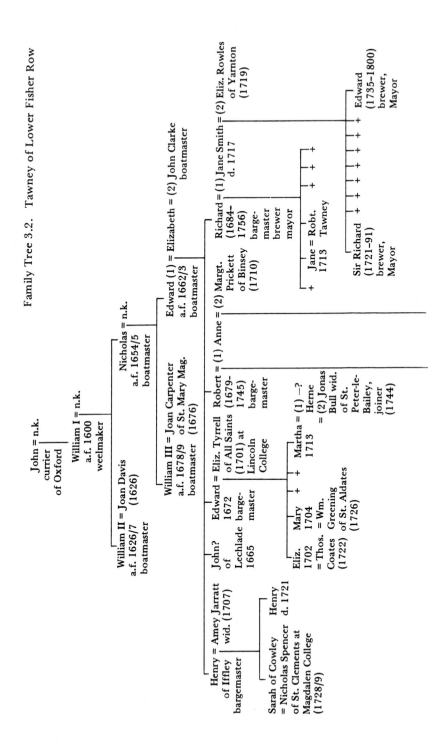

Anne (1703–4)

Elizabeth 1705 = Thos. Lethrom or Latham of Binsey (1724) at St. Mary Mag.

Catherine (1707–8)

Robert 1708 carpenter of St. Aldates = (1) Mary Mouldern (1736) at St. Aldates = (2) Jane Tawney

Mary 1719

Edward d. 1719

Margaret = Michael Cook

Thomas

Sarah = John Taylor

Martha = —— Mitchell

Robert ap. 1755 watchmaker Clerkenwell

Mary 1739

Bradnam 1745 clergyman = Eliz. Jagger (1770)

Henry = Eliz. Treacher of Pyrton (1772) ap. 1761 carpenter

Jane = Theophilus Wharton apothecary

John

Richard = Eleanor Edkins (1799) (1774–1832) engineer Dunchurch co-purchaser of Banbury New Bank

Henry (1775–96)

Robert (1776–1800)

Mary (1778–99)

Charles = Ann Copland of Abingdon (1804) (1780–1853) brewer Mayor co-purchaser of Banbury New Bank

Jane = James Morrell brewer of St. Thos. (1807) at Headington

in Fisher Row for her friends to build her a house.[90] No doubt her brother was responsible; because Thomas Clarke, boat-master of Sutton Courtenay, left bequests to his sister Elianor Chappell in his will, and also to his brother Stephen's son, we can be sure that Thomas was one of the same family as John Clarke the dyer. We cannot be equally sure that the bargeman William Clarke of Culham or the bargemaster, Richard Clarke of Bray, were also relatives, even though persons with these names appeared in Emme Clarke's will.[91] It is, however, much more likely that Thomas Clarke, a London woodmonger was a relative, for in 1668 he was given a licence to marry Elizabeth Robinson of St Thomas's, and she may well have been the Elizabeth Robinson who was living with the recently bereaved Martha Clarke, widow of John in 1667, whose kinswoman she was said to be.[92] Perhaps this Thomas Clarke was Stephen's son Thomas. A family with a boatmaster at Oxford and another at Sutton Courtenay, which often served as an alternative trans-shipment point to Abingdon (as did Culham), and with a woodmonger in London, had the sort of connections which would make for well-organised trade, even if the other two bargemen were not involved. The Clarkes were prosperous by Fisher Row standards. John Clarke the dyer was worth £300 at his death, and his widow Martha spent over £50 on the funeral.

Now when Elizabeth Tawney, widow of Edward, married the boatmaster John Clarke, whose family was so heavily involved in the London trade, it is not surprising that the Tawneys entered this trade too. In 1702 two of Edward's sons, Henry and Robert Tawney, masters of the *Sovereign* and the *King's Arms* respectively, were amongst the Oxfordshire barge-masters who petitioned the Privy Council for protection from the impress for the crews of their boats.[93] For a time four of Edward's sons were engaged in the barging trade, Henry, Robert, Edward, and Richard, though they did not continue on the river.

    [90] *Oseney*, H. 505; Ch. Ch. estates, 7814.
    [91] PROB 11/274/128 (Thomas Clarke); MS Oxf. Dioc. Pprs. c. 28, fos. 83-4 (William Clarke); PROB 11/285/701 (Richard Clarke).
    [92] D. M. Barrett, ed., 'Index to Oxfordshire Diocesan Marriage Bonds and Affidavits, 1661-1850', C 458; MS Wills Oxon. 78/2/5 (Bond Inventory and Account of John Clarke). The inventory was appraised 8 Jan. 1667 and the Poll Tax assessed the following month.
    [93] PC 2/79, 309.

In 1711 John Clarke, their stepfather, died, and it was by his will that the Tawneys came to hold tenements in Lower Fisher Row.[94] John Clarke left little to his own family, but far more to his new wife and her children. To his daughters, Anne, wife of John Prickett of Binsey, and Martha, wife of – Kenwright he left a shilling. He left to Thomas and Matthew, Anne Prickett's sons, £5 each, after the death of his wife Elizabeth, so long as they 'sign up all their right and title' to a tenement in the Fish Row, which was signed over by John Clarke to their mother as a Jointure. Failing this they were to have only a shilling. The same bequest was made on the same terms to William and Martha, the son and daughter of the late John Kensall (a boatman). John and Martha Clarke were each left 20s. To his 'sons-in-law' Henry, Edward, and Robert Tawney and each of their children likewise, £5 each after the death of his wife. To Elizabeth, the daughter of Robert Tawney, he left the messuage in Fisher Row in which her father lived, after her grandmother's death. To his 'loving wife' went all his messuages and tenements, interest on mortgages and bonds, and household goods. His wife and her youngest son Richard Tawney were to have all his 'boating' and 'all tackling that belongs to them'. Richard Tawney was to have £10 out of the 'Principle sum' out at interest, to renew the leases of his tenements when they came up, and he was residual legatee and executor of the estate. Richard's line was to be the wealthiest in the family, though the cadet branch. The Tawneys appear to have been treated better by John Clarke than his own family. Probably his wife had brought him substantial property on marriage or at least an interest in the barge trade up river, and this would explain it, but otherwise there seems something capricious and arbitrary about the will of a man who favours his stepchildren above his own. There was another Clarke who lived in the vicinity not to be found in John Clarke's will. In 1729 Robert Clarke a Quaker inhabited the tenth tenement, as subtenant to Thomas Loader, an Oxford brewer, whose daughter he had married.[95] Was he a relative of John Clarke?

[94] MS Wills Oxon. 121/4/17 (John Clarke).
[95] 'Berkshire and Oxfordshire Marriage Bonds and Affidavits', III (1710); MS Wills Oxon. 139/4/36 (Francis Loader); *Oseney*, II. 503.

Barging, brewing, and malting go together, and so do brewing and nonconformity. Professor Mathias has pointed out the transition from barging to malting was not uncommon on the River Lea, and also from brewing to banking.[96] How often it obtained on the Thames is not yet known. As well as Thomas Loader the Oxford brewer there were Loaders of Harwell who were bargemen 97 but the name was common on the Upper Thames as well. There were Halls too on the river, and the Halls were a major family of Oxford brewers in the 19th century (their Swan Brewery has now been absorbed by Ind Coope). If there is any connection here it was not direct, and anyway the name was, in 1853, the 16th commonest name in England and Wales. It is easier to trace such transitions with uncommon names, and this transition was certainly made by the Tawneys, from barging to brewing and then from brewing to banking.

Before we turn to this classic transition, however, let us look back and try to reconstruct something of the circle in which the Tawneys moved. St Thomas's was even in the 17th century essentially a poor parish, and the number of those who could sign their wills was not high. Book owners were few, for the period covered by inventories (roughly 1600-1730), but one of these was a Clarke, one a Kensall, and one a Tawney: William Tawney, the boatman, who died in 1687 had a Bible and Testament, John Kensall, baker, who died in 1671, had a Bible and other books worth 10s., and Thomas Clarke, fellmonger who died about 1719, had four Bibles, one with cuts, a Prayer Book and 'other books'. Is it simply coincidence that three related families were represented, or did they perhaps make up a group of rather serious minded tradesmen?[98]

The Tawneys were members of the established church. There was little nonconformity in the parish by the late 17th century, though they included three of the most substantial men in the parish.[99] The Tawneys were probably more like Anthony Kendall, the fellmonger, an old-fashioned Anglican

[96] Peter Mathias, *The Brewing Industry in England 1700-1830* (Cambridge, 1959), 328-9, 457-8.

[97] Oxon RO, Quarter Session Records, Mich., 1689, (3).

[98] MS Wills Oxon. 175/2/16 (W. Tawney); ibid. 82/3/22 (Kensall); ibid. 163/3/30 (T. Clarke, fellmonger).

[99] MS Oxf. Dioc. Pprs. d. 708, 61.

with a streak of Calvinism more typical of the 16th than of the 17th century.[100] Such families were not to be found in the parish by the middle of the 18th century, for by 1738 the parish had no Papists, no Presbyterians, no Quakers. No persons of even moderate means lived there any longer.[101] The process by which it lost any social and religious diversity, and became a parish entirely given over to labourers and small tradesmen and craftsmen of an unthinking conformity may have been hastened by the civil disturbances between Jacobite and Hanoverian interests which affected the town intermittently from 1715. During the riots of 1715 the Presbyterian and Baptist meeting-houses were wrecked. These disturbances occurred in a decade of poor harvests and bad trade, and the rioting townsmen were probably as much concerned with these matters as the university was with Jacobitism. The decision of the City Quarter Sessions in February 1715 to exempt the Presbyterian Meeting-House from the Poor Rate may have had as much to do with the destruction of dissenters' meeting-houses as the politics to which they have been ascribed.[102] Such unsettled conditions probably played a part in polarising the haves and have-nots, and hastening the transfer of the more substantial houses from tenant to subtenant, as the better-off moved elsewhere.

By the 1720s the river was beginning to decline, and the Tawney brothers, who had become bargemasters in its palmier days, grew restive. Scope for movement was limited, for the city did not encourage the movement of its tradesmen into new fields, and the alternatives open to bargemen were limited to trades such as wood- and corndealing, and brewing. There was perhaps already a tinge of an interest in woodmongering through the family connection with the Clarkes, and Thomas Clarke the London woodmonger in particular. The marriage of Henry – perhaps the eldest of the Tawney brothers – to Amey Jarrett, widow, may have deepened the tinge to something

[100]   PROB 111388195 (Kendall).

[101]   MS Oxf. Dioc. Pprs. d. 553, fo. 231.

[102]   City, 0.2.3, fos. 26, 33; R. D. Whitehorn 'Presbyterians and Baptists in 18th Century Oxford', *Journal of the Presbyterian Historical Society of England*, VI (1936-9), 229-30; J. R. Green, 'Oxford during the 18th Century', in C. L. Stainer, ed., *Studies in Oxford History* (OHS xli, 1901), 121-79; W. R. Ward, *Georgian Oxford* (Oxford, 1958), 50-97.

stronger, for the Jarretts were a dynasty of Abingdon boat-builders. Henry and his son died young, but perhaps it is not fanciful to see here an interest in the timber trade passed to another branch of the family, for Henry's nephew Robert, son of his brother of the same name became a substantial carpenter and builder.

In 1720 Edward attempted to establish himself as a haber-dasher of small wares, for which he was prosecuted by the City at its Quarter Sessions under the Statute of Artificers. The case dragged on until 1723, when he was acquitted, presumably having desisted. At the end of 1723 when the brothers took the Oath of Loyalty along with other propertied Oxford peo-ple, Henry, the eldest brother, was dead, but Edward, Richard and Robert were still described as boatmen.[103]

Nevertheless, Richard and Robert moved from the declining river trade. Perhaps it was through marrying Margaret Prick-ett, of a Binsey family, that Robert Tawney moved to Binsey, before 1735, and kept an alehouse there.[104] His family was to play an important part in the development of the Tawney dynasty, but it was the youngest brother, Richard, who laid the fortunes of the family. Richard took over the lease of the sixth tenement in Lower Fisher Row in succession to John Clarke. It was divided into two dwellings. In 1714 Richard Tawney, boatman, lived in the northern one, and his mother in the southern. In 1728 he called himself a boatmaster of Binsey, and his mother was no longer living there.[105] By now Richard Tawney was a rising man in local politics. He had been jun-ior bailiff during the mayoralty of John Treacher, the brewer, in 1741/2, and about the same time moved into brewing. The family was prospering, and moving into new spheres both in trade and socially, and to do so it girded its loins, mustering its strength and concentrating its resources. In this strategy marriage played an important part, for it was not easy for an aspiring family to make a socially desirable match without at the same time reducing its capital resources. Only by marry-ing within the family or not marrying at all could capital be preserved. As well, if the family could not afford to increase

[103] City, 0.2.4, fo. 85; 0.2.5, fos. 10, 19, 23, 28, 34.
[104] Ch. Ch. MS estates, 62, fo. 8-9; City, N.4.5; City, 0.3.1.
[105] *Oseney*, II. 498-9.

its standing by marriage, at least it should not encumber itself with new and embarrassing family commitments. Therefore Robert's daughter, Jane married her cousin, the carpenter Robert Tawney in 1742. Her only surviving siblings Richard and Edward never married (see Family Tree 3.2).

It may seem cynical to talk of this marriage as entirely a calculation. It was certainly convenient, but it was probably the most natural thing to the couple themselves. Both probably spent their childhood at Binsey, and had been thrown into each other's company in the round of family visits and ceremonies. No doubt any attraction was smiled on and encouraged. The society they moved in was, wills suggest, like that of John Taylor, the East Anglian maltster, factor, and bargemaster, and characterised by Prof. Mathias as 'a world of cousins'.[106]

A similar concentration of resources was found by Mr Leonard G. R. Naylor in the family of the Tomkins of Abingdon at the same period. They were a family with the same kind of background, which moved from barging to malting, and then, after two marriages of cousins, into banking (see Family Tree 3.3).[107] As a method of capital formation it seems to have been successful on a modest scale.

Richard Tawney, Jane's father, moved into brewing, and when he renewed his lease to the Fisher Row property in 1743, the year after Jane's marriage, he styled himself a brewer. The transition from barging to brewing, like woodmongering, was one of the transitions countenanced by the city, and he had none of the problems which had beset his brother Edward.

The line continued through the marriage of the two Tawney cousins, Jane and Robert. Robert was a carpenter and a widower. By his first wife he had a son who became a watchmaker, and moved to Clerkenwell.[108] Bradnam, the eldest son of Robert and Jane, went to university and became that negligent chaplain of New College whom Parson Woodforde sconced for dereliction of his duty. Henry the second son was apprenticed

---

[106] Mathias, op. cit. 457-63.

[107] Leonard G. R. Naylor, *The Malthouse of Joseph Tomkins* (n.d., no place, privately printed); Gough Berks. 3 (26 and 27); *Hist MSS Comm.*, *House of Lords*, New Series, i (1900), 547-8; MS Wills Berks. 99/59 (John Moore).

[108] City, L.5.5, 10 June 1755; C. F. C. Beeson, *Clockmaking in Oxfordshire 1400-1850* (Banbury Historical Society, iv, 1962), 144.

to his father in 1761, and in 1772 married Alderman Treacher's niece Elizabeth, who was also sister-in-law to Thomas

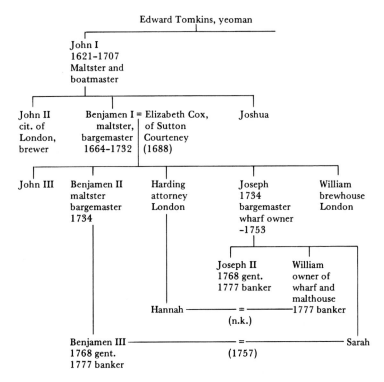

Family Tree 3.3.   The Tomkins Family of Abingdon.

Walker, town clerk of Oxford from 1756 to 1795.[109] This marriage not only linked the Tawney family ever more closely into the power structure of the city, it allied them with other major brewing families, for Alderman Treacher was a brewer and his wife Mary was the daughter of Thomas Loader the brewer of Fisher Row.[110] In the next generation Jane and Robert Tawney's granddaughter Jane Wharton married James Morrell at Headington. The brewery is still in business. The wealthy families of

[109] W. N. Hargreaves-Mawdsley, ed., *Woodforde at Oxford, 1759-1776* (OHS, New Series xxi, 1969) 186; City, L.5.5, 2 July 1761; *JOJ*, 1 Oct. 1772.
[110] *Oseney*, II. 497.

the late 18th century who owned property in Fisher Row formed a caste of sorts, which intermarried.

The Tawneys provided the City with three mayors in the 18th century, Richard I, mayor in the municipal year 1748/9, and his sons Sir Richard and Edward, who were each mayor three times: Sir Richard in 1764/5, 1778/9 and 1790/1; Edward in 1772/3, 1784/5 and 1797/8. They were active at a time when city, university, and river were in decay, and the city was sinking into debt. In 1766, the year Edward entered local politics, an over-ingenious attempt to solve the city's financial problems by offering its representation for cash involved the city in scandal. Richard (later Sir Richard) Tawney and John Treacher were involved, and, along with other members of the Council spent five days in Newgate before being publicly reprimanded before the House of Commons. Negotiations were then continued to sell the representation.[111]

The Tawneys' involvement with water transport was now at boardroom level: they were administrators and investors, first as Barge Commissioners, and after the Thames Commission was set up in 1771 they served on that body too, and they interested themselves in the Oxford Canal.[112]

When Sir Richard died in 1791 he was buried at Binsey, 'the Burying Place of his Ancestors', attended by the Mayor, the Council and a vast concourse of people, and the *Gentlemen's Magazine* carried an obituary. He left bequests to his vast circle of cousins and nephews, but the bulk of the estate went to his brother and executor, Edward.[113]

Edward Tawney and Sir John Treacher both built themselves houses in St Thomas's. In 1808 the vicar was able to report that there were four respectable families in the parish.[114] Edward acquired the freehold of the fifth to the ninth tenements in Fisher Row in October 1796 under the provisions of the 1771 Mileways Act, II Geo. III c. 19, which allowed the alienation of College land. He built a pleasant town house at the foot of Lower Fisher Row facing his malt-house and the

---

[111] John Cannon,' 'The Parliamentary Representation of the City of Oxford', 1754-1790', *Oxon.* XXV (1960),102-8.

[112] Berks. RO. D/TC 25A. *passim*.; - *JOJ*, 8 Jan. 1791.

[113] *JOJ*, 8 Oct. 1791; *Gentleman's Magazine*, LXI (1791) pt. ii, 973; PROB 11/1211/542 (Sir Richard Tawney).

[114] MS Oxf. Dioc. Pprs. d. 571, No. 53,1.

mill and the Castle, across the mill-stream, and a few steps from the brewery where he was in business with Mark and James Morrell. However, Edward had not long to live. He dissolved the partnership in December 1798, and died in March 1800, aged 65, Senior Alderman and Father of the City.[115] Edward Tawney's fortune was extensive, and, like his brother he made generous legacies to his relatives. He left money to the City, and endowed almshouses which were built next to his own house in Fisher Row. These can still be seen, and so can the memorial he had raised to the memory of his parents and himself at Binsey. His household goods were auctioned off, including an elegant eight-day clock, made by his half-brother Robert Tawney and sixty dozen of port. His freehold and leasehold properties came into the hands of the Morrells, who still own his house in Fisher Row and the Brewery in St Thomas's High Street.[116]

The family's interest in canals extended into the next generation. Richard was first Agent of the Oxford canal and later its engineer, stationed at Dunchurch near Braunston, an important junction on the canal. Together with his brother Charles, a brewer, and later a mayor of Oxford, he purchased the Banbury New Bank of Heydon and Wyatt. This passed to the Gillett family in 1822, Richard's second son, Henry, having a share in the business when he came of age. The firm acted as bankers to the Oxford Canal Company.[117] So the final step in Mathias's transition from brewing to banking was accomplished.

For the rest the history of the family can be summarised in the words of the biographer of Richard Henry Tawney, the most eminent member of the family:

R. H. Tawney rarely spoke of his forebears. His father, C. H. Tawney, Principal of the Presidency College in Calcutta, was a distinguished Sanskrit scholar; and behind him the line runs back through a clergyman, a civil engineer who became general manager of the Oxford Canal Company, as Oxford builder and timber merchant, to an eighteenth century

---

[115] *JOJ* 21 Dec. 1798, and 14 Mar. 1800.

[116] PROB 11/1339/243 (Edward Tawney); *JOJ* 31 May 1800, 29 Sept. 1800; City, D.5.15, 37; *Council Acts* 1752-1801, 277-8; conversation with Mr L. Gunther, Head Brewer, Morrell's Brewery, 1 Sept. 1972.

[117] J. J. Tawney, 'Notes on the Tawneys of Oxford' (typescript, 1974), 8; Audrey M. Taylor, *Gilletts, Bankers at Banbury and Oxford* (Oxford, 1964), 5-9; L. S. Pressnell, *County Banking in the Industrial Revolution* (Oxford, 1956), 34-6, 56.

watchmaker of Clerkenwell. In 1819 the civil engineer, Richard Tawney, had joined with his brother, an Oxford brewer, to acquire a major share in a Banbury bank. When, by a fortunate chance the records of the banking house of Gillett and Tawney were given to the London School of Economics (and for want of space were lodged for a time in Tawney's own room) it proved impossible to kindle in the great grandson even a flicker of interest. He took a poor view of men who spent their lives in finance, and perhaps family piety made him wish the connection forgotten.[118]

In the Tawneys we have a highly successful family of barge-masters which moved into and married within the powerful brewing interests which dominated the politics of Oxford in the 18th century. In its structure and kinship patterns the family was very like those of the nonconformist maltsters, bankers, and brewers which have been studied by Professor Mathias in East Anglia. The Tawneys and the other Oxford brewing families into which they married – the Treachers and the Morrells – were, however, staunch supporters of the established church. It might be said that it would be impossible for any business to flourish in Oxford which was not, for Oxford, unlike Cambridge, has never been any friend to nonconformity, but this is a regional difference, reflecting the attitudes of the hinterland. Nevertheless in all other ways the Oxford families had just such characteristics as their nonconformist counterparts in East Anglia. The nature of trade in a society without developed commercial institutions favoured family-based business, and gave it a continuity not otherwise obtainable. Religion no doubt provided a second bond, but it was family rather than religion which lay at the base of trade.

VII. THE GARDNERS OF UPPER FISHER ROW

The Gardners and the Crawfords represent the second type of family, one which failed to make links with trade and the services connected with it, but became involved with the provision of services for moving boats along the river. Such families were unable to diversify out of the barging trade when trade became depressed, and suffered accordingly. Economic depression, with its loss of opportunity, its narrowing of horizons, forced these two related families into a narrow groove. They came

---

[118] T. S. Ashton, 'Richard Henry Tawney, 1880-1962', *Proceedings of the British Academy*, XLVIII (1962), 461. The watchmaker was not a direct ancestor.

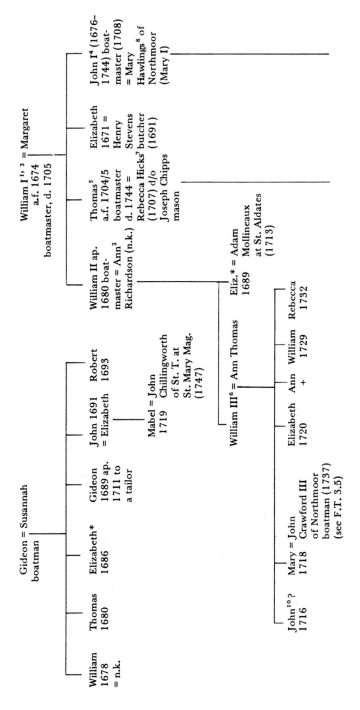

Family Tree 3.4. The Gardners of Upper Fisher Row.

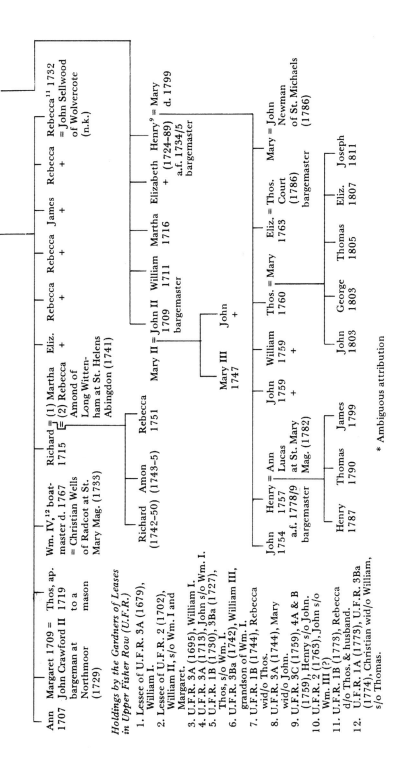

Ann 1707

Margaret 1709 = John Crawford II 1719 bargeman at Northmoor (1729)

Thos, ap. to a mason

Wm. IV,[12] boatmaster d. 1767 = Christian Wells of Radcot at St. Mary Mag. (1733)

Richard 1715 = (1) Martha ≡ (2) Rebecca Amond of Long Wittenham at St. Helens Abingdon (1741)

Eliz. +

Rebecca +

Rebecca +

James +

Rebecca +

Rebecca[11] 1732 = John Sellwood of Wolvercote (n.k.)

Richard (1742–50)

Amon (1743–5)

Rebecca 1751

Mary II = John II 1709 bargemaster

William 1711 bargemaster

Martha 1716

Elizabeth +

Henry[9] = Mary (1724–89) d. 1799 a.f. 1734/5 bargemaster

Mary III 1747

John +

John 1754 a.f. 1778/9 bargemaster

Henry 1757 = Ann Lucas at St. Mary Mag. (1782)

John 1759 +

William 1759 +

Thos. 1760 = Mary

Eliz. 1763 = Thos. Court (1786) bargemaster

Mary = John Newman of St. Michaels (1786)

Henry 1787

Thomas 1790

James 1799

John 1803

George 1803

Thomas 1805

Eliz. 1807

Joseph 1811

* Ambiguous attribution

Holdings by the Gardners of Leases in Upper Fisher Row (U.F.R.)

1. Lessee of U.F.R. 3A (1679), William I.
2. Lessee of U.F.R. 2 (1702), William II, s/o Wm. I and Margaret.
3. U.F.R. 3A (1695), William I.
4. U.F.R. 3A (1713), John s/o Wm. I.
5. U.F.R. 1B (1730), 3Ba (1727), Thos, s/o Wm. I.
6. U.F.R. 3Ba (1742), William III, grandson of Wm. I.
7. U.F.R. 1B (1744), Rebecca wid/o Thos.
8. U.F.R. 3A (1744), Mary wid/o John.
9. U.F.R. 3C (1759), 4A & B (1759), Henry s/o John.
10. U.F.R. 2 (1763), John s/o Wm. III (?)
11. U.F.R. 1B (1773), Rebecca d/o Thos. & husband.
12. U.F.R. 1A (1773), U.F.R. 3Ba (1774), Christian wid/o William, s/o Thomas.

to form a community which was almost entirely one large family.

The tight structure of this family can only be appreciated by a close analysis, without which no reader could be expected to accept the results. In a society like our own, in which family ties are loose, it is not easy to credit, as we

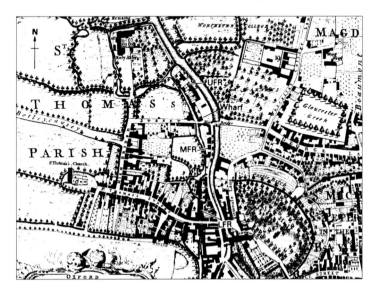

Fig. 3.2. St Thomas's Parish, 1750. Detail from John Taylor's Map of Oxford.

readily do with exotic civilisations, the importance of family ties. In a society which feels so close to our own – we need some other word than 'familiar' – we are too easily seduced into thinking it like our own in ways in which it was in fact very different.

Both the Gardners and the Crawfords lived, for the most part, in Middle and Upper Fisher Row, where there was plenty of room for expansion. The trade could absorb many sons, in crewing the family boat, or captaining the small family fleet, and so small houses of related men sprang up along the bank. The empty land allowed development by a family and encouraged the members of the families to continue in the same business (see Fig. 3.2).

In the development of the barging community it is difficult to assess the importance of the wharf at Hythe Bridge. Until 1719, when it was leased to a victualler, it seems to have been in the hands of men who had no conceivable connection with the navigation. Probably the City discouraged its development in competition with the official wharf at Folly Bridge. By

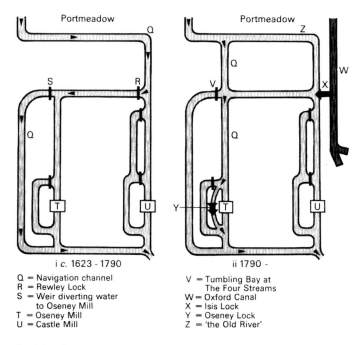

i c. 1623 - 1790

ii 1790 -

Q = Navigation channel
R = Rewley Lock
S = Weir diverting water
        to Oseney Mill
T = Oseney Mill
U = Castle Mill

V = Tumbling Bay at
        The Four Streams
W = Oxford Canal
X = Isis Lock
Y = Oseney Lock
Z = 'the Old River'

Fig. 3.3. The Changing River: the Navigation Channel of the Thames and other Waterways in St Thomas's Parish.

1719, however, the river above Folly Bridge was causing difficulty, and perhaps this led to a reversal of policy. Something of the reasons may be seen in a petition which the Council considered on 10 August 1719, a week before a new lease of the wharf was granted. Francis Stacey, the agent of the waterworks at Folly Bridge, stated that owing to the lowness of the water it was impossible to maintain the city's water supply, and he asked permission to erect a dam on a small stream 'out of the navigation to increase the supply'. The waterworks were in fact competing with the barge traffic for the water supply, reduced already by drought. On 28 August 1719 a tenant was found for the wharf, and the ground was to be 'set out by high stones or posts fixed 10 foot distant from each other for keeping off carts and carriages'. The entry fine was only five guineas.[119] The new wharf would be useful to Oxford traffic from the upper river, but not for through traffic. The recognition of this second wharf came when conditions in Oxford were depressed, and whilst it may have brought welcome trade to Fisher Row, it would be at the expense of Folly Bridge.

The passage of the river above Folly Bridge continued to pose problems. At that time the main navigation channel ran by way of the Bullstake Stream. This stream lies west of the present navigation channel, which is an enlargement of Oseney Mill Stream (see Fig. 3.3). It is now difficult to imagine the Bullstake Stream bearing commercial traffic, for it is now barely navigable by the lightest skiff, but then it was dangerous. St Thomas's parish registers record two fatal accidents there, one in 1686 and one in 1708. In 1721 dissatisfaction boiled over, and the bargemen rioted and pulled the bridge down. Thomas Hearne describes the whole affair.

In the Middle way between St Thomas's Parish ... and Botley, is a Place called Bulstock Bridge. At this Place several Persons have been crush'd to death (by reason of the Lowness of the Arch) at Floud times. Upon wch account a Motion was made to have it pull'd down and built higher, and this Motion was very much countenanc'd and forwarded by the present Vice-Chancellour, Dr Shippen. There being, therefore, so much Encouragm^t, Preparations were made for pulling it down, as I found on Friday, Octob. 13 last, when, walking over it, I found them carrying Planks & other Things in order to make Dams. But then, presently after, I heard of a great opposition, upon very frivolous reasons, some few Persons pretending that 'twould be a Prejudice to Oxford, & I know not what, Notwithstanding w^{ch}, on Monday Octob. 16, 'twas pull'd down by some Bargemen & others, and now 'tis actually rebuilding, the Arch being to be a Yard higher than before, and 'till such time as the Bridge is rais'd, there is to be a Ferry on the South side of the Bridge, & today I saw people ferry'd over, to wch all are to pay a half-Penny a Man, & a penny a Man & horse, all, I mean, as do not pay to the said Highway.

The bargemen involved were indicted for riot at the City Quarter Sessions, and seem to have been picked up as their

[119] *Council Acts,* 1702-51, 113-14.

boats came in to the wharf, for they appear in batches on different days. John Roberts together with Edward Tawney; Charles Pemerton separately on the same day; Thomas and George Howse (two brothers or father and son) with Edward Price (brother-in-law), and John Clark and Thomas Gardner; William Robinson later and alone. All were fined 6s. 4d.[120]

It seems likely that this passage continued to be difficult, and that the wharf at Hythe Bridge rather than Folly Bridge had to be used for the trade above Oxford.

We have no statistics for the period, but the conditions of the two communities at Hythe Bridge and at Folly Bridge suggests that at this period Folly Bridge suffered more than Fisher Row. For at Folly Bridge few families survived the depressed conditions of the middle years of the 18th century, but among the poorer folk of Fisher Row the continuity was not broken, and the community, embryonic in the 17th century, developed as house after house beside the river was built, and occupied by families of boatmen. The dominant family of the 18th century was the Gardners, and most of the other occupants of the Row came to be related to them. The family extended itself under many roofs and the unit of family life was the Row itself. By 1772 13 out of 18 tenements in Upper and Middle Fisher Row were occupied by the Gardners or families related to them.[121]

Given the dynastic tendencies we have seen so far amongst boatmen and fishermen, the future of the Row might be expected to lie with the families who held the original leases of Upper and Middle Fisher Row: the Pemertons, the Potters, and the Shotterills, but nothing can be found to link them with the Gardners. The lack of early parish registers is particularly felt at this point. There seem, though, from taxation returns to have been few Gardners in the parish in the early 17th century.

The first occurrence of the name so far found is in the Lay Subsidy for 1648, when Mr Gardner paid 3s. 6d.; it next appears in the will of Alice Pemerton, widow of William, lessee of the twelfth tenement, Fisher Row, dated 1659. In her will Alice left her daughter, Margaret, the house near Little Hythe

[120] Heame, *Collections*, VII. 292; City, 0.2.4, fos. 122-3; City, 0.2.5, fo. 6.
[121] *Salter, Surveys and Tokens*, 42-3.

Bridge lately occupied by William Gardner.[122] Perhaps Margaret married William Gardner, for the wife of William Gardner I, the founder of the dynasty, was called Margaret (see Family Tree 3.4). William Gardner I bought his freedom for £5 in 1674, giving a bond to follow no trade save that of a boatman or a fisherman – a much narrower restriction than was often imposed.[123] In 1677 he took his first apprentice, Nicholas, son of William Terrill, boatman, one of the family descended from the Backesters of Lower Fisher Row; in 1680 his son William II was apprenticed to him, and in 1687 William, son of William Nichols yeoman.[124] In 1676 his youngest son, John was born. William I prospered, and acquired two properties, tenement 3A in Upper Fisher Row, in 1679, part of Richard Shotterill's old tenement, and the second tenement in Lower Fisher Row in 1681, once occupied by William Terrill.[125]

When William I died in 1705, he called himself a yeoman rather than a boatman. His will made provision for his wife and those of his children who leased no property in their own right. There is no mention of William II, who married Ann Richardson, the girl next door, and who through this marriage held tenement 2, Upper Fisher Row, from 1702. William I left his property in Upper Fisher Row to his son John, and that in Lower Fisher Row to his son Thomas. Each was to pay £10 to his daughter Elizabeth, the wife of the butcher Henry Stevens, who occupied the second tenement in Lower Fisher Row. To his widow he left his boats and wherries, chattels and cattle for her maintenance.[126]

In 1705 the three sons of William I held three properties in Fisher Row. The river trade was still flourishing, and the

---

[122] Salter, ibid., 181; PROB 11/292/340 (Alice Pemerton); MS Wills Oxon. 51/4/7 (William Pernerton).

[123] *Council Acts, 1666-1701*, 71-2.

[124] City, L.5.4, 1677 (Terrill to Gardner); ibid., 20 Sept. 1680 (Gardner to Gardner); ibid., 15 Oct. 1687 (Nichols to Gardner).

[125] For leases of Upper Fisher Row see Appendix III, and for the Second Tenement, Lower Fisher Row see *Oseney*, II. 495-6. Between 1678 and 1693 another boatman, Gideon Gardner, baptised six children in St Thomas's, many confusingly bearing the same names as William's offspring. This, together with their common occupation, suggests William and Gideon were brothers, or perhaps father and son. Ambiguities are often resolved by following the descent of leases, and this evidence probabilifics the view that William, not Gideon was the ancestor of all the families in Upper Fisher Row called Gardner.

[126] MS Wills Oxon. 129/3/14 (Wm. Gardner I).

Gardners had no reason to look beyond it, any more than William Gardner I when he accepted his freedom on condition he took up no other occupation save that of fisherman or bargeman. They were boatmasters rather than bargemasters like the Tawneys, but they held leases and made wills. There is no mention of books in their inventories though. Their horizons were less extensive.

The sons continued to hold property in the Row. William II having served his apprenticeship to his father, married the daughter of a boatbuilder's family. Ann was the daughter of a boat-builder's widow Susanna Richardson, who leased tenement 2, Upper Fisher Row, in succession to the boat-builder, George Potter. In 1685 she married again, her husband being the boatman George Lea. Remarriage probably terminated her legal right to the lease she had inherited, but when the Council granted a new lease to her children Ralph and Ann, they stipulated that they must sublet it to the Leas.[127] Probably for this reason William II and his wife Ann lived in St Aldates, for though their two children William III, born in 1687, and Elizabeth, born in 1689, were baptised in St Thomas's – perhaps an instance of family piety – they married in St Aldates. Even after the death of the Leas their property was sublet. In 1713 a William Terrill was living there, whilst in 1722 the lease was taken over by the butcher, John Nicholls (William II's father had had apprentices with these surnames). John Nicholls did not renew his lease, and after it lapsed in 1763 a John Gardner, perhaps the son of William III, took out a new lease.

William I's son Thomas increased his holding in the Row. He became a freeman in 1704/5, and married Rebecca Hicks in 1707 at St Thomas's. He had already inherited the second tenement in Lower Fisher Row by his father's will in 1705. In the early 17th century this tenement had been held by the fisherman Thomas Hicks. Whether Rebecca was a descendant of this fisherman's family cannot be established. Her father, Joseph Hicks was a mason.[128] Thomas had his ups and downs. When he took his first apprentice in 1709 he was described only as a bargeman, but when he took his next apprentice, in 1717, he was said to be a boatmaster. The difficulties

---

[127] *Council Acts, 1666-1701*, 172.
[128] MS Wills Oxon. 35/1/27 (Joseph Hix the elder).

of the navigation which seem to have become acute in 1719 appear to have affected his fortunes, for when he renewed his lease of the second tenement in Lower Fisher Row on 9 July 1719, Christ Church reduced his fine from £3 to £1 because of poverty.[129] Later Thomas Gardner's fortunes revived and within 11 years he owned two leases in Upper Fisher Row, tenements IB and 3Ba as well as the one in Lower Fisher Row. At his death his widow Rebecca appears to have inherited the lease of tenement IB, and his son Richard held tenement 2. His son William IV had already taken over tenement 3Ba. Widows or sons and their heirs, rather than daughters, inherited leases.

The policy was followed by Thomas's widow, Rebecca, in disposing of her lease of tenement IB in her will. It went to William IV and her late son Richard's child, Rebecca. Her daughter, Margaret, wife of the bargemaster, John Crawford II, despite their numerous children, received no part in this. Margaret was forgiven a debt for £10, and she, together with William IV's wife Christian, divided her mother's clothes. When William IV died in 1772 his widow inherited everything, including the tenement he held in his own right (3Ba) and the half share of his mother's property.[130]

William I's third and youngest son, John I, preserved his inheritance in the Row, and his family extended it. In 1708 John married Mary Hawlings of Northmoor at St Thomas's. Northmoor was to have a special importance to the bargemen and bow-halers of the Row, and more will be said of the connection later. Between 1709 and 1724 they had five children, and in 1718 John took his nephew Henry Stevens as apprentice, receiving £5 from the Charity School towards the boy's apprenticing. Perhaps the poverty that affected Thomas Gardner in 1719 also affected his sister's family at this time. John I inherited tenement 3A from his father, and after his death in March 1744 it passed to his widow, Mary I, and was renewed in May 1744. Mary seems to have died the following February, and by 1763 the occupant was John Gardner II, her son. He also held tenement 2, which lay adjacent to it. When John II died is not known, but his widow Mary Gardner II died about

1779 and, her son John III having predeceased her, she left her leases to her daughter Mary VII.[131] What happened to this Mary is not known. In 1786 tenement 3A was leased to Richard Crawford, boatman.

Henry Gardner, born in 1724, was the youngest member of the family of John I. He grew up in a period of depressed trade. By the time he reached maturity the Gardner family was declining, and so were the fortunes of the bargemen of the parish, though the river trade was at last beginning to look more hopeful, especially below Oxford. New bargemasters were establishing themselves at Folly Bridge.

He extended his family's holding. In 1759 he leased the wharf at Hythe Bridge. He was the first boatmaster ever to do so. In 1764 he had four boats on the Thames, all fairly small, suited to the upriver trade. One was of 65 tons burthen, two of 30 tons, and one somewhere in between – about 160 tons in all. John Grain at Folly Bridge had six boats totalling 295 tons burthen.[132]

The world they lived in was a changing one. Old institutions were declining. Though they themselves were freemen, men like John and Henry Gardner did not take apprentices. The list of freemen in the Poll Book for the 1768 election shows that the number of Gardners in barging was not large: two bargemen, and one bargemaster. The Crawfords were now the largest family, with seven bargemen. [133]

Nevertheless the Survey of Oxford made in 1772 shows the Gardners still strongly represented in the Row, though active bargemen are now almost missing, and this is not obvious in the first place, for the ten tenements appear to be in the hands of three women: Mrs Gardner, Mrs Crawford and Mrs Shillingworth. It looks like a list of lessees of investment property rather than of the actual occupants. A table (3.1) comparing current leaseholders with those listed in the Survey and with those deduced to be in occupation from all available sources, shows that such an impression is misleading, for the leases were

[130]   MS Wills Oxon. 98/165 (Rebecca Gardner); MS Wills Oxon. 98/157 (William Gardner IV).

[131]   MS Wills Oxon. 216/324 (Mary Gardner)

[132]   [John Burton] *The Present State of the Navigation of the Thames considered by a Commissioner* (Oxford, 1764), 41-3.

[133]   MS G.A. Oxon. 4° 6 (3), A true copy of the poll for representatives in the ensuing Parliament for the City of Oxford, taken … 16th-17th March, 1768 (Oxford, 1768).

Table 3.1. Tenements of Upper Fisher Row—Tenants and Occupants.

Tenement	Leaseholders and date of lease	1772 Survey	Occupants deduced from various sources
1A	Rd. Spindler, cook (1762)	Mr Chadwell	William Gardner (1762)
1B	Rebecca Gardner (1759)	Mrs Gardner Mr Gardner, yard[a]	not known[b]
2	John Gardner	Mrs Crawford	Edward Crawford (1759)
3A	Mary, widow of John Gardner I (1744)	Mrs Gardner	? John and/or Mary Gardner II
3Ba	William Gardner[c] (1756)	Mrs Gardner	Christian, widow of William Gardner[c]
3Bb	Jane Collison[d] (1758)	Mrs Crawford	not known
3Ci	Mary Ayres, wid.	Mrs Shillingworth	Francis and Mary Shillingworth[e]
3Cii	do.	do.	do.
3Ciii	do.	Mrs Crawford	do.
4	Henry Gardner	Mr Gardner; house and yard	Henry Gardner

a Probably the yard of (1B, sub-let to Henry Gardner.

b Rebecca Gardner's will (MS Wills Oxon., 98/165) was made in 1759, proved 1772, but she died in 1763. Her son William of Ten. 3Ba and daughter-in-law Christian inherited it.

c William Gardner's will (MS Wills Oxon., 98/157), made 1766, proved 1772, left everything to his wife, Christian.

d Widow of William Collison, slatter. She left 3Bb to Susannah 'wife of my brother William Shillingworth of St Ebbes, slatter (MS Wills Oxon., 97/28) by her will of 26 June 1764. This was investment property.

e *Council Acts*, 1752-1801, p.41. Though no lease to Francis and Mary Chillingworth has been found, by Council Act of 31 July 1761 they seem to have taken over the lease of Mary Ayres, widow. According to Francis Chillingworth's will he was living in St Thomas's in 1788 (MS Wills Oxon., 218/9).

still in many hands. The name Mrs Gardner appears three times and represents at least two different boatmasters' widows: Christian widow of Rebecca's son, William IV, and Mary widow of Rebecca's nephew, John II. Henry Gardner, the bargemaster also lived there and was Rebecca's nephew and Mary's brother-in-law. Who the third Mrs Gardner was is not known.

Family Tree 3.5.   The Crawfords of St Thomas's Parish and Northmoor.

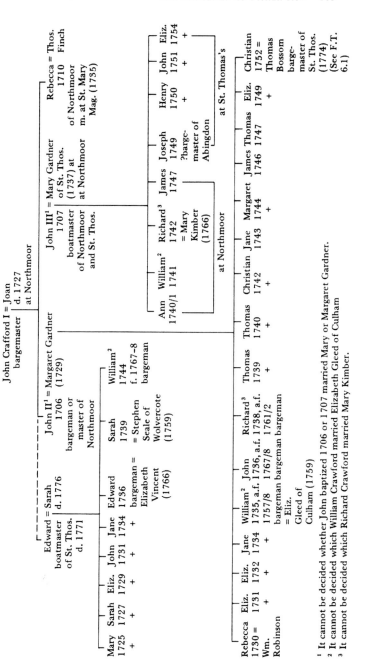

[1] It cannot be decided whether John baptized 1706 or 1707 married Mary or Margaret Gardner.
[2] It cannot be decided which William Crawford married Elizabeth Gleed of Culham.
[3] It cannot be decided which Richard Crawford married Mary Kimber.

VIII. MIDDLE FISHER ROW AND THE CRAWFORDS

In Middle Fisher Row houses had multiplied since 1621, when it had been a bare bank. The property consisted of two leases held from Christ Church, and known as the 12th and 13th tenements. They had been subdivided and developed as investment property in the 18th century. In 1653 there had been three dwellings, built by the Pemertons, and Elianor Chappell had added a fourth in 1656. In 1722 there were seven, and by 1772 there were nine. The houses were smaller, and the occupants, being subtenants in rack-rented property, had no security of tenure such as was enjoyed by the leaseholders of Upper Fisher Row. In the 1772 Survey we have a list of the occupants, not to be found by reading leases for the period. The occupants were, from north to south, the following: Mr Crawford, Mrs Mollineaux, Mr Edward Crawford, Mrs Fletcher, Mr Mollineaux, Mrs Fletcher (in lodgings), Mr Roberson, Mrs Fletcher (in lodgings).[134] The Mollineauxs, the Robinsons and the Crawfords were all related to the Gardners. It is unfortunate forenames are not given.

In Upper Fisher Row the property passed usually to sons or widows, and so the name Gardner is repeated along the Row. In Middle Fisher Row one finds the surnames of men who married into the Gardner family, and the relationship is therefore not obvious at first sight, but it is none the less real. Let us be explicit. The Crawfords were related to the Gardners by the marriage of two Gardner girls to two Crawford men: in 1729 Margaret married John Crawford II at Northmoor and in 1737 Mary married John Crawford III at St Thomas's. The Robinsons were related to both the Gardners and the Crawfords by the marriage of Rebecca, daughter of John Crawford II (above), and his wife Margaret (née Gardner), in 1753 to William Robinson at St Thomas's. The Mollineauxs were related to the Gardners by the marriage of Elizabeth, daughter either of William II or of Gideon Gardner, to Adam Mollineaux in 1713 in St Aldate's parish.

The men of the Gardner family inherited and populated the larger more spacious tenements of Upper Fisher Row, and the families into which Gardner women married populated Middle

---

[134] *Oseney*, II. 503-5; *Salter, Surveys and Tokens*, 42-3.

Fisher Row.[135] In Upper Fisher Row the inhabitants were leaseholders, in Middle Fisher Row they were subtenants. The obscurity which surrounds the lives of most labourers was only surpassed by that of their wives, whose names might not even be recorded in the baptisms of the children they bore. Middle Fisher Row was to Upper Fisher Row as the labourer's wife to the labourer. To turn from Upper Fisher Row to Middle Fisher Row is to turn from an area which is well documented, with its plentiful leases and wills, to a sort of *terra incognita*: subleases are unrecorded, and subtenants have no leases to leave by will.

Even more obscure than the subtenants of Middle Fisher Row were the inhabitants of the tenements kept in lodgings by the lessee of Middle Fisher Row, the widow, Mary Fletcher. These tenements probably provided temporary accommodation for bargemen. In the 1851 Census several of the smallest tenements in Middle Fisher Row were inhabited by two or more canal boatmen, apparently unrelated, living a bachelor existence. These particular houses had different inhabitants at each Census. Some provision for birds of passage would always be necessary in a community devoted to transport. Their inhabitants were perhaps engaged in bow-haling on the river above Oxford.

How bow-haling was organised in Oxford is not known, though it was bound to be on a smaller scale than downstream; the river was smaller, the number of boats fewer and their burthen less. The occupation of bow-haler or hireling was unknown in Oxford, and it seems likely that they were recruited from amongst bargemen out of work between trips, and labourers living near the wharf. The first stage for haling was perhaps as far up the river as Bablock Hythe. Ten miles above Oxford, the river makes a great loop round Wytham Hill, and the road back from Bablock Hythe, where there was a ferry is fairly straight, and would be not much more than four miles. The halers could return on foot at the end of a day. It is, therefore, not surprising to find some connection between the people of Northmoor, the parish in which Bablock Hythe lies, and Fisher Row.

---

[135] For the descendants of the Gardners in Upper Fisher Row in the 19th century, see Fig. 5.2 and Family Tree 5.5.

The trade required organisers as well as manpower, and one would expect these to be alehouse-keepers, pubs being all-purpose institutions on rivers. The first family to have a connection both with Northmoor and Oxford was the Brookings, who probably organised traffic. Tenement 1 in Upper Fisher Row, once Thomas Pemerton's, was held by Richard Brookings, boatman, in 1699. In 1716 it passed to Richard Brookings, the younger, victualler of Bablock Hythe.[136] The Northmoor registers show that he had three children born there between 1717 and 1719, one, Jonathan, becoming a freeman in 1743/4. His next lease in Upper Fisher Row in 1730 described him as a fisherman of Stanton Harcourt, an adjoining parish.

There were other connections between Northmoor and Oxford. Between 1722 and 1724 the Northmoor registers show children born to Thomas Beckley and James Payne, men bearing the surnames of Oxford fishermen. Marriages between Oxford men and Northmoor brides also link the two places; but the families with the strongest links with Northmoor were the Crawford and Gardner families. A consideration of the history of the Crawford family and its connections with the Gardners suggests that the families were heavily involved in supplying and organising this particular type of support service, and goes a long way to explaining why such families should decline rather than prosper. These families were too heavily committed to river transport, too specialised to adapt to changing conditions.

In St Thomas's the first mention of the Crawfords in the parish occurred in 1706 with the birth of a son, John, to John and Joane Crafford. A second son, John, was born in 1706, and a daughter Rebecca in 1710.[137] At this time John had his own boat, for on 10 January 1710 Richard, son of John Folly of Oxford, boatman, was apprenticed to John Crafford of the City of Oxford, bargemaster. However his fortunes declined, and when he supported the application of Elizabeth Chillingworth for letters of administration as executor of her husband's estate in 1717 he was only described as a bargeman.[138]

---

[136] See Appendix III, tenement 1A.

[137] Both sons called John survived. Calling more than one son of the same parents by the same name was common enough, but usually only when the first one had died vacating the name, as it were. Probably when one finds two sons alive bearing the same name, the elder had been weakly and not expected to survive when the younger brother was born.

The family then disappeared from the parish, but it seems clear that, like Richard Brookings before them, they went to Northmoor, though the evidence is circumstantial. In 1727 Joan, wife of John Crawford, died there. It was the first mention of the surname in this small parish. The Northmoor family then proceeded to marry partners from St Thomas's parish. In 1729 John Crawford (Northmoor married Margaret Gardner of St Thomas's at St Thomas's. In 1735 Rebecca Crawford of Northmoor married Thomas Finch of St Thomas's at St Mary Magdalen, and finally, John Crawford of Northmoor married Mary Gardner of St Thomas's at Northmoor. Thus the three children of John and Joane married back into their parish of origin. The marriages made by the Crawfords exhibited their close connection with the river. Though nothing is known of the occupation of Thomas Finch, it seems likely that he was some relative of Edward Finch, who was apprenticed to William Beckley, fisherman, of Oxford in 1718. Two Crawford brothers, both called John, had married two Gardner girls, Margaret and Mary, who were distantly related to each other (see Gardner Family Tree). Margaret married first, and we shall call her husband John II, and Mary's husband John III, though which was the elder brother is uncertain. Both were involved in the barging business.

John II and Margaret married in 1729 and had 16 children born in St Thomas's. The eldest daughter survived to marry, but the next three daughters died young. Three succeeding sons (William, born in 1735, John, born in 1736, and Richard in 1738) all became freemen and bargemen.[139] Most of the remaining children died young; Christian, the youngest, born in 1754, survived. Margaret Crawford, mother of this large family, was remembered by her mother, Rebecca Gardner, lessee of tenement 1B, in her will made in 1759. Mary was then described as the wife of John Crawford, bargemaster, but in Burton's list of 1764 he was not mentioned. The mother forgave her daughter a debt, but left her no share in the residue of her estate, which included her lease. Margaret and John never rose to be full tenants, yet through the marriage of their

[138] MS Wills Oxon. 163/3/26 (Francis Chillingworth).
[139] City, L.5.5, 1757-8, 1761-2, 1767-8.

youngest daughter Christian in 1774 they were ancestors of a branch of the Bossom family, one of the dominant families of Fisher Row in the 19th century (see Family Tree 6.2, The Bossoms).

John Crawford III, brother of John Crawford II, was never a freeman. He and his wife Mary (née Gardner) spent part of their life at Northmoor where four of their children were born between 1740 and 1747. Four more were born in St Thomas's. His position seems to have been more lowly than that of his brother, the bargemaster. He was probably the bargeman John or 'Beauty' Crawford, who was tried at Quarter Sessions in 1757 for stealing 400 crayfish from a stew belonging to Jeremiah Bishop at Godstow, and was sentenced to transportation.[140] Some of his family seem to have moved to Abingdon. In 1795 a Joseph Crawford (perhaps John III's son born in 1749) was involved as a witness in a somewhat obscure series of criminal cases, along with other Abingdon bargemen.[141] A John and Elizabeth Crawford of Abingdon also owned barges of 71 and 114 tons burthen respectively in 1795, and Elizabeth Crawford kept The Magpie.[142]

But who William Crawford, the boatmaster of Lechlade, whom Burton listed as owner of two boats in 1764, may have been – whether a son of John II or John III or even Edward – we do not know.

IX. THE BARGEMEN AND THE COMMUNITY

What were the relations of this community with the world at large? Material is sparse, and after the dense thickets of genealogy almost any generalisation seems rash. Let us take the reputation of the bargemen, and make of it what we can. Bargemen, it was said, were violent and foul-mouthed. They had a reputation for mobbish behaviour and their swearing was legendary. Let us seek the evidence on which this reputation was based.

The first gatherings of Oxford bargemen had nothing mobbish about them. In 1622 the Vice-Chancellor summoned the boatmen to his rooms in Christ Church to forbid their conveying

---

[140] City, 0.2.9, fos. 75, 77; *JOJ*, 16 July 1757.
[141] Oxon. RO, Wi. VI/iv/3, 13.
[142] Bromley Challenor, *Selections from the Borough Records of Abingdon, 1555-1897* (Abingdon, 1898), Appendix, xlii; *UBD*, II. 13.

corn out of town, as it was a time of scarcity.[143] Further down
the river at Marlow where the river trade was longer established the bargemen were involved in a rumbustious election
in 1640 when they supported Bulstrode Whitelock's can-
didacy, as he himself tells us: 'Some disorders and a little
violence there was, but we quickly appeased it, and our party
being much the more numerous, kept the other in the better
awe, who else longed to have been at acts of violence. The
bargemen of the town came in one and all for Mr Hoby and
me; so did generally the ordinary sort of townsmen.'[144] There
is no hint here, though, that the bargemen were more out-
rageous than other electors, though they clearly formed an
identifiable group.

In Oxford bargemen there are still no signs of mobbish behaviour. In 1652 a meeting was held in St Mary's Church at which
the boatmen discussed their grievances concerning the condition of the navigation and the conduct of millers with the
Barge Commissioners.[145] At this time voyages were short, and
boats small. The community was still in its infancy, and may
have had little sense of alienation from the wider community.

This however did not last. Trips lengthened, men were absent
longer, and the Restoration saw a deterioration in attitudes.
In part these were due to changes beyond the banks of the
river. The Puritan Revolution had failed. Attitudes hardened
and wider opportunity receded, though the river prospered.
In September 1680 Monmouth visited Oxford, and was point-
edly ignored by the University. The City however entertained
him. A lampoon was circulated: 'A Ballade on the Duke of
Monmouth's Entertainment at Oxford by the Rt. Worshipfull
the Maior (Mr Pawling) and the Worshipful Alderman and
Bargemen of the City of Oxford'. It was alleged that at the
banquet in Monmouth's honour and at the races the aldermen, including Alderman Wright, had been accompanied by
an enthusiastic rout of bargemen. Why bargemen should play
so prominent a part in the proceedings is not so clear, nor
why the Wrights who were a prominent Whig family well
into the 18th century, were pictured as their patrons. The

---

[143] OU Archs., Hyp. A. 34, Registrum Curie Cancellaii 1622-3, at back, fo. 2.

[144] Mary Reno Frear, 'The Election at Great Marlow in 1640', *The Journal of Modern History*, XIV (1942), 443.   [145] Oxon. RO, CH. N. IX/i, fos. 1-2.

Wright-Hicks connection seems too distant to be of moment, but Wright was a Barge Commissioner, and, in an undated list of debts for tolls 'Lady Wright's boat' appears.[146]

In Oxford in the 18th and 19th century the Whigs and the bargemen were to be associated, but how the association arose and whether they played an active part in the election riot in the 17th century is not known. There is no evidence of it, though their supposed support of Wright suggests it.

Further downstream, where traffic was heavier, bargemen were said to have been active again in the election of 1690 at Great Marlow, whilst at Abingdon in 1698 one of the candidates was said to have sought the bargemen's support by promising to use his influence to gain them freedom from impressment.[147]

In July 1730 the violence of the bargemen was provoked in a gruesome affair which had nothing to do with politics. The relatives of Richard Fuller of Caversham, a capitally convicted felon, arranged for his body to be carried by barge to Caversham. The students however seized the body from the relatives for dissection, and a riot developed. The body was in turn rescued by the Proctors from the students and held till night fell, when it was taken to the waterside. It was ambushed and finally taken over by the students, who carried it to Queen's College where it was 'made a skeleton & the Flesh dispersed up and down'. The case was referred to at the Act of 1733 when the *Terrae Filius* made a satiric survey of the Colleges. Bargemen were clearly involved, and also the undergraduates of Jesus, the Welsh College: 'Methinks, I scent toasted Cheese, sure we are upon the Welsh Borders. See the Fabrick founded by Queen Elizabeth for the Jolly Cambro-Britons ... Here are your Heroes that vanquish Bargemen and carry off the dead Bodies in triumph to be anatomiz'd.' There had been an element of the ritual town-gown violence in this case, as well as of the Tyburn-type riot against the surgeons recently explored by Dr Linebaugh.[148]

---

[146] Wood, *Life*, II. 496; ibid. III. 506-10; MS Twyne-Langbaine 1, fo. 51.

[147] Thomas Carew, *An Historical Account of the Rights of Elections of the Several Counties, Cities and Boroughs of Great Britain, to the year 1754* (London, 1755), pt. ii, 3, 388.

[148] Hearne, *Collections*, X. 313, 315; G.A. Oxon. 8° 61 (3), *The Terrae Filius Speech as*

In 1754 a similar Tyburn-type riot occurred in Oxford during the elections. Bargemen were said to be involved in the
election riot, hired by the New Interest or Whigs. There had
been no contested elections since 1710, and there were now
two, one for the City, one for the County, as well as an uncontested one for the University representative.[149] Electioneering
was in full swing by the summer of 1753. In August *Jackson's
Oxford Journal* noted that the Earl of Harcourt had entertained
100 Freeholders of towns along the Upper Thames: one week
Eynsham, Ducklington, Northmoor, and Standlake, and Bampton, Aston, Coate, and Black Bourton another week. By the
following February, when the Oxfordshire candidates of the
Old and New Interest both held meetings at Chipping Norton
on the same day, the county was at a pitch of excitement. The
supporters of the New Interest broke up their rivals' meeting
at The White Hart, and assaulted the landlord. Fourteen were
arrested, amongst them three with surnames suggestive of the
river. Some time later, in 1756, a former bargeman, Joseph
Best, arrested for murder, confessed to having been hired to
lead the mob at Chipping Norton.[150]

In Oxford itself the canvass continued noisily, and when the
candidates for the city for the Old Interest or Tories conducted
a canvass, about the time for the execution of two highwaymen,
Bryce and Briscoe, election mob and Tyburn-type riot seem
to have coalesced. The canvass took place on 21 March, the
execution, the next day. The body, intended for the University
anatomists, was rescued by the mob. This episode was mentioned a month later, when a letter was printed in *Jackson's
Oxford Journal*, warning the public that precautions had been
taken to prevent the recurrence of such an event.[151] The mob
may well have included bargemen, though at this stage there
was no suggestion of it. The city and university elections passed
off quietly enough, on Monday 15 April, but the County ones

---

it was spoken at the Publick Act (London, 1 733), 19-20; Peter Linebaugh, 'The Tyburn Riot
against the Surgeons' in Douglas Hay, Peter Linebaugh, E. P. Thompson and others, *Albion's
Fatal Tree* (London, 1975), 65-117.

[149] R. J. Robson, *The Oxfordshire Election of 1754* (Oxford, 1949) gives a detailed account of the election, but makes no mention of the constitution of the mob.

[150] *JOJ*, 18 Aug. 1753, 16 Mar. 1754, 26 Sept. 1756.

[151] *JOJ*, 4 May 1754.

held from the 17th to 20th were another matter. The Old Interest guarded the booths, preventing the Whigs from voting, and only through the aid of Exeter College, which was Whig and also strategically situated, were they able to bypass the Tory mob and vote. The irregularities of the poll led to a call for a scrutiny. At the climax of the scrutiny it was reported later that 'a great number of Bargemen and Country Fellows' with the orange cockades of the New Interest appeared and formed a threatening mob.[152]

The elections of 1761 were undisputed. The County families had no desire for such expensive encounters, but to the freemen an uncontested election was a disappointment. There may have been frustration and restlessness. Two days before the election day the execution of Isaac Darkin, a highwayman, took place, 'His body was carried off in Triumph by the Bargemen and most inhumanly mangled in order to prevent (according to his own Request) his being anatomized.' According to James Woodforde he was buried in St Thomas's Churchyard. 'All the College Gates was shut from ten o'clock last night 'till nine this Morning by an Order of the Vice-Chancellor & Proctors.'[153]

No further clear cases of 18th-century Oxford bargemen involved in mob activity have been found, but the accounts of the expenses of the canvass of Lord Robert Spencer and Captain Peregrine Bertie, who were the candidates supported by the Duke of Marlborough and the City in 1774, throw light on the methods by which a mob was raised.[154] The accounts include £212 12s. 6d. distributed amongst alehouse-keepers. In Oxford bargemen with pubs benefited: Edward Crawford, Richard Crawford, Henry Gardner, and John Chadwell, and so did the fisherman Benjamin Johnson. For the day of the elections there were miscellaneous payments, such as for flags and change-ringers. They included payments to 'out of town freemen': at North Hinksey and Cumnor to Richard Hart, at Wolvercote to John Sellwood, at Sandford to John Beckley, at Kennington and Radley to John Mollineaux, at Iffley to R^d Myzell, at Headington to Edmund Walker, at

[152] *JOJ*, 1 June 1754, Robson, op. cit., 115-27.
[153] *JOJ*, 28 Mar. 1761; W. N. Hargreaves-Maudsley, *Woodforde at Oxford*, 33.
[154] MS Top. Oxon. c. 280, fos. 15, 17.

South Hinksey to Anthy. Gardner, at Abingdon to Mr Buswell, at Islip to James Beckley, at Botley to Mr Cummings and at Cowley to Richard Biddle. Four of these payments were to fishermen and freemen: Richard Hart, John Beckley, James Beckley, and John Mollineaux. Almost every place on the river in the list was represented by a fisherman, and John Sellwood the blacksmith of Wolvercote had married Rebecca, granddaughter of Thomas and Rebecca Gardner. They held the lease of tenement 1B, Upper Fisher Row in succession to their grandmother by 1773.

On the whole it was fishermen rather than bargemen who were recipients of the New Interest's funds. Such men often kept alehouses beside their weirs and were thus well placed to treat the bargemen, many of whom were freemen, and bring them in to vote at city elections. A new light is cast on the Earl of Harcourt's canvassing of the hamlets of the Upper Thames in 1753.

The bargemen remained loyal to the Whigs in the 19th century. When John Richard Green was canvassing for Thackeray in the Liberal interest in the city elections of 1857 he was sent to seek the support of a barge-owner said to have many votes at his command. 'The man heard him to the end, and then silently stretched out an open palm, ... "How much is it?" said he.'[155]

The bargeman's reputation for violence both arose from, and was a symptom of, an alienation from society in which he was as much victim as anything. The hardening of public attitudes towards the group is perhaps most vividly brought home by considering the Oxford attitude to the impressment of boatmen. In the 17th century it was marked by compassion, but not so in the 18th century. In 1665/6 the Computus of the Vice-Chancellor recorded £3 'given to the watermen who were press'd here for his majesties service'. In August 1690 the City Quarter Sessions decreed that 'St Thomas parish may have some allowance in respect of several poor families of Boatmen that were pressed into their Majestie's service which are fallen on ye parish.' The press continued to take Oxford men, as it also seems to have taken men from

---

[155] John Richard Green, *Oxford Studies* ed. Mrs J. R. Green and Miss K. Norgate (London, 1901), xxix.

Abingdon, and the bargemasters petitioned the Privy Council for protection in 1702, but to what effect is not known. By the middle of the 18th century feeling was different when the press visited Oxford in search of men: 'Several of the loose People flew to the Woods, others went armed with Hatchets, &c. to defend themselves, and, one of the Bests, being seized, he immediately chopped off his left Thumb to render himself unfit for Service; notwithstanding which, he was taken away with the rest.[156]

The relationship of the bargemen to the wider community was curious. The violence was far from one-sided. The role of the mob was as much conferred as chosen, and the bargemen's violence was manipulated and encouraged when it served the ends of authority.

[156] Wood, *Life*, IV, 68; City, 0.2.1, fo. 31; PC 2/79, 309; *JOJ*, 13 Mar. 1756; Carew, Rights of Elections, 3.

Part II

FROM THE INDUSTRIAL REVOLUTION TO THE
DISINTEGRATION OF THE COMMUNITY

CHAPTER 4

Canal, River, and Row

I. REORIENTATION

The great changes which began to affect England in the late 18th century, and which are roughly lumped together as the Industrial Revolution did not bring industry to the whole country, but their effects were felt everywhere, even in such a rural county as Oxfordshire, and even in a town like Oxford, which was essentially a consumer society, and was to remain so until the 20th century. There was a quickening of economic life: there was more money to be spent, for if Oxford was non-industrial its inhabitants had interests in industry elsewhere. Communications improved, and throughout the Midlands almost every town of any size was linked by turnpike roads and canals.

Improved communications affected different parts of the country differently, and affected different groups within the same community in various ways. The opening of the Oxford canal brought a long period of prosperity to the shareholders, but to the Row it brought high hopes in the first place, then bitter competition, and then a feud rent the community from end to end. Railway competition brought decline, diversification, and dispersal.

Improved communications altered the very geography of the parish. The Row and its environs were radically changed, first by road improvement, then by the building of the Oxford Canal. The Botley Causeway had provided a road to the west for pack-horse traffic at least from the 16th century. The old route ran over Wytham Hill to Swinford Ferry, and so to Eynsham, Witney, and the west. Now a wide turnpike road was built and a bridge replaced the ferry. A road from the city

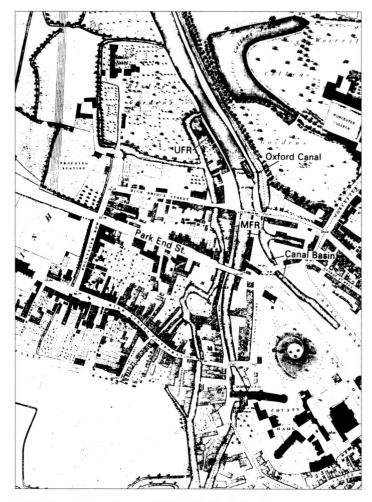

UFR   Upper Fisher Row   MFR   Middle Fisher Row

Fig. 4.1. St Thomas's Parish, 1850. Detail from Robert Hoggar's Map
    of Oxford.

to join the new turnpike was cut from the town centre west-
ward across the site of the Castle moat. It crossed Middle
Fisher Row by means of a new bridge known as Pacey's
Bridge (see Fig. 4.1). It carved through the centre of the large

block of land between Hythe Bridge Street and St Thomas's High Street, through the land occupied by the Hollybush Inn, which for centuries had stood at the end of the Botley Causeway, casting a welcome gleam of light through the night to greet the traveller on his approach to the city. The Hollybush, which stood on part of the site of what is now the Royal Oxford Hotel had to be rebuilt. The route was open to traffic from August 1769, two and a half years after the appropriate Acts of Parliament had obtained the Royal Assent.[1] The new road probably took a certain amount of traffic from the river above Oxford, affecting Fisher Row and its small boats more than Folly Bridge. Pacey's Bridge itself was a foretaste of things to come. Although it was built with a footway along the water's edge below the bridge to connect the two parts of the Row, its building probably accelerated the tendency for the southern part of the Row to turn its back on the barging trade and become involved in the affairs of the parish in general. Fishermen, however, continued to cluster round The Lock until well into the 19th century.

Even greater changes were brought to the Row some 20 years later, with the opening of two canals in the winter of 1789/90. On 19 November 1789 the Thames and Severn Canal was opened, supplying the last link in a chain of waterways which joined the Thames and Severn. It provided a through route by water from the West Midlands and South Wales to Oxford and London. Just over six weeks later, on 1 January 1790, the Oxford Canal was opened, linking the North and the Midlands to Oxford and London by a second route.[2]

The Thames and Severn Canal joined the Thames 32 miles above Oxford at Inglesham near Lechlade, but the Oxford Canal was carried into the parish of St Thomas's itself. The Oxford canal ran from its junction with the Coventry Canal in the parish of Foleshill on the outskirts of Coventry to Banbury, and then down the Cherwell Valley as far as the hamlet of Thrupp, near Kidlington, north of Oxford. Here it crossed to the west side of that long terrace of gravel on which the

[1] E. de Villiers, *Swinford Bridge, 1769-1969* (Eynsham, 1969), 12-17.

[2] Humphrey Household, *The Thames and Severn Canal* (Newton Abbot, 1969), 69-70; Charles Hadfield *The Canals of the East Midlands* (Newton Abbot, 1966), 26.

medieval city of Oxford had been built. It ran down the side of the shelf, with Port Meadow on its west. The Thames lay beyond the Meadow. The old navigable channel of the Thames swung eastwards round the lower end of the Meadow, and for a short distance the river and canal lay side by side. In 1796 a lock (Isis or Louse Lock) was built connecting river and canal just where the river swung westwards again (see Fig. 3.3). At this point too the Castle Mill Stream left the main river, passing down by Fisher Row to the Castle Mill. The Oxford Canal now lay parallel to the Castle Mill Stream as it ran past Upper Fisher Row, separated only by a narrow strip of towpath. An extra arch was added to Hythe Bridge, and river and canal ran side by side under it. Now the canal turned east to form two basins, surrounded by wharves, one for coal, one for other goods. The line of the road which crossed the site was lifted over the canal by a bridge. The area is now filled in. A car park stands on the part nearest the Castle Mill Stream, and Nuffield College stands on the eastern portion. Canal House, built by Richard Tawney the canal engineer in 1827-9, still stands in an elevated position overlooking the site.[3]

The building of the canal and the canal basin in the parish must have caused a major upheaval, but there is no evidence of major disturbances in the last year of the building of the canal, as it approached the city, even though, in the winter of 1788/9, there had been a 50-day frost. For four weeks the citizens of Oxford had distributed food to crowds of as many as 3,679 and 'upwards of four thousand' of the industrious poor.[4] Only in December 1789, near the end of the period is the presence of navvies in the parish noticed in the paper, when 'one of our Canal Navigation men made a public sale of his wife':

After a Conversation about the payment of 5s. as the Purchase-Money, the old Husband very deliberately pulled out a Penny Slip and tied it around the Waist of his Wife, the end of which he held fast till he pocketed 3s. in Part, the Purchaser not abounding in Cash. He then put the Cord into the Hands of the new Husband, and took French leave. The Woman then immediately called for her second Wedding-Ring.

---

[3] Hugh J. Compton, *The Oxford Canal* (Newton Abbot, 1976), 63-4; Jennifer Sherwood and Nikolaus Pevsner, *The Buildings of England: Oxfordshire* (Harmondsworth, 1974), 249.
[4] *JOJ*, 3 Jan. 1789, 24 Jan. 1789.

This was no navvy wedding, but a poor man's divorce of a type noted from time to time in the newspapers. In the comfortable houses of the High Street the paper's stricture might be accepted: 'Wives are now transferrable like Bank Stock'.[5] How it was seen in the little houses of Fisher Row we do not know.

Whatever may have been thought of the changes which were taking place, their extent and the economic consequences were not fully realised. Two new waterways extended the trade of the river: which was it most advantageous to exploit? Probably the bargemen were hardly aware there was a choice to be made. The Thames and Severn Canal was a wide canal, the sort which could be used by any boat which was already used in the river trade to Lechlade. Indeed, the boats which the Thames and Severn Canal Company built travelled on both waterways, first along the canal and then downriver to London. The Thames and Severn was therefore simply an extension of a known route, and it offered young men new openings. But for the bargeman to move on to the Oxford Canal from the river was to make a vast change. He must move from a familiar waterway, with a riverside population with which he was familiar, on to a waterway peopled with strangers. The current-less canal needed new techniques, and, above all, it needed new boats, for the canal locks were too narrow for barges. If the men of the Row did not accept the challenge of either of the canals they could carry on as before, for there was plenty of traffic in the early 1790s coming down the Oxford Canal for transport along the river to London. To see the choice open to the boatmen in its full context we must turn to the development of the river canals.

II. ALTERNATIVE ROUTES

The vision of canals which would join the seas by linking the great rivers of the country, providing inland routes from port to port, and turning inland towns into inland ports, was an old one. In the early modern period the south of England was economically more advanced than the north, and it was natural that such schemes should be first mooted there. In the 17th century a route to join the Thames and Severn was much discussed: it was surveyed by Henry Briggs, the Savilian Professor

---

[5] *JOJ*, 12 Dec. 1789, 6 Feb. 1790.

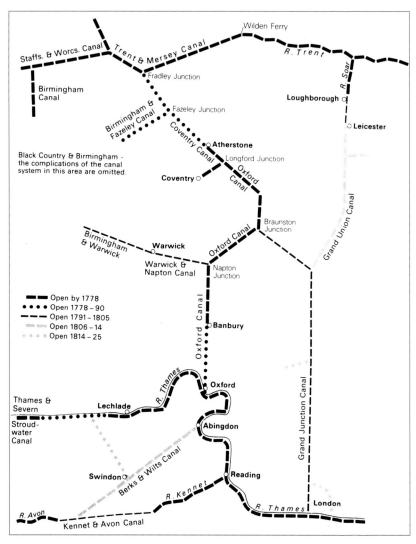

Fig. 4.2. The sequence in which the Canals were opened to Navigation.

of Astronomy; John Taylor, the water-poet, demonstrated that the scheme had some sort of feasibility by rowing to Lechlade, and portaging over the watershed to the Frome, and descending it; Francis Mathews pamphleteered; John Collins caught his death of cold while examining a route; and Joseph

Moxon mapped one.[6] Nothing came of it, and in the 18th century
the initiative passed to the north, and, despite all the 17th-century
interest the Thames was to be the last of the rivers to be linked
into the scheme.

The first step to this end was taken by the passing of two
Acts of Parliament in May 1766. By the act, 6 Geo. III c.96,
the Trent and Mersey Canal was authorised, linking the Trent
at Wilden Ferry with the Mersey by way of the Bridgewater
Canal, which it joined at Preston Brook (see Fig. 4.2). By the
second act, 6 Geo. III c.97, the building of the Staffordshire
and Worcester Canal was authorised. By this act a canal was to
be built from the Severn to the Trent and Mersey, so that when
the two canals were completed the three rivers, Trent, Mersey,
and Severn would be linked by artificial cuts. In 1772 the Staffordshire and Worcester Canal was completed, and enough of
the Trent and Mersey to link the rivers Trent and the Severn.
The link with the Mersey was not made until 1777. It was to be
another 13 years before the link with the Thames was completed.

The year after the Trent and Mersey and the Staffordshire
and Worcester canals received their acts moves were set afoot
to consider linking the Trent and Mersey with the Thames. The
Oxford Canal was first mentioned tentatively in an advertisement in the *Northampton Mercury* for 10 August 1767. The
advertisement for a meeting on the 18th was concerned with
the proposed Coventry Canal, which was to make a junction
with the Trent and Mersey Canal at Fradley and also link Coventry with the collieries around Atherstone, Chilvers Coton,
and Bedworth. The line had been surveyed, and an act was
sought. A canal to Oxford was also to be considered. The Coventry Canal was authorised on 29 January 1768 (8 Geo. III
c.36), and the Oxford Canal received its act (9 Geo. III c.70)
on 21 April 1769.[7] Although work on the two canals started
with expedition, the American War of Independence and its
aftermath made it difficult to raise money for the completion
of these works. Started within three years of the Staffordshire
and Worcester Canal, they were completed 18 years afterwards.

[6] Household, *Thames and Severn*, 13-16; *DNB*, Henry Briggs, John Taylor, John Collins.

[7] Hadfield, *Canals of E. Midlands*, 15-18; PP. Eng. 1870/1vi (184), *Return relating to
Inland Navigations and Canal Companies*, 4-5, 12-13.

Work started on the Coventry Canal on 25 April 1768, and coal was first brought to Coventry in August 1769, whilst the Oxford Canal, which had obtained its act in April 1769, had cut only 10 miles of its length by March 1771. By the end of 1772 the Coventry Canal was completed between Coventry and the coal pits at Atherstone, its capital was used up, and there it stopped for some years, an isolated ribbon of water. It had, nevertheless, a fairly brisk local trade in coal, and was able to pay a dividend of 2 per cent in September 1774 and similar modest dividends thereafter.

Meanwhile the Oxford Canal continued building. In September 1772 200 men and 24 boats were employed by the Company; in 1773 500 men and 60 boats. In 1774, the year the canal was open to Napton, 700 men and 65 boats were employed. By 1775 the canal was only half finished, the last calls on the, shares had been made, and it was necessary to raise a loan by Act of Parliament (15 Geo. III c.9).[8] Work on the junction of the Oxford and Coventry canals was delayed by a long-standing quarrel between the two canal companies over the terms on which the junction of the Coventry and the Trent and Mersey Canal and that between the Coventry and Oxford Canal were to be made. Relations between the two companies had been so bitter that in the winter of 1773/4 the Oxford Canal had contemplated abandoning any such junction and had entered into discussions with the proprietors of the Birmingham Canal about an alternative route. Eventually the Coventry Canal Company took the Oxford Canal Company to law to force it to make a junction. After an order in the Court of King's Bench, a junction was made at Longford on 15 April 1777 and by March 1778 the canal had been completed as far as Banbury.[9] Funds were exhausted. Work stopped.[10] Coal was, however, carried on the finished portion of the canal. From 1778 to 1786 the waterway remained isolated and incomplete, running from Atherstone in the north to Banbury in the south. It served the surrounding area with coal.

[8] J. R. Ward, *The Finance of Canal Building in 18th-Century England* (London, 1974), 101; Hadfield, op. cit. 20-1.

[9] Hadfield, op. cit. 19-20.

[10] Dep. a. 16, Accounts, 20 Apr. 1878 and 20 Aug. 1878.

The linking of the Thames into the canal system progressed slowly. In 1779 talks between Birmingham and Oxford interests were reopened. Meantime the Trent and Mersey Canal attempted unsuccessfully to obtain a bill to force the Coventry Canal to make a junction with it at Fradley. At length a compromise agreement was reached at Coleshill on 20 June 1782, between the various interested canals. It was contingent upon Birmingham and Fazeley promoters obtaining an act to cut a canal to join the Coventry Canal at Fazeley. By this agreement the Oxford Canal was to be completed to Oxford by the Oxford Company, whilst the Coventry Canal completed their canal as far as Fazeley. The section from Fazeley to Fradley was to be completed in two sections, the southern by the Birmingham and Fazeley Company, the northern by the Trent and Mersey.[11]

In 1786 both the Oxford and Coventry Canals raised loans to complete their lines, and work recommenced. The final sections of the Oxford Canal were built rapidly over the next four years. The progress of the canal can be plotted by advertisements in *Jackson's Oxford Journal* for the sale of coal as new wharves opened along the line of the canal. In May 1788 coal was available at the Company's wharves at Aynho, Heyford, and Enslow Bridge; in February 1789 it was available at Wolvercote. On 3 October 1789, before the canal was open to Oxford, advertisements appeared for coal from the canal at Eynsham, on the Thames above Oxford. A connection with the Thames had been achieved by way of the Duke's Cut, a short private canal built by the Duke of Marlborough from the Thames above the King's weir near Wolvercote to the Oxford Canal.[12]

The Oxford Canal opened on 1 January 1790, but by then a canal, authorised 14 years after the Oxford Canal, had already fulfilled the old 17th-century dream of linking the Thames and Severn.

The building of the Thames and Severn Canal had been facilitated by the construction of the Stroudwater Canal, which

[11] Hadfield, op. cit. 22-4.

[12] Dep. a.1 6, Accounts, 5 Aug. 1790: 'Labourers work at junction at Wolvercote and purchase of Wharf £356. 6. 11½'; Kingsley Belsten and Hugh Compton, 'EynshamWharf, Oxfordshire', *Journal of the Railway and Canal Historical Society*, XIV (1968), 45-6.

was completed from Framilode on the Severn to Stroud on 24 July 1779.[13] The continuation of the line by a new canal to join the Thames was well received. It was supported by the West-Midlands canals as it provided a through route from the Midlands by the Severn and the Thames to London, at a time when the Oxford and Coventry canals were at a standstill for lack of money. The London market was a desirable one, and the canal system until this time had been entirely provincial. The scheme attracted Londoners also, and according to a contemporary account the new line was surveyed in 1782 'at the desire of several opulent private persons, chiefly merchants of London'.[14] They obtained their act, 23 Geo. III c.38, on 17 April 1783. From the beginning it was viewed as a scheme of great importance, and there was no difficulty in persuading people to subscribe to the initial issue of shares. The Oxford Canal had had an authorised share capital of £150,000 in shares of £100 each, but only 1,223 shares were originally taken up; the Thames and Severn, for a line only a third as long had an authorised share capital of £130,000, all of which was taken up, and even more finance would have been available had it been required. The subscribers to the Oxford Canal had been largely local. Only eight per cent of the capital was subscribed outside Oxfordshire and Warwickshire, and the dons of Oxford colleges subscribed 13 per cent of the share capital. The subscribers to the Thames and Severn came from further afield: the Staffordshire and Worcestershire Canal took up 25 per cent of the shares, whilst J. R. Ward has identified 61 per cent of the shares as emanating from London.[15] The canal was built swiftly, in order to forestall the Oxford Canal, and the junction of the Canal was made at Inglesham, a short distance above Lechlade, well before the Oxford Canal was finished.

Looked at from a strictly commercial point of view, in 1790 the Thames and Severn Canal linked with the Thames must have seemed a better waterway. The Oxford Canal had taken 20 years to build, and the Thames and Severn only 6½. Certainly the Oxford Canal was 91 miles long, and the Thames and Severn only 28¾ miles, but the Thames and Severn was a

---

[13] Household, *Thames and Severn*, 19-21.

[14] J. Phillips, *A General History of Inland Navigation* (4th edn., London, 1803) 211-12.

[15] Ward, *Canal Finance*, 64-5.

wide canal, capable of taking barges and trows, and the Sapperton Tunnel was an engineering work of such magnitude that the King himself had visited it; the Thames and Severn was supported by well-run Midland canal companies and the money of the metropolis, whilst the Oxford Canal was a local affair, supported by local money. So it must have seemed in 1790. Yet the Oxford Canal was to prosper, and the Thames and Severn Canal was never to fulfil its initial promise.

The primary cause of the failure of the Thames and Severn Canal was that it was linked to that unregenerate natural river, the Thames, subject to incalculable delays which were no longer tolerable in a period when artificial cuts could provide more reliable transport. The Thames and Severn was connected with the Thames (so was the Oxford Canal), but it was connected with it at a higher point, from above Lechlade (see Fig. 3.1). This was a disadvantage in itself. As well, although after the establishment of the Thames Commission in 1770 the river had been improved, the improvements had begun in the lower and more profitable districts of the river, and they moved upstream slowly.[16] By 1784 work was only about to commence at Whitchurch, and nothing had been done further upstream. In 1784 the Thames and Severn Canal proposed the building of a canal from Kempsford to Abingdon, to bypass the upper river, but this scheme came to nothing, and the Thames and Severn remained hostage to the state of the Upper Thames.[17] By 1790 the Commissioners were still at work in Abingdon, and the river above this was still in poor shape.

Above Oxford things were even worse, and it was this part of the river which affected the Thames and Severn so adversely. Some river improvements took place in the 1790s, the Thames Commissioners reacting tardily to the pressure of the Thames and Severn Canal Company. It was at this time that the course of the river on the west side of Oxford was altered radically, and the river assumed the form we know today. In the 1790s the Bullstake Stream ceased to be the main navigation channel, and the mainstream was turned down from Medley by a new

[16] For the progress of the work on the river a chronology is provided by H. S. Davies, in his unpublished thesis, 'The Thames Navigation Commission, 1771-1867' (Reading University), 84-108.

[17] L.J. Dalby, *The Wilts and Berks Canal* (Lingfield, Surrey, 1971), 4.

cut into Oseney Mill Stream, which was widened to take traffic, and a pound-lock built near Oseney Mill (see Fig. 3.3). The old line of the navigation channel from Medley to the Castle Mill Stream was abandoned, save a small section used by traffic coming down from the canal on to the river by means of Louse Lock.[18] The raising of the level of the pound between Medley and Oseney Lock probably preserved a sufficient head of water to serve the Castle Mill Stream, for there do not seem to have been any complaints. The city, however, no longer took much interest in the Castle Mill, which was leased out. As well as these alterations to the river at Oxford, improvements were made to the locks above Oxford, but they were not very satisfactory, and the Upper Thames continued to pose problems for the Thames and Severn Canal, until a new route by way of the North Wilts Canal and the Berks and Wilts was opened in 1819 (see Fig. 4.2).

After the canals opened, the newspapers spoke of the varied cargoes of goods which now came along the waterways from north, cast, and west, but coal was the most important item, for sea-coal had always been expensive: the long trip by keel from the Tyne, through London, and up the river added considerably to the price. In 1769 a hundredweight could cost as much as 3s.[19] Once coal started to come down the Oxford Canal and the Thames and Severn, the monopoly was destroyed and sea-coal could not compete with Warwickshire and Staffordshire coal which sold at from about 1s. 2d. to 1s. 6d.[20] – coal price varied according to the season and quality as well as distance from the pit and the trade upstream in coal above Reading fell away. This upset the balance of trade upstream and down. Formerly corn had been carried down to London, and coal back; now there was an imbalance which meant that whilst there was always plenty of lading waiting to go to London, the boats at London must wait to make up a cargo, or travel at a loss; but if they waited for a cargo they gained a reputation for unreliability, and cargo piled up on the wharves up-country. Ultimately the failure to solve this dilemma, taken

---

[18] City, P.5.23; Joseph Sills, *Report Of the State of the Navigation of the River Thames between Radcott-bridge and Abingdon* (London, 1796), 22-3.

[19] *JOJ*, 18 Nov. 1769; 9 Dec. 1769.

[20] *JOJ*, 31 July 1790.

with the unpredictability of the Thames, doomed the Thames and Severn to serve little but local business.

Whilst the Thames Commissioners slowly continued their work of river improvement, they threw one lock after another out of action, thus delaying and hampering the river trade.[21] Such inconveniences were doubly galling, for with the outbreak of war with France trade increased. A large volume of supplies for troops required transport to the south-east, to the towns nearest the channel ports, and coastal trade was anxious to switch to inland routes, if efficient and reasonably priced transport became available. Yet the Thames and Severn Canal was unable fully to exploit the situation. Originally the Company had set up its own fleet of barges, some working on the Severn, and some on the Thames and Severn, and some all the way to London. The books of the company are interesting in providing a full day-by-day picture of the running of a river carrying business. They also show in detail the difficulties under which the company was labouring. The business had been started initially by the company to give an impetus to trade on the new waterway, but as the prospects of the canal did not improve and private carriers did not appear, they were forced to expand their fleet to keep trade going. In 1800 they had a fleet of 'more than 50 vessels', and about 31 of these were engaged in the trade down the Thames. The efficient surveillance of this fleet trading on two rivers as well as the canal was beyond the capacity of the Canal Company, and dissatisfaction with them as carriers meant that with the return of peace in 1801 they lost trade. In the next few years they began to disperse their fleet to such as would take the boats.[22]

Meantime the Oxford Canal flourished. Its shares had increased in value with the completion of the line, and the payment of the first modest dividends in 1791. By 1793 the share price stood at £200.[23] Because the Canal joined the Thames many miles below Lechlade, it gained some benefit from such improvements as the Commissioners had made to the river, and it provided the shortest inland route by water to London from the Midlands, and the most efficient. In 1795-7 the boats

[21] See, for example, *JOJ*, 2 Aug. 1794 and 16 Aug. 1794.

[22] Household, *Thames and Severn*, 94-110.

[23] Ward, *Canal Finance*, 101.

of 82 traders in Warwickshire and Staffordshire were registered for trading down the Oxford Canal, and whilst many perhaps only occasionally traded the full length of the canal, there was also an unknown number of Oxfordshire traders on the waterway as well. Some of the boats traded down from the Trent and Mersey, even from as far as Harecastle, north of the Potteries.[24] During the war some coastal trade which had formerly passed by the Trent and Gainsborough and around the coast found its way down the canal.[25] Indeed, though the traffic on the canal was still to increase, at this time it came from further afield than it was to do later, and the variety of goods carried was greater. Its management was aggressive, and from 1794 it encouraged trade by offering premiums on trade passing, certain locks along the Thames, at Abingdon, Caversham, and Benson, later also at Whitchurch and Wallingford.[26] On 19 July 1793 water-carriage from Manchester and the Potteries by regular weekly stage boats was advertised in *Jackson's Oxford Journal* by Francis Joules of Stone in conjunction with Messrs. Wyatt and Grain, two bargemasters of Folly Bridge. They had come to recognise that the future lay with the Oxford Canal rather than the Thames and Severn. Despite its auspicious beginnings the tonnage on the Thames and Severn was to be at best a little over one ninth of that carried by the Oxford Canal, even in its most prosperous years, when it had managed to bypass the Upper Thames.[27]

The route to London by way of the Oxford Canal still used a considerable length of river, and as early as 1791 and 1792 rival schemes were proposed to provide a route to London entirely by canal. One of these schemes, the London and Western Canal would have incorporated almost the whole length of the Oxford Canal, and was therefore favoured by the Oxford Company. The second scheme, for a canal to be known as the Grand Junction Canal, however, won the day. This canal stretched from a junction with the Oxford Canal at Braunston in Northamptonshire to the Thames at Brentford, and traffic

[24] Staffs. RO, QR UB1, Register of Boats and Barges, 1795; Warwicks. RO, QS. 95/4-8, Register for Boats and Barges, 1795-6. Warwicks. RO, CR 1590/1, Oxford Canal Letter Book, 1791-1801, 310.

[25] PRO RAIL 855/110, letter of R. S. Skey, 11 Nov. 1801; RAIL 855/111, pt. i, letter of William Parkes, 3 Mar. 1803.

[26] Dep. a. 16. [27] PP. Eng. 1870/lvi (184) 12-13, 20-1.

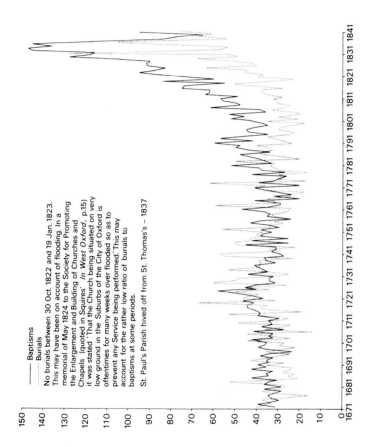

Fig. 4.3. Population of St Thomas's Parish, 1672-1841.
Births and Deaths by Calendar Years.

from the Midlands used only a small part of the Oxford Canal compared with what it had used formerly. Undeterred, the Oxford Canal struck a shrewd bargain, claiming compensation for the tolls which it no longer received. Heavy compensatory tolls were charged. The Oxford Canal was empowered, for instance, to charge 2s. 9d. for every ton of coal which passed off the Oxford Canal on to the Grand Junction Canal, whilst the new canal had to guarantee the Oxford Canal an income of £10,000 a year. Once this arrangement had been made the Oxford Canal Company withdrew its opposition to the Grand junction. The Oxford Canal had managed to make the success of its rival the basis of its economic fortunes. Though the route from the Midlands to London by Oxford and the Thames was abandoned after the Grand Junction Canal opened in 1805, the Oxford Canal waxed wealthy. In 1806 the Oxford Canal paid a dividend of 16½ per cent, by 1809 it paid 25 per cent, in 1811 it paid 31 per cent. This was maintained until 1819, when it rose to 32 per cent. By 1824 it paid 34½ per cent, at which figure it remained until the threat of railway competition forced the company to put money into the improvement of its line.[28]

Clearly the soaring dividends were no indication of the actual trade of the Oxford Canal itself. The tonnage figures for the busy northern part of the canal above Braunston which was still part of the through route from the Midlands to London were very different from those for the section below Braunston, which had lost its importance in the canal system. Figures which do not distinguish the two parts give us little idea of the trade to Oxford, or of the prosperity of the canal boatmen who plied this section of the canal.

On paper the dividends of the Oxford Canal suggest a brisk and busy canal – one of the success stories of the Industrial Revolution. It is easy, if we look at statistics to have this view reinforced when we see how Oxford grew after the canal was built, and even more how the working-class suburbs increased. Whilst the population of Oxford doubled between 1801 and 1841, a substantial rise for a southern town, the population of St Thomas's more than tripled (see Fig. 4.3). It expanded with the vigour of an industrial town in the north of England,

---

[28] Hadfield, op. cit. 108-9,159.

such as Preston. In 1801 its population was just over 1,000; in 1841 it was over 3,700. Two of the other poorer, low-lying suburbs, St Ebbes and St Clements, showed the same sort of spectacular growth.

Surely the canal had brought trade, coal, industry, population, and employment to these places? The appearance is delusive. Oxford expanded, but it developed no new industry to absorb this population. Indeed, the vast increase of population in the poorest parishes is difficult to explain entirely. In part at least it was due to the deep distress of the surrounding countryside – a distress which found expression in the activities of 'Captain Swing'. Oxford has always been a magnet even to stolider men than Thomas Hardy's Jude, in *Jude the Obscure*, who saw it as a beckoning town of golden opportunities. Certainly the beginning of every term brought openings for some, but these too often ended with the term. The economy of Oxford was hopelessly dependent on the university, expanding and contracting with its season. Unemployment and under-employment were endemic in St Thomas's throughout the 19th century. So, when, for whatever reason, trade grew slack on river or canal, alternative employment was almost impossible to find, and rivalries became bitter. The spectre of want stalked the men and women of the Row.

III. ALTERNATIVE FUTURES

At the beginning of the canal era, however, in the early 1790s, the atmosphere of canal carrying was euphoric. The year 1793 marked the start of a period of canal mania, which was to sweep many small men into incautious enterprises. By 1797 such men were often in difficulty, and it was in this year that an important struggle between the waterways for the trade of the Oxford Canal took place. The protagonists were brothers, William and Thomas Beesley (see Beesley Family Tree 5.1). William Beesley was engaged in the barge trade from Oxford to London, and Thomas was a cost-bearer employed by the Thames and Severn Canal Company, which was already in difficulties. A letter from an official of the Thames and Severn Company to the Oxford Canal Company tells the story. Evidently William Beesley claimed a monopoly of all goods being trans-shipped at the Canal Wharf from canal boat to river barge, and, even when there were more goods than he could deal with, was only prepared to subcontract for a very large consideration:

Sirs,

Having been informed that there were considerable quantities of goods lying at the Oxford Canal Wharf waiting a conveyance to London, by far a greater quantity than the present Boats working from the wharf could convey in a short or convenient time, we desired our Costbearer Thomas Beesley to apply for a Freight, which he did, and was informed that William Beesley had contracted with the C⁰ to convey all Goods that passed their Canal, and upon application to him he demanded £10.0 for permitting any boat to take in a freight, which was of course declined; As it does not appear probably that the Company should grant an exclusive privilege to William Beesley or any other Man to load the whole of the Merchandize passing their Canal, but upon the contrary, that they wish to give encouragement to everyone who promotes the Interest and dispatch of the Canal, we have taken the liberty of addressing you ...[29]

Bad feeling persisted, and another brother, Samuel, who also captained one of the Thames and Severn barges seems to have taken his brother Thomas's part. In October 1799 William was before the City Quarter Sessions charged with assaulting Samuel Beesley, and had to enter into a recognisance of £20 to keep the peace for seven years towards his brothers, Thomas and Samuel. They also had to enter into similar bonds. It was a period of obscure violence which is glimpsed in the Docquet Book for the City Quarter Sessions at that time, involving other men as well. The Beesleys were clearly hot-blooded. In 1800 William Beesley was up before the court again, this time for assaulting Thomas.[30]

Who were these two brothers? Though the name was new to the Row in 1789, the Beesleys had been in the parish since the 17th century, and had married into the Establishment of the Row. The Beesleys were related to the Gardner family through a grandmother. Their mother, Jane or Ann Molineaux, was the daughter of Adam Molineaux and his wife Elizabeth Gardner (see Beesley and Gardner Family Trees).

William Beesley had moved into Middle Fisher Row in 1789 when he took over the lease of the 12th and 13th tenements, Fisher Row, from Christ Church.[31] At this time he

[29] RAIL 855/106, letter of Jona. Sills and Son, 19 Dec. 1797.
[30] City, 0.2.11, Mich. 1799, Trin. 1800, Epiph. 1801. See also Easter 1798 and Trin. 1799.
[31] *Oseney*, II. 504.

called himself a fisherman. In the 1790s he rebuilt this part of the Row, perhaps with an eye on the increasing population of the parish. Where there had been seven tenements in Middle Fisher Row when he took it over, there were 15 tenements at the time of his death in 1802. He was a wharfinger, the owner of two barges, the *William* and *Mary* and *The Pattern*,[32] and he was also the landlord of the pub at the corner of Middle Fisher Row and Hythe Bridge Street. In his time it was called The Fishes. Later renamed the Nag's Head, it was to be an important canal boatman's pub. William Beesley was a man of some power in the Row, and well placed to exploit the trade from the canal to the river.

His younger brother Thomas held another important property in the Row. On 1 May 1795 he leased tenement IA Upper Fisher Row from the City (see Appendix III). This was the tenement immediately adjacent to The Lasher. At the time of his fracas with his brother he was perhaps the Thames and Severn Canal Company's most trusted costbearer.[33] Thomas Beesley however set up as an independent bargemaster about 1798.

Competition continued between the Thames and Severn Company and a group of Oxford bargemasters, among whom William Beesley was prominent, and an attempt was made at Oxford to set up a similar company to the Thames and Severn's carrying company, to be known as the Oxford Boat Company. This company would carry on behalf of the Oxford Canal Company between Oxford and London.[34] The plan came to nothing however, with the bankruptcy in May 1801 of the timber-merchants and bargemasters, Aris and Taylor, who had, like William Beesley played a leading part in the scheme. It took a little time to arrange an auction of their stock, which was extensive, and, before it took place, the goods of Thomas Beesley of Upper Fisher Row had been sold up for the benefit of his creditors. This included his barge, which lay at Iffley.[35]

[32] RAIL 855/110, inventory, 19 Jan. 1801.

[33] Gloucs. RO:TS 110. Letter Book of the Thames and Severn Canal Company, *passim*; Q/RR1, Register of Barges and Trows … 1795.

[34] RAIL 855/110, see especially Aris and Taylor's 'Observations', and the letter of Messrs. Hopkins, Couling, and Beesley, 16 Jan. 1801.

[35] *JOJ*, 23 May 1801.

The demise of the Oxford Boat Company, the collapse of Aris and Taylor and also of his brother must have affected William Beesley; and with the signing of the Peace of Amiens on 27 March 1802, and the inevitable reduction in trade which peace brought to the canal, William Beesley's affairs seem to have become confused. He died intestate in July 1802 with an estate of under £2,000, but his affairs were in disorder, and clearly too difficult for his widow and administratrix to deal with. In October Middle Fisher Row was up for sale, though it was long before the estate was finally wound up.[36]

The quarrel between the brothers was a watershed in the history of the Row. William's descendants continued to be connected with the canal, and for long Middle Fisher Row reflected William Beesley's interest in the canal trade, and more canal boatmen lived there than in any other part of the Row. Thomas Beesley, and his descendants continued in Upper Fisher Row, and remained loyal to the river. The families were to be the two leading families of the Row. When we deal with the canal boatmen, willynilly we shall find ourselves dealing at every turn with William's descendants; when we deal with bargemen and fishermen, Thomas's family will occupy us. The futures of the families were to be very different, and we shall deal first with the canal boatmen – 'William's children'.

CHAPTER 5

The Canal Boatmen and the Row

I. A NEW SORT OF BOATMAN

Canal boatmen were an entirely new sort of boatman unknown to the inhabitants of Fisher Row before 1790, although they had been developing as a group from the time the Trent and the Severn had been linked by artificial cuts in 1772, when the length of the boatman's trips had increased so that canal boatmen started to live on their boats. They became an extraordinarily colourful group with their own distinctive dress, style of boat decoration, and customs, which were found on all the narrow canals of the Midlands.

We have no first-hand accounts of the earliest canal boatmen but the description by the Birmingham writer George Mogridge, already quoted, suggests that by 1822 they already provided a familiar yet picturesque feature in an everyday landscape.[1] Our earliest description of the boatmen and their boats at Oxford probably dates from about seven years later, and comes from the childhood memories of a daughter of the geologist William Buckland, then one of the Canons of Christ Church:

This old-world corner of Oxford, with the high earth mound adjoining the Gaol, or Castle, as it was then called, was always full of mysterious interest to the little people. There were no railways then, and several gaily-painted barges were often to be seen moored along the Canal Wharf, supplying the city with coals, salt or pottery. However grimy their cargo might be, the owners contrived to keep fresh and bright the gay lines of colour on the sides of the little cabin at the end of the long black hull. Dr Buckland, or occasionally a good-natured bargee, would lift the children into the empty barge and allow them to peep into the snug little

[1] See 5-6, above.

abode, reeking with the savoury smell which issued from a black iron pot on its small hob...[2]

Such accounts show that already a tradition of brightly painted boats was developing, though the descriptions only adumbrate the full and luxuriant decoration described for the first time by John Hollingshead in 1858. The tradition was to continue as long as working narrow boats plied on the canals, and is even now lovingly preserved by devotees of narrow boats. After describing the traditional arrangement of the cabin Hollingshead continues his description of the boat *Stourport*:

> The boatman lavishes all his taste: all his rude, uncultivated love for the fine arts, upon the external and internal ornaments of his floating home. His chosen colours are red, yellow, and blue ... The two sides of the cabin, seen from the bank ...present a couple of landscapes, in which there is a lake, a castle, a sailing-boat, and a range of mountains, painted after the style of the great teaboard school of art. If the Stourport not match many of its companions in the freshness of its cabin decorations it can eclipse every other barge upon the canal in the brilliancy of a new two-gallon water-can, shipped from a bank-side painter's yard, at an early period of the journey. It displayed no fewer than six dazzling and fanciful composition landscapes, several gaudy wreaths of flowers, and the name of its proud proprietor, Thomas Randle, running round the centre upon a back-ground of blinding yellow.[3]

The development of such a form of boat-decoration suggests a close-knit group of people with a strong community of interest. Such a group need not, however, be bound together by family ties. Community of interest and a desire to mark off an exclusive group can erupt into fanciful forms, as with the decoration of the jackets of Hell's Angels in our own day, or the development of private languages and nicknames among railwaymen, navvies, and schoolchildren.[4] On the fly-boats, which were the express service of the canals, with boats worked round the clock by shifts of men, nicknames were used as an expression of the solidarity of the group, a group, which, by the nature of the work, consisted entirely of men. In 1822 the crews of some of Pickfords fly-boats rioted for an increase in wages, and when four of them were brought before the

Life and Correspondence of William Buckland *A Glossary of Railwaymen's Talk* *The Railway Navvies*

magistrates they excited a certain stir. The four men had been pursued by Bow Street runners from London into Warwickshire where they were taken at Ansty:

viz., - John Maxwell alias Redman, Peter Hand alias St Peter, Thomas Owens alias Stour, and William Pickering alias Shiner. The prisoners were all youths between 17 and 20 years of age, but their robust and manly appearance excited the attention of the Magistrates who could not help remarking the contrast between them and the generality of London prisoners brought before them: – They were severally asked how they came to have nicknames in addition to their real names and they said that those on the canal had *two names*, and were known by their bye-names better than their real, that their nicknames were expressive -as for instance, Pickering the 'Shiner' was originally a white-washer in Birmingham, and on commencing his present employment on the canal he was designated by the appellation of 'Shiner' from a suspicion of having been previously engaged in shining 'Tizzies, Bobs, Half-Bulls and Bulls', of the manufacture of his town.[5]

Casual labourers like Shiner seem to have drifted onto the canal to work fly-boats, but it is clear from Hollingshead's account that canal boatmen, like the bargemen, often lived in close-knit communities:

Not far from Braunston in Northamptonshire ... we came upon a small boatman's village. It was the only place we had seen on our journey where the people on the land seemed to belong to the people on the water; where everybody knew everybody, and seemed glad to see everybody, and where there was some provision made for a boatman's requirements ... This boatman's village consisted of only a few houses, all crowded round a lock and a bridge. There was a boatman's bookmaker's, from the recesses of whose workshop came a most deafening clinking of hammers closing rivets up, showing clearly the metallic character of the article produced. There was a boatman's tailor's and hosier's, with many pairs of bright blue thick worsted stockings shining through the small window ... Women were leaning over garden-rails in little front-gardens on the towing-path, talking to boatmen; while other women in barges were coming out of cabin-doorways to join in the conversation, followed by children, who appeared one after the other, as the first got out of the way of the second, and the second of the third, like the figures that come through an archway on the top of the automaton toy-clocks ... Inquiries were being made on land and water respecting journeys, families, relations, cargoes, provisions, and persons passed on the road ... Close to the lockgates, was a long low-roofed tavern, grocer's and butcher's, all in one, kept by a female relation of our commander.[6]

[5] *Morning Chronicle*, 30 July 1822.   [6] Hollingshead, op. cit. 359.

Fisher Row was to become in the 19th century the home of many canal boatmen, and the 1841 Census makes it clear that the members of the group were closely related. How did the canal boatmen come to penetrate the tight-knit community of river bargemen which had developed there in the 17th and 18th century? How closely were they related to the bargemen and fishermen of the Row, and how often did the bargemen and fishermen move from the river on to the canal? In this chapter we shall be concerned with attempting to answer these questions and with analysing the structure of their families.

II THE BOATMAN AND HIS WORK[7]

Work on a canal was very different from that on a river, and this was reflected in many aspects of the canal boatman's way of life. The canal was an artificial, planned, and controlled waterway from which delays, uncertainties, and hazards of river transport had been largely removed. Only one horse was needed to tow a boat on the still waters of a canal. Modern pound-locks were used everywhere, and these required very little water or muscle to move boats from one level to another. Delays through water shortage were therefore uncommon. On the river delays had been frequent, for flash-locks were profligate in their use of water, and since water was used for milling as well as navigation, millers and bargemen waged continual war. On the canal the water served one end only, the working of the navigation. At locks procedure was different: on the river barges assembled and went through the flash-lock together. On the canal boats went through one after the other, and there was competition in getting to the next lock ahead of other boatmen.

A canal boat required only two people to work it – one to steer and one to lead the horse and work the locks. The work did not require great strength, and a second man could be replaced by a boy or a woman. Originally canal boats, like river barges, were worked by all-male crews, but quite early, by 1820 women and families were found living on the boats and

---

[7] This account is largely based on 'Evidence of the Select Committee On Sunday Trading on canals and navigable rivers and railways', *House of Lords Journal*. LXXIII, Appendix 2, 6-50.

working them.[8] In this, of course, the canal boatmen were unlike bargemen, who invariably had homes ashore.

Two types of boat were used on the canal. The first was the 'slow' boat. These only worked during daylight hours, and often they were run by families. The 'fly-boat' we have already described as supplying an express service. To do this it travelled round the clock. It was manned by a double crew, working in shifts, and the horses were changed at intervals along the canal at boat-stations. Only carrying firms in a big way, like Pick-fords, ran fly-boats. The setting up of a fly-boat service was a complicated and expensive business: agents had to be established; horse-stations maintained, with their horse-keepers and horses. They were only introduced on busy major routes, and by the time they were developed the Grand Junction Canal was built and the Oxford Canal had little more than local importance. Only Pickfords and Crowley and Co. had agents in Oxford. They may not have run fly-boats, for there is no clear evidence that they had horse stations on the southern part of the canal. They maintained a presence, as was necessary for firms claiming to supply an extensive network of services, but perhaps little more than this.

The slow trade was therefore the important part of the trade on the Oxford Canal. Because Oxford was not an industrial centre, boats run by manufacturing companies were all but unknown. On the Oxford Canal boats were usually owned either by collieries or merchants dealing in salt, coal, corn, tiles, and the like. In the 1790s the coal-merchants Ward and Holland had 17 boats, Thomas Polley 10, and Eaton, Hopkins and Co. seven.[9] These were the largest merchants. On the whole the size of fleets decreased. In 1841 the Wards, who were the most substantial family of coal-merchants in Oxford in the 19th century had only 12 boats.

As well there were a number of boatmen who owned their own boats. These boatmen have come to be called 'Number Ones' in recent times, but the term came in late, and is probably of nautical origin. Usually canal terms are almost perversely

---

[8] Harry Hanson *The Canal Boatmen, 1760-1914* (Manchester, 1975), 53-8. The first known case of a wife on a boat on the Oxford Canal was in 1816. PRO RAIL 855/114.

[9] Warwicks. RO, CR 1590/1, Oxford Canal Letter Book 1791-1801, 310.

a-nautical, as if the boatman feared that the press-gang might be waiting at any corner for him to demonstrate some familiarity with nautical matters to seize him as a particularly likely recruit. These small men sometimes worked as subcontractors for large carrying companies, sometimes on commission, employed by coal-merchants or collieries, sometimes apparently in partnership with relatives who ran businesses as coal-mer-chants or publicans. On the Oxford Canal the number of owner-boatmen must have varied from time to time, but it was probably always comparatively high, as there was little competition from large carrying companies. When boats were first registered under the Canal Boats Act of 1877, a third of the Oxford boats were owned by independent boatmen, and Mr Harry Hanson found this to be the second highest proportion in any registration district for the years 1879-84.[10]

On all boats the responsibility of selecting and paying the crew lay with the captain of the boat. If he was an employee he would receive payment for the trip, and from this he would pay for the hiring of the crew and the cost of maintaining his own horse. Whether he was self-employed or not, the master of a boat was an employer of labour, though it might be simply that of his own family. In many ways his outlook was that of a small capitalist. His ambition was to own his own boat (if he did not already do so). Often the only time when the boatman was likely to feel himself an employee was when, as a young man, he worked for some master as a step on the way to becoming a boat-owner himself. Working on a fly-boat was the quickest way to earn enough money to buy a boat. Pay on slow boats was less. Often the young boatman worked on the family boat as mate, waiting for the boat to come his way on the death of his father. His position was somewhat like that of the son of a husbandman with a few strips, before enclosure, waiting to step into his father's shoes, often working away from home until that time might come, or hoping to 'make his fortune' and take up acres of his own. For the young boatman a period of service was a preliminary to the captaincy of a boat. When he achieved it, he felt himself to be very much his own master.

[10] Hanson, *Canal Boatmen*, 110.

The first boat in was unloaded first, and unless there were plenty of hands to unload, a boat arriving a few minutes after another might have to wait several hours until the other boat was dealt with before receiving attention. Then while the first boat set out with another load and an order for a return load, the second might have to await both. In such a situation it is not surprising that the canal boatmen were highly competitive.

The working of the canal boat was a long, slow, monotonous business. The boatman's waking hours revolved round the business of getting the boat forward, maintaining the slow movement of the boat by every means within his power. For him the day had no division of work and leisure. In the normal way waking and working were one and the same. As with most outdoor work, it was the weather that decided whether working conditions were good or bad. For the vigorous young boat-man however the life of the fly boatman was undoubtedly appealing. His shifts of work were clearly defined; he worked the best boats and the fastest horses, and if his pay was low, he had no responsibilities.

Despite the long hours of unremitting labour, the crises caused by accidents to horse or boat, and declining health and vigour at the end of a hard-working life, the older boatmen would appear to have been better off than most southern labourers in the 19th century, and their housing was often superior. Their cabins might be small, but the traditional fittings were well planned and space-saving. Because pay was by the trip and was therefore a form of payment by the piece, speed was important. The more trips a boatman could fit into the year, the better his income. Delays of all sorts cut his income, whether they were due to natural causes, delays in turning round the boats, or delays along the route.

The boatman alternated periods when the boat was on the move, and every muscle was strained to speed the boat, with periods of enforced inactivity, when the boat was at the wharf. The length of these periods of waiting were beyond the control of the boatman, and depended on the state of trade, the availability of cargoes, and on the rhythm of the working week of the men on the land.

In the Black Country the rate of work in the manufacturing districts varied over the week. Work started sluggishly on Tuesday, after the celebration of Saint Monday, and passed through a crescendo of activity to a pitch of frenzy as deadlines were met and orders fulfilled and parcelled up on the Saturday. In many collieries a similar rhythm prevailed, though it was less hectic. There were few cargoes early in the week, more later. Saturday night and Sunday, all carriers agreed, were the busiest time of the week for boatmen, as they cleared the wharves of the products of other men's labours. Like clergymen, who also work on Sunday, boatmen were usually at work when other men were at leisure, and like the clergy too, they spent their leisure thrown very much in the company of their own kind.[11]

As the boatmen's families moved onto the boats their links with the wider community became ever more tenuous, and as the social centres on the land which they patronised catered for them almost exclusively, boatmen had very few points of contact with the men beyond the banks of the canal, even in the parish which they called their own.

III. THE SOCIAL FRAMEWORK OF CANAL LIFE

Two institutions impinged on the boatman's life, and played an important part in shaping his environment. The first was the boatman's pub, and the second was the boatman's chapel. The first drew the boatmen together as a community, the second set them apart from the wider community of the parish. Both reinforced their isolation.

With the opening of the new trade, pubs were needed, for the pivot of the boatman's world was the pub. In the passage

---

[11] 'S.C. on Sunday Trading', 1841, Q. 238 and Q.1174-6. The notorious example of this type of working was that of the nail-makers, but the witnesses at the Select Committee on Sunday Trading made it clear just how general this method of working was and how widespread was the shortage of cargoes at the beginning of the week and how congested the wharves were at the end. The situation, described in Lancashire in 1842, shows the way this state of affairs arose in the collieries: The Monday after the pay is always a holiday: indeed in many collieries it is never expected that they should return to their work on that day, and I am informed by the proprietors that many of them will not settle to work before the middle of the week following the pay. In this manner the drawers are kept half employed for two days at the beginning of the reckoning (this is the Lancashire way), and towards the end of it they are worked past their strength. This has arrived at such a pitch at Mr Harrop's colliery, and the inconvenience of having the boatsmen and banks-men standing idle for two or three days ... became so intolerable that Mr Harrop devised a scheme... (PP. Eng. 1842/xv (380), *First Report of the Commissioners on Children's Employment*, 124).

already quoted from Hollingshead a boatman's pub was mentioned. It was run by a relative of the captain of the boat on which Hollingshead was travelling.[12] Such pubs were remarked by various observers of canal life, but the fullest description is to be found only in 1875, when there was much agitation to improve the working conditions (and thereby the morals) of boatmen. The account is not as deeply tinged with moral condemnation as many descriptions of boat-life of that period. This pub was probably typical:

The canal-side town 'public' is a thing to be remembered. You come on it suddenly, hiding modestly in a dark hole or corner of a dark wall. Its dirty little windows display weird and fearful compounds ... I find the grimiest of low-ceilinged tap room, a truly savage and barbaric 'tap' wherein is dispensed the thinnest and flattest beer I have ever yet come across ... Greasy wooden 'settles' and battered wooden tables furnish the apartment, and there come the 'jolly bargemen' to make merry. The walls have two distinct and clearly defined rows of black lines, indicating the presence of greasy backs and heads, and when the boatmen have mustered, 'harmony' reigns ... The ballads peculiar to boatmen possess either the humour of the not specially decorous country ditty, or the sentimentality of the Holywell-street 'lay' as retailed in fluttering tissues pinned to ragged sheeting in 'shy' corners ... The choruses are frequent and tremendous. The 'harmony' is often relieved by a little step-dancing.[13]

No such vivid account of the Oxford boatmen's pubs in their heyday has been found. Yet, vivid as this account is, it is all eyes and ears, and lacks any sense of context. The boat-man's pub was not only a social centre, it had an important part in the web of transport and commerce. Here goods were left, horses stabled, messages collected. The pub-keeper himself might double as agent to carriers or coal-merchants, or be a coal-merchant himself.[14] To the boatman he might act as post

---

[12] See above, p. 201.

[13] *Birmingham Mail*, 5 Mar. 1875, quoted in George Smith, *Our Canal Population* (new edn., London, n.d.), 77.

[14] We have no hard evidence of pub-keepers as agents in Oxford itself, but with the coming of the railways we have evidence of how naturally coal-merchants turned to pubs as agencies. When the Buckinghamshire Railway station first opened in Oxford in 1851, new coal-merchants established themselves dealing in railway coal, and in their advertisements they informed the public that orders could be left at various public houses. J. and J. Watson received orders through the Lamb and Flag in St Gile's, the Civet Kitten in Cornmarket Street, and J.J. Faulkner's Temperance Hotel as well as the New Coal Wharf at Botley Station. (*JOJ*, Sept. 1851). Charles Beesley received orders at the King's Arms, Summertown or the station (ibid., Sept., 1851). John Smith at the Plough Inn,

office, bank, pawnbroker, employment exchange, employer, or
tommy-master. The position of a pub by a wharf could be
ambiguous: centre of social life and source of exploitation.
Where the landlord was also an employer, as he might well
be if he were also a coal-merchant, part of the wages were
usually paid in drink. This was very common amongst the
coal-whippers on the Thames, as Henry Mayhew showed so
vividly in the *Morning Chronicle* and *London Labour and
the Poor.* Thus Lawrence Levi in 1830 described himself as
a 'constant man', one who drank regularly at a pub where the
landlord acted as an agent, supplying labour to unload the
Tyneside colliers.[15] On some canals and rivers boatmen also
needed to be 'constant men':

It is a common thing for the keeper of a public house to combine with his business of publican that of a broker for canal boats and other river craft, with the
result that the waterman who can empty the greatest number of pint pots down
his throat in a given time, or who is the most successful in running up a score at
the broker's swipe shop, is also the most successful in obtaining a remunerative
cargo; and it sometimes happens that if the broker is not a publican himself, he
is in league with someone else who is...[16]

The larger the employer, the more remote the connection of
employees and employers, the more likely the relation was to
be exploitative.[17] In a period where cash was in short supply,

St Aldate's, the Horse and Jockey, St Giles, the Vine Inn in the High Street or the Royal
Oak in St Clement's (ibid., Sept. 1851). Just as the railways had taken over the word wharf
to describe coal depots on waterless sites, so it seems they probably took over from the
canals the use of pubs as agencies, as they did many other aspects of the early organisation of the trade.

[15] PP. Eng. 1830/viii (380), *Report of the Select Committee on the State of the Coal
Trade*, 187-8.

[16] PP. Eng. 1892/xxxvi, pt. ii (C.6795-v), *Royal Commission on Labour, Minutes of
Evidence: Group B*, 289.

[17] It was always difficult for Select Committees to find evidence of truck in its most
pernicious forms, as witnesses feared for their jobs. There is no doubt that in the Black
Country it was found on some canal routes. The evidence is of a sort which evades retri-
bution: a nickname and a ballad. At Pelsall there is a canal bridge still known as Tommy
Shop Bridge (Tom Langley, *The Tipton Slasher: his Life and Times* (Halesowen, n.d.,
11). The bitter ballad, from which two verses are quoted, deals with the trade from High-
fields, Bilston, to Runcorn at the mouth of the Mersey:

The boatsmen now I bring in,
That sails from high fields to runcan;
The boatsmen and their wives,
They curse him at the junction (i.e. 'the high field devil').

and in an economy in which barter and the doing of favours and services was a sort of commerce, it is often difficult to say where truck began and ended.[18] If the boatman's wages might be partly paid in drink, the publican might also be paid in goods by the boatmen or accept payment in kind: 'Further back ... hung sets of second-hand clothing, announcing the fact that you might pay for your beer in other things than money, as many others had done...'[19] Where the publican was related by marriage to the boatmen, and had perhaps been a boatman himself at some time of his life, it seems likely that some degree of payment in kind went on, but in such a situation it was not felt to be exploitative. This was probably the situation in Oxford.

Whatever the pub's economic functions might be, we must not stress them to such an extent that we overlook its social function. In the pub the rivalries of the cut were forgotten, and friendship ruled. The pub drew the community together. Perhaps no more vivid testimony to this is found than in the custom observed amongst boatmen at Braunston, the junction of the Oxford and Grand Junction Canal. Though it was noted in the 20th century, it was probably an old custom rather than new:

The hospitable custom of the place was that when any one came in, lest he should be kept an instant waiting for refreshment, someone handed him

And all belonging to the branch
That know the art of boating
Wish the tiller down his throat,
It would be a means to joke him.
    Fal de ridle ral, etc.
When they had done their runcan voyage
And go to receive their money
One half stops for hay and corn
The other half for Tommy.
Then to the tommy shops we go,
To fetch our weeks provision,
Their oatmeal, sugar, salt and soap,
Short weight and little measure.
    Fal de ridle ral, etc.

'The Tommy Note', printed by T. Bloomer (fl. 1800-40) and reprinted in Michael and Jon Raven, *Folklore and Songs of the Black Country* (Wolverhampton, 1965), 53.

[18] The extent to which a village economy could manage with little money changing hands is beautifully described in Raphael Samuel's 'Quarry Roughs' in Raphael Samuel, ed., *Village Life and Labour* (London, 1975), 141-263.

[19] Mark Guy Pearse, *Rob Rat – a Story of Barge Life* (London, 1878), 29.

a mug from which to take a draught. This was always offered and always accepted. Then when the new-comer's beer arrived, before taking it, he brought it to whoever had been his host, and punctiliously paid off his score.[20]

Table 5.1.   The landlords of the boatmen's pubs of the Row – *c.*1797–1903.

The Nag's Head	The Running Horses	Source
c. 1797 William Beesley ('The Fishes')	–	*Universal British Directory*
1823–4 Thomas Farmer = Rachel Latham d/o Francis Latham keeper of The Turk's Head, St. Thomas's Parish	Christopher Collier = Ann g.d/o Wm. Beesley ('Racers')	*London & Provincial New Pigot's Directory for 1823–4*
1830 do.	Caroline Howkins, sis./o C. Collier ('Race Horses')	*Pigot's Directory, 1830*
1824 Edward Thomas Cox	William Fisher 2nd husband of C. Howkins	*Pigot's Directory, 1842*
1847 do.	William Howkins s/o C. Howkins	*Kelly's Post Office Directory, 1847*
1854 John Redman = Mary Ashley (1838)	do.	*Kelly's Post Office Directory, 1854*
1863 Samuel Spindler great nephew of Wm. Beesley	do.	*Dutton, Allen and Co., 1863*
1883 T. H. Spindler s/o S. Spindler	Thomas Albert Cook	*Kelly's Post Office Directory, 1883*
1903 John Howkins (several of this name—not possible to identify individually— see Howkins family tree	Alfred Henry Phillips	*Kelly's Post Office Directory, 1903*

For the boatman whose home was elsewhere, the pub provided, almost literally, a 'home from home', for the pub-keeper's families were often spread along the banks of the canal. For the Oxford boatman, his host would often be known from childhood, and often a relation.

By far the most important of the canal pubs in Oxford were the Nag's Head at the top of Middle Fisher Row, and The

---

[20] Edmund Vale, *By Shank and by Crank* (Edinburgh and London, 1924), 238-9. Women did not participate in this ritual. 'more than once a woman from the barges came in ... took her ale a little apart from the men and without the customary dole, and went out again'.

Running Horses at the bottom of Upper Fisher Row. Probably they replaced 17th- and 18th-century alehouses which had stood on their sites, or near them, serving the barge trade, but almost nothing is known of them. So far as we can tell, the Nag's Head (formerly the Fishes) was older than the Running Horses. Throughout the 19th century either one or both pubs was run by families which were intimately related to the families of the canal community (see Table 5.1). In this survey of the boatman's environment we shall not do more than mention them; for, we shall return to them shortly. Here we shall describe briefly other lesser pubs.

One of the most interesting of these was The Packet. This pub had town connections which the others lacked. It was situated in George Lane on the north side of the road, not far from the entrance to the canal basin. It is possible that it was on the site of the present pub known as the Welsh Pony. Owned by Hall's Brewery, it was in the hands of Ann Luker in 1830.[21] Ann's husband was presumably the original of 'Filthy Lucre', known to readers of Cuthbert Bede's *The Adventures of Mr Verdant Green* as a pub-keeper patronised by undergraduates with a taste for the Fancy, and given to such sports as ratting. Dogs for this sport, according to Cuthbert Bede, were bought from boatmen. Presumably they were Staffordshire terriers imported from the Black Country where this sport was popular. At that time, it would seem The Packet provided some sort of frontier post between the boatmen and those undergraduates who had a relish for a 'Tom and Jerry' existence, and fought a sort of running battle with the Proctors. By 1887 it was leased to Edward Beauchamp, probably one of the Eynsham family of boatmen.[22] Another Beauchamp had kept a beer-house in Hythe Bridge Street in the 1840s: in the Census of 1841 John Beauchamp was mentioned, and again in 1848 he appeared in the Police Report Book as having a beer-house open after midnight.[23]

---

[21] *Oxon.* RO., MS DD Pprs. Hall's Brewery c. 29, 25 Nov. 1850 (Lease, Trustees of William Hall's will to Ann Luker).

[22] Ibid., 4 July 1887 (Alexander William Hall to Edward Beauchamp).

[23] MS Top Oxon. b. 145, Police Report Book, from 8 Aug. 1848, fos. 68, 81, 17-18 Apr. and 29-30 May 1849.

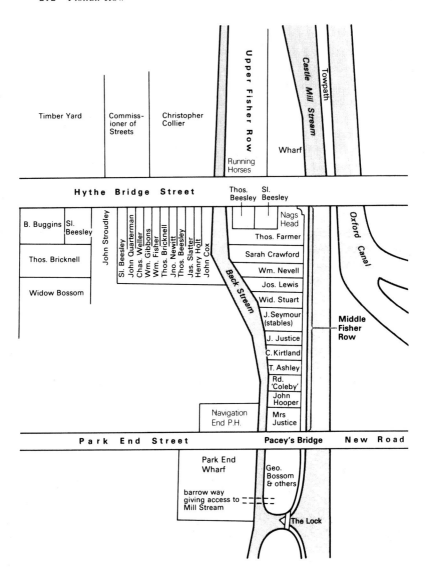

Fig. 5.1.   Diagrammatic Plan of Middle Fisher Row and Hythe Bridge Street in 1829 (based on Benjamin Badcock's Survey. See *Oseney*, II, pp. 603, 618, 620-2).

The Navigation End stood at the foot of Middle Fisher Row, at the side of Pacey's Bridge, on the corner of Park End Street. James Pacey, the landlord, was said by the Census of 1841 to be a coal-merchant. It seems likely that his pub served the Park End Wharf (see Fig. 5.1). This small wharf was used by new boatmen carrying coal from the Park End Colliery in the Forest of Dean, by way of canals leading into the Thames from the west. The landlord had a connection with coal merchants and boatmen. By 1849 the pub was in the hands of David Hickman who had married Martha Pacey, daughter of the former landlord. At this time there was a boatman called William Ashley Hickman who may have been related already to both families. In 1829 Thomas Ashley the coal-merchant had a yard in Park End Street,[24] and Edward Ashley, a boatman, and a witness at William Ashley Hickman's marriage, was also presumably a relative.[25] Such a connection of boatmen, coal-merchant and pub-keeper was typical, and we shall see it on a larger scale with the two major pubs of the Row.

The extent of the canal boatman's community can be plotted from the position of its pubs, for wherever there was a canal boatman's pub there, one may be sure, were boatmen's houses. Thus the Running Horses lay at the foot of Upper Fisher Row, and up the Row northwards stretched the houses of boatmen intermingled with those of bargemen and fishermen. At the top of Middle Fisher Row stood the Nag's Head, and boatmen's families lived down the Row from it. In the newly-built tenements of Hythe Bridge Street, more boatmen lived near the beer-shops of John Beauchamp and Thomas Brown. At Pacey's Bridge, near the Park End Company's Wharf, boatmen connected with the river trade were to be found especially at the south end of Middle Fisher Row, and the north end of Lower Fisher Row. Then again, in St Mary Magdalen Parish, at the foot of George Street, and in George Street Mews, near the entrance to the canal basin and close to the George and Dragon there lived a few more boatmen.

The canal boatman's pub sprang up naturally as a response to needs felt within the community; the boatman's chapel was provided from without, in response to needs which were not

---

[24] *Oseney*, II. 617.
[25] St Thomas Marriage Register, 13 Jan. 1831.

at all obvious to the boatmen themselves. The boatmen in Oxford were as assiduously baptised, married, and buried as any other members of the parish, and, if otherwise they seldom went to church, they were not alone in this. Missions sprang up as canal boatmen became a clearly identifiable occupation group. Some of the missionary activity sprang from a genuine concern for the spiritual and educational welfare of the families, some from a feeling of guilt that boatmen should, by the nature of their work, be forced to labour on the Sabbath, and that the comfort of the community was supported by men who were becoming ever more estranged from the church, as if the comfort of the majority depended on the damnation of a minority. Others saw missions as having a sort of antiseptic effect against moral contagion – the metaphor gained hideously in its overtones after 1832, with the first appearance of cholera in the Midlands – cholera which was undoubtedly sometimes canal borne:[26]

Those foul reeking waters, which bear along the huge masses of coal and ironstone through all parts of the country – navigated by one of the most neglected, and, I fear, abandoned classes of our fellow subjects – are forcibly associated in our minds with that current of dark pollution, which, issuing from this district year after year, circulates its baneful influence throughout the mass of community.[27]

The Boatman's Chapel was itself a recognition by the community that the boatmen were 'a race apart'. The chapel was one of many founded about this time, 1839, and it will be worth our while to consider the various strands of belief and aspiration from which it seems to have developed, for this was a period of religious and social ferment.

Some work for boatmen seems to have started in the Birmingham area about 1824, where a Mr Beazley and a Mr Lord were active, and where a Mrs Edmonds or Edwards ran a Sunday School for boatmen's children at the Crescent and Aston Locks. A somewhat incoherent account of this activity may be made out in the ramblings of George Charles Smith, 'a strange, paranoid itinerant Baptist preacher, who played an important part in the foundation of missions to seamen which

[26] *Berrow's Worcester Journal*, 28 Jun. 1832, 18 July 1832, 27 July 1832.

[27] William F. Vance, *Sermons: with a Voice from the Mines and furnaces* (Wolverhampton, 1853), xvi-xvii.

developed in the aftermath of the Napoleonic Wars.[28] This Birmingham mission seems to have been run by nonconformists. The evangelical Naval and Military Bible Society, which was run by both dissenters and members of the Church of England, and was concerned in part with the welfare of discharged sailors, also showed a sporadic interest in boatmen from 1825.[29] The Paddington Boatmen's Chapel was founded in 1828 by Captains Gambier and Elliot, two well-born young naval officers who sprang from this particular background. These men were deeply influenced by Edward Irving, the magnetic minister of the Scottish Church in Regent's Square, who was later hounded from the church as a heretic and founded the Catholic Apostolic Church. The activities of the group can be followed through the pages of the *Canal Boatmen's Magazine*, and also through George Charles Smith's *New Sailor and Soldier's Magazine*. In addition, these canal missionaries espoused Sabbath Day Observance, took some interest in abstention, and also in the protection of animals. It was in Smith's *New Sailors Magazine* that the idea of a floating chapel for the bargemen of the upper Thames was first put forward in a letter of April 1828, written by Samuel Hopkins, the Oxford nonconformist coal-merchant, of Friars Wharf in St Ebbes.[30] However, nothing came of the letter. Possibly Hopkins continued actively to promote the welfare of boatmen, for St Ebbes was the only parish in Oxford which sent petitions to the House of Lords in favour of preventing Sunday working on canals during the next decade.[31] Sunday working on canals by both fly-boats and narrow boats had increased on canals in the 1830s, as the canal interests sought to speed transport in face of the threat of railway competition. Boatmen had become, in the eyes of the boatmen's missionaries, 'British

---

[28] *DNB*, George Charles Smith; George Charles Smith, *Birmingham; or No Preaching: being a narrative and correspondence respecting the proceedings of various persons in Birmingham to the British and Foreign Seamen's and Soldiers' Friend Society* (London, 1828), 17-18.

[29] *Reports of the Proceedings of the Naval and Military Bible Society*, (1827), 34; (1828), 33, 43; (1829), 31, 33-4, 40; (1830), 32; (1831), 38-9. The sale of Bibles and Testaments had now started to fall away.

[30] *The New Sailors' Magazine* (June 1828), 248. Under various names this magazine ran from 1828 to 1861.

[31] The petition from St Ebbe's for the better observance of the Sabbath, *The Journal of the House of Lords*, LXIX (1837), 311.

slaves', who 'toil and work, day and night, week and Sundays – for what? to enrich their masters.'[32] If Hopkins was one of the instigators of such a petition, another was probably Henry Bulteel; H. B. Bulteel was one of the small group of under-graduates who pioneered the sport of rowing in Oxford, about 1817. He became a fellow of Exeter, and, in 1826 curate of St Ebbes. Here he became a popular preacher of outspoken and alarming opinions. He had his licence withdrawn by the bishop in 1831, and became an Irvingite in 1832. He had his own chapel in St Ebbes where he had a popular following.[33] The Bulteel Controversy was a curtain raiser to the drama of the Oxford Movement. Hard on the heels of the Bulteel Controversy came Newman's *Tracts for the Times*. We do not know whether Henry Ward and his son William, the founders of the Boatmen's Floating Chapel, were initially high or low church. When the chapel was consecrated by the Bishop of Oxford, Henry Ward's letter was business-like rather than informative. There are no clues either in the architecture of the chapel, which was described as being in the 'Egyptian style'.[34] There is no trace here of the Gothic so beloved by the Tractarians, but this may be because it was built too soon. Its architect, John Macduff Derick was an early convert both to Tractarianism, and to Oxford Gothic. Three years later he was to build St Saviour's Church, Leeds, whose vicar was none other than Dr Pusey himself, and the church was intended to be a 'monument of renewed Anglican faith'. As for the Ward family, they were themselves to prove staunch supporters of Anglo-Catholicism, giving land by the canal near their wharf for the building of St Barnabas's.[35] But that lay in the future.

At the time that the Floating Chapel was built, the parish of St Thomas was enjoying the longest pastorate that it had experienced since the days of Robert Burton. It had usually

---

[32] See for example, 'The Fly-boatmen', *The Canal Boatman's Magazine*, New Series, III (183 2), 15-17.

[33] *DNB*, Henry Bulteel; W. E. Sherwood, *Oxford Rowing* (Oxford, 1900), 8.

[34] MS O.D.P. c. 2171 (9) and (11); MS O.D.P. c. 436 468-75; *JOJ*, 8 June 1839, 11 Jan. 1840.

[35] Nikolaus Pevsner, *The Buildings of England: Yorkshire and the West Riding* (Harmondsworth, 1959), 326; Arthur Tilney Bassett, *S. Barnabas' Oxford* (London, 1919), 12.

passed rapidly from one perpetual curate to another, many staying no more than a year. John Jones, however, was the incumbent for nearly 20 years. Though his interest lay in Welsh poetry and orthography – his bardic name was *Tegid* – he seems to have been a popular and conscientious clergyman, repairing the church, and founding a small school in the parish. In his time the church was well attended. There is no sign that he had any interest in Tractarianism. Nor had such early admirers of the chapel as the Church Pastoral Aid Society, who held it up for the emulation of clergy faced with the problems of expanding populations in industrial areas, for which the Church's provisions were inadequate.[36]

In July 1837 the new wedding registers were introduced, with printed forms. John Jones wrote in his a few lines of Welsh verse, which may be translated thus: 'Ah, who will be alive when this register is complete? Who will be the last one? There are many leaves and they will not be filled by me.'[37] John Jones made his last entry on 28 November 1841, and Thomas Chamberlain, his successor, made his first marriage entry the following May. He was to be the incumbent of the parish for 50 years. If there is doubt about the doctrinal position of John Jones there were no doubts at all about Thomas Chamberlain. He was one of the most ardent Tractarians in Oxford, and he made St Thomas's a centre for High Church worshippers. Under Chamberlain, as under John Jones, the Boatmen's Chapel was in the hands of a chaplain. In 1839, the year of its foundation, six marriages of boatmen took place, but over the decade as a whole the average number was 3.1. As the local boatmen had always, apparently, been married in church and had their children baptised regularly, it seems unlikely that the establishment of the floating chapel altered matters. In the past this aspect of the work of the parish had been conscientiously carried out, and so it continued.

When, in his peregrinations, George Charles Smith visited Oxford and viewed the chapel, he crystallised into the experience of a day something of the feverish pressures that were at

---

[36] DNB, John Jones; T. W. Squires, *In West Oxford*, 15; *Church Pastoral-aid Society Report* (1939), Appendix, 47.

[37] I am grateful to Mr F. J. King, formerly of the Bodleian Library, for translating these lines for me, and to Dr D. M. Barratt for asking him to do so.

work in the city and parish, and reflected on them in his own idiosyncratic fashion:

Friday took the stage for Oxford ... Walked out and went through the colleges of the university, distributing papers. A most shocking set are some of those dissipated youths at college, training up for the bottomless pit. What a prospect for the next generation! They have almost destroyed the Temperance Society here. Met Mr Ellis, our former agent ... Visited with him the boatmen and gave books; walked with him down to the boatmen's chapel ... Called on Mr Ward, the gentleman who has built it. Called at the Rev. Mr Bulteel's: conversed with Mrs B about the terrible influence of Dr Pusey's self-righteous semi-popery heresy, that is making such fatal progress in the university. Oh! how hard Satan works.[38]

IV. THE FORMATION OF THE CANAL COMMUNITY

When the Oxford Canal was first open and the long, narrow, unfamiliar boats came down to the Oxford Wharf, they were crewed by an assortment of men who came from all over the place. Some came from the Black Country, some from the collieries round Coventry, some brought salt from Shirleywich, some china from the Potteries. Some brought agricultural produce from near at hand. Some of these men were veterans of the Midland canals which had 20 years' start on the Oxford Canal, and some were raw recruits from the countryside through which the canal passed. Some must have come from Oxford itself, some perhaps even from the river, though this seems unlikely at this stage, for with the increased trade to London brought by the canal there was plenty of work here at first. But where they came from, or however disparate their origins, they developed into a distinctive group with their own customs. Some of these boatmen were to settle in the Row, and by the Census of 1841 had transformed it into a canal community, though it still contained a few bargemen, and an important group of fishermen. How the boatmen were able to infiltrate the close-knit community which already existed is the first question to which we must turn our attention.

The material on which to base an answer to this question is not very promising apart from the parish registers. We have a list of the occupants of Middle Fisher Row in 1802, and a survey of the occupants of Lower and Middle Fisher Row in 1829. We also have a survey of the occupants of Hythe Bridge

[38] *New Sailors' Magazine* (1839), 229.

Street, where some canal boatmen also lived, and the Boat and
Barge Register compiled under the Act 35 Geo. III c.58. Each
county made its own register, and although that for Oxfordshire is lost, those for Warwickshire and Staffordshire will
prove useful when we consider immigrants.

Table 5.2. Comparison of the number of boat and bargemen in St Thomas's
Baptismal Register, 1813-23.

	Bargemen	Boatmen
1813	12 (both groups aggregated)	
1814	5	6
1815	1	7
1816	4	4
1817	2	5
1818	4	4
1819	2	8
1820	1	2
1821	1	6
1822	0	6
1823	1	10

But first we may use the parish register of baptisms to construct a list of boatmen's families, as these give the father's
occupation from 1813. There are, however, problems about using
this register. On the whole the parish registers are excellent in
this period, as befits a college living. But when occupations
were first given in 1813, the clerk did not distinguish between
canal boatmen and river bargemen, calling them 'boatmen'
indiscriminately. This was a serious omission. The number of
bargemen was declining fast, partly because the trade of the
Thames was now ebbing away, partly perhaps because canal
boats were already moving out on to the river and goods were
no longer being trans-shipped into barges to make the trip down
the Thames. In the period 1814 to 1818, though the number
of bargemen never exceeded the number of boatmen, numbers
were equal in two years: after this they declined steadily (see
Table 5.2). In 1813 it seems probable that the chances of a man
being a canal boatman or a river bargeman were about equal,
and it is even conceivable that there were more bargemen than
boatmen, for we do not know just when the shift from a pre-
ponderance of bargemen to one of boatmen occurred.

This failure to make a distinction in the parish register of 1813 means we must handle our early material with caution. Nevertheless, it will be worth while to reconstruct the boatmen's families backwards as well as forwards from 1813, being particularly careful with any family whose occupation has been attributed to it on the basis of an entry in the 1813 register (see Table 5.3). This affects the first couple on the list, John and Elizabeth Bossom, whose children were born between 1791 and 1816. In 1813 John was said to be a 'boatman', but by 1816 when their last child was born, he had become a fisherman. In the difficult and uneasy years in which England came to terms with returning peace and poverty, men often moved from one job to another, adding to our problems. The names on our listing which raise doubts are, on the fact of it, 1-4 and 6: Bossom (1), Gibbons (2), Hooper (3), Ashley (4), and Justice (6). The Bossoms were almost certainly bargemen and came of a family of the same type as the Beesleys. The surname Gibbons was known on the river at this time, though later it represented an important dynasty of canal boatmen of which, they were the forebears (see Gibbons Family Tree 6.5). The Hoopers were a major 18th-century dynasty at Folly Bridge, which lingered into the 19th century in diminished numbers, whilst the name Justice has been found on the river in the 18th century, but was never prominent. For the Ashleys we have independent evidence that the family was on the canal, for they were baptising children both in Oxford and Birmingham, and probably came from Warwickshire.[39]

Yet one finds some very solid 19th-century families established before 1812, often with local connections. Those who commenced in the next few years were less fortunate, for the years after the Napoleonic Wars were difficult and unsettled. Of five boatmen's families who baptised their first babies in 1813 only one had children's baptisms spanning even four years (14). Until about 1821 evidence of hard times stares out from the registers. An attempt has been made to exhibit this in the italicised comments of Table 5.3. Again, from 1819, some large, stable families established themselves and by the mid-'20s the second generation of families such as the

---

[39] Information from Mr W. G. Bowen who is working on this family tree.

Table 5.3.   The incidence of Canal Boatmen in St Thomas's Parish, according to the Baptismal Register, up to 1829.

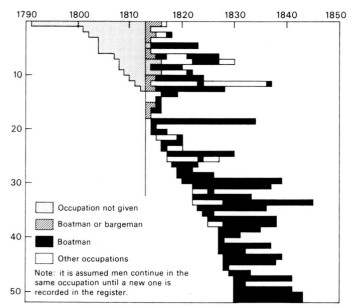

Key: 1. John & Eliz. Bossom *1816 fisherman.*   2. Saml. & Mary Gibbons (Smith). 3. John & Eliz. Hooper *1815 linen dealer, 1816 bargeman.* 4. Jos. & Phoebe Ashley. 5. Wm. & Maria Fisher (Beesley).   6. John & Ann Justice.   7. Thos. & Mary Bricknell (Bossom) *1817 waterman, 1818 bargeman.*   8. Thos. & Hannah Hands *1816, 1827, 1829 fisherman.*   9. Jos. & Christian Shepherd. 10. Edward & Ann Higgins *1816 labourer, 1821 in Workhouse.*   11. Rd. & Mary Edwards (Beesley).   12. Jas. & Jane Preedy (Bridgewater)*bargeman in 7 out of 10 entries.*   13. Wm. & Mary Dix (Stewart).   14. John & Elinor Burnham *1813 soldier, 1815 bargeman.*   15. Wm. & Mary Radbourne *1813 labourer.* 16. Jos. & Ann Barfoot.   17. Thos. & Eliz. Cordingley (Collis). 18. Wm. & Ann Marshall.   19. Ab. & Mary Ann Darby (Ashley). 20. Wm. & Sarah Ford (Matthews).   21. Ralph & Esther or Alice Higgins. 22. Thos. & Eliz. Hooper *1815 soldier, transported 1820.*   23. John & Hannah Price.   24. Chas. & Avis Streak *1816 in workhouse, 1819 labourer.* 25. Jos. & Jane Lewis (Beesley).   26. Wm. & Anne Spindler (Beesley) *boatman only 1823, otherwise bargeman.*   27. Isaac & Margaret Westwood. 28. John & Anne Higginson *1821 Anne died.*   29. Wm. & Caroline Howkins (Collier) *1826 Wm. died.*   30. John & Sarah Howkins (formerly Ashley). 31. John & Ann Paish.   32. Wm. & Mary Bishop *1822 fisherman.*   33. John & Sarah Matthews (Hands).   34. Robt. & Mary Leverett (Mires) *1822 labourer.* 35. Jos. & Anne Cooper (Leverett).   36. Jos. & Lydia Ashley.   37. Chas. & Mary Bull.   38. Wm. & Eliz. Fisher (Collis) *1825 labourer.*   39. Wm. & Eliz. Bossom (Mailing).   40. Chas. & Margaret Alder.   41. Jas. & Louisa Grant. 42. Jos. & Susannah Watson.   43. Rd. & Eliz. Basson.   44. Jos. & Sarah Clements. 45. Thos. & Mary Ashley.   46. Sl. & Mary Lewis (Curtis) *1831 Sl. died.* 47. Geo. & Mary Ashley (Hooper).   48. Ed. & Mary Anne Ashley (Beesley). 49. Fredk. & Michel Collier *1830 Michel died.*   50. Wm. & Martha Gibbons. 51. John & Sophia Seymour (Gibbons).   52. Thos. & Edith Taylor.

Gibbons (2 and 52) and the Fishers (5 and 40) had become well settled.

Whilst all these families would have regarded themselves as belonging to the parish of St Thomas, this did not necessarily mean that they had homes ashore. By the 1820s many families on the canals were living on board their boats, and in 1841, the coal-merchant William Ward estimated only two out of 12 of his boatmen had homes 'on the land'.[40]

How many families of boatmen infiltrated Fisher Row, and what were their particular characteristics? In 1829 Benjamin Badcock made a Survey for Christ Church of its property in St Thomas's parish, and this included part of Lower Fisher Row, the whole of Middle Fisher Row, and Hythe Bridge Street.[41] It will prove useful in our investigation (see Fig. 5.1). We shall omit Lower Fisher Row, for, apart from the presence of several members of the Bossom family, fishermen and bargemen living as subtenants in the first tenement, it no longer offers much of interest. We shall concentrate our attention on Middle Fisher Row, and the southern side of Hythe Bridge Street, where an overflow population of boatmen lived. We shall compare the surnames on this list with the list we have constructed of boatmen of the parish, and we shall also use a listing of the inhabitants of the Row made in 1802 to show which were the longest established families in Middle Fisher Row.[42] Unfortunately we have no similar listing for Hythe Bridge Street. The Survey includes 14 dwellings in the Row and a stable, and 12 in Hythe Bridge Street. In Hythe Bridge Street only four boatmen's surnames are repeated, but in Middle Fisher Row there are 11 repetitions (see Table 5.4).

What can we learn from this comparison? There seem to be four lessons. Firstly, that the older-established a boatman's family was, the more likely it was to have become accepted: for all the first seven families of boatmen had managed to gain a footing in Middle Fisher Row or Hythe Bridge Street. This eminently reasonable deduction must, however, be strongly modified, for four of these seven families could well be barging families in origin, and, therefore, much more likely to be

[40] S.C. on Sunday Trading', Q. 865.
[41] *Oseney*, II. 602-3, 621-2.
[42] *JOJ*, 9 Oct. 1802.

Table 5.4.   The assimilation of boatmen into Middle Fisher Row and Hythe
Bridge Street.

Order of appearance in baptismal register and time span	Order of appearance in parish register, and name	Surname of occupant of M.F.R. or H.Br.St. in *Badcock's Survey, 1829*	No. of appearances
?1. 1791–1816	John and Eliz. *Bossom* *	Bossom	1
?2. 1801–13	Saml. and Mary *Gibbons* (née Smith)	Gibbons	1
?3. 1802–18	John and Eliz. *Hooper*	Hooper	1
4. 1804–13	Joseph and Phoebe *Ashley*	Ashley	1
5. 1804–22	Wm. and Maria Fisher (née *Beesley*)	Beesley*	3
	Wm. and Maria *Fisher* (née Beesley)	Fisher*	1
?6. 1804–13	John and Ann *Justice*	Justice	2
7. 1807–26	Thomas and Mary *Bricknell* (née Bossom)	Bricknell	1
13. 1812–27	William and Mary Dix (née *Stuart*)	Stewart*	1
25. 1817–29	Joseph and Jane *Lewis* (née Beesley)	Lewis	1
51. 1829–42	John and Sophia *Seymour* (née *Gibbons*)	Seymour (stable only)	1
	Stephen and Mary Ann Judd† (née *Neville*)	Neville*	1

* Surname present in the list of occupants appearing in an auction advertisement of William Beesley's property, *JOJ*, 8 Oct. 1802.

Italicisation of names indicates the surname of the spouse which was connected with the Row in 1829.

† Only said to be a boatman after the birth of his children (as parent in 1843 marriage register, and 1851 Census.

regarded with some favour. Indeed, even if some of the barging families were not particularly closely linked with the inhabitants of Middle Fisher Row, in the face of invasion by totally foreign boatmen from outside Oxford, any differences might be forgotten as they closed ranks. This is our second lesson. The third is that families which lived near the canal were, sooner or later, likely to become related to the newcomers, through the marriage of their daughters. So we find four names which had survived from Middle Fisher Row in 1802 linked by marriage with canal boatmen (Beesley, Fisher, Stewart, and Neville). The earliest of these marriages was of Maria, daughter of William Beesley of the Fishes, the pub at the top of the Row, to the boatman, William Fisher (see Family Tree, 5.1). It occurred during her father's lifetime, and was to be followed by later marriages between her sisters and other boatmen, as we shall see shortly. Fourthly and finally, we can see how newcomers gained a footing in the area by marrying a bargeman's or boatman's daughter (Bossom, Beesley, Gibbons). This is a situation we shall see repeated. It was the women who gave stability to this community.

Table 5.5. Immigration into St Thomas's Parish by Staffordshire and Warwickshire boatmen.

1795 S. and W. Registers		1813–29 Parish Register of St. Thomas—Boatmen
Captain	Owner	
Darby, Abraham of Tipton	Thomas Bailey of Sedgeley	Abraham and Mary Ann Darby (née Ashley)
Edwards, Richard		Richard and Mary Edwards (d/o William Beesley of the Fishes, later Nag's Head)
Fisher, Thomas of —	Rd. Whitehouse of —	William and Maria Fisher (d/o William Beesley of the Fishes, later Nag's Head)
Lewis, Richard of Stoke	Sampson Neville of Stoke	Joseph and Jane Lewis (d/o William Beesley of the Fishes, later Nag's Head)
Price, Thomas of Shirleywich	Charles Moore of Shirleywich	John and Hannah Price (née Ioins); William of St. Giles—a boatman? and Rachel Price (d/o Thomas Farmer of the Nag's Head)

Marriage was also an important factor in deciding which of the families from Warwickshire and Staffordshire settled in Oxford. We can identify some of these immigrants by comparing the names on our list of boatmen, 1813-29, with the Warwickshire and Staffordshire Registers of 1795 for boatmen on the Oxford run (see Table 5.5). The names common to both lists will not provide an exhaustive list of immigrants, for some families like the Ashleys came down the canal later. Nor will it show families which started as boatmen in 1795, but later moved into some other occupation connected with the canal. The Rounds, for instance became coal-merchants, and the Farmers succeeded the Beesleys as landlords of the Nag's Head. And, of course, it does not contain childless or unmarried men. We can only link boatmen who remained boatmen between 1795 and 1813-29.

Only five names are common to both listings, and it can be seen from a glance that four of the five surnames exhibit a common characteristic. The boatmen bearing these names and settled in the parish had some sort of connection by marriage with the landlord of the Nag's Head. In three cases it is clear and close, for three immigrants married daughters of William Beesley (see Family Tree 5.1). The connection of the Price Family with the Nag's Head is less direct and more uncertain. It is not with the Beesley family, but with the Beesleys' successors, the Farmers. Thomas Farmer of the Nag's Head was certainly connected with boating people for his own son Robert was a boatman.

What made the Nag's Head the focal point for the immigrants? The canal pub was a social centre for all boatmen, but the method of trade on the canal also made such marriages likely. William Beesley, its landlord in the 1790s, had been a wharfinger and bargemaster as well as a pub-keeper, and it will be remembered that he had been prominent in an attempt to organise the trade from the canal on to the river. In this he was fulfilling one common function of the pub-keeper, and on the canal, as on the river, trade and marriage frequently ran together.

The Boat Inn at Oldbury near Tipton and Smethwick seems to have fulfilled a similar function for Oxford boatmen at the northern end of their run. In 1828/9 *Pigot's Directory* listed it as acting for such agents as Whitehouses and Pickfords. Its landlord was William Fisher. In 1826 an incident occurred which takes us into the very bar of this pub and introduces us to its customers.

In January 1836 a boatman called Joseph Simpson went to The Boat at Oldbury at about five o'clock one evening. He had in his pocket two five-pound notes, drawn on Dudley Old Bank. One of these he changed with the landlady for four pounds in notes and 20 shillings in silver, and while he was asleep the money was taken from his pocket. In court, evidence was given by Jane, the wife of William Fisher, the

Family Tree 5.1.   The Beesley Family of St Thomas's, Part 1.

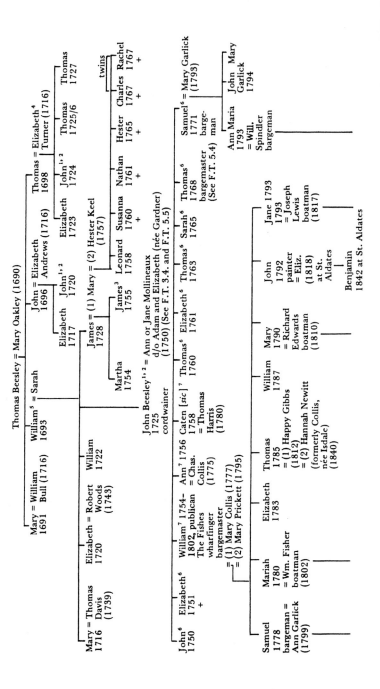

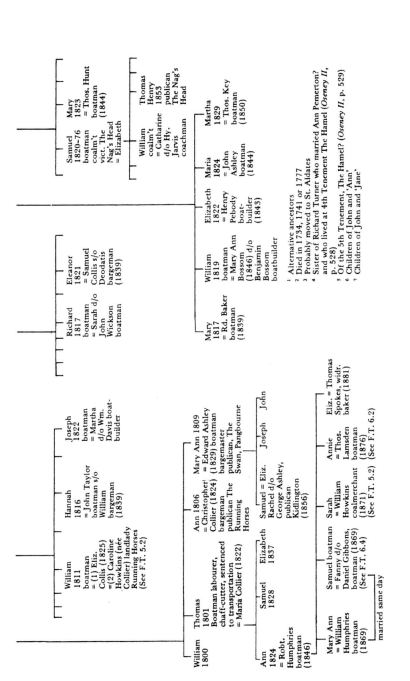

landlord; and James Perry and Richard Price also gave evidence.[43] Price was one of the names common to our registers, and, had the parish register been considered into the '40s, we should have found Simpson to be a name common to both lists too. In 1795 a James Simpson of Oldbury had worked a boat on the Tipton to Oxford run, whilst in 1844 Ellen Bossom, daughter of a bargeman, Charles Bossom, had married one Joseph Simpson, boatman.

The historian, in dealing with possibilities, faces two temptations: to screw up the causal nexus too tightly and assume that each possibility is an actuality, or to refuse to regard any possibility as worth considering. At this distance it is often impossible to discriminate between the casual coincidence and the causal connection. Both look like conjunctions which may be repeated; and as the eye tends to pick out of the welter of experience the patterns which interest it, or to carve them out of an unpatterned matrix, these possibilities must not be overstated. Nor, however, should we dismiss such matters too lightly. In turning over the possibilities, we may learn much about the way business was conducted at the sub-literate level. Not all that seems likely will have been the case, and we cannot tell just which possibilities were realised; nevertheless something of the truth will have been uncovered, and as more is explored and experience accrues the greater will become the ability to discriminate.

It would be to connect events by too tight a chain of causation to state categorically that William Beesley and William Fisher were setting up a carrying business between the two pubs, and that William Fisher's brothers-in-law came to be involved in it. We don't even know who the William Fisher at Oldbury was. Yet something was going on. At the very least, is it not likely that in the golden circle of the bar (and of the barmaids also, perhaps) these young foreign boatmen found favour, and that commissions came their way? These were not the 'constant men' exploited at the docks, but rather, as the old glee says:

> If you've *never* been the lover of the landlady's daughter,
> Then you *cannot* have a second piece of pie.

---

[43] Salop RO, QR 305165, Jan. 1826.

How long Mary Beesley continued to run the Fishes after the death of her husband is not known. If she continued to keep the pub for some time, it is easier to understand how her daughters came to meet and marry boatmen from Staffordshire and Warwickshire, but even if she left it fairly soon, a circle of acquaintances and friends had built up which made it easy for the other girls to meet such men, once the eldest daughter had married amongst them. A community was forming, and the pub played an important part in building it.

V. THE COMMUNITY OF THE ROW, 1841-71[44]

By 1830, the year after Badcock's Survey, the Oxford Canal was in its prime. Toll receipts for the Oxford Canal reached their highest level in that year, at over £90,000.[45] The lean post-war years were well behind, and there had been six years of good trade. Although there were already rumours of railways, it had been a period of consolidation. After the first

---

[44] The Census Returns from Fisher Row and Medley appears as follows:

> 1841   H.O. 107/891
> Lower Fisher Row: Enumeration District 11, pp.1, 26-8
> Middle Fisher Row: "   "   11, pp.29-32
> Upper Fisher Row: "   "   12, pp.10-16
> Medley: 11, p.32
> 1851   H.O. 107/1728
> Lower Fisher Row: Enumeration District 9b, nos. 138-63
> Middle Fisher Row: "   "   9c, nos. 103-19
> Upper Fisher Row: "   "   9c, nos. 65-102
> Medley: 9c, no. 123
> 1861   R.G.9/895
> Lower and Middle Fisher Row:
>   Enumeration District 15, nos. 14-53
> Upper Fisher Row:
> ('Hythe Bridge')   "   "   15, nos. 54-83
> Boats on the Canal
> and River   "   "   15, nos. 218-30
> R.G.9/896
> Medley: 17, nos. 180-2
> 1871   R.G.10-1440
> Lower and Middle Fisher Row:
>   Enumeration District 15, nos. 23-60
> Upper Fisher Row: "   "   15, nos. 70-99
> Boats at Hythe Bridge Wharf:
>   Enumeration District 15, nos. 61-9
> R.G.10/1441
> Medley: "   "   17, nos. 225-30

[45] Charles Hadfield, *British Canals* (revised edn., 1959), 177, 215. The figures given here differ slightly. They are perhaps from two different sources, but the trends are the same.

heady years in the 1790s, the canal had at last settled to a humble and humdrum round, with a trade whose staple cargoes were coal for Oxford and the towns near the canal, and corn for the manufacturing towns of the Midlands, and the collieries. It was a local trade, run on the whole by local Oxford merchants and small boat-owners.

In 1841, the date of the first Census in which occupations were given and individuals were particularised, the canal community was stable and relatively prosperous, and its trade had scarcely felt the breath of railway competition. Oxford had as yet no line to link it with the railway network, and even the Great Western line from Bristol to London was three weeks from completion. The Census was taken on the night of Sunday 7 June 1841, and the Great Western route was completed from Bristol to London on the 30th. On 12 June 1844 a branch line was opened from Didcot to Oxford, and this provided Oxford with its first actual railway station. Oxford now had an efficient railway service to London, as it does to this day. The station however, was not situated in St Thomas's parish, as it now is, but lay across the river beyond Folly Bridge, on the west side of the road to Abingdon and the south. The effect of the building of this railway was slow to make itself felt in Fisher Row. There was no dramatic reduction in the number of boatmen in St Thomas's until after the next Census.

The Great Western Railway ran parallel with the Wilts and Berks Canal from Swindon for many miles eastwards, and it successfully destroyed, as it was intended to do, the trade of that canal; it also took much of the remaining trade of the river. A few towns, like Abingdon and Dorchester, which had formerly got their coal from the Wilts and Berks, and had no railway station, now looked elsewhere for their coal. As the canal declined, some of its boatmen turned to the Oxford Canal as an alternative source for coal, and in the 1840s receipts for tolls on traffic moving from the Oxford Canal on to the river increased by just over 20 per cent between 1843 and 1847.[46] By the time of the 1851 Census the immigration of families from the western and defunct parts of the canal system was a pronounced feature of the Row. So the effect of the building

[46] Compton, *Oxford Canal*, 115.

of the first railway to Oxford was to increase temporarily the trade of the Oxford Canal.

Towards the end of the 1840s the coming of the railways was felt in a variety of ways. Navvies crowded into the parish from time to time in connection with the building of one line or another; new pubs sprang up to cater for them, such as The Engine and Tender in Hythe Bridge Street, and they crowded the cheap lodging houses and narrow courts of St Thomas's High Street. One does not find them in Fisher Row in the 1851 Census. The two groups, with their pronounced characteristics would be unlikely to mix.

The Census of 1851 was taken on Sunday 31 March, and by the end of the summer coal was being advertised in the *Oxford Journal* at two new railway stations in the parish, those of the Buckinghamshire Railway and the London and North Western Railway. The 1851 therefore reflects the last weeks of the pre-railway period on the canal. Change hung over the community, but it was still to come.

In 1841 there were 52 tenements running from The Lasher at the top of Upper Fisher Row to the house Edward Tawney had built on the corner of Lower Fisher Row and St Thomas's High Street. They formed three small sequences of terrace housing; a patchwork of old and new cottages, cottages which could be subdivided further to take in more people if need be, as they were to do in 1851. In 1841 the Census showed that the Row housed 18 canal boatmen, three bargemen and six fishermen in all, 29 men all occupied in some way with boats. Altogether in the whole parish there were 43 men involved in barging, fishing, and canal boating, so that the Row, with 67.4 per cent of the total had clearly the largest concentration of boat-people; Hythe Bridge Street, with eight boatmen and a bargeman, carried an overflow as in 1829. The canal boatmen's hold on the Row was most tenuous in Lower Fisher Row, for while there were six boatmen there, they seem to have inhabited the half of Edward Tawney's Almshouse normally inhabited by almsmen. This seems to have been a purely temporary arrangement. The inhabitants were six men sharing the accommodation in pairs, and having little connection with local families. They were probably the crews of the boats of Pickfords or Crowleys, the canal carriers. As well as the canal boatmen living ashore, the Census mentions 11 males and 12 females in boats by the wharf, but it gives no further information about them. Short as it was, Middle Fisher Row, with only 15 households held 7 boatmen or 46 per cent of the whole. This was a larger proportion than in Upper Fisher Row, which, despite its 27 households held only 5 boatmen or 18.5 per cent. In Middle Fisher Row William Beesley's interest still seemed to persist.

Similarly Upper Fisher Row still bore the impress of Thomas Beesley in having three barging and five fishing families living there. The fishermen of Upper Fisher Row were all members of Thomas Beesley's family. Another fishing family, the Bossoms, were represented by three fishermen living elsewhere: one in Middle Fisher Row, one in Lower Fisher Row, and one at Medley, where in time they were to establish a considerable colony. In 1841 32 canal boatmen lived in the parish. This, however, must have been only a fraction of the total of Oxford boatmen. Can we estimate the full number?

The question cannot be answered straight from the Census, for it is difficult to estimate what proportion of the canal population of the parish was present on the night of the Census. As we have seen, William Ward, who had 12 boats on the canal in 1841, told the Select Committee on Sunday Trading that only two of his boatmen had homes ashore. How typical his employees were of the Oxford boatmen in general we do not know. At the same time he estimated that his boatmen only spent one Sunday in four or five in Oxford. This is more likely to be typical for we know that Sunday was the busiest day of the week on the canal. The Census, taken on a Sunday night, was therefore taken when boatmen were most usually away from home.

In gauging the population of the boatmen in the parish and their families we would do better to base our estimate on the St Thomas's baptismal register. In 1831-40 the average number of baptisms was 12.2, and in 1841-50 12.0. If the birthrate was 30-40 per 1,000 we might expect a population of between 300 and 400 boatmen and their dependants belonging to the parish. When Henry Ward built his chapel to seat 150 persons, presumably this was the largest number of boat-people he envisaged ever being in Oxford at one time.

1 *(top)*. The Castle Mill *c*. 1857, by J. H. Le Keux

2 (*bottom*). Hythe Bridge, Wharf and Canal *c*. 1835, by P. Dewint.

Left

3 (*top*). Lower Fisher Row, 1951, showing The Lock.

4 (*centre*). Middle Fisher Row and The Nag's Head, *c*.1909.

5 (*bottom*). Upper Fisher Row, *c*.1885.

7 (*right*). The Floating Chapel, *c*.1860.

8 Mrs Rose Skinner and Miss Jean Humphries emptying a boat at Juxon Street, 1956.

In Loving Memory of

HANNAH BEAUCHAMP
DIED JULY 9TH 1899
AGED 70 YEARS.
ALSO OF
ABEL LAMSDON,
SON OF THE ABOVE
WHO DIED SUDDENLY AT MOIRA
JUNE 14TH 1897.
AGED 32 YEARS.
ALSO OF
HARRIET HUNT,
DAUGHTER OF THE ABOVE
DIED AUGUST 20TH 1906.
AGED 50 YEARS.
The will be done.
ALSO JOSEPH LAMSDON
29TH 1933, AGED 78 YEARS.

9 The Tombstone of a family of Boatmen, Oseney Cemetery.

Whilst it is disappointing that the Census can give us only a glimpse of the community, we should expect no more. By the nature of the canal boatman's job he was a man on the move. If the Census had listed all the members of the community, it would have been an ideal listing, rather than an actual one. We can learn more about this community from such an actual listing in which the working community is frozen for us on one day, just as Pompeii, suddenly overwhelmed and petrified, can tell us more of the past than any Museum reconstruction. Let us turn from numbers to individuals and examine the Census in detail.

Table 5.6. Distribution of canal boatmen in St Thomas's Parish according to the censuses, 1841–71.

	1841	1851	1861	1871
High St., St. Thomas	1	1	0	0
Holly Bush Row	2	1	0	0
Hythe Bridge St.	8	4	0	0
Lower Fisher Row	6	0	1	0
Middle Fisher Row	7	8	4	0
Upper Fisher Row	5	13	5	2
Elsewhere in St. Thomas	3*	7**	3†	8‡
Total	32	34	13	10

   * 2 adolescents (later acquitted) in gaol; 1 at Rewley.
  ** 6 at 91 Clarendon St., Jericho; 1 at Jericho Gardens.
   † 1 in Nelson St., Jericho; 1 at Bridge St., Oseney Town; 1 at Medley (probably a waterman).
   ‡ 2 at Mill St., Oseney, 1 being retired; 1 at Rewley Place in Jericho; 1 at Medley (living on a houseboat—probably a waterman); 4 in Jericho, 1 each at Canal St., Jericho Gardens, Wellington St., Nelson St.

VI. STABILITY AND CONTINUITY

We have come back to the place from which I originally started on my search: the detailed returns of the 1841 Census of Fisher Row. My investigation has moved forward so slowly through the centuries that now, coming on it in context, it is with a sense of shock that I realise this is the document in which I first discovered the community in Fisher Row.

The way in which one first approaches any place or subject affects the way in which one sees it ever after. For me

Birmingham is two cities, one secret, deserted, and romantic; the other both hectic and humdrum – a place where cars hurtle along great motorways on pedestrian occasions. I entered Birmingham first from the canal one Easter Sunday at dusk. We moored the boat at the top of a flight of locks, walked under a bridge topped by a church whose spire climbed towards the sky; we passed boats moored in a basin, and walked through a door into an empty street. When I go there now by train or car I have difficulty in combining my two images of the city.

I therefore approach the 1841 Census again with some curiosity. When I first read it, I knew nothing of the Row and its history, and nothing of the generations of bargemen and fishermen who had gone before the canal boatmen, and I certainly did not see it as a community of closely intermarried families. How differently I should see it now, having studied the Row so intensively (see Appendix V).

On returning to it, however, my first feeling was one of amazement. It seemed as if the whole web of kinship had disintegrated and vanished. On first sight the turnover of population seemed enormous. In Upper Fisher Row there were five boatmen, Watson, Beesley, Howkins, Bull, and Farmer. None bore the same surname, and only two of the five men appeared in any subsequent Census, one having given up boating, and both having moved house. In the face of such evidence it was difficult to feel convinced that this was an occupation in which son followed father, and boatman married boatman's daughter. But if, as we have been told, a boatman spent only one Sunday out of four or five in Oxford, the probability of any particular boatman appearing in the Census twice was somewhere Between 1 in 16 and 1 in 25. It is also true that the houses in Upper Fisher Row were not arranged in strictly linear order. There were small courts, so that if the enumerator walked round them one way on one occasion, and the other way the next time, the sequence of houses in the list would be different on each occasion. Even allowing for this, if the run of returns for the four Censuses 1841 to 1871 is considered, it becomes clear that the boatmen moved house frequently, and it remains difficult to believe that this was a stable community of closely related families. Closer study reveals how false this impression is.

In any community the sense of stability and continuity may vary even where quantitatively the turnover is the same. It depends who stays and who goes. If its main social centres are in the hands of the same families over many generations, this gives a strong sense of continuity, even though the turnover of members of these families is high. In the community at large again, if the new families are constantly on the move it makes little difference to the community. Like summer visitors in a fishing village, they have little effect on its structure. If, however, it is the older families which go, the continuity and stability of the life of the community is undermined. So we find it in the Cotswolds and the Lake District where the sons of the village cannot afford to buy the village's houses, and they are sold to affluent newcomers. In such villages the oldest families will often be found, if at all, living in council houses on the edge of the town.

The pub was the only indigenous social institution in the boatmen's world, and in Fisher Row the pubs were in the hands of a few families which were intimately related to the boatmen of the Row, and also to each other. This gave a sense of continuity to the Row. As well, despite all appearance of change the same families persisted from generation to generation amongst the canal boatmen. Certainly Upper Fisher Row had altered since the 18th century, when house after house was occupied by sons of the Gardner family, and the occupants of house after house bore the same surname. It was more like Middle Fisher Row in the 18th century, where there were many surnames, but nearly all of them were those of families into which daughters of the Gardner family had married.[47] For as we have seen it was through marriage with daughters of the Row that boatmen entered the community, and here we see the consequence of this, spelt out in the diversity of boatmen's names in the Census. When relationship is traced in the male line, continuity is immediately apparent, for men do not change their names on marriage. We are following the grain of the records; in following continuity through the female line we cut across the grain. Names change in each generation.

[47] See 166-7.

The Oxford community of canal boatmen was matrilocal. Because the boatmen were always on the move, when a
woman married a boatman she seems to have stayed in the
community in which she had grown up, and where she knew
everyone. When Hollingshead described his canal community,
and noted the woman in her doorway talking to the boatman
on the tow-path, he depicted something which symbolised the
life of the community: the man on the move, the woman at
home. Women gave the community stability.

Through the women, too, the families of the old 18th-century
Establishment were perpetuated in the Row.[48] Most of the
families of the Row, fisherman, bargemen, or canal boatmen
formed, by the time of the 1841 Census, one kin. Let us now
consider in turn the three stabilising influences on the Row,
which gave it continuity in the face of apparent change: pubs,
women, and family.

First, then, the pubs. The two pubs of the Row faced each
other across Hythe Bridge Street, the Running Horses on the
corner of Upper Fisher Row and the Nag's Head on the corner
of Middle Fisher Row. The houses of the Row formed terraces
behind them. There they stood, like the captains of opposing
football teams, or, even more, like the fruitful parents on a
brass, facing each other, their offspring ranged behind them,

---

[48] There was probably a latent matrilocality in most groups of English people until the very
recent past. In any matrimonial crisis — whether a marriage went on the rocks or a husband was
posted overseas, a woman 'went home to mother', not to her mother-in-law. The importance of
the relation of the mother and daughter is more commonly recognized in working-class than in
upper-class life, though Dorothy Crozier noted it among the wives of Victorian Empire build-
ers. It did not stretch to the lawmakers of the upper class, and perhaps for this reason the Law
of Settlement made the wife's settlement depend on the husband's, so causing a great deal of
unrecognised suffering. The Law of Settlement could bear particularly hard on the widows of
canal boatmen, should they have the misfortune to be thrown on the parish. The story of Sarah
Cartwright illustrates the plight of such a woman very clearly. Sarah was born at Bedworth,
where her father had a settlement. She married a boatman, Edward Cartwright at Warwick in
1813, and he died 15 years later in the Manchester Infirmary. She was examined about her settlement six weeks after his death, in August 1828. She had heard her husband say that he had
been born at Wombourn, five miles from Wolverhampton, and that if ever she required relief
she must apply there. Her husband had two uncles living somewhere near Wombourn. She had
met one of these, Jackman Cartwright, on the canal at Manchester two or three times. He lived
with the other uncle, a nailer, near Wombourn – that is, if he were still alive. (Warwicks. RO,
DR225/326/162). A month later an order was made for the removal of Sarah and her two young
sons to Wombourn, a place of which, from her evidence, she seems to have had only the haziest
notion (Warwicks. RO DR225/333/183).

Family Tree 5.2.   The Howkins Family.

William Howkins (1) = Caroline Collier = (2) Wm. Fisher
boatman 1795–1826 | publican
b. Willoughby | Running Horses

John Howkins = Sarah Ashley, widow of John Ashley,
boatman | boatman (1820) at St. Mary Mag.
b. Willoughby
near Braunston 1798

Children of William Howkins (1):

- Eliz. 1819
- William 1821 publican Running Horses = Susannah
- Mary 1823
- Hannah 1825 Landlady University Friars' Entry
- Henry 1826 boat-man
- Ann 1820 = Benj. Collis (1847) smith
- Thomas 1823–4
- Emily 1824, St. Mary Mag. = Saml. Tolley boatman (1845) s/o Sl. Tolley boatman
- John 1827 boatman = Mary Corbey d/o Thomas labourer (See F.T. 5.3)
- Caroline 1828 = Jas. Peake cabinet-maker (1853)
- Susah 1829 = Thos. Bayliss (1852) labourer
- William c. 1831 publican George & Dragon = Eliz. d/o Thos. Beesley fisherman. (See F.T.5.4)
- Fanny 1836
- Henry 1838
- Mary Ann 1841

Children of Henry Howkins:

- Eliz. 1847 = Thos. Spokes Nags Head = Betsey Harris
- William 1850 coalm't = Betsey (1868)
- Caroline 1852 = Jacob Beesley willow-merchant (1880) (See F.T.5.4)
- John 1853
- Edwin 1855 coal-porter
- Clara 1857
- Julia 1859
- Joseph Bishop 1859 brewer = Mary Ann Collier d/o William, boatman
- John 1866 coalm't

Children of John Howkins (and Mary Corbey):

- Eliz. Ann 1849 1851 = E. Fisher, engineer (1870)
- Mary Ann 1851
- Thos. 1852
- Eliza. Ann 1853
- John 1856
- Jane Julia 1859
- Willm. Henry 1860 ink-maker = Lucinda Ashfield (1883, St. B)
- Edwin 1862 = M. E. Bowler (1885)
- John
- Susan 1864 = G. F. Bull (1885) greengrocer

Children of William Howkins (c. 1831):

- Caroline 1850
- William 1852 coalm't = Sarah d/o Robt. Humphris boatman (1871) (See F.T. 5.1)
- Harry J. 1854
- Rosa 1857
- Julia 1861
- Fanny 1863
- Clara Sophia 1865
- Alfred Fredk. 1866
- Kate Rosina 1869
- Walter Syd. 1870
- Harriet Margaret 1871
- Anne Amelia 1866
- Laura Maud
- Joseph James 1875

for each Row contained a quota of the relatives of the pub-keeper living in its hinterland.

We have seen how, through William Beesley's daughters' marriages, some canal boatmen from the Midlands gained a foothold in the parish. In 1841 some of his descendants were still found at the top of Middle Fisher Row. A grandson who was a boatman, Richard Edwards and second house from the Nag's Head with his family shared the a carter's family. Two generations of William's descendants lived next door, in the third house from the pub. William Beesley's daughter, Jane Lewis, and her husband who was a boatman, shared their house with their married daughter and her husband, who was a boatman, too, and also with their unmarried daughter, Mary. She married into the Ashley family in 1844, and was to be found living with her husband, a boatman in Middle Fisher Row in the 1851 Census. By that time the Ashley family were the dominant family in Middle Fisher Row and held the Nag's Head.[49]

By 1841 William Beesley had descendants in Upper Fisher Row, and especially near the foot of the Row.[50] His rascally grandson William Fisher II had married the widow who ran the Running Horses, Caroline Howkins (see Family Tree 5.2). She was probably his second wife, and he soon deserted her.[51] Next to the Running Horses, in Hythe Bridge Street lived Samuel Beesley, William Beesley's eldest son. He shared his house with his niece, another granddaughter of old William Beesley, Eleanor Collis (née Edwards). Her husband was a member of a family related several times over to the Beesley family. Near the top of Upper Fisher Row lived Samuel's son, Thomas. There were other Beesleys in Upper Fisher Row in 1841, but they were not descended from William Beesley, but from his brothers.

Some time after William Beesley's death the Nag's Head had passed into the hands of Thomas Farmer, and then to Edward Thomas Cox. The Farmer family had some interest in the canal, and so, probably did Cox, but it was not strong and their families were not extensive.[52] During their time the Running

---

[49] For this part of the Ashley family see the Beesley Family Tree, 5.1.
[50] See Family Tree 5. 1.   [51] *JOJ*, 16 Mar. 1844.
[52] The Cox family and the Farmers may have been related, for there had been a marriage

Horses was coming to the fore as an important pub for boat-men. The first landlord of whom we know anything, and perhaps its founder, was Christopher Collier who held it in 1817. In 1824 he married Ann Beesley, daughter of William Beesley's eldest son. No doubt this was why her father Sam-uel Beesley was living next to the pub at the time of the 1841 Census. His presence was an indication that the Run-ning Horses itself had come for a time into the hands of a descendant of William Beesley. Nor was this the only time. Christopher Collier, the landlord of the Running Horses had a sister, Caroline, who married a canal boatman in the parish of St Aldates in 1819. He was one of two brothers, both boatmen, William and John Howkins, who both settled in St Thomas's parish. Caroline's husband, William, died in 1826, and per-haps about this time Christopher Collier relinquished the pub to his sister. By 1841 Caroline had remarried, and her second husband was William Fisher II, grandson of William Bees-ley. After William Fisher abandoned her, the pub passed to her son, William. This was but the beginning of a dynasty of pub-keepers and coal-merchants who were intimately related to the boatmen of the Row over a long period (see Table 5.1 and Family Tree 5.2).

The Ashley family only held a pub in the Row for a short period, and even then by marriage, but they were enmeshed, like the Howkins, in the network of kin descended from Wil-liam Beesley, and they held pubs elsewhere on the canal and river too. John Redman, who held the Nag's Head at the time of the 1851 Census was a newcomer to the Row, and at first sight had no connection with it. He had been born at 'Melsham' [Melksham] in Wiltshire, according to the Census; according to his marriage lines he was the son of a clothier. His origins remind us of the distressed condition of that county following the decline in the manufacture of woollens. When he married at Kidlington in 1838 he was a boatman, and he married Mary Bowen Ashley, the daughter of the boatman, Thomas Ashley. Thomas Ashley had lived a somewhat peripatetic existence (if the adjective can be used of a boatman), for Mary and her

between a Robert Farmer and a Margaret Cox in St Giles on 17 July 1791. Both names appear in the 1795 Boat and Barge Register for Warwickshire. Edward Thomas Cox's widow married an Abingdon bargeman (MS DD Pprs. Hall's Breweries c. 31).

sister Ann had both been born at Pontypool. He had probably been engaged in the coal trade from Wales and Somerset by way of the Wilts and Berks Canal and the Thames to Oxford, for the Ashley family had connections with the Park End Wharf and probably also with the pub which stood nearest to it, the Navigation End.[53]

In 1841 the Ashleys were only represented in Middle Fisher Row by one household, an extended family containing one Bowen, two Redmans and three Ashleys. Between 1841 and 1851 more Ashleys moved into Middle Fisher Row, perhaps as they withdrew from the Wilts and Berks trade, and began to carry coal from the collieries supplying the Oxford Canal. By the time John Redman was landlord of the Nag's Head, there were at least three other households of Ashley kin, including that of John Ashley, who had married the granddaughter of William Beesley.

Between 1851 and 1861 the Ashleys almost entirely withdrew from the Row. In the 1850s even the Thames trade around Oxford dwindled almost to nothing, and, when the family withdrew from Oxford, part of the family moved to Kidlington, and part moved down river to Whitchurch and Panbourne. At both places members of the Ashley family were publicans. A marriage in 1856 at Kidlington shows the family reinforcing kinship ties by a double marriage. On 8 July Elizabeth Rachel Ashley, daughter of George Ashley, coal-merchant and publican of Kidlington, married Samuel Joseph Ashley, bargemaster of Pangbourne, son of Edward Ashley, bargemaster of the same place.[54]

In the 1880s the Ashleys were still at Pangbourne, at the Swan, a pub 'well known to boating men'. There Mrs Ashley owned 'several barges, one or two of which may generally be seen at the coal wharf' according to an artist who frequented the river.[55] The Pangbourne Ashleys were descended from Mary Anne Beesley, for Edward Ashley, their progenitor, had married a granddaughter of William Beesley of the Nag's Head, and she was sister to Ann Beesley, who had married Christopher

---

[53] For the Navigation End see 213.
[54] See Family Tree 5.1.
[55] George D. Leslie, *Our River: an artist's life on the River Thames* (London, 1888), 147.

Collier, keeper of the Running Horses. The publicans at Pang-bourne and Kidlington were probably brothers, and related to those at the Nag's Head and at the Running Horses. This line of the Beesley family which tied together the keepers of public houses on the canal and river only emerges from time to time, and its extent can perhaps never be fully recovered. How much more is there to find? In 1890 Benjamin Beesley, landlord of the Greyhound, the public house at the junction of the Oxford and Coventry Canals in the parish of Foleshill, Warwickshire, registered a boat called *Competition* (Coventry 190); five more boats followed between then and 1906.[56] Old William Beesley had a son John, a painter, who married in St Aldate's parish in 1818 where he had one son Benjamin in 1824 and then vanished from the parish register. Is this Benjamin to be identified with the publican of the Greyhound, and was there, therefore, another grandson of William Beesley at the top of the Oxford Canal, just as there was a granddaughter or great granddaughter down the line of the river at Pangbourne?

When John Redman left Navigation House, as the Nag's Head became in his time, it was the end of the Ashley dominance of Middle Fisher Row, but the Beesleys continued, for the new landlord was Samuel Spindler grandson to Samuel, brother of old William Beesley of the Nag's Head (see the Beesley Family Tree 5.1). Samuel's daughter, Ann or Ann Maria or Maria, as she variously called herself, had married William Spindler, a bargeman, in 1816 and it was her son Samuel who became the new landlord. The name Spindelow was found in the 18th and early 19th centuries in Lower Fisher Row, and also in Upper Fisher Row in connection with tenement 1. As late as 1809 they had been fishermen. The name was thus well known in the Row, though whether its inhabitants could state what relation (if any) the new landlord of the Nag's Head bore to earlier Spindelows, any more than we can, is a matter of speculation. Samuel Spindler, the new landlord, had been a boatman in early life, and as landlord he combined his business with that of a coal-merchant, like other landlords before him.

Samuel Spindler was one of the only two boatmen in the Row whose wills have been found. When he died in 1876

---

[56] Coventry City Record Office, PH/Reg/ 1/1, Coventry Canal Boat Registers, 1879-1914.

he was worth £800, and had six children amongst whom he left his goods. The stock of the Nag's Head was divided between his two daughters, and one of his sons, Frederick George, who got his piece of freehold building land in Botley Meadow. He divided equally between all his children his 'Boats, Barges, wagons, Horses, implements and stock in trade' as a coal-merchant. A son, Thomas Henry, succeeded him at the Nag's Head.[57]

Throughout the 19th century and into the 20th century the boatman of the Row could be assured that at one or other of the major pubs in the Row, and sometimes at both, they would be served by families which had a close connection both with the canal, the pubs of the Row, and sometimes with those along the river and canal too.

Now for the women. It was the women who anchored the boatmen to the Row. As we have seen, in the first place, it was through marrying women of the Row that boatmen from elsewhere entered the community, and, through the presence of their wives at home, whilst they were away on their trips, a continuing relation between the boatmen and the families of the Row was maintained.

The boatmen came and went, so that the boat-people's community ashore was largely one of women, often living together, helping and supporting each other in the absence of their husbands. These households were not necessarily based on a home ashore at all times. During the life-cycle of the family it was easier to maintain a home ashore at some times than at others. A home ashore was always regarded as desirable, but it was not always economically possible. The age of the children, their number, the ability of the wife to earn a second income at home, whilst the elder children helped run the boat, the responsibility for dependent relatives, the possibility of sharing a house: such factors governed the decision to keep up a home on the land. The movement of the families from one house to another, which can be seen sometimes in the Census, may reflect the alternation of periods when the family

---

[57] Oxon. RO, M and G 23/1 (Spindler). No search however has been made for wills in Somerset House; J. C. Valters, *Oxford Post Office Directory, 1880* (Oxford, 1880).

were able to maintain a home ashore and those when they could not. The boatman's family was one of changing size and shape, taking in dependants at times, or splitting into two parts, a section on the land, dominated by the mother, and one on the water where the men and children worked the boat together. At other times again the family afloat formed a nuclear family working the boat together.[58]

Let us take concrete cases. In the 1851 Census we find a category which is peculiar to it, the 'boatman's wife'. Such women were the heads of their respective households in the absence of their husbands. In 1851 there were four such women in Upper Fisher Row: Mary Howkins, Ann Humphries, Elizabeth Bowell, and Jane Berry. We shall examine their households, starting with the youngest and working to the oldest.

At the time of the Census Mary Howkins was 21 years old. She was living at home with her mother, the widow, Elizabeth Corbey. Her infant daughter was living with her, though her age is incorrectly given as 12 years old. It was nearer 12 months. Mary was probably still recovering from the birth of her second daughter, Mary Ann. This baby's name does not appear in the Census, though she survived, grew up and married (see Family Tree 5.2). Mary Howkins also appears in the 1841 Census. Then she was still a child, and under her maiden name, Mary Corbey, she was living at home with her mother, sister, and brothers.

When Mary married, she married the boy next door, John Howkins. John was a boatman, and the son of a boatman. His father, John Howkins senior was brother-in-law of Caroline Howkins, the boatman's widow who kept the Running Horses. Caroline's own brother had, as we have seen married a Beesley, so that John Howkins was connected with the Row's Establishment.

The Corbeys themselves had some standing in the Row, even though Thomas Corbey, Mary's father, had been a labourer. Mary's mother belonged to an important family in the Row (see Family Trees 5.3, The Corbeys, and 6.1 The Bossoms). She was the daughter of the bargeman, William Bossom, who in turn was the son of Thomas Bossom, the bargemaster who

---

[58] See Appendix IV, Upper Fisher Row, 1841-71.

Family Tree 5.3.   The Corbeys.

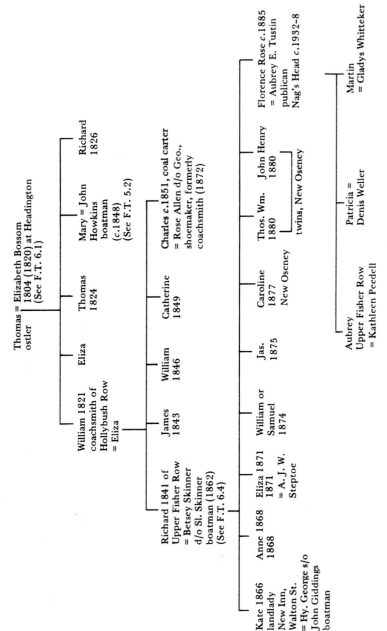

had leased some property in Upper Fisher Row. The lease of one of Thomas Bossom's tenements in Upper Fisher Row came into the hands of Elizabeth Corbey, so that they were not subtenants, like most of their neighbours, but tenants in their own right. In 1851 Mary Howkins was living in her mother's house, but neither she nor her children are found in the Row in the next two Censuses, although she and her husband had 15 children baptised in the parish between 1849 and 1871, and John remained a boatman throughout this period.

There are many similarities between Mary Howkins and the next boatman's wife whom we have to consider, Ann Humphries. Ann, who was 26, was the wife of Robert Humphries, who was also, like Mary Howkins's husband, the son of a boatman. They had married in St Thomas's in 1846. Ann herself was the daughter of Thomas and Maria Beesley (née Collier), and therefore a granddaughter of old William Beesley of the Nag's Head. Her mother was probably a sister of Mary Howkins's aunt-by-marriage, Caroline Howkins, who was also a Collier. So there was some sort of family tie between the two young women. At the time of the 1841 Census Ann, too, had been a girl, living at home with her parents, but unlike Mary she was not living with her parents in 1851. She lived next door. In 1851 she had a son of two, Samuel, and was presumably pregnant, as her next child was baptised in June. By the time of the next Census they had disappeared from the Row. Ann and Robert Humphries had eight children baptised in the parish altogether between 1848 and 1864, and only one of these children appears in the Census. (Robert Humphries remained a boatman throughout the period.) Their daughter Fanny was living as a boarder in the house of a widowed seamstress in Lower Fisher Row at the time of the 1871 Census. That these two large families all but entirely escaped the Census for the parish whilst their families were growing up underlines how small a fragment of the boat-people's community we can recover from the Census alone. They passed out of observation as their families grew older, and as they moved into an expensive period in the life of the family, with many mouths to feed, they probably gave up their home ashore.

In both these cases we observed these families initially when the mothers were young and still dependent on their parents. In the next case we see the relation of mother and daughter at a different stage. Elizabeth Bowell, aged 45 in 1851, had been born at Lechlade, and we know nothing of her parentage. She was probably the wife of William Bowell, of whom we know even less. Her household in 1851 was a household of girls: an adolescent daughter, Jane, aged 15; then Mary, aged four; and an infant granddaughter. She already had two married children, one daughter being married to Benjamin Bishop. Benjamin was a boatman, and so was his father. When he was born, in 1822, the parish register put his father down as a fisherman, and noted that he had been married at Nuncham [Courtenay]. The name Bishop, like the name Spindelow had connections with the lessees of the first tenement in Lower Fisher Row. In 1743 a Jeremiah Bishop of Godstow, fisherman, had held its lease. We have seen now how long the dynasties of fisherman could be, and how tenaciously the river families clung to the river. It would almost be more surprising if there were no connection between the fishing and boating families than if there was. In 1851 Elizabeth Bowell had headed a house full of girls; in 1861 it had become a house of unattached adults. Both Elizabeth Bowell and her daughter Jane were now widowed, and the only other inmate was an unmarried son of 24, a coal-porter. Had the canal been more prosperous he might well have been a boatman. Jane had married a boatman, Isaac Bond, outside the parish, and there had been a son, Thomas Isaac Bond, born in St Thomas's in 1855. In 1871 Elizabeth Bowell was no longer head of a household, but a dependant. She was living in the house of her daughter Jane, now remarried. Jane's second husband, Mark Yeatman was a stonemason, and the family lived at 8 Hythe Bridge Street. Next door lived Elizabeth and Benjamin Bishop, so that Elizabeth Bowell had two daughters living beside her in her old age. The care of parents fell upon daughters, who were often repaying care lavished on their own young when they themselves were absent with the boats, or were managing single-handed in the absence of their husbands.

The fourth boatman's wife was Jane Berry, estimated to be 60 in 1851. Her household contained only one other member,

Emma Berry, her unmarried daughter, aged twenty. Little is definitely known of the family. The mother was born at Finstock, the daughter at Eynsham, and it seems very likely that they were part of an Eynsham boatmen's family. In the next Census they can be identified in the same house (though Jane's name is now given as Mary, which was probably correct) and the house was headed by Thomas Berry, a boatman of 72, Mary being 72, and Emma 27. Thomas Berry had been born at Fulbrook. By 1871 Mary (or Jane) seems to have been dead, Emma had married a bricklayer's labourer and was living in Hollybush Row, and her father, Thomas Berry, was living with them.

These boatmen's wives seem to fall into two groups: the very young, who, in the absence of their husbands were semi-dependent on their parents, and the elderly who were semi-dependent on daughters. The point at which dependence tipped from one sort to the other is not clear. Perhaps we can clarify the natural history of the boat-woman's life a little further. The families of the younger women were still small, and their children still babies. The families were at an age when it was not easy for husband and wife to work a boat together, for it requires two people to work a boat efficiently, and the young children would claim a good deal of attention. As well, the pregnant woman was less agile than usual. Until one of the children reached an age at which some jobs could be delegated – and this could be very young in deed – the management of a boat by husband and wife was not easy, and the husband might well take a job where pay was good, leaving his wife with her parents, or near to them. Once these first difficult years were past, wife and children could provide the necessary help in running the family boat. As the size of the family increased the same money must also be spread over a larger family and the home ashore became an expensive luxury. The young boatman and the elderly were more likely to be able to afford a home ashore where the wife could stay whilst her husband was working the boat, than in middle life. Elizabeth Bowell, in 1851, seems to have reached the age when a regular home ashore could be afforded. But she was caring for her son's child at this time, and it seems likely that the crew of more than one boat was supporting this household.

VII. CANAL BOATMEN AND THE EXTENDED FAMILY FISHERMEN AND THE NUCLEAR FAMILY

Our account of these families ashore makes it clear that they had a matrilocal tendency, and were therefore often extended families. We do not have to look only at households headed by boat-women. We can take another example. Let us take the 1841 Census for Middle Fisher Row (see Appendix VI for the Census return for Middle Fisher Row). Let us assign a letter, A, B, etc., to each household, starting with the Nag's Head, and consider the relationships of the inhabitants of each house in turn. We shall find a rich variety of combinations of relatives in many of these households. Nuclear families, consisting simply of parents and their children, were in the minority. Of the 15 households only four, G, H, I, and M, were nuclear, two generation households. Three of these were families of boatmen who were comparatively new to the canal. There was also one old (K), and one middle-aged couple (O). Two women, one old and one youngish, also live together (L), and are not known to be related. In the remaining eight tenements of Middle Fisher Row the extended family held sway. The following seem to be the relationships:

Tenement A: Couple plus wife's kin
Tenement B: Grandmother, daughter and children
Tenement C: Grandfather, daughter and husband, children and lodgers
Tenement D: Grandparents, son, 2 unmarried daughters, 1 married, husband and children
Tenement E: Parents, children, husband's kin (mother?)
Tenement F: Aunt, married niece and children
Tenement J: Grandmother? Aunt's parents, grandchildren
Tenement N: Family with elderly female

It would be interesting to know if in 1772 the families under each roof were extended families, as they so often were by 1841. In 1772 the barging families were even more closely related than those of 1841. Were they so often extended before the women moved onto the boats, and before help was needed in caring for the children left ashore? Or did the sharing of a house simply cut down the expense of keeping up a home on the land as well as the home afloat?

The canal boatmen were not the only boat-people in the 19th century. The fishermen had increased in number, and where the canal boatman's web of kinship ran submerged below the surface, that of the fishermen is obvious. It can be seen in house after house of fishermen bearing the same surname in Upper Fisher Row. The fishermen's families formed a distinctive group: they were stationary, territory-bound, and patriarchal, and lived in nuclear families forming a striking contrast to the matriarchal, extended, women's households of the canal families.

The Beesleys who were fishermen were all descended from William Beesley's rival for the barge trade, his brother Thomas. After being ousted in the struggle for a share in the trade off the Oxford Canal, Thomas Beesley and his family turned their backs on the canal. How they became fishermen is a story we shall reserve for the next chapter, here we shall concentrate on their family structure, which forms such a remarkable contrast to that of the canal boatmen.

In the past the fishermen had developed long dynasties, and the occupation had passed from father to son. Normally only one son had followed in his father's footsteps, for the fishery, like a farm was limited in the number of people it could support. In the 17th century, with its high mortality rate, the problem of finding a successor in the male line had often been acute. In the 19th century, a time of teeming fecundity, and lower mortality rates, the problem was not too few sons, but too many. The problem was made more acute by the high rate of unemployment which afflicted St Thomas's throughout the 19th century, so that men had to make their livings as best they could on a scratch-as-scratch-can basis.

In this situation, not just one son but many of the sons of Thomas Beesley became fishermen (see Family Tree 5.4). Nevertheless, one can see that primogeniture of a sort was practised, for the elder sons were favoured over the younger. The households of the fishermen contained nuclear families without exception. None contained married daughters and their children. Had any of the descendants of Thomas Beesley I married boatmen and produced children, perhaps things would have been different; but they never did. In this they

Family Tree 5.4.   The Beesleys of St Thomas's Part II (see also Family Tree 5.1).

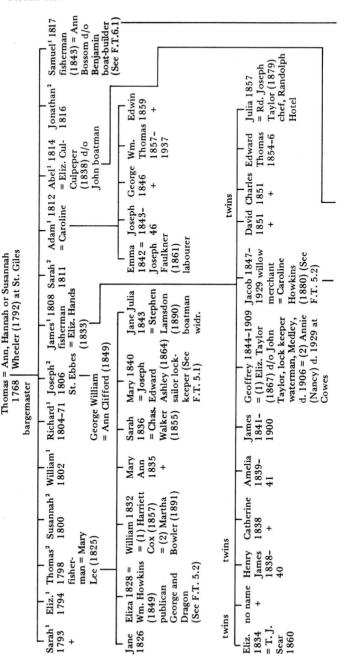

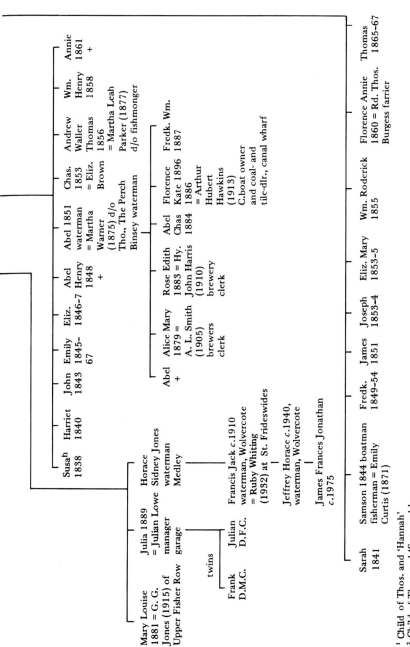

¹ Child of Thos. and 'Hannah'
² Child of Thos. and 'Susannah'

were unlike Thomas's two brothers, William and Samuel I.[59] William had, of course, died a long time before the 1841 Census, but Samuel I, who was a bargeman, had a daughter, sometimes called Ann, sometimes Maria, and sometimes Ann Maria, who married a boatman, and was living with her father at the time of the 1841 Census. After her father's death she shared her home with a daughter, Mary, who married a boatman Thomas Hunt (see Appendix V). If, however, adult daughters of fishermen were living at home, it was because they were unmarried.

Let us turn to the Census to see the structure of the family of Thomas Beesley, the fisherman, and the favoured position of elder sons (see Family Tree 5.4). Thomas Beesley I first leased the tenement beside the Lasher at the top of Upper Fisher Row in 1795 (see Table 5.7). He continued to lease it through the ups and downs of his career, though in 1818, during the difficult years which followed the Napoleonic War it was subdivided, and the southern part assigned to the wharfinger Samuel Steane. This tenement by The Lasher was of course a prime situation for a fisherman. Thomas was living there at the time of the 1841 Census. At this time his son Thomas II lived next door, to the south, in the first of Steane's tenements. Thomas's second son, William, had died in infancy, and his next two sons seem to have found themselves fisheries in other parishes. Richard, the third son, was a fisherman, living in St Aldate's parish,[60] and Joseph, the fourth, in St Ebbe's.[61] James, the fifth son, is not mentioned in the 1841 Census, though in subsequent years he lived next in order down the Row. Adam, the sixth son, was unmarried and lived at home with his father. Abel I, the seventh son, lived in the southernmost and last of Steane's tenements. The eighth son had died in infancy, and the ninth son, Samuel III, was living with his bride of two months' standing further down the Row.

[59] There were two Samuel Beesleys who must be distinguished. The other one was the eldest son of William Beesley, and the uncle of the one with whom we are now dealing (see above, 239). Only seven years separated the two men, one being the youngest of his generation, the other the oldest of the next. Both married women with the same surname, Garlick.

[60] St Algate's Marriage Register, 18 Spet. 1856; Census RG 10/893 Enumeration District 2, 266.

[61] Freeman of St Ebbe's, 1832, 1841, 1851, 1863, and 1879.

Only two of the brothers lived in Upper Fisher Row in 1851. In 1861 there were four brothers, and several of them had sons in their households already working as fishermen. Thomas II's only son, William, never became a fisherman. He lived near the foot of the Row, further down even than Samuel III the ninth son.

Table 5.7.   The decendants of Thomas Beesley the Elder of the first tenement Upper fisher row their tenements and occupations 1841-71.

	1841	1851	1861	1871
Tenement IA	F †, S6	S1	S1	S1
IB	S5		S5†, S5S1	S5†, S5S3
IIA			S6	S6
IIB or IIIA	S7	S7	S7†, S7S1 or 2	S7†, S7S1* or 2
IIIBc			S9†, S9S1† S9S2	S9*†, S9S2*
IV	S9†			

† bargemaster then fisherman.
* waterman.
F = Thomas Beesley the elder; S = son of F; S1 = first son of F, and so on.
S1S1 = first son's first son, and so on.
Note: Most of the leases of Upper Risher Row were subdivided and carried more than one house. The occupation of say tenement IB in no way indicates sole occupancy.

By the default of William, James's sons were now the most senior amongst Thomas I's grandsons in the Row, even though James was but the fifth son. In 1861 the three younger brothers, Adam (sixth son), Abel (seventh son), and Samuel III (ninth son) were still fishermen, and Abel and Samuel had sons following in their footsteps. By 1871 though the eldest three brothers still called themselves fishermen, and so did James's third son, who was still under his father's roof, the two youngest brothers and their sons called themselves watermen.

VIII. KIN AND COMMUNITY

Despite the entirely different structure of the fishermen and canal boatmen's families many of them were connected in a network of kinship stretching back continuously in the past to the 17th century bargemen of the Row, the Gardners.

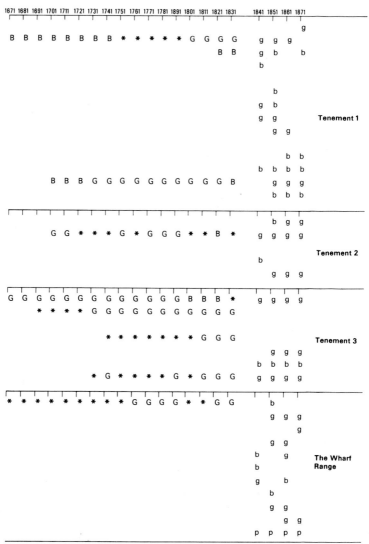

Fig. 5.2. Distribution of the Gardener Family in Upper Fisher row by deceniums – from leases, 1671-1831, and from the Census, 1841-71.

The different limitations and demands of the different occupations which they followed had resulted in differences which
ultimately divided the two groups as markedly as if they had
been two tribes.

Yet this connection can be traced. Both the Beesleys and
the Bossoms, the other major barging family of the Row were
descended by marriages on the female side from the Gardner family (see Family Tree 5.5, the Common Descent of the
Bossoms and Beesleys). The Howkins, the Colliers, and the
Collises were also large groups of kin who were drawn within
this network sooner or later. It is instructive to exhibit the extent
to which the inhabitants of the Row were linked into this network of kin. A diagram has been drawn up to exhibit it for the
Gardner family (see Fig. 5.2) and its direct descendants in Upper
Fisher Row. Collaterals are not included. Thus, the family of
William Howkins of the Running Horses remains outside this
network of kin, though his mother Caroline Collier probably
had siblings who married into both the Beesley and Bossom
families, and she herself, by her second marriage, became the
wife of a grandson of William Beesley of the Nag's Head.

The diagram uses the Census for the period 1841-71. It has
been possible to use material from the City Lease Books to
construct a table of the lessees of the tenements from the
17th century at 10-year intervals. Often, of course, lessee
and occupant were different persons, but this cannot be got
around. In fact, the lessee in the Row, more often than not,
occupied at least one of the houses even where they had been
subdivided, and they sublet the remainder. There was less
investment property at an earlier period than later on, and,
as the property was divided up into smaller and smaller units
the lessee was less and less likely to be an occupant. In 1841
the property in Upper Fisher Row was held on nine leases, but
only three lessees were occupants: Thomas Beesley, the fisherman at the top of the Row, Elizabeth Corbey and Benjamin
Bossom, about the middle of the Row. Even the pub-keeper
at the foot of the Row did not hold the lease of the Running Horses. He was a subtenant of Morrells, the brewers (see
Appendix III). Even despite these provisos, it is clear that if
the Gardner kin held a large proportion of the leases in the
period before 1841, a high proportion of the subtenants were

also Gardner kin during the period thereafter, and quite a large proportion of this kinship group were boat-people of one sort or another too. In 1841 33.3 per cent of all occupants were Gardner kin; in 1851 31.5 per cent; in 1861 44.8 per cent, and in 1871 37.9 per cent.

Family Tree 5.5.   The Common Descent of the Bossoms and the Beesleys from the Gardners.

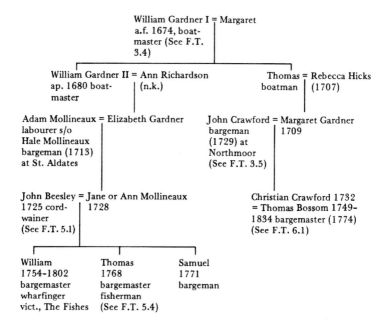

The two groups lived side by side in the Row, like men of different cultures, almost as if there were a colour bar, and there was little intermarriage. Some sort of scale of desirability of marriage partners may perhaps be glimpsed in the marriages of the sons of Thomas Beesley I. Five of his seven surviving sons married within the parish, and the second marriage of another son is recorded in St Aldate's parish. The eldest married someone of whom nothing is known except her name, Mary Lee. Richard, the third son, and the next surviving, married as his second wife a pub-keeper's daughter, and so did

Family Tree 5.6. The Beesleys of Upper Fisher Row: Contrasting Occupational Patterns.

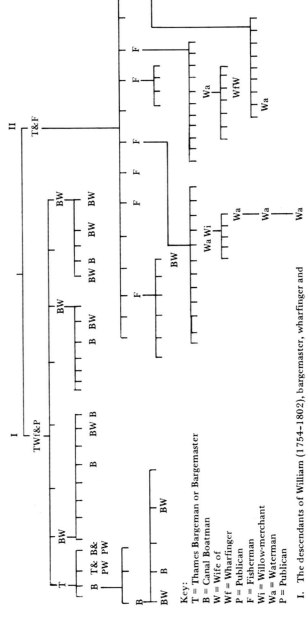

Key:
T = Thames Bargeman or Bargemaster
B = Canal Boatman
W = Wife of
Wf = Wharfinger
P = Publican
F = Fisherman
Wi = Willow-merchant
Wa = Waterman
P = Publican

I. The descendants of William (1754–1802), bargemaster, wharfinger and
landlord of the Fishes, later the Nag's Head.

II. The descendants of his brother Thomas (1768–), bargemaster, then
fisherman.

Note: The Tree shows only boat-people of various types, and others involved in the trade of river and canal.

Adam, the sixth son. James, the fifth son, married a daughter of Thomas Hands, sometime a bargemaster, sometime a fisherman, and the lessee of property in Upper Fisher Row, in which James and his wife lived. Such marriages were esteemed. Abel I, the seventh son, married a boatman's daughter, Elizabeth Culpepper. The name is otherwise unknown in the parish. Samuel, the next surviving, ninth and last son, sank very low, for he went over to the enemy, married a member of the Bossom family, with which the Beesleys had a long-standing feud, and occupied a house as subtenant to his father-in-law, Benjamin Bossom.

We must be careful, nevertheless, not to overstate the differences between the two groups to such an extent that we cannot see them as forming a single community. The fact that three of these seven Beesley marriages were with girls who lived in the Row is surely evidence that it was. We should however, see it as a community in which there were all sorts of distinctions and social gradations. Differences of occupation marked one of the most basic of all. Sometimes descendants of Thomas Beesley I might marry boatmen's daughters, as Abel Beesley did, but only Jane Julia actually married a boatman. She was the youngest daughter of Thomas Beesley II, and according to the 1871 Census she looked after her parents in their old age. 19 years later, in 1890, still a spinster, she married a widower, the boatman Stephen Lamsden. One wonders how two elderly people from such different backgrounds got on together (see Family Tree 5.6, The Beesleys of Upper Fisher Row: contrasting occupational patterns).

CHAPTER 6

The Decline of Fisher Row

I. THE TIMETABLE OF DECLINE

It is easy, and mistaken, to see Fisher Row achieving full flower with the development of the canal community, and decline setting in when it started to decay with the coming of the railways. Even as the canal boatmen were settling into the Row, the barge trade was in decline, and whilst the Census of 1841 showed more fishermen in the area than at any time since the end of the 16th century, there was something unnatural and untimely about this.

The fortunes of the fishermen, the bargemen and the canal boatmen did not follow the same course. The origins of the decline of the bargemen must be looked for well before the coming of the railways, and of the fishermen even earlier, perhaps from the beginning of the 17th century. The demand for fish had been influenced by the practice of fasting and by the size of the population of Oxford, and it is difficult to gauge the extent to which the decline of the one was offset by the growth of the other. With the opening of the barge trade at the beginning of the 17th century, some fishermen turned to barging, so that whilst it is possible to talk of the fishermen as a declining group from this time, and the bargemen as developing in the 17th and 18th centuries, it was often a case of the fishermen changing jobs rather than abandoning the community. In the 19th century the canals first brought new trade to the Thames, and then as the network of canals extended, superseded it and rendered river transport almost obsolete. The redundant bargemen then reversed the trend of the earlier period, and turned back to fishing. Initially this movement back to fishing may have seemed wise,

for in the latter part of the 18th century the population of
Oxford started to increase and, presumably, so did the demand
for fish. However, the number of men expecting to make a living from it was large, and the waters limited.

The cutting of the canals was but a foretaste of more radical
changes to come, and it was these changes which ultimately
destroyed the fishermen. The fishermen were casualties of the
forces which changed England into an industrialised society.
They did not acquiesce in their fate, but the battle involved
issues larger than they realised: it was a collision between two
worlds, a battle between the champions of the old pre-industrial
society and the champions of the new industrial one which
superseded it. On the one hand we have a world in which a
man's position in life was settled by his birth, and the power
and privileges he enjoyed, depending on the status of his family
and their friends. In such a world the family was of primary
importance. A man's first duty was to his family, and the idea
of disinterested public service barely existed. The actual perquisites of office might or might not enrich a man's family
directly but the power and standing they brought encompassed
a man's family through patronage. In England the extended
family seldom existed as a household except as a special case,
but obligations to kin stretched beyond the nuclear family.
Although the fishermen and bargemen of the Row were not
part of the ruling oligarchy, they were part of the privileged
section of Oxford society, for they were freemen and usually
the sons of freemen. As such, though they might be illiterate, and sometimes poor, they had rank in the city which was
denied to even the wisest, wealthiest, and most cultivated man
of independent means, unless he were a freeman too. All this
was regarded as right and proper in a world where the outsider
was regarded with suspicion, as one who might divert to himself what was the birthright of the freemen.

In an industrial society ability and money, the hall-mark of
ability, gave merit, and were regarded as qualifications for the
exercise of power. Impartiality, equality of opportunity, and
justice were contrasted with nepotism, privilege, and corruption. Yet to the poor, uneducated yet privileged freemen the
new system seemed weighted against him. Inarticulate, he could
not easily defend his rights, nor was he usually sufficiently

well-to-do to buy the advocacy to put his case convincingly. For such men the old system had provided institutions which protected him from naked competition. In a world of equal opportunity he was outstripped. The new world in his eyes embodied a new ruthlessness. In few cities was the franchise as wide as in Oxford, so that it was natural that here opposition to reform should agitate the poorer freemen. For most it meant a diminution of old rights and a loss of privilege; for the fishermen, however, the new society also imperilled their living and their whole way of life, for their right to fish the free waters was threatened.

The coming of the railways affected the whole community. The position of the fishermen was further undermined, for the railways brought large quantities of sea-fish in prime condition on to the market at a reasonable price. They administered the *coup de grâce* to the river and they also affected the canals, which lost much of their trade to them. Having rendered the barging trade largely obsolescent in the first flush of industrialisation, the canals now suffered the same fate in the next wave of technological improvement.

The canal community declined slowly. There was no struggle or protest. A canal system dies first at its extremities. As trade declined the Oxford families of canal boatmen turned away from the local community and became more closely identified with the wider community of canal boatmen, and finally moved away from Oxford to the heart of the system, where trade still circulated. One way and another the community was all but dead by the end of the 19th century. And yet, it is still not quite dead, for it lives on a little while yet in the memories of old men and women. In the last chapter we shall see what light human memory can cast on this community which we have reconstructed from so many diverse records. In tracing the decline of the community in detail, however, we must go back to 1790, to the year in which the Oxford Canal was opened.

II. COMPETITION AND FEUD: THE BOSSOMS AND THE BEESLEYS

The opening of the Thames and Severn and the Oxford Canals brought competition to the river and dissension to its bargemen.

Family Tree 6.1. The Bossoms (tentative).

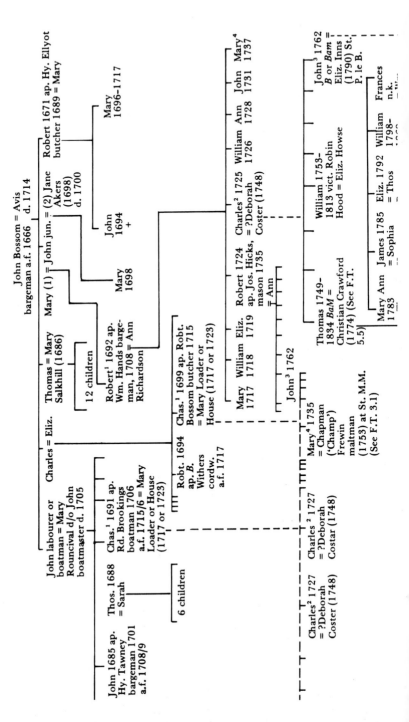

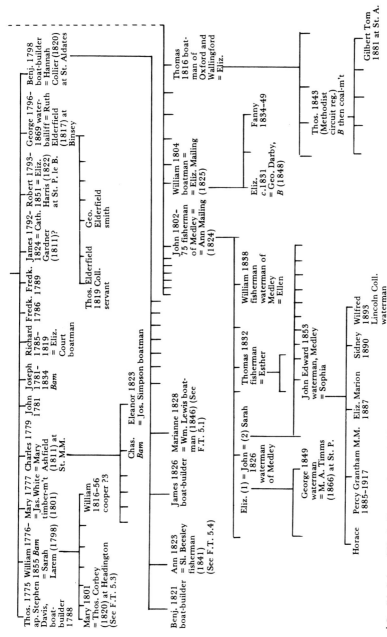

¹ Possible father of Charles Bossom who married Deborah Costar.
² Possible spouse of Deborah Costar.
³ Possible ancestor of the Bossoms of Medley.
⁴ Possible spouse of Chapman Frewin.

We have already seen how the Beesley brothers, William and Thomas, quarrelled over the trade from the Oxford Canal on to the river so that the family was split into two parts with different interests: William Beesley's descendants becoming involved in the canal trade; Thomas's descendants remaining on the river. Each of these branches of the family had a well-defined sphere of interest, and from this time they seem to have co-existed in the Row without further conflict. Where there was no clearly defined demarcation of interest, trouble was likely to occur, and this rivalry was probably the original cause of the feud which developed between the two leading families of the Row in the early canal period, the Bossoms and the Beesleys (for the Bossoms, see Family Tree 6.1).

The feud weakened the community, for feeling ran so high in the early 1820s the families were almost in a state of war. Presumably this was at least a part of the reason for the departure of a segment of the Bossom family to Medley. The antagonism of these two leading families also prevented them from acting in concert when the fisheries were jeopardised, and later prevented their co-operation in developing alternative employment as watermen.

In many ways the Bossoms and the Beesleys were very alike. In the female line, as we have seen, the Beesleys were descended from the Gardners. One important branch of the Bossom family who lived in Fisher Row could also claim descent from the Gardners. Both families were prolific, and, in a period when infant mortality was much reduced, they were over-blessed with sons. Charles Bossom produced nine children, including eight sons between 1749 and 1762, and some of these were bargemen. John Beesley produced a mere five sons out of 11 children between 1750 and 1771, but four of the sons grew up to become bargemen or bargemasters. Thomas and Christian Bossom produced 12 children between 1775 and 1798, but 11 were sons, and some grew up to become bargemen too. Starting in 1793, Thomas Beesley produced a family of 13 children, nine being sons, and seven growing up to become bargemen and fishermen. It is indeed fortunate that the two families' fertile periods did not overlap more than they did, for feuding is likely to be most marked between men who are close in age.

The experience of the two families was similar, for both were caught up in the trade of the river when it was artificially flushed by the wartime boom, and both suffered when peace brought recession and unemployment. Families which, with their numerous sons, would have brought success to a bargemaster in an expanding economy, suffered severely when employment was short. As in Northern Ireland at the moment, large numbers of underemployed young men provided a fertile source of recruits for feuding.

The first sign of bad blood between the two families occurred within a month of the opening of the Oxford Canal. The canal opened on New Year's Day, 1790, and on 30 January *Jackson's Oxford Journal* reported:

Last Tuesday Morning a pitched battle was intended to have been fought in Gloucester Green between Beasley and Bossom, a couple of Bargemen, for deciding a Difference that had happened upon the River, and a Wager of One Guinea, but by the Prudential Efforts of the Magistrates of this City the Crowd was dispersed – The Combatants immediately went out of the jurisdiction was well as the County, and in a Field a little above Botley, after a very short Contest, Beasley proved victorious, having among other injuries fractured one Rib of his Antagonist.

No further case reached the pages of the *Oxford Journal* for another thirty-two years. How far it smouldered or flared into incivilities upon the river we do not know, but perhaps it was a matter of generations, and depended on the presence of hot-headed contemporaries. In 1790 the protagonists were probably John Bossom I, the youngest brother of Thomas Bossom who was 27 at that time, and Thomas Beesley I who was 21. By 1822 when the next bout of feuding occurred, a new generation of Bossoms and Beesleys was ready for battle.

We shall, however, consider the fortunes of the two families in the interval, dealing with the Beesleys first and more briefly, as we have already encountered them. We shall only be concerned with the descendants of Thomas Beesley I, who, after his momentous quarrel with his brother William in 1797 turned to the river whilst his brother concerned himself with the canal and its trade. It was not an easy time for bargemasters, and even in these years of war-flushed trade, it was the men with the longest purses who flourished, while smaller men went to the wall. *Jackson's Oxford Journal* shows quite a run of bankruptcies among smaller bargemasters and coal- and corn-merchants during the war years. By 1801 Thomas Beesley was in financial trouble. On 20 May he was granted licence to assign his lease of the property in Upper Fisher Row to John Flory of Abingdon, a fisherman who may have been a relative, and on 23 May the *Oxford Journal* carried a notice of the sale of his goods for the benefit of creditors. The sale included house-hold goods from the house in Upper Fisher Row, and his barge 'now lying at Iffley'. His brother William died the following year, also in financial difficulties.

The Beesley family now entered a period of eclipse. Little is heard of Thomas Beesley, apart from the birth of his children. In 1811 when he renewed his lease to his property in Upper Fisher Row he called himself a fisherman, but this does not seem to have been a settled occupation, for when his children were baptised in 1814, and thereafter, he was said to be a bargeman.

Nevertheless when Thomas Beesley took a lease of tenement 1A in 1795, which lay beside The Lasher, he took a fateful step. When all else failed his family had two assets to exploit: firstly, as freemen they had the right to fish the free waters, and secondly, they occupied a tenement which had natural advantages for fishermen. It was inevitable that the family should become fishermen. In 1818 Thomas Beesley was probably still finding it difficult to make ends meet, and he divided his tenement into two parts, the southern being demised to Samuel Steane, the wharfinger of the Oxford Canal, who subdivided his part and sublet it.[1] The northern part by The Lasher continued in the hands of Thomas Beesley I, though it was occupied by his son, Thomas II. Thomas I was now said to be 'of Blenheim Park, fishermen'. Later he moved back to Fisher Row, and his descendants continued to live at the top of the Row to within living memory (see Appendix III, Tenement IA) The tenement which the son occupied was described as having The Lasher to the north of it, and in the lease of 1852 the City also leased to Thomas Beesley the Ham adjoining The Lasher, a long narrow strip of land, between the wall of Rewley Abbey and the Thames. This later became the site of the osier works of his nephew, Jacob Beesley. In the early 19th century, however, it was waste ground, and was used

---

[1] See Appendix III.

by fishermen to beach their boats and dry their nets. Before 1824 however, it seems likely that the Beesley family had begun to treat it as their own.

We must now turn back and consider the progress of the Bossom family especially in the first thirty years after the opening of the rival canals. The Bossom family had been connected with boats and the river for a very long period, as their family tree demonstrates, and they had been in the parish at least since the 17th century, as had the Beesleys. Unlike them, however, the males of the family had always been connected with the river. It is possible that through marriage with the Howse family the 19th-century Bossoms could claim descent in the female line from the family of the first boatman, John House, who took out his freedom in 1583. Unfortunately, however, at this point the family tree is full of ambiguities: it, is at best a setting out of probabilities. The only reason for presenting it is that the reader would be even worse off without it. There were three different Charles Bossoms all more or less of an age who could have married Mary House. In the next generation a Charles Bossom who married Deborah Costar seems to have been the ancestor of either all or about half the Bossoms in the parish, but which Charles Bossom was his father, and which Mary Bossom his mother? Or was he a son of Robert Bossom, and if so, of which? Nothing is certain. It is a farcical situation. It seems all round most likely, however, if the evidence of leases is closely considered, that the 19th century Bossoms were all descended from Charles and Deborah and that the Bossoms who played so important a part in the history of the river in the early 19th century were brothers. This is the possibility shown in the family tree.

The eldest of these putative brothers was Thomas who married Christian, the youngest daughter of John Crawford II and Margaret Crawford (née Gardner). She was the descendant of the two great barging families of Upper and Middle Fisher Row (née Family Tree 5.5). Given these antecedents it is not surprising that Thomas Bossom should take up property in Upper Fisher Row. In 1800 he leased the property immediately north of the wharf, once held by Henry Gardner, cousin to his wife's mother. His real opportunity seems to have come after the crash of the Beesley family – in 1801 Thomas's bankruptcy, and 1802 the death of William Beesley. By 1804 he leased the wharf, the wharf range of buildings, and some tenements to the north: in all about half the Row.[2] In 1805 he was in business as a bargemaster, with two barges lying at Brooks Wharf in London, awaiting orders. In 1812 he was listed as owning three barges, whilst his son-in-law, the timber-merchant, James White owned four.[3] Only one barge was owned by a Beesley. As the Bossoms waxed, the Beesleys waned.

Some at least of Thomas Bossom's other children had a connection with the river. There are, however, problems in identifying his sons and distinguishing them from their cousins or even from their younger uncles, William and John. Which of these Williams, for instance, was lock-keeper at Medley from about 1823 to 1838? Which William married Elizabeth Gunn in 1821, which Elizabeth Mailing in 1825, and which Elizabeth Basson in 1838? All were boatmen at least when their children were born. In a family so traditional in the naming of its children, so dedicated to riverine occupations, such questions may remain undecidable. It is not surprising that in the reconstitution of families for demographic purposes such families must be put aside. It is impossible to establish with certainty the length of such individuals' lives, so as to estimate mortality rates. It is therefore necessary to remember that where such violent surgery is performed, the selected remnant of the par-ish may not be truly representative, as it excludes the most successful families of the parish, from the point of view of sheer survival.

In 1814 Thomas Bossom who was now in his 65th year applied to the Council for licence to let his wharf to his son-in-law James White. In this same year a William Bossom was granted the lease of tenement IB, and so became a near-neighbour to the Beesleys, at the top of the Row.[4]

The Bossoms had now achieved their maximum holding in the Row, and in the lean post-war years they grew less prosperous. In January 1817 James White, the timber-merchant,

---

[2] See Appendix III.

[3] *JOJ*, 12 Jan. 1805; Zachary Allnutt, 'A List of Barges on the Thames remeasured in August-September 1812', quoted in Thacker, *Highway*, II, 120-1.

[4] See Appendix III.

was bankrupt, and the *Oxford Journal* announced a meeting of his creditors at The White Horse, Broadway – this meeting, in a Worcestershire town, is a reminder of how far-flung a timber-merchant's trading connections might be. In March the wharf, some tenements and stables, and 'a long and well established Public House, called the Running Horses' were up for sale. Eighteen months later, in 1819, William Bossom relinquished his lease to his tenement near the top of the Row.[5]

The Bossoms were feeling in their turn something of the depression that the end of war brought to the carrying trade, just as the Beesleys had done after the Treaty of Amiens. As the Beesleys had watched the Bossoms take up the trade in which they had foundered, and prosper with the renewal of war with France, it is not surprising if they harboured feelings of bitterness and envy; especially as they, who had probably employed the Bossoms in their own days of prosperity were now, in all probability, their servants. It was a small community, and the change would be obvious and poignant. To the Bossoms there may well have been much satisfaction in the situation, especially if the memory of the battle in 1790, won by a Beesley, was kept green. Their own difficulties which beset them after the Napoleonic wars would therefore be made doubly bitter by the Beesleys' enjoyment of their discomfiture.

Like the Beesleys, in their hour of need, the Bossoms turned to fishing as a way of making their livings. Like the Beesleys they were freemen, and like the Beesleys and all other free-men, they had the right to fish the Free Waters. And, like the Beesleys too, they leased property beside a sluice in Fisher Row. We do not know when the Bossoms first occupied the little houses which had been built just below The Lock, in Lower Fisher Row, for they were subtenants, but it seems likely that they did so when they turned to fishing, for they were traditionally fishermen's tenements. In the Poll Book for the 1820 election John, John, and William Bossom were listed as fishermen, whilst Badcock's Survey, of 1829, shows that John, John, and Richard Bossom lived to the south of the Lock, with George Bossom as the lessee of the tenement just

---

[5] *JOJ*, 4 Jan. 1817 and 8 Mar. 1819 (The tenant and landlord was Christopher Collier); Appendix III, Ten. IB.

to the north of it.[6] No site could have suited fishermen better
– apart, that is, from the tenement by The Lasher at the top
of Upper Fisher Row, and that was held by the Beesleys. The
very position of their houses thus made them rivals for control of the water of the Castle Mill Stream, as the millers of
Oseney and the Castle Mill had been centuries earlier. Feeling
between the two families grew bitter in the 1820s. The very
position of their houses exacerbated the feud.

III. THE FISHERMEN AND THEIR COMMON RIGHTS

In times of economic stringency common rights had a value
that they did not have at other times. Men must make the
best of what is available to them. At this time Port Meadow
and the Fisheries were seen as doubly valuable by the freemen in general. In the difficult times in which this is written (1977) allotments are in great demand, and flower gardens
are dug up and vegetable gardens planted. After the Napoleonic wars the Beesleys and the Bossoms were not the only
people to turn to their common rights. Other freemen became
more conscious of their value, and determined that they should
be protected. In 1820 the freemen felt Port Meadow to be
threatened, and the City Council received a petition from the
freemen complaining that a new lock had been built by the
Thames Commissioners to their great injury.[7] The lock in question was probably Medley Lock, for if the water there was held
up too high, the Meadow flooded. The petition was referred to
the Port Meadow Committee, which was also to recommend
a suitable man as water-bailiff. The days were long past when
men paid for the privilege, and expected to make a good thing
out of the perquisites of office. The water-bailiff no longer
held his own court at which miscreants were amerced. Cases
came before the City Court. Since 1783 a salary had even
been attached to the position, but it was not always possible
to fill it.[8] The lack of prosecutions in the early 19th century
suggests that the waters were under little or no supervision
at that time. In 1820 no appointment was made, but the slow

[6] *Oseney*, II. 602-3. This evidence particularly suggests the Bossoms we are con-cerned
with were very closely related.

[7] City, B.5.5, Council Book, 1813-32, 16 Mar. 1821.

[8] *Council Acts, 1752-1801*, 155, 187, 195.

machinery of local government turned to consider the condition of Port Meadow.

Ten months later the Committee reported, and ordered that its report should be appended to the acts of that particular council meeting, but it was not inserted, for a blank space divides the acts of that meeting from those of the next.[9] A year later the freemen requested the establishment of a joint committee of the Council and the freemen: 'The latter body being equally interested in the said common with the former – nor are we aware of any authority or custom by which the power of making Bye Laws for the regulation of the said Meadow is vested solely in the Members of the Council Chamber'.[10] At the time of the Municipal Corporations Act it was generally complained that the Council was drawn from the freemen, who formed only a small portion of the population of the city and did not represent it. Clearly even the freemen did not feel that their interests were adequately represented in 1822. This feeling was to grow stronger after the passing of the Municipal Corporations Act, when the election of the Council was no longer in any way their prerogative, and the relations of the freemen and the Council became even more strained.

As a result of this petition the Mayor convened a meeting of the freemen before the month was out, and a joint committee of eight members of the Council and 16 freemen was set up. George Bossom, one of the younger sons of Thomas Bossom, served on this committee.

Perhaps the meetings of this committee sharpened the freemen's appreciation of their rights, and gave a new twist to the sense of resentment the Bossoms felt towards the Beesleys. They saw the Beesleys as infringing the rights of the freemen in general, and sublimated their bitterness, which essentially arose from economic causes beyond the control of either party. Resentment and dissatisfaction boiled over into riot in 1822 in which a Beesley's orchard was destroyed. The affair is not mentioned in the newspaper at the time, but a case was brought against '—Bossom and others' by one Beesley, and the case went to the Beesleys. The case is in some ways obscure. It is not clear which of the Beesleys was injured, nor which property

[9] City, B 5 5, 29 May 1821.
[10] Ibid., 12 Apr. 1822.

belonging to the Beesleys was invaded. At this time a certain Samuel Beesley was a stable-owner who leased a certain amount of land. It is possible that he was the injured party, but it seems more likely, as the case unfolds, that the land invaded by the Bossoms was the Ham at the top of Upper Fisher Row, by Rewley wall on which boats were beached and nets dried (see p. 267). The case was probably brought by Thomas Beesley I or his son: it was reported in the newspaper as follows:

A very general sensation having been excited in this City by the causes of Beesley against Bossom and others, and the proceedings being brought now to a close by the award of Mr Sergeant Peake, to whom they were referred at the last Lent Assizes, it may not be uninteresting to our readers to have a short statement of the whole matter laid before them:

In October, 1822, a considerable number of persons entered into a garden in the possession of the plaintiff, and utterly destroyed it — they cut down all the trees, and trampled into the earth the crops of vegetables. Some idea may be formed of their havoc and devastation from the fact that nearly 200 trees were cut down valued at about 10 *l*. Not yet content, however, some of the defendants came again on the night of the 5th of November, and completed their work of desolation by burning the remains of their former vengeance — Application was in vain made for redress to those who had committed this outrage; and the plaintiff was reduced to the alternative of either submitting to it, or seeking redress at law. Actions were consequently brought, and the defendants, who were freemen of Oxford, and who contended that the garden had been formed out of the bed of the river, and usurped by the plaintiff, in derogation of their rights, put in pleas in justification of what they had done. The whole case was gone into before Mr Sergeant Peake, who, having heard the evidence on both sides, decided the issues in favour of the plaintiff, and awarded to him 30 *l*. damages for the first trespass, and 10 *l*. for the second; and having so disposed of the more immediate matters in dispute, the award goes on thus:- 'And whereas in addition to the matters pleaded by way of defence to the said actions, it was made a question before me, and insisted on by the defendants, that they, as freemen of the city of Oxford, were entitled to enter the plaintiffs close, and to lay boats there on for the purpose of repairing, and also to dry fishing nets thereon. Now I do award and determine, that the said defendants are not were entitled to hold and enjoy the same close, absolutely freed and discharged from any such claims'.[11]

A sequel to this affair seems to lie in the Council Acts some six years later, when the Beesleys' position was regularised. On 18 November 1831 the Council Acts record that Thomas Beesley was to pay a quit rent of 10s. for an encroachment

[11] *JOJ*, 19 Feb. 1825.

on the east side of Rewley Wall, and at the same meeting —
Bossom was required to pay a quit rent of 2s. 6d. yearly for
an encroachment on the river Isis under the wall of the canal
wharf. This strip of land, opposite Middle Fisher Row can still
be seen, with a door in what was formerly the canal wharf
wall. By such even-handed rulings, perhaps the Council hoped
to lessen the antagonism of the two families who were to be
called at a later date the Montagues and Capulets of the Isis.

Meantime the Port Meadow Committee concerned itself with
improvements, and in 1823 £50 was granted for repairs. In June
1824 a committee was appointed to inquire into the extent of
the fisheries, and a day was set aside to make a circuit of them,
when the presence not only 'of such Old Fishermen but of all
other persons who are interested' was solicited. Again the need
for a water-bailiff was stressed. On 11 November 1824 a report
was tabled, and ordered to be printed and circulated. No copy of
this report has yet been discovered, though a draft of the extent
of the waters has been found (see Appendix II). Finally, two
months after Sergeant Peake had settled the case of *Beesley* v.
Bossom and others in favour of Beesley, the Council appointed
George Bossom as water-bailiff.[12] In the light of later events
it seems a strange appointment, but the extent and bitterness
of the feud lay in the future. As well, the Bossoms defence in
the case *Beesley* v. *Bossom* had been that the Beesleys were
encroaching on the freemen's rights, and so they appeared the
self-appointed defenders of these rights. The general effect,
however, was that from now on not only were the Beesleys (like
other freemen) fishing controlled and regulated waters, but the
controller of these waters was their enemy.

If this is how the Beesleys saw it, there is no reason to
believe George Bossom saw the matter in this light. George
Bossom was an able and intelligent man. By 1828 he had also
become a member of the city police force and was to rise still
higher. In his first four years as water-bailiff he prosecuted
his cousin John Bossom (or perhaps his uncle) twice, and only
one member of the Beesley family, as far as is known. This
was Sarah Beesley, who was taken up for selling freshwater
fish out of season in the market.[13] Perhaps the prosecutions

[12] *JOJ*, 16 Apr. 1825.
[13] *JOJ*, 19 Aug. 1826, 14 Feb. 1829 (John Bossom); ibid., 14 Apr. 1827 (Sarah Beesley).

of John Bossom made John Bossom for a time an honorary Beesley, however, for one finds him involved in aiding one of the Beesley family in escaping the law. Yet, in Fisher Row, which was a much intermarried community, family ties may make for alliances at first not obvious, and perhaps this was so in this case. The Thomas Beesley involved in this case was probably Thomas Beesley, son of Samuel Beesley, who married Maria Collier. Now John Bossom's cousin Benjamin, brother to George, was married to a Collier as well, so there were perhaps more things than meet the eye in this case. Nor was the crime for which Thomas Beesley was tried as simple, capricious, and straightforward as it appeared in the paper. He was tried for murder, but the jury returned a verdict of manslaughter, and he seems to have served only seven years, rather than being transported for fourteen years as reported in the paper; for in the parish registers there is a gap of only seven years, from 1828 to 1837, in the run of his children (see Family Tree 5.1).

The case arose out of a fracas between some Oxford men and the inhabitants of Wolvercote. The village of Wolvercote borders Port Meadow, and has rights of intercommonage on it. From time to time there had been a certain amount of ill-feeling, and some horseplay between the people of Oxford and those of Wolvercote, and it was not always clear – even perhaps to the inhabitants – where one ended and the other began. The occasion in 1829 may have started as an incident in what amounted in part at least to a dispute over boundaries. On the afternoon of 2 July the inhabitants of Wolvercote had seen a group of young men from Oxford, including Thomas Beesley and William Newman, driving their cattle, ducks, and geese on the meadow in a violent manner. Two Wolvercote men, Robinson and Eeley went out 'for the purpose of pro-tecting their property' and to ask them to desist. 'Tom, you ought to know better than to destroy poor men's prop-erty', said Robinson. 'Do you mean to say I have got one [a duck] in my pocket', Beesley had asked, and in his pocket a duck had quacked.[14] The two Wolvercote men were attacked and retreated to Wolvercote, pursued by the 'ruffians', one of whom struck Robinson and knocked him into a ditch. At

---

[14] The account is drawn from the newspaper report of the incident, *JOJ*, 11 July 1829; *JOJ*, 18 July 1829, and from the account of the trial, *JOJ*, 6 Mar. 1830.

Wolvercote they challenged the whole village to fight. They then returned to the meadow and 'proceeded to vent their fury on the cattle and the poultry', Eeley and another man armed with bludgeons now attacked them, and blows were exchanged. The Wolvercote men again retreated and went into the public house called the Plough (which still exists). Various of the inhabitants of the village had assembled to watch the proceedings. Four of the men, including Thomas Beesley came over 'from Lower Wolvercote to the Plough, and Beesley took the bludgeon from Eeley, and rushed on the crowd who were quietly standing by and attacked them. Newman fell on Robinson, whilst Beesley attacked a young man, John Barrett (perhaps the son of Lord Abingdon's gamekeeper) whose back was towards him. He struck him a tremendous blow on the head. The two men Robinson and Barrett were taken to the Infirmary, where Barrett died the next day. The four Oxford men were arrested soon after, but Thomas Beesley and William Newman were rescued by some of their friends, who took them 'over the water', that is, into Berkshire. On 25 July John Bossom and Robert Newman were charged at Abingdon with rescuing the two men from the custody of John Thomas and William Saxton, and John Tubb was indicted for aiding Bossom and Newman in escaping from the constables, [George] Bossom and Keats, at Sandford on 4 July. Thomas Beesley and William Newman had, however, been successfully rescued for a time at least. An advertisement for their apprehension with a reward of £50 appeared in the *Oxford Journal* on 18 July. Thomas Beesley was described in some detail, and as we seldom get a description of any member of the community, it is given here:

about 30 years of age, about 5 feet 7 inches in height, middle sized, light complexion, rather freckled face, rather dark hair, whiskers a little sandy, has the appearance of a boatman or bargeman, had on a pair of fustian trousers, red plush waistcoat, with brown fustian sleeves, and a pair of half-boots, a black leather cap bound round with fur; walks rather stiffly with one leg.

Despite this detailed description it seems to have been some time before he was recaptured. The trial took place the following March. No one seems to have raised the question of George Bossom being implicated in the escape of his cousin, John

Bossom. He had certainly shown him no favour earlier, and continued to be regarded as a zealous officer. When the New Police were established in 1836 he became an Inspector, and by 1841, he was Governor of the City Gaol.

IV. REFORM AND RIGHTS OF COMMON

The fishermen of the Row were inevitably freemen, and so were most of the bargemen, and as such, they were amongst that privileged minority of Englishmen who had the franchise before 1832. It has been estimated that in 1801 about 3 per cent of adult males had the vote, and in 1831 less than 500,000 in a population of about 20,000,000 persons. This privilege came to the Oxford freemen as members of a borough in which all freemen were enfranchised, and in which being a freeman was still a matter of considerable importance economically. It was still impossible to be a tradesman in Oxford without being a freeman, and therefore the number of freemen was higher than average, being about 1,400 in a population of about 20,660 persons, or one in fourteen, over three times the average national representation.[15] The fishermen and bargemen of the Row were often illiterate and sometimes poor, but in this they were not unusual amongst the freemen, who covered a wide social range. This was noted, with disapproval by the Commissioners' inquiry in 1833:

The consequence of this [the treating and drunken proceedings at council elections] is, that the respectable and instructed portion of the freemen [tradesmen and shopkeepers] studiously absent themselves from the elections, and ... the annual vacancies are generally filled up by the votes of less than 500 persons, consisting of the inmates of the workhouse who, on election days, have a holiday for this purpose — and of the most indigent, illiterate and worthless inhabitants of the city.[16]

Oxford was, in fact, one of those places whose franchise was regarded as too wide, by most of the supporters of the Reform Bill, and too democratic as well as too corrupt. In such boroughs it was the intention of the reformers to disenfranchise the less 'respectable' portion of the electorate, whilst giving the vote to persons, assumed to be respectable, who could fulfil certain property qualifications. The fact that the

[15] PP. Eng. 1835/xxiii, pt 1 (116), *First Report of the Commissioners on Municipal Corporations*, 33.
[16] Ibid., Appendix, 99.

freemen of such boroughs as Oxford retained their vote was due to the Tories and not the reformers, and they retained it in the name of privilege rather than democracy. Only in an attempt to gain the support of waverers in the House of Lords at the 11th hour – in the third, revised, Reform Bill introduced in December 1831 – was the freemen's franchise allowed.

Had the original intention of the reformers been pursued, the political power of the freemen of Oxford would have been extinguished. Furthermore, during the progress of the second bill the Tories managed to insert an amendment which increased the powers of county landlords, 'the Chandos clause', and to counterbalance this a further clause was inserted to allow the county vote to borough freeholders worth 40s., but not wealthy enough to qualify for the borough franchise. There was little freehold land in Oxford, and this clause probably benefited most the inhabitants of the newly developed free-hold land in St Ebbes, opened up in the 1820s. It was from this area that the only petitions emanated in favour of reform.[17] Here striving, serious artisans were buying small houses for which they were beholden to none of the great Oxford land-lords, the colleges, whose property was in the main leased out on 40-year leases, and who dominated the property market.

Because of the struggle involved in passing the Great Reform Bill it failed to reduce the privilege against which it sought to wage battle, or at least, the privileges of those it considered unmeritorious. It affected the freemen of Oxford only by diluting the political powers of the freemen by injecting a new group of voters. In the first election after the passing of the Act in March 1833, 1,408 freemen voted, and 904 householders.[18]

In the Municipal Corporations Act of 1835 privilege was again attacked, and this act's provisions were to affect the freemen of Oxford far more seriously than the Reform Act itself. Its progress was reported fully in *Jackson's Oxford Journal*. The bill was brought forward by Lord John Russell. A Committee had, he said, examined more than 200 corporations.

---

[17] R. J. Morris, 'The Friars and Paradise: an Essay in the Building History of Oxford, 1801-1861', *Oxon*. XXXVI (1971), 80; PP. Eng. 1830-1/iii (263), *Reports of the Select Committee on Petitions in favour of Parliamentory Reform*, 7.

[18] *JOJ*, 17 Aug. 1833.

He would not list the abuses, but some were so strong that he could not forbear to notice them. Norwich, Oxford, Cambridge, and Liskeard were cited. In his opinion, one of the first objects of these corporations ought to be to represent the owners of property in these towns, to take care of their interests, and to give due protection to those who were liable to pay the expenses of the government.[19] A week later the newspaper reported Lord Stanley as saying that it was a main principle of the bill to take from the self-elected corporations the control of the corporation funds, and to vest them in the control of the inhabitants of the borough.[20] 'The following information respecting provisions of this bill may prove interesting to our readers', announced the journal. The bill provided that no freedoms should in future be granted, and that no freemen (as such) should vote in Council elections.[21]

In the following issue a warm debate between the reformers and the supporters of freemen's rights was reported. On 11 July it was reported Donald Maclean, member for Oxford, raised the question in committee as to whether the property of the old corporation should be vested in the new? What would happen to Port Meadow?[22] Similar questions were being raised by other towns with property in land or charities. The old corporations were defended when the matter was argued by counsel before the House of Lords, and Sir Charles Wetherell, in their defence, called, among others, the Town Clerk of Oxford. His comfortable and complaisant assertions provoked an outburst from local reformers in a letter to the *Oxford Journal* in August 1835, on 'the corrupt Corporation of this City', signed by 26 persons, some later prominent Liberal members of the council. *Jackson's Oxford Journal* which was a Tory paper printed a reply immediately, dealing with each signatory in turn:

> One Bookseller to lead the van
> And three who cobble *Cordovan*
> Painter and a Tailor,
> second 'ninth part of a man',
> And to screw up the well-wrought plan
> Carpenter and Nailer...
> A *Hatter* to—no Royal Highness,

[19] Ibid., 13 June 1835.
[20] Ibid., 20 June 1835.
[21] Ibid., 20 June 1835.
[22] Ibid., 11 July 1835.

A *Whitesmith* noted for his shyness!
A Chemist effervescing...

The bill however became act. The Municipal Corporations Act (5 & 6 Will. IV c. 76) was less like the overhaul of an old machine than its replacement by a new model. Though the freemen retained the parliamentary franchise, they lost the exclusive right as freemen to appoint the council and its officials. The new electorate consisted of male, adult householders of premises rated for the Poor Rate who had fully paid such rates and also those of the borough. They must have been in occupation of such a property for two years, and also lived in or within seven miles of the borough in that time. Aliens, those in receipt of parish relief or charities of the town were excluded from the franchise. The qualification was low, but it excluded many of the poorer freemen. The style of the corporation was changed from 'The Mayor, Bailiffs and Commonalty' to 'the Mayor, Aldermen and Burgesses'. The bailiffs, who had been responsible for law and order, together with constables, were replaced by the Sheriff, a new official, and the New Police. Port Meadow (it was held) came under the Sheriff's control, and also the Free Waters. Port Meadow and the fisheries remained to the freeman, but in what fashion was to be debated. According to the Act it reserved 'rights of the freemen in common lands, &c. as fully and effectually, and for such time and such manner as they, by any Statute, Charter, Bye Law, or Custom in force at the time of the passing of that Act might or could have been acquired or enjoyed in case that Act had not been made', (5 & 6 Will. IV c. 76 § 2). Reports of Council Meetings henceforth appeared in the press. Clearly the reformed council saw itself as adopting a more open and democratic form of government. It was also to be free from the abuse of the city's funds. Expenditure on such self-indulgent activities as feasting were to be curtailed. There would be no beer and circuses – nothing which smacked of bribery and corruption. Lord John Russell had regarded as the worst sort of city government that in which a self-interested oligarchy, ruled with the support of a portion of 'the lower class ... whose votes they bought and whose habits they demoralised'.[23] The new regime was to be more austere. Their

[23] *Parliamentary Debates*, XXVIII, col. 545.

effort to come to terms with the old saturnalia of the riding of the franchises supplies a picture of their attempt, and its failure to impose this new mood on public life. The attempt at reform of a ceremony whose function was not understood has an importance in the history of the fisheries which makes it worth considering in detail.

Under the old council the bounds had been ridden whenever a mayor held that office for the first time, but not on any sub-sequent appointment of the same man. It had been a jolly occasion, much enjoyed by the freemen, and involving a certain rumbustiousness and 'horseplay, with beer, cheese, and cakes supplied to all and sundry at traditional halting places, and feasting by the mayor and his party, at Godstow. The ceremony lasted the full day, for the bounds of the city were perambulated partly on foot, partly by boat. Ditches must be crossed, planks carried, and many miles must be traversed. Nevertheless, the ceremony was no idle frolic, for by it the freemen instructed each mayor on taking office of the bounds of the city, the Meadow, and above all of the free waters. Indeed, on their perambulation it often seems it is the limits of the free waters which are delimited more than the actual physical boundaries of the land.[24]

Under the new council such ceremonies were to be reduced in number and expense. They were to be triennial. The city drummer was deprived of his post. The bounds were first perambulated under the new dispensation in July 1837, shortly after the accession of Victoria. It was a decorous occasion, and the freemen played no part in it. The Mayor, several of the Council, and the City officers made the circuit as far as Godstow, where they were joined by the rest of the Council and 'numerous friends', and then 'the whole party', sat down to 'an excellent cold dinner followed by a profusion of rich wines and a splendid dessert',[25] as the Journal reported. The account was no doubt read with anger and resentment by the freemen, for three years later ceremonies were brought back and perhaps even embellished.

The day started soon after eight in the morning, with the city drummer in the van. At the Free Water Stone 'an old

---

[24] I owe this observation to Dr Janet Cooper.
[25] *JOJ*, 22 July 1837.

freeman on whom has been conferred the title of the King of the Sclavonians made his appearance according to ancient custom',[26] and greeted the Mayor. At Hogacre Ditch he put in his claim for toll 'for the benefit of old and decayed free-men'. At Godstow the '*worthies* or poorer class of freemen were most liberally entertained by the Mayor in Godstow Meadow with beer and cheese'. Yet freemen were not allowed to fulfil their most important function. In demarcating the bounds of the city the Sheriff relied on the antiquarian researches of Mr W. Joy. Beer and circuses had been restored, but the teaching function exercised by the old men of the town and the continuity of this teaching were lost. With a triennial perambulation mayors might hold office without ever receiving this instruction in the bounds of the franchises. It is not surprising therefore that in modern times the full extent of the fisheries is no longer known by the Council.

Despite the apparent deference paid the freemen by the council in this second perambulation of the bounds, this was but an intermission in hostilities. Feeling ran high amongst the freemen. Who controlled the city's commons – the Meadow and the Fisheries? The Council assumed the right to be theirs on the basis of Clause 6 of the Corporations Act which stated that 'the newly created body corporate shall be capable in law, by the Council of the Borough, to do and suffer all such Acts which then lawfully they and their successors might do or suffer by any name or title of Incorporation'. In June 1837 they set to work. A committee was set up to frame bye-laws for their regulation. In March 1838 Alderman Sadler brought a petition from 210 persons praying for the better regulation of Port Meadow, and prayed that a hayward and a herdsman be appointed.[27] It was urged that fines be imposed for transgressing the laws of the fisheries also, but the legality of imposing such fines being uncertain, the question was left over until the Committee had considered the matter. A week later the Council received the report of the Committee. The bye-laws proposed that the Fence Months be extended and run from 1 March to 1 June, and all nets should be scaled by the Sheriff. In this time no fish might be taken in the city waters or fresh water fish exposed for sale, under certain penalties.

[26] Ibid., 18 July 1840.   [27] Ibid., 24 Mar. 1838.

For a first offence this was 20s. and costs; for a second offence
£5 and costs or three months in gaol; for the third offence
offenders were liable to disenfranchisement. A water-bailiff to
enforce the bye-laws was to be appointed, and one John Bossom was put forward.

When Alderman Sadler proposed that the new bye-laws be
accepted and sent to the Secretary of State he met with opposition.[28] Mr Talboys sprang to the defence of the freemen. He
questioned the legality of the bye-laws. They had powers to
make laws for the good of the borough, but he did not think
they had the power to disenfranchise the freemen. He thought
the fisheries were adequately protected and such an exercise of
power was uncalled for. It was preposterous to disenfranchise
freemen for illegally fishing three times in the city waters.

The bye-laws were sent to the Secretary of State and
sanctioned by the Government. Talboys then wrote to Lord John
Russell 'and the consequence was that his Lordship sent a second letter, stating that certain things would not be sanctioned'.
There was much bitterness and vituperation. Mr Thomas Sheard
blamed the confusion over the bye-laws on Lord John Russell's
'listening to the petty communications of interested parties,
instead of attending to the statements made by the constituted authorities'. The resolution about disenfranchise merit
was then expunged.[29]

The new water-bailiff now set to work. The John Bossom
who had been appointed to the post was almost certainly the
very same John Bossom who had helped in the rescue of Thomas Beesley, and later escaped – a man already twice arrested
by George Bossom for fishing offences. Since that time he
had become somewhat steadier it would seem, for he had
been appointed lock-keeper at Medley on the dismissal of a
William Bassoon.[30] On 15 September 1838 the first proof of
his activity may be seen, at the City Sessions, when Joseph
Beesley was charged with assaulting John Bossom the water-
bailiff.[31] However, John Bossom was not entirely regenerate.
On 24 November Mr Sheriff Hastings reported a breach of
duty on the part of John Bossom the water-bailiff. He had

[28] Ibid., 31 Mar. 1838.
[29] Ibid., 19 May 1838; D. A. Talboys, *the Proposed bye-laws* (Oxford, 1838).
[30] Thacker, *Highway*, II. 106.   [31] *JOJ*, 15 Sept. 1838.

been laying a net of improper size at Medley to catch eels, and the Council was to consider the matter.[32]

The problem of the position of the freemen of cities and boroughs and of their commons was not one which affected Oxford only. A Select Committee was established to inquire into their position, and the corporations were asked for information. The position and attitudes of the reformed council are clearly exhibited in the answers to their questionnaire by G. P. Hester, the Town Clerk. The developing tension is clear.

To their second question Hester replied that there had been no alteration in the right of common or the fisheries, except that the council have no power, under the acts regulating corporations, to grant any money for the necessary repairs of the bridges and roads in Port Meadow, or for draining it, which, with some other improvements, was much needed. Then to the question as to whether the council claimed to have any custody or control over any property which was or had been applied to the individual use or benefit of the freemen, he replied that the Council claimed control

of Port Meadow and the fisheries by way of trustees to the freemen, and for their benefit; but their power has been questioned ... The council are very desirous to let Port Meadow to a lessee for the benefit of the freemen; it is estimated that it would produce 1,000 *l.* per annum; and if they could not let it, they are desirous to stint and otherwise regulate the common, and also enact bye-laws for preserving the breed of fish. It is doubtful whether their interference would be well received by a majority of the freemen.[33]

The anomalous position of the Meadow led to some of the freemen making a large claim. Under the Reform Bill 40s. freeholders in cities, who did not meet the property qualification in such cities, were entitled to vote in the county elections. If it could be proved that the freemen's rights in the Meadow and the fishery amounted to a 40s. freehold, then the freemen contended, they would be entitled to vote not only in the city but the county election. Eighty freemen sent in a claim for registration in St Thomas's parish in respect of their rights in Port Meadow and the fisheries. The grounds for qualification were queried and the case came up before the revising barristers. In

---

[32] Ibid., 24 Nov. 1838.
[33] PP. Eng. 1840/xi (465), *Select Committe on Freemen of Cities and Boroughs,* Appendix, 193-4.

such cases the revising barristers would select and try the right in one case, and the judgement was then applied to the others.[34] The case selected was that of Thomas Beesley, junior, fisherman of Fisher Row. The freemen, said their lawyer, a Mr Maley of Bicester, possessed rights of fishing the city waters and grazing their cattle, subject to certain restrictions; but the soil of the Meadow was in the Corporation. The number of freemen was about 2,400, and the extent of the Meadow about 400 acres, and if let these would be worth about £3 an acre. The fisheries extended several miles. Thomas Beesley the claimant proved that he had exercised his right of fishing in the waters many years, and had cut the sedge and rushes *'a good deal in his time'*; that he earned 30 *l.* a year *regularly* by fishing and cutting'. However, he had to admit he could not get so much if all the freemen exercised their rights. Mr Maley submitted he had shown a prima-facie case. Mr Brunner, the Recorder, submitted that the freehold of the meadow lay in the Corporation, and that the Meadow and fishery could not be shown to give the freemen a value of even 20s. a year, even if under the Act the freemen had acquired freeholds for life.[35]

The decision was followed with much interest in the town. The question, it was said, was whether the benefit of Port Meadow to the freemen amounted to an estate of 40s. a year, and to this the answer was no. The land not owned by the corporation was enjoyed jointly with Wolvercote and Binsey, who had rights of intercommoning. It was common by reason of vicinage, and did not amount to sufficient to grant a right of franchise. It was, he said, referring to Blackstone, 'an excuse for what is, in strictness, a trespass'.[36] The judge next turned to deal with the land in the fee of the corporation, and proved that here there could be no right of common either.

A right of common vested in the Corporation it cannot be, since the Corporation cannot have common over its own land. Nor can it be a right of common in the freemen, since it appears from the note to Saunders, which we have already cited, that they cannot prescribe for such a right. It follows, that the privilege must have originated in some arrangement

[34] J. Alun Thomas, 'The System of Registration and the Development of Party Organisation, 1832-70', *History*, New Series, xxxv (1950), 81-3.

[35] *JOJ, 25 Spet. 1841.*

[36] W. Blackstone, *Commentaries on the Laws of England* (5th edn., Oxford, 1773), II, 33.

anciently made amongst the members of the Corporation as to the mode in which this property was to be enjoyed; and considered as we think it must be in that point of view, it is insufficient to confer the franchise. It is a mere license, rendered indeed irrevocable by the Municipal Corporations Act, but not amounting to a freehold tenement.

The freehold of both Meadow and fishery he held to be vested in the body politic, and if this were not so, then 'the only alternative would be to hold that the land is vested in the Corporation as a trustee for the freemen, in order that they might enjoy the right of pasturage ... whether it is this or a license is a question of evidence'. And he held the evidence cogent that it accrued by way of license, not of trust 'And if it had accrued by trust, then it was not sufficient to confer the franchise.' Had the decision been different, the *Oxford Journal* noted, there would have been at least 2,000 claims the following year.[37]

The decision attempted to deal with a baffling problem. As W. G. Hoskins has remarked, the origin of common lands 'is a most obscure problem in English history: yet it is not an academic problem, for it has its living repercussions down to the present day'.[38] The feudal maxim *Nulle terre sans seigneur* used opportunistically sometimes as statement of fact, sometimes as edict, was used by lawyers to justify the claims of manorial lords to common land, but it did not apply so neatly to the lands of towns. So long as the freemen to whom a charter had been granted were the rulers of a town the question did not arise, but when Parliament by act of parliament handed over the power to another group, then indeed, what had happened to the ownership of the freemen's common lands?[39] All common land is private property, say W. G. Hoskins and L. Dudley Stamp in their book based on their work for the Royal Commission on Common Land, 1955-8; and even they were puzzled by Port Meadow: 'who actually owns the common does not seem to be clear.[40]

---

[37] *JOJ*, 9 Oct. 1841. This seems unlikely as only people who did not have a sufficient property qualification to vote in the city election could qualify as 40s. freeholders for the country vote. Many freemen would qualify to vote in city elections on grounds of property. Only the poorer freemen would have gained a double vote. D. G. Wright, *Democracy and Reform 1815-1885* (London, 1970), 38-9.

[38] W. G. Hoskins and L. Dudley Stamp, *The Common Lands of England and Wales* (London, 1963), 7.

[39] F. W. Maitland, *Township and Borough* (Cambridge, 1898, repr. 1964), 1-17.

[40] Hoskins and Stamp, *Common Lands*, 4, 131.

V. THE BEESLEYS v. THE REFORMED COUNCIL

The feeling of the freemen about the Meadow and the Fisheries was deep and emotional, and their attitude was the more intransigent because they had lost control of the council, and felt fearful of any threat to their rights to the Meadow and waters. In the time of the Peasants' Revolt, in 1381, the peasants had made claims to lost rights to hunt chases and have free warrens (and warrens included fisheries), and to govern boroughs through their own corporations. They looked to a past when they had freedoms which they claimed had been unjustly usurped and which had been embodied in the ancient charters of Canute and Offa.[41] In the same way the freemen of Oxford put their trust in ancient charters. 'Port Meadow', one said 'was given by the Conqueror in 1070, and they had enjoyed it for 773 years, and it was recorded in the vellum books'.[42] Perhaps their intransigence was all the greater for the fact that the Sheriff was now the member of the new council who had to do with the Meadow and the fisheries. Around Robin Hood had gathered all the legend of social discontent of the 15th and 16th centuries, and the Sheriff of Nottingham had been the very image of the corrupt ruler, of injustice in high places.[43] We can only speculate on whether the freemen of Oxford cast the Sheriff of Oxford in a similar role. Certainly the Beesley family, with their insistence on their inherited rights, and their defiance of authority behaved as if they were all but reenacting the legend.

From the time of the passing of the Municipal Corporations Act, and the new corporation's attempts to control the fisheries, the Beesley family was in constant trouble. As the Bossoms had attached themselves to the establishment in various ways the Bossom-Beesley feud and the war with what they regarded as wrongfully usurping authority mingled; privilege and family feud becoming intertwined. In the 1840s the two seemed inextricably tied together. Indeed, with the Bossoms policing the waters it must frequently have been difficult for the Beesleys to tell where law enforcement ended and vendetta began.

[41] M. H. Keen, *The Outlaws of Medieval Legend* (London, 1961), 162-3.
[42] *JOJ*, 2 Dec. 1847.
[43] Keen, *Outlaws*, 149-50

In 1838, as we have seen, Joseph Beesley assaulted the newly
appointed water-bailiff, John Bossom, and shortly thereafter
John Bossom was suspended for setting nets illegally. On
22 May 1841 Sheriff Hunt reported to the Council that the
Beesleys had been found with their nets unsealed in the fence
months, so contravening the new regulations. All had acknowledged their transgression and promised not to repeat it, save
Joseph Beesley, who was to be prosecuted. At the end of the
same year James, brother to Joseph, was prosecuted for illegal
fishing on the evidence of John Bossom of Medley Pound.[44] In
1843 James Beesley was again in trouble, reported for pasturing
cattle for his brother-in-law, a non-freeman, on Port Meadow.
The evidence was given by William Bossom, the hayward. Two
months later George Bossom laid evidence against two of the
other Beesley brothers.[45] Samuel and Richard Beesley were
charged at the Hustings Court with illegal fishing and threatened with disenfranchisement. On the advice of their lawyer, Mr
Brunner, they pleaded guilty, were reprimanded and forgiven.[46]

Bitterness between the two families was not limited to
the river and the meadow. Nor was it total. In 1841 one of
the Beesley brothers, Samuel, married Ann, the daughter of
Benjamin Bossom. This, however, did not lead to any permanent rapprochement. In the Row the feud continued. Indeed
intermarriage may have added a further dimension to the bitterness. In 1844 Abel, Samuel Beesley's brother, was fined in the
City Court for insulting one Ann Bassoon.'[47] In 1846 an Ann
Beesley was gaoled for fourteen days for insulting Elizabeth
Pebody. Elizabeth Pebody (née Lewis) was a granddaughter of
William Beesley, and her brother, William Lewis, had married
a Bossom earlier in the year.[48]

The real struggle, however, continued on the river and in the
meadow. The Beesleys were now in an isolated position. In
any town with fisheries there is always a danger that the professional fishermen will arouse bad feeling by exploiting the
fisheries, or being thought to do so. At a time when the population of the town had increased rapidly and pollution was
heavy, fish were likely to decline with or without the help

[44] *JOJ*, 18 Dec. 1841.   [45] Ibid., 5 June 1843.
[46] Ibid., 19 Aug. 1843.[47] Ibid.   [47] 4 May 1844.   [48] Ibid., 20 June 1846.

of the fishermen, but the freemen blamed the decline on the fishermen, and particularly the Beesleys. Whilst the freemen in general might be anxious to prevent the Council's controlling the waters, they also felt that the waters needed some protection from the Beesleys. As the sport of angling was increasing in popularity, so the need for regulation impressed itself on the freemen. Idealists on the Council also were inclined to think that the waters should be free to everyone. This view was, however, political dynamite.

The isolation of the Beesleys was probably further increased in 1844 with the opening of the Great Western Railway link to London by way of Didcot. River fish had now to compete against excellent and very cheap sea-fish. Locally river fish was perhaps all but superfluous except as a free supplement to the larder. Whilst the fishermen might cling to their occupation and adapt only slowly, the townsmen had now little to gain by their activities.

In 1846 the condition of the fisheries was deteriorating and a joint committee of freemen and members of the Council was set up to consider the situation. 'Nothing could be more wretched than the state of the fisheries of this city', according to the Mayor. Hester, the Town Clerk, urged that it was necessary that some arrangement be made 'to render the city waters a source of amusement to others, beside those who obtained a living from them'. The law was that the fisheries should not be drawn until the Mayor and the Corporation had had their fishing at Michaelmas, but now the waters were drawn long before that.[49] Alderman Sadler said that they did not wish to rob the fishermen of their living, but they should fish 'in a proper manner'. An act of Parliament would however, be necessary if the waters were to be regulated. Mr Faulkner pointed out that even if the sheriff had not the power to enforce bye-laws, every freeman bound himself to observe the bye-laws on taking up his freedom. Every freeman must protect his rights. 'Some did', he continued 'and a little too much, for one family (the Beesleys) looked after the fisheries day and night – (loud laughter) – it was no longer free water, but Beesley water ... if a poor man wanted a fish dinner he must go to Mr Beesley and pay for it.' Apart from pugilism, he

[49] i.e. dragged with a draft net, a species of seine net.

continued, amusement was lacking in Oxford, and angling should be encouraged.[50]

Six months later another joint meeting of the Council and the freemen was held. The drawing of the city waters was held to be particularly harmful and destructive of fish, and a bye-law was generally approved, imposing a fine for drawing the waters, and for the confiscation of nets. Water-bailiffs were also to be appointed – 'To look after one family' as a voice from the hall remarked – and this also was passed. The Beesleys alone objected to both measures. The Town Clerk, Hester, attempted reason. The law against drawing the water might press hard on certain persons and the Beesleys had prepared nets at great expense for a draught at Michaelmas and they ought to have compensation. He himself was ready to do his part he announced amid cheers. The meeting ended and the Beesleys announced they would go 'a-drawing in defiance of all the world'.[51]

The Beesleys set out to test the validity of the bye-laws. At Michaelmas James and Joseph Beesley drew the free waters as usual, from Folly Bridge to the boundary. When it was reported to the Council Hester said he understood that they had done so on the advice of a learned serjeant in the neighbourhood.[52]

The Council satisfied themselves meantime in prosecuting some non-freemen who had helped the Beesleys drag the nets and sought legal advice themselves. Sergeant Manning and Mr Alexander gave their opinion that the Council and Common Hall had the right to make bye-laws governing the fisheries.[53]

Two months later new bye-laws were submitted to the freemen and the Council, and it was decided that two waterbailiffs were to be established.[54] Yet two months later an Angling Society was formed, with Hester, the Town Clerk, as President and Treasurer. The society was to rent waters for itself, and, to ensure that both the city bye-laws and national laws regarding fisheries were enforced, eight part-time water bailiffs were to be appointed. The men chosen lived along the banks of the river, being mainly pub-keepers (like Richard Alder of Binsey

[50] *JOJ*, 25 Apr. 1846.
[51] Ibid., 26 Sept. 1846.
[52] Ibid., 3 Oct. 1846.
[53] Ibid., 13 Feb. 1847.
[54] Ibid., 17 Apr. 1847 and 12 June 1847.

and William Lipscombe of Godstow), or lock-keepers like William Wyatt at Iffley or (inevitably) John Bossom at Medley.[55] These appointments were announced at the end of August, just a month before Michaelmas when the waters were traditionally drawn.

Around Michaelmas the rumour circulated that despite everything the waters would be drawn again, and on 27 September the Sheriff announced in *Jackson's Oxford Journal* that he would prosecute anyone attempting to draw the free waters.

On the same day a deputation from the fishermen visited the Town Clerk, G. P. Hester, who wrote a letter in the *Oxford Journal* addressed to his 'Brother Freemen'. The fishermen had told him that they had no other means of supporting their families save by catching and selling fish. Their object was to represent to their fellow freemen through the Town Clerk, that the bye-laws bore heavily upon them, and that they were unnecessarily strict. Whilst Hester had no intention of abandoning impartiality he pointed out that they were a class of men brought up to this mode of earning their livelihood, and were probably incapable of earning any other. Perhaps netting fish should be allowed. The fishermen themselves suggested certain changes in the fence months, and asked that they be allowed to use hoop nets in February and something larger than a minnow net to catch live bait.[56] The waters were not drawn that year at Michaelmas, but no time was really allowed by the fishermen for a response to their plea before they started drawing the waters again. On 10 October Thomas Beesley was taken up fishing with a net of less than statutable mesh, whilst on the 30th the *Oxford Journal* advised its readers to call at the Town Hall and see the net lately taken by John Bossom the water-bailiff. That zealous officer of the law featured in the neighbouring column of the paper also, in a report of the Sheriff to the Council on illegal fishing. Four nets had been seized and in three cases fines imposed. The first was that of George Ward, the second a Beesley; the third John Bossom, water-bailiff. The Beesleys continued defiant. A year later, on 21 October 1848, *Jackson's Oxford Journal* reported a case against Thomas Beesley for the recovery of a fine of £2

55 Ibid, 28 aug. 1847.   56 Ibid., 2 Oct. 1847.

'for breaking one of the bye-laws'. Mr Brunner again acted
for the fishermen, and the case came up before the County
Court. In this case, *Mayor of Oxford* v. *Thomas Beesley*,
Brunner called attention to the 92nd section of the Municipal Corporations Act as to the power of making bye-laws. The
fisheries were not, he held, vested in the Mayor and Corporation. Hester, for the Mayor and Corporation held that they
were, but the benefit thereof lay in the freemen. The judge was
of the opinion that the property remained in the Corporation
and freemen, and adjourned the case to the next meeting of
the County Court. On the next court day the case was again
deferred, though Mr Hester said it was of consequence that the
case be settled, as the defendant kept on drawing the waters.
Thomas Beesley, on being asked if this were so, replied that
'he had, and should continue to do so; it was his birthright'.[57]

He was as good as his word. The case came up finally in
January, 1849, and Brunner acted for the brothers. He was,
he said, 'acting as the willing advocate of a set of poor men
whom he conceived there was an attempt to crush'. The case
went against the Beesleys.

The city Archives contains a petition from the family:[58]

To the Mayor, Aldermen and Citizens of Oxford in Common Council assembled −
The humble Petition of the undersigned Thomas Beesley the younger, Richard
Beesley, Adam Beesley, Abel Beesley and Samuel Beesley
Sheweth −
That your Petitioners have severally had judgments given against them by the
judge of the County Court at Oxford for the Penalty of forty shillings and Costs upon
each of them, for impugning one of the City Bye Laws made for the regulation of
the Fisheries.

That your petitioners consider the Bye Laws to be injurious to them and materially
to abridge the birthrights and the ancient usages of the Fishermen; but they admit that
the Bye Law against draught nets upon which the judgments against them have been
obtained, may be a beneficial regulation.

That your Petitioners, upon being summoned in the County Court sought legal assistance (which was granted gratuitously) in order that the Question might be raised
as to the jurisdiction of that Court as well as to their rights and privileges as Freemen
− but the judge, having decided against them, they submit to such judgment; they
are however too poor to pay the penalties and Costs − particularly at this season of
the year.

[57] Ibid., 25 Nov. 1848.
[58] City, F.5.4, fo. 252.

They therefore throw themselves on the mercy of the Council and promise to withdraw all resistance to the Bye Law against Draught Nets.[59] But reserving to themselves all lawful means of persuading their brother Freemen to rescind or alter the said Bye Laws — and they pray that upon their submission and promise the council will be pleased to direct that the judgement against them shall not be enforced.

It was signed by five of the Beesleys, and it then continued with an addendum in another, and less than copperplate hand:

Gentelman if you please if siging [sic] wont do you must give us some time after the fence monghts To pay the money by installments. We are all so very poor at this time.

This seems to have been the nadir of the Beesleys' fortunes and of their popularity with their fellow citizens. The younger members of the family began to diversify, though the family were not to give up their connection with the river, and with fishing.

New cases were to come up involving the Beesleys and the rights of the freemen. They came to a head again 20 years later when the situation had altered considerably, and the Beesleys became almost popular heroes in the city, for their defiance was now directed against another authority, one which threatened the authority of the whole city.

VI. THE BEESLEYS *v.* THE THAMES CONSERVANCY

The coming of the railways had proved all but fatal to the river as managed under the Thames Commissioners. In 1853 a series of letters by the Revd Vaughan Thomas described the condition of the moribund navigation in detail. The trade was all but gone, owing to railway competition:

Trade, prosperous trade, may be said to have taken flight from the District, and may now be seen in the heavy-goods train, whirling onwards at the rate of 12 or 14 miles an hour, whistling in derision as it passes by the Thames and Canal navigations, and by its speed mocking the drowsy barge (that emblem of the old slowness of traders and the torpid course of their commercial transactions) which would reach the rail trains terminus in four or five days and nights after it, and then return in eight or ten days more, if it escaped being grounded in its passage home.[60]

The Thames and Severn boats were rarely seen in Oxford. In 1854 an observer reported: 'in the past four days he had seen

---

[59] Now by the new bye-laws, printed in *JOJ*, 17 February to 1 June.
[60] *JOJ*, 26 Mar. 1853.

a Thames and Severn barge at Hythe Bridge; it had brought a sort of small coal, which its master called 'Tambies', for the worthy Mr Ward, for malting and brewing purposes. The men seemed as much surprised as the spectators, at such an unusual arrival...'[61]

Whilst the upper river was declining, the Thames below Staines was passing under new management. This part of the river had formerly lain within the jurisdiction of the City of London, but in 1840 the Crown claimed lordship, holding its prerogative to be the bed and soil within the ebb and flow of the tide. The dispute simmered for many years, and the condition of the river deteriorated whilst its status was in question. The City capitulated in 1856 and the Thames Conservancy Act, 1857 (20 & 21 Vict. c. 147) was passed immediately. The river was now controlled by the Conservators, who included nominees of Crown and City. Finance was put on a sounder footing. The old colourful pageantry of the City, the Lord Mayor and his watermen, passed with the abolition of the city's control. Amendments were made under the Thames Conservancy Act, 1864 (27 & 28 Vict. c. 113), which allowed (Section 65) the power of making bye-laws to protect fish and fisheries; to register and control fishing boats; to prohibit improper nets and determine the fence months for certain varieties of fish. Waterbailiffs were to be appointed, with power to enter boats and seize nets (Section 66). Under Section 67 private fisheries were excepted from all bye-laws except those for the preservation of fish, the prohibition of unstatutable nets, and the enforcement of fence months.

The Thames navigation under the Commissioners was slowly grinding into bankruptcy. The decline may be traced in its accounts,[62] but for most people the situation was brought home sharply by a report of January 1865: the Commissioners were £300-400 in debt; no further expenditure was to be undertaken until liabilities were met; staff to deal with emergencies would be kept on; in areas liable to flooding permission was given to maintain the works of the river at the expense of the interested parties. The Commissioners regretted these steps, but 'it could not be expected that gentlemen in the

---

[61] Ibid., 7 Jan. 1854.
[62] Oxon. RO CH N IX/iii.

discharge of a public duty would subject themselves to personal responsibility'.[63]

Previous to the passing of the Thames Navigation Act, a Select Committee was set up, and interested parties submitted their petitions. St John's and Lincoln College, Abingdon and Reading Corporations sent in their objections supported by personal representations by their agents. The Mayor, Aldermen, and Citizens of Oxford only sent in an unsupported petition against the bill.[64]

New powers, improved finances, greater control of the river were sought. The floods of the winter of 1865/6 gave a sense of urgency to the matter: 'thousands of acres of land, with many roads and footpaths, vast areas of urban land, and even streets, had been for several weeks under the water; lands had been deluged, traffic interrupted, and human health undermined'.[65] Despite the name of the bill, drainage, sewerage, and pollution concerned the Commons more than navigation; fisheries were barely mentioned, and it seems likely many people were unaware of the powers, which, under what one might call 'The Etcetera Principle', passed to the Conservators. Under the act, (29 & 30 Vict. c. 89), which received the Royal Assent on 6 August 1866, the old Commission was terminated, and 'from the passing of this Act the Conservators shall have the same Powers and Authorities over and with respect to the Thames and Isis from Staines to Cricklade as they have by virtue of the Conservancy Acts over and with respect to the Thames below Staines' (Section 41). In 1620 the Water-bailiff of the Thames had attempted to impose his jurisdiction on the citizens and fishermen of Oxford. He required that warrants be sent to the constables of the city to send men to their court and to warn millers and fishermen of the city to appear with their nets and gynes (engines – i.e. weels and traps) to be measured. The city had replied haughtily that they had 'free liberty and jurisdiction within or selves for wch we pay his Matie a great feefarm. We derive it from anciaunt grants ratified by the king and we have Bailiffs and other officers of this

---

[63] *JOJ*, 7 Jan. 1865.

[64] PP. Eng 1866/xii (391), *Minutes of Evidence before the Select Committee on the Thames Navigation Bill*, 2-3.

[65] *Parliamentary Debates*, CLXXXIV, cols. 762-3.

Citty that have authoritye to settle the assize and measure all nets, used within the waters in our jurisdiction.' It would be 'a greate thraldome to or citizens to be subiecte to the authority of Mr Waterbayliff'.[66]

But in 1866 Section 41 gave the Thames Conservancy powers to issue new bye-laws which the freemen were to regard as a 'thraldom' indeed, and in their report for the year 1869 the Conservators reported with much satisfaction that the fishing in the river, which gave pleasure to so many, was considerably improved, and attributed this to the exertions of their officers in suppressing illegal fishing. Oxford itself was to be the subject of such exertions the following year.[67]

According to Hester, the Town Clerk, the Sheriff had intended to bring a case against the fishermen earlier, but 'was crabbed off by the Mayor in order to conciliate the offenders and get their votes for Mr Harcourt'.[68] 18th-century practices continued into the 19th century.

In July 1870, Joseph Beesley and his son William, of St Ebbe's were summonsed for illegal fishing. Hester prosecuted, and Brunner, now a very old man, defended. The Water-bailiff of the City, William Venables, proved they were fishing in the Back Stream of the Castle Mill with flew-nets. Cross-examined, he admitted that this part of the river was not navigable, and the freemen fished there with flew-nets by custom. Brunner submitted that there was no case to answer, for the stream was not navigable, and the water was the freemen's birthright. Hester held that whether the river was navigable was irrelevant. It was all part of the Thames, and Sergeant Manning had established that every branch of the river was to be taken as part of the river itself. Brunner insisted on his clients' right to fish. The water was not under the control of the Conservators, it was a private fishery, and by Section 13 of these bye-laws they were exempt. The case was reserved. It aroused great interest, and the court was surrounded by a crowd of freemen. On 20 August the *Oxford Journal* reported the two Beesleys were fined 10s. and costs, and the Bench hoped a case would go

---

[66] City, F.5.2, fo. 28.

[67] PP. Eng. 1870/1vi (436), *General Report of the Conservators of the River Thames for 1869*, 1-2.

[68] Berks RO, DIEH 08. Letter from George P. Hester to J. K. Hedges, dated 8 May 1869.

forward to Queen's Bench for a final settlement of the dispute. Just over a month later a serious disturbance took place in Port Meadow Stream involving six members of the Beesley family: Abel, Adam, Samuel senior, Samuel junior, James junior, William, and two other persons. On 23 September they were involved in a fracas on the meadow, when Captain Eldridge of the Thames Conservancy attempted to measure their nets.[69] They had refused to allow him to do so. When Captain Eldridge, 'the Von Tromp of the Upper Thames' as the defence later dubbed him, returned with the Sheriff, the Inspector of police, four constables, and the Mayor's Sergeant and the Water-bailiff, the Beesleys were fishing. The officials took a punt and set out to capture the nets, remembering, no doubt, their entitlement to enter boats and seize them. As they tried to do so their punt capsized, and the Beesleys then attacked them with punt poles. James Beesley escaped, but the others were charged with assault. The case caused great excitement, and the prisoners were cheered when they entered the dock. After a remand the six Beesleys finally apologised for the assault, for which they were fined £5 each and costs, apart from James, who got three months' hard labour.[70] This, however, was but a part of the matter. Captain Eldridge preferred a charge of illegal fishing which came up in November. The prosecution pointed out that before the passing of the act relating to the Conservancy of the Thames, notices were issued which all might have seen, calling on people to assert their rights and have them inquired into. Everyone who had a right had only to make a complaint and oppose the passing of the Act. The Act had, he claimed, 'clearly done away with any right which these defendants had supposed they had' – and also they had used illegal nets. The case was related once again, and it was pointed out that the Beesleys had been fishing in a manner legal under the 1847 bye-laws. However, the Von Tromp of the Upper Thames 'did not concur in them', and fines were imposed: Samuel Beesley was fined 15s. and costs, the others 1s. each and costs. And 'the case caused great excitement about the Court'.[71]

[69] *JOJ*, 24 Sept. 1870 and 30 Sept. 1870.
[70] Ibid., 8 Oct. 1870.
[71] Ibid., 12 N.I. 1870.

Brunner died in March 1877 in his 81st year, and did not see the long dispute ended. A further case was brought by the Conservancy in February 1878 against Samuel Beesley and his son-in-law, Richard Burgess, for fishing with illegal nets. The defence was based upon the legitimacy of the grant of the fishery to the freemen: the rights of the freemen were recognised as early as the time of Henry I, confirmed by a charter of Henry II, by John and Edward III. Were these rights, confirmed in the Municipal Corporations Act, to be abrogated and swept away by the bye-laws of the Thames Conservancy? The Conservancy was not impressed. Later statutes repealed earlier ones. The freemen had no rights. Mr Gough, the Beesley's lawyer, applied for leave to take the case to a superior court, and leave was granted, but no evidence has yet been found that the Beesleys did, or could afford, to take the matter further.[72]

In the history of the dispute over the freemen's rights the part played by the Town Clerk seems disingenuous, to say the least. He at least, must have been aware that the position of the city's fisheries needed clarification. If the fishery was a private fishery it should have been registered. If not, special provision should have been written into the Act. Why did the petition of the Mayor, Aldermen, and citizens about fishing go to the Select Committee unsupported, unlike those of Reading and Abingdon? It does not seem possible to plead ignorance, for when private fisheries were being registered and the Harcourts of Nuneham Courtenay were putting together evidence of their claim in 1866, Hester, who was something of an antiquarian, provided them with information. Along the Thames there must have been much searching of deeds to establish the rights of private fisheries.[73]

Hester stood entirely for the authority of the newly constituted commission and against the aspirations of the freemen, and hoped with the extinction of the freemen's rights in the free waters that the old tension between the freemen and the city council would end. His involvement in angling also made him an interested party in the 1840s when the society was

[72] Ibid., 23 Feb. 1878 and 9 Mar. 1878.
[73] MS D.D. Pprs. Harcourt, letter of G. P. Hester to the Revd W. Harcourt, dated 12 Dec. 1866; PP. Eng. 1884/viii (321), *Report from the Select Committee on the Thames River Preservation*, 312-56.

founded, and this interest continued. In May 1869 he wrote 'The Oxford Otters (i.e. the fishermen) are about 20 and the Anglers 500. Therefore there ought to be no netting.'[74]

VII. DIVERSIFICATION AND THE DISPERSAL OF THE FISHERMEN

Railway transport had undermined the market in freshwater fish, and the Conservancy Act brought an end to widespread commercial fishing, and despite the cases of 1870 and 1878, the fishermen seem to have seen the writing on the wall.

The rise and decline of fishing as an occupation in the parish can be seen in the number of fishermen's children baptised at St Thomas's (see Table 6. 1). The last to call himself a fisherman was the redoubtable Abel Beesley. When his son Abel was born in 1878 Abel Beesley called himself a fisherman. Doing so, even then, may have been as much a salute to a family tradition already moribund as a clear statement of fact. No doubt he fished; the Beesleys continued to be occupied on the river, but he was probably more accurately described as a waterman, a man involved with pleasure traffic, as he was when his second child was born in the following year.

There had always been some pleasure-boating on the Thames, but so long as the river was busy with commercial traffic it was relegated to the quieter parts. It provided an alternative occupation for bargemen as it tended to flourish as soon as commercial traffic fell away. At the time when the barge-men of Fisher Row turned to fishing, the bargemen of Folly Bridge, who were seldom freemen (and could not therefore fish the free waters), turned to catering for pleasure-boating. When rowing developed as a sport, the watermen of Folly Bridge were closely associated with its development.

The sport first became popular on the river at London and spread to river-side schools like Westminster and Eton, then, at the end of the Napoleonic Wars, to Oxford.[75] Here

---

[74] Berks. RO, D/EH 08, Letter of G. P. Hester to J. K. Hedges, dated 18 May 1869.

[75] The John Johnson Collection, the Bodleian Library, Box Sport 13, Regattas and Rowling, contains a splendid cut with two views, one entitled 'Sailing for the Silver Cup with a View of Daniels Life Preservers, 1806'. Surely one of the earliest cases of sport and advertising combined. The second shows 'Rowing for the Prize Wherry' (Published 21 Aug. 1806 by T. Hughs, No.1 Stationers Court, London).

Table 6.1. Decline of Fishermen in St Thomas's Parish 1813-90.

Date	Number of baptisms in families whose fathers called themselves fishermen	Number of surnames
1813–20	3	2
1821–30	12	4
1831–40	11	2
1841–50	15	2
1851–60	13	2
1861–70	4	2
1871–80	1	1
1881–90	0	0

undergraduates from these same schools fostered it, and local boat-people catered for it. As new bridges removed the traffic across the Thames at London more and more watermen turned to catering for this new and growing interest. Regattas started first in the London area, and were reported, like other sports on which men laid wagers, in Bell's Sporting Life. Like racing it started as a popular sport, and was taken up by the gentry, but never entirely taken over. As a spectator sport the Boat Race involved the whole populace, though local regattas were more plebeian occasions despite the claims of one broadsheet emanating from The Seven Dials:

> From Westminster to Chiswick,
> Folks like mussles line the beach,
> An old duchess lost her snuff box,
> As she stood on Chelsea Reach.
>
> ...
>
> There's flutes and fifes, and fiddles too,
> Pianos, harps and drums.
> While some are picking pockets,
> Others take them as they come.
> Oh! there they go a butcher crew,
> There's pink and orange too,
> I will bet a half a crown on red
> And seven bob on blue.[77]

[76] W. B. Woodgate, *Boating* (London, 1889), 26-41.
[77] John Johnson Colln., Sport 13, (Broadsheet, *The Ground Thames Regatta,* Published by M. Birt, Printer, 39 Great St Andrew Street, Seven Dials, London.

In Oxford the sport grew up on the river below Folly Bridge, and in St Aldate's the number of watermen increased early as the baptisms of watermen's children show: three in 1821-30, eight in 1831-40, 11 in 1841-50, 30 in 1851-60. Here the rise after the building of the railways is seen clearly. In 1850, at the funeral of one of their number, they made an impressive showing: 'The body was conveyed in a hearse, on each side of which three watermen with blue jackets and white trowsers walked as under-bearers; then followed the relatives and friends of the deceased, after which 14 watermen in deep mourning walked in pairs...'[78]

In the early days of rowing undergraduates and watermen had rowed together, developing the new art. Stephen Davis, the boat-builder was the acknowledged authority on the sport.[79] This idyllic condition did not continue. Watermen were banned from rowing in matches after 1823 ('No hired watermen') 'though watermen coxed and coached crews for many years thereafter.[80] Class feeling was strong in the sport. Arthur Hughes in *Tom Brown at Oxford* makes the captain of St Ambrose's boat voice the heresy that watermen were usually better rowers than were undergraduates: 'I only say that a gentleman's flesh and blood and brains are just the same, and no better than another man's. He had all the chances on his side in the way of training and most of the prizes ...'However his crew 'soon talked themselves back' into 'a renewed consciousness of their natural superiority'. This superiority was finally formalised and enshrined in 1866 in The Laws of Boating: 'Amateurs must be officers of Her Majesties Army, Navy or the Civil Service, members of the clerical, medical or legal professions, of the Universities of Oxford, Cambridge, Dublin, Durham, Edinburgh, Glasgow, St Andrews or Aberdeen, and the Queen's Colleges in Ireland, of Eton, Westminster and other public schools, or of any club not composed of tradesmen or working mechanics...'[81]

Such attitudes did not lead to easy relations between rowing men and such commercial traffic as remained on the river.

[78] *JOJ*, 17 Aug. 1850.

[79] J. Hewlett, *Priggins, the College Scout* (3 vols., London, 1841), I. 78-9.

[80] W. E. Sherwood, *Oxford Rowing* (Oxford, 1900), 8-11; James Pycroft, *Oxford Memories* (London, 1886), II. 72.

[81] Given in Argonaut [E. D. Brickwood], *The Arts of Rowing and Training* (London, 1886) 145-8.

Wherever Regattas were held the river was shut to commercial traffic. This meant taking over and obstructing a Royal River, on which navigation had rights of way, but constituted authority had now turned against the boatman who claimed these ancient legal rights. Such attitudes must have played some part in the alienation of the boatman from the community. An incident, which occurred on the boat-race course, near Folly Bridge, in 1864, is particularly startling. For once the boatman speaks:

On the 12th of May, between seven and eight o'clock in the evening, I was with my boat near Folly Bridge, Oxford. I had been waiting there for about an hour for the race to finish. The racing had been over about 20 minutes, and the gentlemen had got out of their boats. I started my horse over the Bridge. It is a towing path bridge, and no people had any business there by rights, except those belonging to the water. It is a way that people go down the river side. I had got two or three yards before I was first stopped ... I did not by myself ... knock anyone, except it might be when they started knocking it [the horse] about. I did not strike anyone from first to last. I was stopped and they rushed in upon me. Cook used a punt-pole, he punched me on the breast with it several times; he was in a punt; the path was crowded then. A gentleman struck me with an umbrella several times ... he struck at the horse, and he tried to poke me in the face. Then they catched hold of me ... I cannot say it was either of the defendants. I was covered with blood, and do not know. I was taken back to Oxford by a City policeman. I do not know why they took me in charge. I think my ribs were bad from their trying to push me over the rails.[82]

Cook and the man with the umbrella were fined 30s. each. However, later, under an Act of 1894, legislation was passed to 'regulate' the traffic. As Lord Desborough of the Conservancy Board told a Royal Commission in 1907, 'At the University Boat Race the bridges are blocked up by barges across them and at Henley and other regattas we have powers given under the Act of Parliament to help regattas.'[83] The law giving precedence to barges over pleasure boats was also abolished.

Henley Regattta had been founded in 1839, and it and many lesser regattas flourished on the river as the barge trade fell away. Whilst they delayed commercial traffic, the boatmen's feelings towards them were undoubtedly ambivalent.

[82] *JOJ*, 21 May 1864.
[83] PP. Eng. 1907/ xxxiii, pt. i (Cd. 3717) *Royal Commission on Canals, Second Report, Evidence and Appendices*, 345.

Henley provided a great meeting place for boatmen, and a week of saturnalia, as they came together to carry the racing-boats down the river to Henley, and then, after the pleasure of Henley itself, with all the drinking, the odd jobs, and perks that it provided, they brought the boats back.[84]

Though the boatmen of St Thomas's probably enjoyed Henley as much as anyone, the inhabitants of the Row had nothing to do with the development of rowing as a sport. When the sport of rowing took over the river below Folly Bridge, other types of pleasure-craft were banished to the Upper River. Men went 'down the water' to row, and 'up the water' to mess about in boats. The Bossoms, when they emigrated to Medley, were engaged mainly in supplying the demand for punts, wherries, and skiffs.

On the upper river the families of fishermen were engaged in perfecting their own form of racing – punt-racing, using the fisherman's punt in the first instance. Punt-racing is first heard of in Oxford at the City Regattas, which were started two years after Henley, in 1841. No details of the participants in this regatta are given, but in 1842, we have a more detailed account. There were two punt races for watermen. The first, having a purse of 15s., was won by S. Beesley; the second, the punt-race for beaten men, by A. Beesley.[85] The Beesleys maintained their position in ensuing regattas. After 1845 there no more City regattas until 1858. Enthusiasm had been intense, but no clubs were founded, so no enduring framework was established to perpetuate them, and city rowing went into eclipse.[86]

In this interim the Beesleys continued active as punters, and so did the Bossoms. Indeed the old feud was pursued here, and not without bitterness, for the supporters of each family could turn any occasion into a cause for battle. Punt-racing was well suited to augment dissension. In 1898 the author

[84] Interviews with Mr Jack James (4 Oct. 1968), Mr W. H. G. Round, (c. June 1968); Mari Prichard and Humphrey Carpenter, *A Thames Companion* (Oxford, 1975), 120.

[85] *JOJ*, 28 Aug. 1841, 20 Aug. 1842.

[86] The Local History Dept., Central Library, Oxford, OXFO 797 1 contains a collection of Oxford city rowing club pamphlets, including W. H. Allnutt, *notes on Oxford Royal Regatta, 1841-1891* (n.d., Oxford), reprinted from the *Oxford Times* of 1891.

of the Badminton Library article on punt-racing remarked revealingly:

> The status of punt racing all over the river has much improved. At one time it was very much of the rough-and-tumble order, owing to the jostling and fouling introduced into the races, which were mostly between watermen; for some time, however, deliberate fouling has been prohibited, and if one competitor deliberately interferes with the other, he is liable to be disqualified on an appeal to the umpire.[87]

From this account of punt-racing, fouling and cheating seem almost built into the pursuit, and differences between the participants inevitable. Certainly it proved so in the race Between Sampson Beesley and John Bossom, junior, of Medley, which took place on 19 July 1849, and resulted in a case at the Small Debts Court the following year.[88]

The race was for £2, fouling was prohibited, and he who did so would lose the race.

> On starting, Beesley took the lead, but Bossom came up on him just before Binsey Gate, when Beesley, finding that Bossom was about showing a good lead, and likely to win the race, determined to prevent it, and drove him into the Bank of Port Meadow, keeping him in that position for nearly 30 yards. The umpires, who were together at that time, decided that in consequence of this fouling the race was at an end, and that Bossom was entitled to the stakes. In consequence of bets having been made as to the time of punting the distance, Bossom proceeded onwards to the winning post at Godstow, and Beesley did the same, and succeeded by a little management in getting there first, when he and his friends demanded the stakes, which the stake-holder refused to give up to him, and which he afterwards handed over to Bossom, in accordance with the decision of the umpires. A bet upon this race was made between Adam Beesley and Luckett, and the stakes, amounting to 10s. were placed in the hands of James Stroudley.[89]

At the conclusion of the race Beesley demanded the stakes of Stroudley, who refused to give them up, in consequence of which he was waylaid by Beesley and his party and compelled to give them up the money. A summons was then obtained against Beesley, to answer the charge in the City Court, but it was settled out of court, and Beesley returned the money and

---

[87] P. W. Squire, 'Punting' in R. P. P. Rowe and C. M. Pitman, *Rowing* (London, 1898), 258.

[88] *JOJ*, 31 Aug. 1950.

[89] Thomas son of John Bossom sen. was apprenticed to a James Stroudley, cabinet maker, whilst A. Luckett was a neighbour of Benjamin Bossom in Upper Fisher Row.

paid the expenses of the summons, witnesses, etc., amounting to £1 5s. A statement of the case, however, was sent to *Bell's Sporting Life* for their adjudication and a decision upon that statement was given in favour of Beesley. In consequence of this decision Beesley again applied to Stroudley to hand him over the amount deposited in his hands, but Stroudley replied that he had already given it up to Luckett.

Interest in rowing was picking up too by 1850. The College Servants formed a club in August 1850 on the model of a college club. They rowed their opposite numbers at Cambridge, and a return race took place later in the season:

> Then stroke for stroke and oar for oar
> Away the two crews went,
> And after struggling long and well,
> The Cam to Isis bent.[90]

This club was the first of many: the Neptune (1863), the Falcon (1869), The Hannington, and many others followed over the years, some connected with firms, others with social groups sometimes with church affiliations – the Clarendon Press, the Gas Works, Morris Motors, the YMCA, the Phil and Jim (St Philip and St James). In Oxford rowing became a sport for everyone.[91]

Or rather, not quite for everyone. The Bossoms and the Beesleys continued to develop punting, treating it as something between the duel, the joust, and the prize-fight. In 1853 S. Beesley took on Emony of Eton, 'the Eton Pet', for a purse of £10, and won by a hundred yards, demonstrating (as *Jackson's Oxford Journal* remarked) 'that there really was a man to be found, who, in his calling, was superior to their "Pet" whom they had hitherto regarded as having no "rival near his throne"'.[92] In local regattas, which started again in 1858, the Bossoms and Beesleys were the main competitors in watermen's punt races, and the inevitable winners. In the 1860s, when W. E. Sherwood was a child, he says that the regattas were suspended owing to the hostilities of the watermen, the two families, the Bossoms and the Beesleys, to whom most

[90] 38442 d. 27, 'Oxford University and College Servants Rowing Club Centenary, 1850-1950', 1-7.
[91] OXFO 797.1.
[92] *JOJ*, 30 Apr. 1853.

of the watermen were related, and who were 'the Capulets and the Montagues of the Isis'.[93]

The 1870s and 1880s showed an enormous growth in the pleasure traffic of the river. Houseboats of great size and splendour were found on the lower reaches of the river, rowing caught the popular imagination, Henley became fashionable, modes for the river were popular, Punch made jokes about it, novels were written about it, such as Jerome K. Jerome's *Three Men in a Boat*. At Oxford the world of Zuleika Dobson and of Eights Week was underpinned by the watermen of Folly Bridge and Fisher Row. The river was haunted by artists, and described by naturalists. Railway excursions carried fishermen from London Anglers' clubs to such towns as could be reached by rail, and their handbooks described each reach of the river. Henry W. Taunt wrote his New Map of the Thames, listing hotels, firms hiring boats, and fishermen who could supply their services, boats, and bait to the amateur.[94]

At this time punt-racing became recognised as a sport, and Abel Beesley its greatest professional exponent. In 1877 he defeated E. Andrews in a match for £100, and became professional champion of all England. The Professional Punting Championship became an established event in England in 1886 at Maidenhead, and he won the event six years running. He retired then, still undefeated, and trained many amateurs at Maidenhead in the summer months, including W. H. Grenfell, Amateur Champion (1888-90), later Lord Desborough, Chairman of the Thames Conservancy.[95]

In the winter months Abel Beesley continued in the Row as a fisherman. He was a son of Abel Beesley, fisherman and waterman; seventh son of the fisherman Thomas Beesley who had worked for the Thames and Severn Canal Company as a young man. He lived at 4 Upper Fisher Row, died between 1923 and 1926, and after his death a Mrs Beesley continued in the house for perhaps another ten years. His cousin Jacob at the top of the Row outlived him by a few years, dying in

[93] W.E. Sherwood, *Oxford Yesterday* (Oxford, 1927), 54.

[94] R. R. Bolland, *Victorians on the Thames* (Tunbridge Wells, 1974), provides an amusing illustrated account of this period of the river's history, with a good, short biography; Barnes, *Rail and Rod*; Henry W. Taunt, *A New Map of the River Thames* (Oxford, 1872).

[95] Squire, 'Punting', 285-7; *JOJ*, 23 July 1892.

1929, and Jacob's son, Horace Sydney Jones Beesley, moved to Medley to take over the business of the boat-owner, Geoffrey Beesley, who had died in 1909, leaving no heir. The Wolvercote family of watermen are descended from him. Other branches of the family have now left the river.[96]

VIII. THE RAILWAYS AND THE CANAL

The decline of the canal system was due to the railway. A more primitive machine for transport was superseded by a more sophisticated one; but the effects of competition were neither immediate nor simple. Some of the effects of the coming of the railways on waterways have already been referred to, but we shall do well to deal more systematically with the matter here, even at the risk of some repetition.

The opening of the railways acted as a *coup de grâce* to the ailing barge trade. Natural rivers had already suffered severely from the building of efficient artificial systems of waterways. By the 1841 Census only three bargemen were left in Fisher Row. The Oxford barge trade had not yet felt the effect of railway competition at that time, but with the opening of the Great Western Railway from London to Bristol in June 1841, three weeks after the Census, the trade of Berks and Wilts Canal and of the Thames below Abingdon moved to the rail-ways. There were, however, a few towns, like Abingdon, which were not on the railway, and which now turned for their coal from the foundering Wilts and Berks to the Oxford Canal. Some families involved in the trade moved to Oxford. We have already seen this movement reflected in the 1851 Census. These men were, however canal boatmen, not bargemen. As the canals started to fail, they did so at the extremities of the system, and the boatmen moved in towards the living heart. They swelled the population of canal boatmen, so that there were slightly more in Oxford in 1851 than in 1841; but this was a sign of decay. If the community of canal boatmen in the Row was fully blown in 1841, it was a little overblown by 1851.

In 1844 a branch line from Didcot to Oxford was built to connect Oxford with the Great Western. The station lay south-west of Folly Bridge. It had little effect on the inhabitants of Fisher Row, but must have had a considerable effect on the

---

[96] Interview, Messrs. Beesley, 20 May 1975.

great bargemasters of Folly Bridge and St Ebbe's, for their wharves were placed on the market almost simultaneously with its opening.[97]

Although the first railways scarcely affected the canal boatmen of Fisher Row, they affected public attitudes and board-room policy radically. It was the age of the railway. Canals were seen as old-fashioned and cumbrous. The work-grimed and rough canal boatman with his absurd beflowered boat must have epitomised the bad old unenlightened days, just as the neat, uniformed, disciplined corps of railwaymen epitomised progress and enlightenment. The battle against the railways had been fought by the canals with every device available, and they were now seen as symbolising petty vested interests cramping and crippling new, bold, and splendid schemes. The compensation they claimed in looking after their shareholders did not endear them to the public. When they lowered their tolls and freight charges to hold their traffic it was assumed, rightly, that the companies' charges had previously been too high. That the new prices were uneconomic, and that the companies were often being forced to lower them to the point where they could be ruined and run out of business, and the railways reap the advantage, was lost on the public. Ebenezer Elliott 'the Corn-Law Poet' caught the popular mood.

> Who's a dead canal to sell,
> Worth a skinn'd cats clothing?[98]

No one was interested in canals; no one wanted to know. By 29 November 1851, when £100 shares were advertised for sale in the *Oxford Journal*, it was remarked that they now paid £12 per cent per annum, and that 'in the past this company had paid a very large dividend'. In 1802, when the company paid only 11 per cent £100 shares had sold at £275, but then the canal was a 'rising concern'.[99] What the shares realised in 1851 it would be interesting to know.

And yet the policy of cutting tolls was, on the face of it, successful. The tonnage carried on the canal remained over

[97] *JOJ*, 24 Feb. 1844; ibid., 29 June 1844.

[98] [Ebenezer Elliott], *More Verse and Prose by the Corn Law Rhymer* (London, 1850), II. 42.

[99] J. Phillips, *A General History of Inland Navigation* (4th edn., London, 1803), 342.

400,000 tons throughout the 19th century as may be seen in Table 6.2.

Table 6.2. The trade of the Oxford Canal.[100]

	Gross Tonnage	Revenue	Amount paid to shareholders
1828	450,000	£89,300	£60,740
1838	520,000	£86,600	£53,594
1848	420,000	£56,000	£35,729
1858	400,000	£24,700	£14,291
1868	482,000	£24,700	£15,185
1888	450,000	£22,843	no figures given
1898	421,000	£19,260	no figures given

IX. MEASURING DECLINE

Trade was not, however, sustained on all parts of the canal equally. The northern parts of the Oxford canal formed a section of the through route between London and Birmingham, Coventry and the North, and in 1830, according to Mr Charles Hadfield, this part of the canal accounted for 67 per cent of the traffic. Figures for the trade on the southern part of the canal have proved elusive, but there seems to be general agreement that it suffered most of all.[102]

The Census bears this out and suggests a serious decline in the numbers of Oxford boatmen between 1851 and 1861. In 1851 there were 34 boatmen in the whole parish and in 1861 there were 13. The fall was of the order of 60 per cent. Between 1861 and 1871 the fall was less steep, from 13 to ten. As for the Row itself, in 1861 the numbers of boatmen had kept up better than in the parish in general. They had fallen from 21 to 10 – just over 50 per cent; but by 1871 they had fallen from 10 to 2, a fifth of the 1861 figures, and a tenth

---

[100] PP. Eng. 1870/lvi (184), 12-131 PP. Eng. 1906/xxxii (Cd. 3184), *Royal Commission on Canals, First Report, Evidence and Appendices*, Appendix 1.

[101] Hadfield, *British Canals*, 215-16; PP. Eng. 1907/xxxiii, pt. i (Cd. 3717), 16. In *Q*.33230 the engineer for the Oxford Canal was asked for this information, but only figures for 1898 and 1805 were supplied, PP. Eng. 1907/xxxiii (Cd. 3719), *R.C. on Canals, Second Report, Returns*, 84. By 1907 there was said to be too little traffic on the southern section to justify widening it, though the engineer Mr Chamberlaine believed that if it were, trade would improve (PP. Eng. 1907/xxxiii (Cd. 3717), 14.

of those for 1851 (see Table 5.6). Boatmen were moving to Jericho, the new working-class suburb, north of Worcester College,
which had been until recently pasture and market garden. Here,
in this outpost of St Thomas's, bounded on the west by the
canal, two new parishes grew up in the 19th century, St Paul's
(1839), and St Barnabas's (1869).

Decline is also clear in the parish register, and most markedly in the marriage register. Between 1841 and 1850 there
were 30 marriages of canal boatmen; between 1851 and 1860
only 5. But the movement of boatmen out of the community
and up into Jericho does not fully account for the fall, for there
were only two marriages of boatmen at St Paul's in those two
decades, both between 1841 and 1850, so that the revised total
of marriages in both parishes was 32 for 1841-50. There is no
other change.

The marriage register shows decline in its most melodramatic
form. In comparison the baptismal registers show only a modest
fall in the baptisms of canal children. There were 122 baptisms
in 1831-40, 120 in 1841-50, and 105 in 1851-60. A great fall
came in the next decade, and an even more marked fall in 1891-
1900 (see Table 6.3).

The discrepancy between the number of marriages in the '40s
and '50s is teasing. The number of marriages is not unduly
swollen in the '40s because of the presence of the boatmen's
chapel, which had been founded quite recently, for the proportion of births to marriages in the '40s is just about what might
be expected (a little low, but the families were fecund). Though
we have no figures for marriages in the '30s, it is possible also
to recognise the names of many boatmen in the marriage registers even in periods before occupations are given, and though
these cannot be regarded as completely satisfactory identifi-
cations, it does look as if the figure for marriages at this time
was quite normal and figures for baptisms are almost exactly
the same as for the next decade. In the '50s there is, however,
a puzzling disproportion between the number of marriages and
baptisms: it moved from one marriage to four baptisms in the
'40s to one in 21 in the '50s, to one in seven in the '60s, one
in around six in the '80s, and one in 13 in the '90s.

It may be thought that labour spent in accounting for this
decrease is wasted, and that boatmen were simply giving up

marrying, but if so, why did they not give up having their babies baptised too?

Table 6.3. Marriages of boatmen and baptisms of their children by decades, St Thomas's Parish, Oxford.

	Baptisms	Marriages
1814-20	55	—
1821-30	90	—
1831-40	122	—
1841-50	120	30
1851-60	105	5
1861-70	49	7*
1871-80	29	5*
1881-90	26	2
1891-1900	7 (3 living afloat)	1
1901-10	11 (8 living afloat)	1
1911-20	37 (37 living afloat)	2

* Including a double wedding.

Note: The occupations of marriage partners are only given from 1837. Registers of baptism have only been examined up to 1918.

X. THE CHURCH, THE BOATMEN, AND THE FUNERAL OF FANNY BOSSOM

One factor which may have affected the incidence of marriages in the parish after 1851 was that alternatives to church marriages were available. Civil marriage was recognised, and in 1851 a remarkably high rate of civil marriage was noted in Oxford. The national average was 3.9 per cent, but in Oxford it was 24 per cent.[102] The same factors which made civil marriage popular in Oxford generally probably operated on the boatmen too.

Oxford had been the cradle of Tractarianism, and its influence in Oxford was strong. Under Tractarian influence the demands of piety were rising, and were probably too great for

[102] T. Allen and W. A. Greenhill, Report on the Mortality and the Public Health of Oxford during the years 1849-50. (The Ashmolean Society, Oxford, 1854), Appendix A, 5-7. The percentages of marriages performed outside the Anglican rite included the following: All England, 13.8 per cent; Londn, 7.02 per cent; Norwich, 30.31 per cent; Oxford, 30.10 per cent; Southampton, 24.93 per cent. I am grateful to Mr Christopher Day for showing me this Report.

the boatmen, whose major interest in the church seems to have lain in the celebration of the three rites of passage. The church was becoming more demanding as its secular role as the registrar of baptisms, deaths, and marriages was given up. The new freedom this brought the clergy to demand a higher spiritual understanding of marriage and loyalty to the church – such indeed as the 'gathered' churches had always required – was recognised and exploited. In the face of such demands the boatmen seem to have turned to places where less was expected of them, either in the established or dissenting churches. Indeed, it was about 1851 that the Seamen and Boatmen's Friend Society was established by nonconformists to serve the floating population in the Midlands.[103]

That high demands would be made by the incumbent of St Thomas's parish was certain, for Canon Thomas Chamberlain who ministered to the parish from 1842 to 1892 was closely associated with the Tractarian movement, and was the least tractable of Sectarians. Nor was Chamberlain a tactful man, and by 1846 he was at loggerheads with his churchwardens over pews and church renovations and improvements.[104] Their antagonism was, however, probably initially due to other matters. Some shared the opinions (as reported by his son) of Mr Sherwood, the brewers' agent, who lived at the foot of the Row in the Tawneys' former house. 'Our Parish Church, to which we should have naturally gone, was S.Thomas', but that was terribly in advance of the times, and had vestments and altar lights, and Sisters of Mercy, and all sorts of strange horrors, which were utterly anathema to an old-fashioned churchman like my father.'[105]

In 1847 matters between the Canon and his parishioners had reached such a pitch that the church wardens reported at the Archdeacon's visitation that the church was 'nearly deserted by its parishioners'.[106]

Yet in some ways the canal boatmen and Canon Chamberlain were people in the same position at this time – men with their backs to the wall. Chamberlain found himself placed in

---

[103] *The Waterman*, II (1910), 209; ibid. III (1911), 37-8.
[104] *JOJ*, 24 Oct. 1846, and 19 Dec. 1846.
[105] Sherwood, *Oxford Yesterday*, 18-19; T. W. Squires, *In West Oxford* (Oxford, 1928), 20-1.
[106] *JOJ*, 19 June 1847.

a hostile parish, whilst the boatmen felt the threat of the railways hanging over them, and their livelihood endangered.

Though the threat of the railways was unrealised in the 1840s, change was imminent. By 1849 the navvies were in Oxford itself, and the papers were full of progress reports of railway construction. In early July the parish witnessed an impressive ceremony, the procession of the navvies in their white slops as they followed the bier of one of their fellows, killed in an accident, on its way to the new burial ground at Oseney.[107]

Three weeks later another funeral was reported, of an even more spectacular sort. It was the funeral of Fanny Bossom, the daughter of a Mrs Bossom, laundress of Fisher Row, widow of William Bossom, a boatman.[108] To Chamberlain, no doubt the funeral was in some sort an attempt to reach out to his parishioners, a demonstration of his concern for them. It was probably also seen by the boatmen in much the same way, a sort of counter demonstration to that funeral procession of the navvies, something through which the boat-people demonstrated their corporate strength in the face of the threat symbolised by the navvies. The result was altogether bizarre and unfortunate:

On Tuesday last a funeral took place in St Thomas's parish church, which, on account of the unusual form and ceremony attending it, excited more than ordinary interest ... It appears that Fanny Bossom, a girl of 16 years of age, of exemplary character, and daughter of Mrs Bossom, laundress, of Fish-row, St Thomas's, died of consumption, and the Vicar undertook the arrangement of the funeral. We hear that he was present at the laying out of the corpse, and had the arms of the deceased laid across the breast, and a cross of nails placed at the head and foot of the coffin. The funeral was fixed to take place at half-past nine, and about that time the procession left the Fishrow. On reaching St Thomas's church, it was joined by the children of the school, who preceded the bier, and scattered flowers along the way, while a large attendance of the choristers and singing men chanted the service. On entering the church three clergymen, in surplices, assisted in the ceremony, and the choir chanted portions of the service, as well as at the grave. On the conclusion of the service the mourners and many others re-entered the church and partook of the holy sacrament, but several who did not anticipate being required to do so, declined, in spite of the remonstrances of the Vicar.

[107] Ibid., 7 July 1849.
[108] Ibid., 28 July 1849.

This sad, ludicrous incident can only have increased the sense of alienation of the canal boatmen underlining the economic cause of their disintegration as a community. Everywhere the decay of the trade brought hardship, boatmen who had been able to maintain a home ashore were giving it up, moving on to their boats, and losing touch with the wider community.

For the older men, with families to support, there was no alternative form of occupation to which they could turn. They had grown up on the canal, they knew no other way of life, and they dared risk no change. Younger men, however, unmarried and without ties, would be the first to leave the canal, moving off with the navvies, perhaps, to dig new railways; later, perhaps, like many simple, brave young men joining up and seeking excitement and glory fighting in the Crimea. The canal failed to hold the cohort of young marriageable men who grew up as the railways came into being.

XI. THE DARK YEARS

In the years after the opening of the railways, competition was cut-throat, the condition of the canals was deteriorating owing to the straightened circumstances of the canal companies, and the canal boatmen whose plight had aroused public concern in the '30s and '40s were forgotten, save by those who continued to work amongst them. In Oxford the Floating Chapel continued to serve the boat-people, and each year a sermon was preached in aid of it, often by some very eminent cleric. In 1854, for instance, the sermon was given by Dr Pusey:

The Rev. Dr Pusey, Canon of Christ Church, preached at St Mary's Church on Sunday last, in aid of the Oxford Boatmen's Floating Chapel ... The fact of Dr Pusey's having consented to advocate this laudable institution drew a very large congregation, notwithstanding that the annual Trinity Service at New College Chapel was taking place at the same time ... The discourse was more appropriate to the day (Trinity Sunday) than to the special occasion of its delivery, as it was confined almost exclusively to the mystical unity of the Trinity.[109]

The *Oxford Journal*'s criticism was captious, for it was the custom to devote the proceeds of the collection, not the substance of the sermon, to the boat-people. When Dr Jacobson spoke of their condition in 1852 this seems to have been

[109] Ibid., 17 June 1854.

exceptional. He gave a gloomy picture of their situation. He compared their lot to that of the gipsy – a comparison frequently made later: '... men who were not taken away from the land of their birth, who were not sent to the ends of the earth, who did not remain on the broad seas, but yet who laboured under the burden of spiritual destitution ... with no settled place of abode, no local ties, but ever moving to and fro, they seldom hear the sound of the same church bell on two successive Sundays –gypsies of our inland waters...'[110]

It was easy for the casual observer to see the boatman with his family living aboard the boat as rootless wanderers, for men do not carry, obviously displayed, the evidences of their origins and the strength of their ties to places and to social groups. Only familiarity with the individuals, or research can reveal such things. Yet the situation Dr Jacobson described was becoming truer with every year, as the boatmen of Oxford moved away on their boats.

The boatmen were not only becoming an isolated group, they were also a special case, and a forgotten one at that, so far as the lawmakers were concerned. They slipped through the net of legislation devised to improve the lot of working men and women in the next decades, until, in a sensational series of articles and letters to the papers, George Smith of Coalville (not to be confused with George Charles Smith) described the condition of the boat-people, and agitated for legislation to improve their position. He claimed that 'there are 100,000 men, women, and children living, working, and floating on our rivers and canals in a state of wretchedness, misery, immorality, cruelty and evil training that carries peril with it'. Moreover, he claimed:

Not 5 per cent of the men, women, and children can read and write; and I have it from the men themselves that nine out of ten are drunkards – they buy rum by pints and drink it like water. In the little village of Braunston, near Rugby, there are ten public-houses adjoining the canal in a distance of a little over a mile, at which the boatmen, their wives, and children are to be seen at any time of the day. One boatman who has worked between the Potteries, Birmingham, and London during the past forty years, does not know of half-a-dozen boaters who are members of a Christian Church. He further says that two parts out of three of the men

[110] Ibid., 27 Mar. 1852.

and women living as husbands and wives are unmarried. If my estimate of 100,000 be true, and 1 am led to believe it is under the mark, we have 22,400 men, 22,400 women, and 72,000 children, which may be termed, 'our canal population'; out of this number, we have 13,000 men and 13,000 women living together in an unmarried state, and 40,000 illegitimate children living, floating, and working in connection with canal boats.[111]

Smith's disclosures aroused a storm of comment, denying or confirming his evidence. Smith throve on publicity and controversy, and kept up a remorseless campaign, aided by the press in crusading mood. Bemused, blinded by statistics, conscience-stricken, and browbeaten, the House of Commons, passed two acts in 1877 and 1884 (the second amending the deficiencies of the earlier panic-ridden legislation).[112] Under these acts boats were inspected and registered, and a host of regulations were made to improve the living conditions on the boat – to improve hygiene, improve general maintenance, to prevent overcrowding, and prevent adults and adolescents of assorted sex sleeping with each other, except in explicitly approved combinations. As *The Times* had foreseen in 1877: 'The floating home of the 'bargee 'is to be invaded. Its privacy is attacked. Its liberty appears doomed to pass away...' Because the canal boatman's work-place and home were the same, powers of inspection were granted which would not have been tolerated in homes ashore, where conditions were often rather worse. Even the first Inspector of Canal Boats was to report that the cabins of the majority 'are a perfect paradise compared with some of the dwellings of the working classes'.[113]

Nor was this the only form of inspection to which the boat-people were subjected, for the Canal Boats Acts concerned themselves with the education of the children, and attempted to make the children attend school whenever the boats were moored for as much as a few hours. Under such a scheme the children, naturally shy and apprehensive away from the world of the canal, were new boys whenever they went to school,

---

[111] George Smith, F S A, *Our Canal Population: A Cry from the Boat Cabins, with a Remedy* (new edn., London, 1878), 140.

[112] 40 & 41 Vict. c. 60 and 47 & 48 Vict. c. 75. For a discussion of this legislation see Roy M. MacLeod, 'Social Policy and the "Floating Population": the Administration of the Canal Boats Acts 1877-1899', *Past and Present*, XXXV (1966), 101-32.

[113] *The Times*, 4 June 1877, quoted in MacLeod, 'Social Policy', 111; PP. Eng. 1886/xxxi (C.48440, *15th Annual Report of the Local Government Board*, 73.

and apart from boatmen who were able to leave children at home to be educated, most boatmen evaded and resisted this requirement. In this they frequently had the co-operation of the teachers, who regarded these newcomers as an intrusion, and as an unrewarding addition to their work-load.

The boatmen had fiercely resented the light in which they were presented by George Smith in his attempts to rouse public opinion. Some might style Smith the boatman's friend, but the boatmen regarded him as having betrayed them. In a thinly fictionalised account of a holiday as passengers on a working boat by two emancipated young women of about 1890 an account is given of a meeting with George Smith, and of his being berated by a canal boatwoman. The campaign had fed the boat-people's sense of being an outcast group, whilst the new legislation increased their incipient paranoia.[114]

XII. FROM THE WORLD OF THE ROW TO THE WORLD OF THE CUT

In these dark years the community of canal boatmen had become more isolated and introverted, and when public interest was focused upon them it did nothing to encourage their integration with the rest of society. They felt themselves even more outsiders. We must now turn to the Row and see how its families fared in this period.

The 1850s saw the end of many names which had been familiar for two generations on the canal. The Ashely clan vanished from Middle Fisher Row. The Lewises, the Farmers, the Fishers, the Bakers, and the Judds also disappeared. Some seem to have died out, like the Lewises, other moved away. The Bakers for instance, moved to Kidlington, probably to Thrupp. Here three of Richard Baker's children married Between 1864 and 1872, but none married boatmen.

As the trade decreased and families moved up the canal, Thrupp assumed a new importance. Thrupp was situated on the canal just above the junction of the Duke's Cut and the Oxford Canal, and was well situated to serve either the Oxford trade, or such trade as still remained to towns such as Eynsham on the river above Oxford. The Census of 1871 reveals little of interest about this hamlet, but there were 22 boats

---

[114] V. Cecil Cotes, *Two Girls on a Barge* (London, 1891), 134-6.

Family Tree 6.2.   The Skinners.

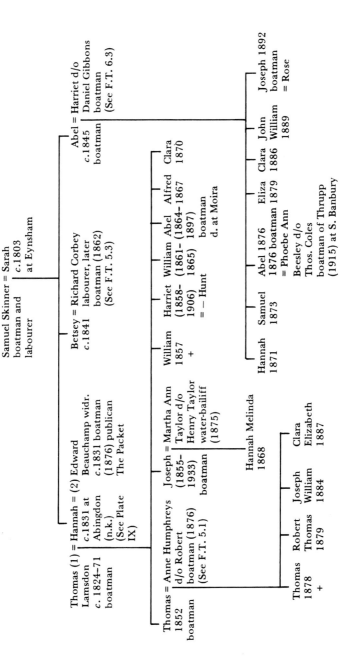

from Thrupp which appeared from time to time in the pages of the book of the canal Boat Inspector for the Bicester Union between 1879 and 1920.[115] Most of these were registered at Banbury, some at Coventry, a few at Oxford, and one finds members of both Oxford and Eynsham families claiming to be of Thrupp. For some families it formed the first stage in their movement up the canal.

If some Oxford families were drifting away, up the canal, some also moved into Oxford. The Skinners and Lamsdens came from Abingdon or Eynsham – the Census is not consistent. They came in the '40s rather than the '50s, presumably because railway competition was already affecting the river a decade before the canal.

One has therefore an apparent break in the surnames of the boatmen of the Row before and after 1851. New surnames came in and old ones vanished, but the change was usually more apparent than real. The importance of the female line must not be forgotten, for it was not only strong, it was conservative. Through the women links were formed with the old community. Thus the children of a boatman called Samuel Skinner entered the parish through marriage (see Family Tree 6.2, The Skinner Family). Mary Corbey, daughter of Elizabeth Corbey, nee Bossom, had married the boatman John Howkins. Her nephew Richard married Betsey Skinner in 1862, and her brother Abel married Harriet, daughter of Daniel Gibbons. Both men married into families that were old-established. Their sister Hannah had already married Thomas Lamsdon, another boatman from outside Oxford. All set up important families of boatmen in the parish. When Hannah, who had been widowed a few days before the 1871 Census, remarried, in 1876, one Edward Beachamp, a boatman, she had no doubt helped his assimilation into the community. Certainly when he became landlord of The Packet about 1880, her kin could supply him with just such customers as a boatman's pub required. They prospered and became boat-owners in a modest way. Like the Skinners they increased, and became one of the most important families of boatmen in the last years of the community.

[115] Oxon. RO, Dew VI(d)3 (provisional number), Registers of Inspections of Boats, Bicester Sanitary District, 1889-1921.

For some years after 1861, such marriages of boatmen as occurred tended to be entirely between members of the boating community, as can be seen in Table 6.4. In the two decades

Table 6.4. Intermarriages between boatmen and the daughters of boatmen in St Thomas's Parish — 1861-1920.

Decade	Number of boatmen	Number of boatmen who are sons of boatmen	Number of daughters of boatmen	Number of boatmen who marry boatmen's daughters
1861–70	8	6	11	8
1871–80	5	5	4	4
1881–90	2	1	5	0
1891–1900	1	1	2	0
1901–10	2	2	3	1
1911–20	0	0	0	0
Totals	18	15	25	13

between 1861 and 1880 there were 13 marriages of boatmen and 15 of boatmen's daughters, and 12 intermarriages of a boatman and a boatman's daughter. In the three decades between 1881 and 1910-15 boatmen and 10 boatwomen married, but there was only one marriage between a boatman and a boatman's daughter. Men were marrying out of the parish,or were moving out of the business; women were marrying men in other occupations, and their function of integrating men from outside the tight knit world of the Row, of acting as anchorman to the family on the boat was being relinquished. The community therefore passed through two stages; in the first, the community turned in on itself, became ever more determinedly introvert, almost claustrophobically narrow. It then began to turn away from the parish, moving into the world of the cut and losing its links with the shore.

Something of both these trends may be seen in the family displayed in the will of Daniel Gibbons, who died in 1889. His is the only will that has been found of a man of St Thomas's who called himself a boatman. He was probably exceptional in owning property, and its disposal seems to be the reason for making a will. In this he resembled Samuel Spindler, and he also had property at Botley comprising two houses worth £309. This would be unusual wealth for a boatman. He

Family Tree 6.3. The Gibbons.

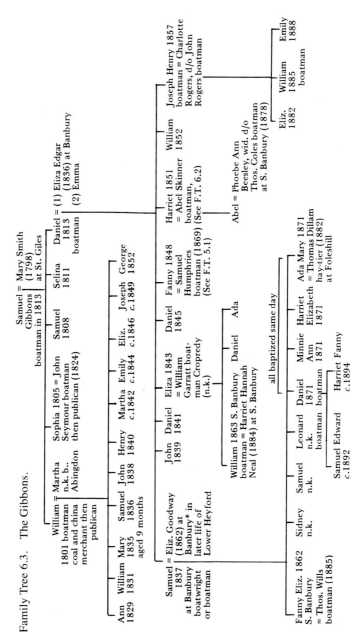

* The children and grandchildren of Samuel and Elizabeth Gibbons whose baptismal dates, if any, are lacking, are known from Boat Inspectors' reports; those of William and Martha Gibbons from the Census.

divided his estate between his wife, three sons, and three daughters.[116]

Daniel Gibbons belonged to one of the oldest families of the canal (see Family Tree 6.3). He was the youngest son of a boatman, born in 1813, which was the first year in which occupations are given in baptismal registers. If his father was a boatman during the period when his children were being baptised, he was on the canal from at least 1801, when his eldest son was born. Possibly the family had come from the river. The name is found at Abingdon and Culham at that time. The names of Daniel's sisters suggest, though, that the family had felt the influence of the Midland canals. Selina and Phoebe were names much favoured at Foleshill, the parish in which the junction of the Oxford and Coventry Canals had been made. One, or perhaps two, of Daniel's brothers were boatmen, like him. His sister Sophia married a boatman, and the Phoebe Gibbons who married the boatman Edward Fisher was perhaps another. Both William Gibbons and John Seymour, Sophia's husband, became pub-keepers in Jericho in later life. Daniel, however, remained a boatman to the end. When he died in 1889 'of Fisher Row' he divided his estate between his wife, his three sons, and three daughters. His daughters were Harriet, wife of Abel Skinner, the boatman, and Fanny, wife of Samuel Humphries, another boatman. One of his sons may have become a waterman, the other two were boatmen, one of whom was living at Lower Heyford at the time the will was made. His eldest son, Samuel followed him as a boatman, and so did their sons. One of these, Leonard was still on the Oxford canal in 1938, but he was living on his boat; he had probably never known any other home. When children he and his siblings were frequently encountered by the Inspector of the Bicester Union, on their boat. Joseph, the younger son, married an Eynsham boatman's daughter, Charlotte Rogers in 1881, and they had two children, including a son, William. Joseph's boats were registered at Banbury; those of a William Gibbons, probably his son, though said to be of Longford, at the top of the canal, had his boat registered at Towcester, on the Grand Junction Canal.[117] For one living at Longford the Grand Junction

[116] Oxon. RO M and G 23/2 (Gibbons).
[117] Bicester Reg. of Inspections, *passim.*

Canal was as accessible as the Oxford Canal. To live there was to have access to commissions to work on two different routes. Boatmen in the Midlands could range over more routes than a boatman settled in Oxford. This consideration must have weighed heavily with the boatmen.

When it is said that the families moved north it is difficult to produce statistics. We are dealing with a mobile group, often only glimpsed fleetingly, in a great variety of records. The old contrast between the family whose business was to be always on the move, but who yet was embedded in a tight-knit, small, land-based community had gone. Perhaps the best evidence of the movement can be seen in the fate of the 51 boats which were registered on the Oxford Canal Boat Register, made under the Canal Boat Acts of 1877.[118] It was first made up in 1879, when the 51 boats consisted of seven from the Thames below Oxford, 38 from Oxford, and six from the canal (two from Thrupp, one from Kidlington, two from Cassington, and one from Banbury). 16 of this number were sold to boat-owners of one sort or another, up the canal, none down the river below Oxford; two to Heyford; six to Banbury; two to Napton; three to Sephton brothers at Tusses Bridge, at the top of the Oxford Canal; one each to Hinckley and Rugby. After 1879 more boats were added to the register, and when sold to a local owner might be re-registered there with a new number. Though there were 100 boats on the register before it closed in 1925, many had been registered more than once, and some had been broken up. Ten were noted as being in the same ownership, but the masters had moved away to the north, and registered their boats elsewhere.

On the Oxford Canal there had been little activity by the big carrying companies, and the boats were mainly run by coal-merchants, like William Ward, who might own several boats, or even a small fleet; or they belonged to the boatmen who ran them. As railway competition increased, more and more coal-merchants gave up their boats – why own boats, and em-ploy boatmen, when the railway would take care of this side of things entirely? As their number declined, the boatmen were increasingly thrown on their own resources. They had little ability to combine to seek out contracts and became dependent on working for coal contractors in the Midlands,

---

[118] City, Oxford Canal Boat Register (awaiting cataloguing).

who dispatched them to firms which had placed orders with them.[119]

Even if they lost their homes ashore, whilst they kept their own boats they might still think of themselves as Oxford men temporarily employed in the north, but as commissions decreased, and the length of time taken on journeys increased as standards of canal maintenance fell, it became a struggle to keep a boat. The boatmen became increasingly vulnerable to ill-fortune: frosts and drought, which halted the boats, accident or illness – these were things they could no longer take in their stride. Boatmen were then forced to mortgage or sell their boats. There were few buyers in Oxford, and so the boats were bought by coal contractors or perhaps boat-builders like the Sephtons, or Nurser Brothers.[120] Living on a hired boat, working for a Midland firm, it became increasingly difficult for a boatman to regard himself as of Oxford. When he took a house on 'the land, or again bought a boat, if ever he did so, he was likely to regard the Midlands as his home. One finds those who managed to retain their own boats a proud group indeed.

Several events occurred in 1894/5 which affected the boatmen seriously, and hastened the flight to the north. A great drought in 1893 held up trade on the canal for weeks. This was followed in 1895 by frosts and then floods. Trade suffered. The canal company experienced serious loss of revenue, for in 1894 it lowered its charges in the hope of attracting trade. The sacrifice was in vain. Trade did not increase. Maintenance costs became harder to meet just when repairs from the ravages of extreme weather became pressing. All things seemed to conspire against the company and its boatmen.[121]

In 1902 Wards, the coal-merchants sold off their fleet of canal boats to another local firm, King and Co., and within a

[119] PP. Eng. 1909/xiii (CD. 4840), *R.C. on Canals,* Third Report, Evidence and Appendices, 17.

[120] Coventry City RO, PH/Reg/1/1, Coventry Canal Boat Register. Sephtons, the boat-builders bought many boats, which they often kept for quite a short period. It seems likely that when a boatman could not pay his bill for the repairs he mortgaged it to the boat-builders. It would be interesting to see the business papers of such a firm, who may well have acted as a sort of bank or money lending organisation to the boast people.

[121] PP. Eng. 1896/xxiv (C. 8429), *Report of the Committee of the Council of Education, 1895-96,* Education of Canal Boat Children, 160; Cornish, *Naturalist on Thames,* 5-10; PP. Eng. 1909/xiii (Cd. 4840), 12-17.

year nearly all the boats were resold to firms in the north.[122] In the same year the Council withdrew its support from the boatmen's chapel, now no longer a floating chapel, but a conventional brick building. By now the parish register showed that nearly all the children baptised were living on canal boats, not ashore. When they came to be baptised, there were usually two or more 'done' at the same time from one or several families. They were something of a round-up. Few children bore Oxford names. The church had now only an occasional influx influence on them. In 1902 the last marriage between a boatman and the daughter of a boatman took place in St Thomas's. The community was now too shrunken and its young too few for it to perpetuate itself. One or two boatmen lingered on, just as one or two of the Beesleys did too, but the community which had once peopled the Row with brothers and sisters, cousins and aunts, was dead.

Old Joseph Skinner, master and owner of his own boat, and a member of one of the families which had come from the river to the canal when the railways were first built, continued to ply the canal long after the Second World War, stopping only when the tow-path was damaged and could not be used by his mule. He was the last of the Oxford boatmen, but his boat was Coventry -registered, and when he retired he went to live on his boat at the junction of the Oxford and Coventry canals, in an area where a few boatmen might still be found.[123]

---

[122] Oxford Canal Boat reg., *passim*.
[123] Coventry Canal Boat Reg. No. 490, registered 28 Nov. 1924.

History and Memory

I. PHYSICAL DESTRUCTION

For a little while yet the community held a semblance of life. There were still boatmen who brought coal from the Midlands to the wharf, and called for a drink at the pub. Outwardly the Row still looked the same to the casual visitor. A romantic and sentimental man of letters visited Oxford in the first decade of the 20th century and described the Nag's Head. He wanted to hire a boat:

Mr Phipkin indicated a public-house called the Nag's Head. 'If yer ever want a bargee in Oxford,' said he, 'look for him there'...

In reply to my suggestion, the landlord brought in whisky and water to the little parlour of the Nag's Head, where I have no doubt private transactions have taken place ever since the canals were opened. It is an old inn. The floors are strewn with sawdust. The benches are well-worn and polished. Through the door from the bar comes the sound of thick laughter, heavy voices, and the brittle clink of glasses. One glance within reminded me of drinking-houses along the quay-side in Marseilles.[1]

Yet the vital spark was dead. The last marriage between a boatman and a boatman's daughter had already occurred and the community had now fallen below replacement level. The last generation would grow old and then there could be no more.

The railways had killed the community, and now only the shell remained, and the motor car would destroy that. Its end came with the revival of road traffic as the motor car came to outrival the railways. The first step in the disintegration of the fabric of the Row was due to the widening of Pacey's Bridge,

---

[1] E. Temple Thurston, *The Flower of Gloucester* (London, 1911), 31-2.

in 1922, to carry the increased volume of road traffic.[2] Two houses were pulled down, but this was the least of the damage; the new bridge was built lower than the old one and acted as a barrier across river and Row. The footpath which had passed under the bridge, linking Middle and Lower Fisher Row, was omitted, and there was no headroom for boats to navigate through its arch.

It was now impossible for boats to pass down to the Castle Mill. Perhaps this was the last straw for the mill. In 1929 it was demolished, and the mill-wheel which had turned since before the Conquest was still. It was 800 years since Robert d'Oili, Keeper of Oxford Castle, had granted the houses on the weir-ham of his mill to Oseney, and now, with the mill gone, the Bank had lost its function. It would not be long before the houses on the Bank suffered the same fate.

No barges now came to the wharf by the Running Horses, for the river trade was moribund, and in 1938, the pub lost its licence. In the following year the Nag's Head was pulled down, and when it was rebuilt the old stables for the canal horses were not replaced.[3] The pub was expanded and modernised and its door no longer opened on to the Row. It opened on to Hythe Bridge Street, as if the brewers who owned it sought a new type of custom.

The basin of the canal was sold in 1936 to Lord Nuffield, and the coal-merchants who had offices by the wharf moved up the canal to the wharf at Juxon Street.[4] The basin lay derelict and rotting throughout the Second World War, and in 1954 it was filled in. The western part of the site became a car park, while on the eastern section, Lord Nuffield, Oxford's most munificent son, the car magnate, raised his college. It was the proud gift of a self-educated man. The car has made the road the most successful mode of modern transport, and the college stands over the moribund canal like a triumphal arch, a symbol of success over a broken rival.

In 1914, when several houses just south of The Lasher in Upper Fisher Row were pulled down, new Council houses were built; but in 1954, when all the houses between the Nag's

---

[2] MS Top. Oxon. d. 505, The Minn Collection, St Thomas's parish, fos. 159, 239-43.

[3] Ibid, fo. 217.   [4] Compton, *Oxford Canal*, 145.

Head and Tawney's Almshouses were demolished, nothing was erected in their place.[5] A new block of flats was built next to the almshouses, and the rest was turned into a municipal garden.

The parish has always been a centre for transport. It has seen one form supersede another, and adapted to each in turn. Now the double-decker buses sway along its narrow streets to the bus station at Gloucester Green just over the borders of the parish to the cast. The forecourt of the London and North Western Railway station has become a tyre retread business, and acres of its track are covered by a car-park for commuters who still travel to London from the surviving station. The parish is a palimpsest scored with changing transport systems, but the people who served these obsolescent systems have gone. The community in Fisher Row has vanished.

II. THE LIVING MEMORY

And yet the Row lives on in the memory of men and women who spent their childhood in the parish or the Row. The Row they remember is but a shadow of the teeming community it once was, but nevertheless their recollections confirm and supplement what has been deduced from archival material. So much of the strivings of ordinary men and women escapes the record. It is of no interest to officialdom; it is not concerned with the ownership of property or the maintenance of order or the collection of taxes: but if we would know how men lived in the past it is of interest to us. In this book we have so far moved from the past forward, towards the present. We have now reached a period within living memory. Now we shall look from the present to the past, and our sources will be the memories of men and women.

The historian may ask many questions of his material, and ask in vain. He must school himself to accept that fact. But living men and women who were children in the last years of the community tell us things we could not otherwise know, and confirm what we, with infinite toil in the archives, have come to suspect. We must not expect too much, for the interests of boys and girls of 10 or 12 cannot be expected

---

[5] MS Top. Oxon. d. 505, fo. 270; W. A. Pantin, 'Houses of the Oxford Region, I – Fisher Row, Oxford', *Oxon.* XXV (1960), 121-5.

to coincide with those of the social historian. For old people, however, the past has a reality and interest the future no longer holds, and their minds return to it. When asked about the Row, many recalled it in great detail:[6] '... but I tell my husband that almost every night when I go to bed, I go down the Fisher Row and St Thomas and St Giles Fair and Tumbling Bay in my mind...'[7]

Memory is capricious, though, in what it preserves, and to coax it is to run the risk of overtaxing it. There is a twilight area of uncertainty, of things we think we remember, but may have been told, or even dreamed, or wish we had been told. It must be treated gently.

These memories showed though, how influences were felt in the parish in ways of which the historian had no glimmerings. The power of the Castle loomed over the Row, as perhaps one might expect from pictures of the area, for the Castle mound and the tower of St George's in the Castle still stand over the lower part of the Row. The County Gaol is situated within the walls of the Castle, which rise up from the water of the Castle Mill Stream opposite the foot of the Row. The Row reverberated to the sound of the Castle bell whenever an alarm was sounded. In concentrating on the Row, in looking in on the inhabitants, it is easy to forget the view from the Row itself. In the twelfth century the houses of the Bank had been owned by the keeper of the Castle, and the menace of Norman power hung over the Row. Even in the 18th and early 19th centuries the power of the law was grimly visible in the Row, for executions took place on the Castle Mound. It is not surprising that when a body was to be rescued from the gallows to save it from the anatomist it was from the Row that a mob was recruited. They lived nearby and they acted as a group, their sympathies easily aroused.

---

[6] People's memories of the Row were sought in various ways. Where possible introductions were used, but an appeal for information was also solicited in an article by 'Anthony Wood' (Mr Don Chapman) entitled 'Do you recall life down at Fisher Row?' in the *Oxford Mail* for 4 March 1974. This evoked a most generous response in the form of letters, interviews, introductions, the loan of books, pictures, and other useful material. This section of the book is drawn largely from help received from these people, who are thanked in the Acknowledgements.

[7] Mrs M. Massarella, letter, 19 Mar. 1974.

The very economy of the Row was affected by the Castle. The father of one of the women who had grown up there had mended the shoes of the young policemen, whilst her mother had done the washing of the young, unmarried policemen. They were often country lads, and their underclothes were often so full of holes that her mother had been ashamed to hang them out. No doubt earlier there had been work for laundresses and cobblers as well.

Territorial loyalties divided the parish. Many bore witness to the fact that the Row and St Thomas's High Street were worlds apart. For the inhabitants of the Row to go 'up the parish' was to move into alien territory. According to one of the inhabitants of the Row St Thomas's High Street was 'a dreadful sort of a place'. 'When the Turk's Head turned out,' said another, a former coal-labourer, 'there were knife fights.' He had seen women fighting, and the men did not intervene; they bet on it. The police never went there singly. It was all little alley-ways, crammed with Italians with their hurdy-gurdies, said a third. Tramps lived there in cheap lodging-houses at a penny a night. A man who grew up in St Thomas's High Street, a son of a skilled craftsman, gave the view of an inhabitant: many decent families had to live there, cheek by jowl with this wild element. To him the bargees of Fisher Row were 'a rough people – sort of gypos'. On the other hand, an inhabitant of the Row, who had lived next door to a family of canal boatmen for many years found them 'very nice people'. In the 1860s, when the Sherwood family lived at the foot of the Row, on the corner of St Thomas's High Street, it seemed to W. E. Sherwood as if all the fights of the neighbourhood took place beneath their windows.[8] Here, the Row and St Thomas's High Street confronted each other.

Whatever may have been the territorial allegiances of the Row, the strongest economic influence on the southern part of the Row was exercised by the Breweries, Morrells and Halls. The Sherwoods themselves were connected with Morrells brewery. W. E. Sherwood's father had been the brewery agent in 1861, and they occupied Richard Tawney's old house. 'The picture of Fisher Row', wrote one man, referring to a photograph of the Row, 'brings back memories of the high and low. The Sherwoods (ex-Mayor) in the first big house, and the

<hr />

[8] Sherwood, *Oxford Yesterday*, 8.

Berrys, the live-bait sellers in the last one in the picture...'
Near the Sherwoods, in Lower Fisher Row, lived humbler
employees of the brewery. They lived, as did the Sherwoods
themselves, in tenements rented from the brewers. The rent
of these little houses was low, sometimes no more than 2s. a
week, much what it had been 100 years earlier. In 1802 the
Widow Crawford had paid almost exactly that (£5 4s. 0d. a
year) for her tenement in Middle Fisher Row.[9] In Lower Fisher
Row a man might live in a brewery-owned house, work for
a brewery all his life, and after his death his family might
visit the brewery weekly to collect a pension. Further up the
Row the influence of the brewery waned and occupations had
been diversified.

A former inhabitant, Mrs Burden (née Kilby) conducted me
along the Row, and revealed new aspects of it to me. We paused
as we passed along the path by the new municipal lawns and
gardens, whilst she indicated the sites of houses now gone.
The houses near The Lock had been liable to flood, and so
were those at the foot of Middle Fisher Row. Some were built
with floors below street level; yards scarcely existed where
the Row was at its narrowest. Back yards had been important, for no space was wasted. Their own yard had housed
rabbits and a goat. The houses in Middle Fisher Row had been
built on a smaller scale than the houses in Upper Fisher Row,
having one room on each of three floors. The inhabitants of
Upper Fisher Row, Mrs Burden observed, had thought themselves socially superior. This, though, was familiar, for the
difference in standing Mrs Burden observed was reflected in
the leases of the past. All the little houses of Middle Fisher
Row were built on the land of the 12th and 13th tenements
of Christ Church's Fisher Row leases, and this was investment property from the 18th century, whilst the property of
Upper Fisher Row was largely occupied by its leaseholders.
In the 18th century bargemasters and their sons had lived
in Upper Fisher Row, whilst the names of the families into
which their daughters married were repeated in Middle Fisher
Row, in the Survey of 1772. It was easy to discover the names
of the occupants of Upper Fisher Row but those of Middle
Fisher Row were usually unknown, for subtenants left little

---

[9] *JOJ*, 20 Nov. 1802.

trace before the advent of the street directory. Perhaps because the leases of Upper Fisher Row were in many hands, it still stands, whilst grass covers Middle Fisher Row. We paced the garden and climbed the steps to the road and Hythe Bridge. Only here did we pass anyone who looked as if they lived in the area. Perhaps they were not strangers, and had known each other long ago: 'I look at them and they look at me, but we don't speak...'

Life had been hard, and the struggle was not forgotten. One man, an acute observer, who would not give his name, came to tell me of the 'destitution' of the parish: 'A man of forty looked old and worn out with worry on how to exist.' The worry of how to exist was a constant preoccupation in a parish where underemployment was chronic. The words brought to life the evidence of various citizens, employed, as 'messengers' at the 1857 Oxford elections, in an investigation of corrupt practices: 'What is your occupation?' – 'To go about and get what I can.' A lamplighter, who worked at night, being asked if he had the days to himself, replied 'I have a large family and I am obliged to work day and night if I can get it.'[10] Similarly, in Headington Quarry, on the eastern outskirts of Oxford, Raphael Samuel found that making a living was a matter of stringing together a series of bye-employments. It was 'a family affair rather than a matter for the man of the house alone'.[11]

In the face of these descriptions of the variety of ways in which a living was put together, the neat attribution of a single occupation to each worker in the 1841-71 Censuses seems implausible. Other conditions in the parish may have altered, but not this. In the early years of the twentieth century the man who could rely on regular employment was indeed fortunate. Railwaymen, printers, and some other skilled craftsmen, some (though not all) college servants, were in this group, but for many more employment was seasonal. A man who laid gas mains might have only about four winter months of full employment; a college waterman might have no work in the long vacation. Many trades were slack at this time, for the town

[10] PP. Eng. 1857, Session 2/viii (170), *Select Committee on the Oxford City Election Petition*, 25-6.

[11] Raphael Samuel, 'Quarry Roughs' in Raphael Samuel, *Village Life and Labour* (London, 1975), 183-207).

alternated still between boom in term and recession during the vacation.[12] Men must find what work they could. Thus one man, a cobbler, also sold live bait, acted in the summer as a ferry-man, and also at times as a coal-labourer. Some went into the country in summer, haymaking. One at least went poaching in Wytham and Bagley woods to supplement the larder, whilst fish from the river was sold from door to door. Emptying coal-boats was a regular job until strikes interrupted the flow of boats in the early '30s. After this men were drawn from the labour exchange. At that time men desperate for work would walk out to Kidlington to meet the boats there and travel back aboard, having secured the job of emptying them. No possible source of income was overlooked.

If the men were often engaged in a series of bye-employments, so were their wives and children. The load carried by the women was often heavy, for work had to be fitted into the management of large families, and there was little evidence of any shar-ing of household chores by men or boys. Women of the parish were still engaged in laundry work, like some of the boatmen's wives of Upper Fisher Row we encountered in the Census. The woman who took in the young policemen's laundry has been mentioned. Another, a widow, who received a certain amount of support from the church and the con-vent, worked in the laundry at the convent; others worked for schools.[13] Yet others worked as charwomen in private houses, or scrubbed the floors of nearby pubs and shops. Often young children accompanied their mothers when they went out to such jobs; or an elder sister would look after the younger children. Women who worked in factories, however, had to leave their young behind, but there were few such jobs going. Mr Harry Ayres recalled that his mother had worked in Hyde's Factory in New Inn Hall Street, earning 3s. 6d. a week. Here corduroy trousers were made. 'She smelt of corduroys,' he said. According to him, the chil-dren had seen little of her. Nevertheless, she had come home at lunch-time to feed them, sending someone out to buy bread and jam for the meal.

The osier works at the top of Upper Fisher Row, run by the Beesleys, provided seasonal work for the women from about

---

[12] Messrs H. Ayres, W. C. A. Molyneaux, Mrs Burden.
[13] Mrs Burden, Mrs Massarella, Mrs J. Lowe (née Beesley).

April through the summer. First they peeled the rods, later they wove them into various shapes. This seems to have been a cheerful time, and the children ran in and out among the workers. One man remembered his mother telling him how she worked there before he was born, making lobster pots which were sent to the south coast.[14]

Girls found employment in a variety of jobs. They were indeed conditioned to it young. A don's wife recalls a little girl in whom she had a particular interest (having rescued her from drowning) as she saw her at play: 'She generally wore a man's cap back to front (like the washerwomen of my childhood) and a bit of sacking, and had a little tub in which to wash her doll's clothes.' Mrs Burden (née Kilby) told me how she had been employed when she was 10 years old to scrub out a shop at 5.30 in the morning before going to school. On Saturday mornings work could be had chopping up oranges for marmalade at Frank Cooper's marmalade factory.[15] This brought in a few coppers. For this reason it was probably preferred to the child-minding which fell to schoolgirls when their mothers were out at work.

When the girls grew older they might go into service. The daughter of the widow, already mentioned, was one of these. 'As I told you before we almost lived in the church', and perhaps for this reason her going into service was aided by gifts both pious and useful. 'I still have the prayer-book presented to us by Dean Inge in Worcester College when we left school. Also they gave us a tin trunk of clothes, and found us our first job in domestic service ...'The first job she held was that of between maid, 'that was everybody's lackey, and had all the dirty jobs to do, and my time off was from two to five one afternoon a week ... I wouldn't like to see those days over again. I was a drudge at every one's beck and call; but I think it taught me to keep my own home clean, and to do the corners before the middle.'[16] There is often a hidden predatoriness in good works, perhaps not entirely absent here. The almost endless labour of these maids of all work was commented on with pity by a coal-labourer, but was part of the nature of things to the inhabitants of North Oxford.

---

[14] Mr A. Tustin, Mrs J. Lowe.
[15] Mrs Masarella, letter, 19 Mar. 1974.   [16] Ibid.

The laborious lives of these girls instilled Victorian middle-class standards of housekeeping, and it survives in their homes to this day. The meticulous housewifery of such former inhabitants of the Row cannot be surpassed, though it was equalled by the best of the canal boats: 'The cabin is part of the boat-woman's self-expression as well as her home; by its appearance and cleanliness she proclaims her self-respect and standing in the boat society.'[17] As the group became divorced from the rest of society, together with the painting of the boats, cleanliness became part of the mystique of boating. This would not be missed in Fisher Row where cleanliness was a matter of fierce pride: 'however poor we were, mother was always spotlessly clean'. By cleanliness people were judged with a knowledge-able eye – for many indeed were laundresses. Mrs Cripps for instance was said to look so nice in her black dress with leg-of-mutton sleeves and 'a very, very clean white apron'.

Employment for boys was on the whole less common and more spasmodic. They might run errands to the covered market in town, or earn a few coppers helping Mr Cripps, the drover, herd his beasts to the slaughterhouse opposite Morrells Brewery. Singing in the choir at St Thomas's brought in 2s. a quarter, but it also brought two treats: a pantomime at Christmas, and a trip down the river to Nuneham with its emus and deer park. Two of my informants had been choir boys, and Mrs Massarella (née Cox) had a brother who had moved on to sing in the choir at Exeter College: '... anyway there was an advert in the *Oxford Times* for boys for Exeter College choir and lo and behold my brother passed, but although he got paid quarterly, which was a help also, the Vicar, Rev. T. H. Birley, didn't like it very much. Imagine a boy born at 6 Fisher Row in an Eton suit and cap and gown. If he had been crowned king my mother couldn't have been more proud.'[18]

It is easy now to see how natural it had been for the under-employed bargemen of the early 19th century to turn to fishing, exploiting their position as freemen in fishing the free waters. The cluster of bye-employments which went with it naturally at that time-rush gathering, osier-growing, hiring out boats for pleasure-had, indeed, become for the fishermen

[17] A. J. Lewery, *Narrow Boat Painting* (Newton Abbot, 1974), 24, 92.
[18] Mr H. L. Webb, letter, 5 Jan. 1977.

the main source of income by the end of the 19th century, probably because of the ban on their traditional nets. By the turn of the century some of the Beesleys had become relatively prosperous. Mrs Julia Lowe (née Beesley), daughter of Jacob Beesley, who owned the osier works at the top of the Row, spoke of her father owning osier beds at Iffley, Binsey, and Long Hanborough, and of his buying rushes from an old woman who smoked a clay pipe at Leafield. She had accompanied her father to Leafield and other places when he bought rushes. Jacob Beesley also owned a farm at Binsey, and had cattle there and on Port Meadow, as well as owning property in the Row. He had built two houses at the top of the Row, behind the gate which divided their land from the rest of the Row. The land beyond the Lasher where the osier works were situated – called 'The Flam' by one of the inhabitants of the Row-was quite extensive; there they grew vegetables and fruit and kept ducks and chickens. They had two ponies and a trap.[19]

Fishing still played a part in the economy of the Row. In giving an account of the various bye-employments to which their parents turned, two people mentioned that their fathers had sold live-bait for fishing. One had sold fish from door to door. Fishing was also an important pastime in the lives of the parish, and a common topic of conversation. This emerged vividly from a letter from Mr H. L. Webb, attempting to throw light on the link between barbers and fishermen in the 17th century:

In the years before the 1914 war and the thirties there were no such things as electric or safety razors, only cutthroats, of which quite a few hadn't got one. In those days almost everyone made a point of being clean and shaven on Sunday, so everybody went to the barbers on Saturday, or Sunday morning. As many as 15 to 20 would be waiting, the lather boy or apprentice lathering one chair, the barber shaving in the other. Now, this is the connection between the fishermen and the barber's, whilst waiting, the conversation naturally turned to angling (the roach are going well at the Sheep-wash, there's big pike at Louse Lock, the chub's feeding well at Turn, how about a turn in Potts Stream or an afternoon at Hinksey). The times I listened and been fascinated as a boy.

J. J. Faulkner had long ago pleaded for the use of the Free Waters for the benefit of all Oxonians, and such a letter shows

---

[19] Mrs J. Lowe.

the reason for the popular opposition to the Beesley's monopoly of the fishing in the last century. There would always be a demand for live bait amongst local fishermen. Selling live bait could make a useful addition to the family income.

The Row was no longer an enclave inhabited almost entirely by boat-people. It had become apart of the wider community, and the Beesleys were prominent and respected members of it. They were remembered by everyone in the parish. Abel Beesley was remembered as an old man – something of a 'Gentleman john', better off than anyone else in the Row. His wife had outlived her husband, dying at 80 or thereabouts. She was recalled sitting in the sun outside her house. The sons had died young, but the daughters had married well, and were remembered. Florence, 'Floss', had married 'the manager at the wharf', Hubert Hawkins, the owner of several boats on the canal at the end of the First World War. Rose kept The Fishes at North Hinksey, whilst Alice had married a Mr Smith of Hall's Breweries.

Abel's pre-eminence as a punter was not always remembered with great clarity and it was the last inhabitants of the house of The Flam who were most clearly remembered. I was told by two men repairing a motor-bike outside their house in Upper Fisher Row that the house at the top of the Row had belonged to an old man called Jones until recently. His wife, May, was a Beesley, a family who had been big people round here at one time ... Mrs Jones – she could punt – a man couldn't touch her. The Beesleys had been great punters.[20] Abel was less clearly remembered than May Jones, who had been their neighbour.

Few of the old inhabitants are left there. Most are scattered on housing estates on the outskirts of the city. All the same, the memory of the parish is still kept alive. Just as the old inhabitants of St Ebbes, which was cleared for re-development some years ago, keep its memory green, so in St Thomas's books in which St Thomas's is described are treasured. Inter-views with old people are published in the *Oxford Mail* and prompt more reminiscences. The Mayoralty of Olive Gibbs, daughter of a family which had lived in the parish from the 17th century, is a matter of local pride. Her father,

---

[20] Interview with two unidentified inhabitants of Upper Fiser Row, 7 Nov. 1973.

Lazarus Cox, lived his whole life in the parish, dying only recently aged over ninety. During the year of Olive Gibbs's office the former inhabitants of the parish held a reunion, and parties of the 'Tom-Rags', as they call themselves continue to be held each year. In this they follow a precedent set by the dispersed families of St Ebbe's. There is a ground swell of local pride and nostalgia which still binds old families of the parish.[21]

At the beginning of this century, most of the inhabitants were poor, and a common experience of life bound them together: but in this the boatmen had no part. In good times their boats gave full employment to the family. When trade was slack, as it was almost all the time after the opening of the railways, the boat was a ball and chain, tying them to one occupation, and preventing them from taking up such casual employment as was available to other occupants of the parish.

Employment on the canal might be scarce, but they must be waiting, ready to seize any opportunity which might come their way.

How did they get work? Well, you had to seek it where you could-see. You used to watch the outride-you knew when he would be down from the collieries-and you watched. There he'd go, bowler hat, umbrella, strutting along. He'd go and call on the coal-merchant and you waited, and when he came out, you went in, and you took the coal-merchant's man-his agent-and you treated him – whisky and so on – that was the way-and after a bit he'd say, well, he'd send you a postcard to Sutton Stop – and off you'd go. And there'd be another boatman waiting for him after you, and another ...[22]

Whatever one makes of Jack James's account of how the boatmen got jobs, it is clear that any machinery there had been had entirely broken down, and methods were, at best,

[21] *Oxford Mail*, 28 Nov. 1974.

[22] Interviews with Jack James, Stoke Bruern, 4 Oct. 1968. The interview was written up by notes made at the time. Mr James's accent was thick, and it was not easy to follow the logical connections of his ideas. Anthony Wood got a slightly different reply or perhaps interpreted it differently – when he asked much the same question some months later: 'The colliery agents or outrides as we used to call them used to meet in his office [Hubert Hawkins'] on Market Day. That was when the market was in Gloucester Green. Then over they come to the Greyhound, and we'd sleer over to the Greyhound after them to find out where the next loads of coaling were coming on. Of course, in those days we were competing with the Great Western – and we could hold our own' ('Meet Jack James', *Oxford Mail*, 3 Feb 1970).

ad hoc. Nothing could be taken for granted, and planning was impossible. The boatman lived from hand to mouth.

It might be said that many other inhabitants of the parish lived in a hand-to-mouth fashion too, but in fact the whole pattern was very different. The pattern of employment of the boatmen drove them into the company of their own kind, and prevented their mixing with the parish, whilst other members of the parish were continually thrown into each other's company. This can be seen very clearly in their different shopping patterns.

In the parish those with steady jobs were able to plan and store provisions. They made jams and country wines, for which their children gathered dandelions and blackberries. The daughter of a skilled craftsman in steady employment remembered these occasions with pleasure. For poorer families, however, sugar and jam were things bought as required. Thus the son of a gas-fitter – a seasonal job – remembered his mother sending out immediately before lunch for a halfpennyworth of jam. Where livings were hand to mouth, so was housekeeping. Food was bought as need arose, for immediate use: a halfpennyworth of tea and sugar, half the bottom of a cottage loaf for three farthings, and a halfpennyworth of milk. This made a meal for a family. For lunch a child might buy himself a halfpennyworth of rice pudding. Broken bread from Boffins and Coopers, the bakers, and broken cheese from Grimbly Hughes, the Cornmarket grocer, provided cheap food. Often the pennies earned in the morning were spent on the food that was eaten during the day. Sunday dinner was more lavish. The makings would come from the market: 2d. for giblets at Tyrrells or for half a sheep's head, 2d. for 'all sorts' (mixed root vegetables); this provided a good meal. A sheep's head could be roasted at the bakery for 2d., together with roast vegetables and a Yorkshire pudding. Few people had an oven of their own.

Such provisioning in pennies and halfpennies was not possible for the boatman. Nor was it possible for him to earn in the morning the bread for the day. He was paid by the trip, and provisioned his boat accordingly. Thus in 1858 a fly-boat for four was said to be victualled in the following manner: 'The victualling of the vessel consists in shipping a sack of potatoes, a quantity of inferior tea, and about fifty pounds of meat at the beginning of the voyage; while large loaves of bread, weighing upwards of eight pounds are got at certain places along the line of the canal.' Four large men with navvy-like appetites and taste in food, working for a well-run company no doubt ate more than the owner and captain of a family boat who hardly knew where the next load was coming from, but the method of victualling remained the same. The boater was, however, often forced to go into debt in the process, and he therefore dealt with victuallers who catered for his kind. Jack James described dealings with the Lovelocks, the owners of such a shop on the Grand Union Canal at Long Buckby:

> They were good to the boaters, They'd help them when they had nothing. Lend them money.
>
> Mrs Lovelock would say, 'How are you, Harry? Are you alright for money? Do you need a pound?'
>
> 'Oh yes,'he'd say, 'I reckon I'm alright. And if I did borrow, I'd have to pay it back.'
>
> 'Come on, Harry, sure you don't need a pound?'
>
> 'Well, ten bob perhaps'– then she'd give him ten shillings, and after the boat was revictualled and corn got on board for the horses they'd go down to Dickinsons and get their cheque. Dickinsons always paid by cheque ... and they'd take it straight back to Long Buckby and hand it over the counter, and she'd refill the starn cupboard, and reckon up – the groceries last week and then this week – 'And don't forget the ten bob you lent me', the boaters would say. They were straight.
>
> She'd reckon it up and take it out of the cheque and get the boat men to make their mark on the back of it ... And they didn't have any banks. The shopkeeper was their bank. They wasn't the only one. There were the Beesleys at the Greyhound at Sutton Stop. They were old boaters. When they went ashore they got other people to run their boats ... Polly Beesley ... but that's going back a long way – 1901 or 2 ... they came from the Thames, the Beesleys did.[23]

As the machinery of canal transport disintegrated, its workers looked within their own group for support, and grew ever

---

[23] 'Sutton Stop' is the junction of the Oxford and Coventry Canals. Benjamin and Mary (Polly) Beesley appear first in the Foleshill Parish Baptismal Register in 1877 as boaters, the name being given as 'Bearsley'. By 1884, at the birth of their second daughter, Benjamin was a publican of Hawkesbury (Sutton) Stop. Between 1890 and 1906 six boaters belonging to Benjamin Beesley (said in 1890 to be of the Greyhound Inn, Foleshill), were entered on the Coventry Boat Register (Coventry City Record Office, PH/Reg./1/1). No evidence that the family did come from the Thames has been found. The marriage of Abel Beesley's daughter into a family which included canal clerks at the wharf at Hawkesburymay give some weight to the suggestion that Benjamin Beesley came from the Thames. The names Beesley and Bearsley, however, are found in Foleshill parish from time to time.

more clannish, and more isolated. It was perhaps typical of their mistrust of the world of people on the land that no interviews with former boatmen arose out of the appeals for information from ex-boat-people, and the only interviews with boat-people of the Row were with two men (both now dead) who for long acted as interpreters of the boat-people's way of life to the growing number of 'noddy boatmen' (canal enthusiasts in cabin cruisers). These men had overcome the boatmen's natural caution in dealing with people off the land, and were regarded as oracles. Their tales have frequently been recounted, and, through no fault of their own, had come to have some-thing of the quality of an oft-told rosary.

In interviewing the other inhabitants of the parish and the Row I was aware over and over again of an almost painful search for exactitude. One old lady presented me with a list of mistakes in detail which had crept into her evidence on our first meeting. This had been carefully typed out by her son. These people were volunteering information and they were anxious that it should be as accurate as possible. Not for nothing had so many sons of this parish become printers at the University Press.

I felt in talking to boat-people, and reading interviews by others, that words were used more impressionistically. They were conveying an impression of their world to an alien, to a total outsider. Emphasis and exaggeration were necessary to get points home. They were on the defensive, and their pride in this world led them at times to embellish the truth. The decoration of the boats was marvellous and fantastic, and at times something of the same fantasy crept into their description of the boatmen's world. So it was when an old boatman recalled a wedding: 'You see they all reckoned to get here for Banbury Fair, if they could, a lot of the boat people. There might be five or six weddings, but there were two holidays to have a wedding.'[24] Such should be taken as a description of the ideal rather than the actual. Only two double weddings are recorded before 1923, in St Thomas's,[25] and it is doubtful

[24] 'Working the Cut: Reminiscences of a Boatman' (interview of Arthur Coles) by Christine Bloxham, *Cake and Cock Horse*, VI (1975), 21.

[25] On 12 Apr. 1869 the boatman Robert Humphries' daughter Mary Ann and his son Samuel, who was a boatman too, both married. Mary Ann married the boatman William, son of William Humphries, boatman, and Samuel married Fanny,

whether after this date there were enough boatmen on the Oxford canal for such an event to occur anywhere along its banks. This was the perfect wedding as boatmen envisaged it. All rites of passage were important. If, however, one turns again to consider baptisms we find that multiple baptisms involving different families were quite common, and commonest when the canal community was at its peak. Between 1813 and 1820 only 8 per cent of boatmen's baptisms were multiple, by 1841-50, 34 per cent. By 1881-90 the figure was approximately 7½ per cent. But between 1891 and 1914 there were only seven years when more than one family was having its children baptised, so that the number of such double baptisms was limited. Nevertheless out of 20 families baptising in these 'possible' years four or 20 per cent of the baptisms were multiple. In Oxford, where the standard of pastoral care was high, it was unusual for children of the same parents to be baptised together unless they were twins, but in the early 20th century, when almost all the boatmen were living on their boats, such baptisms were common, and five families baptised two or more children between 1908 and 1917. Baptisms, like weddings, were occasions of importance to boat-people, and may well have gained in significance as the community dwindled. At such a time any increase in numbers was surely a matter for rejoicing. It also gave an occasion for the members of the community to come together and strengthen their ties. In this, perhaps, lies the kernel of truth in the boatman's account of marriage celebrations.

The world of the boatmen had become by the beginning of the twentieth century so remote from that of the inhabitants of the Row, that it is not surprising that memories of them were, on the whole, slight and superficial. It is agreed the boats were 'beautiful', 'very clean', and 'everything was polished', but very few boatmen lived ashore. Most were here today and gone tomorrow, there was no chance for children to get to know them. One exception had been the James family. Mrs James had kept a house ashore so that the children could go

daughter of the boatman Daniel Gibbons. On 18 Dec. 1896 another brother and sister married. Thomas, son of Thomas Lamsden, boatman, married Anne, daughter of Robert Humphries, and Harriet Lamsden married John Faulkner. All were boatman and sons or daughters of boatmen.

to school. Perhaps for this reason Mr James was to become the most accessible of all boatmen to the outsider, and a moving spirit in the establishment of the Waterways Museum at Stoke Bruern. Only Mrs Burden (née Kilby) remembered them

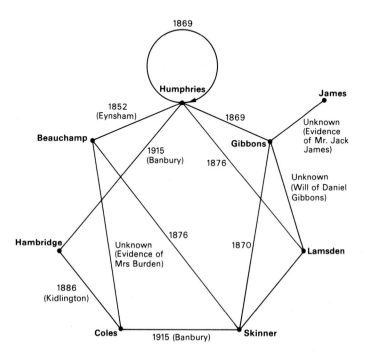

Fig. 7.1.   Marriages between families of canal boatmen listed by
               Mrs Burden.

in detail and by name. She had lived next door to the Beauchamp family as a girl, and had even slept on a canal boat. She listed for me the following boatmen whom she remembered:
   George James
   Mr and Mrs Humphries
   Joe Lambsden
   Mr and Mrs Beauchamp
   Mr Gibbons
   Mr Skinner
   Mr Hambridge.

Mrs Burden also referred to the Coles family, though she did not necessarily know them. If we consider these families it is possible to see how close-knit this group of boatmen was, for they formed, quite literally, one large family. All were related by marriage. It is not possible to indicate exactly how they were related, because we only know the Christian names of a few of them from Mrs Burden, but we know there were marriages between these families, and there may be others of which we do not know, for not all took place in St Thomas's parish. The least closely integrated into the group, so far as we know, was George James, brother-in-law to Joseph Gibbons. The Gibbonses were related by three marriages to other families in this group, as also were the Beauchamps, the Skinners and the Coleses. The Hambridges and the Lamsdens were related by two marriages to the group, and the Humphries by four; two branches of their family were linked by the marriage of cousins (see Figure 7.1).

In the 1930s L. T. C. Rolt converted a working narrow boat for cruising at Tooley's Yard at Banbury, and whilst there, and on his travels, he came to know boatmen at a time when some commercial traffic still survived on the Oxford Canal. His observation bears out the evidence adduced here of the close family ties which existed between families:

> It is exceptional for the boatman to marry 'off the land' and so, since the boating community is a small one, everyone appears to be related to everybody else either by blood or by marriage or both. The boatman seems to carry in his head this complex genealogical tree. As he nods to the steerer of a passing boat he will most likely explain: 'That's Joe so-and-so as married our Auntie Rose's girl. Uncle Jack that works for the Limited now, married his Dad's first wife's sister.'[26]

But if they married amongst themselves, they were marrying now as much outside Oxford as inside, and only two of these families, the Humphrieses and the Gibbonses were in the parish before 1840 – the Humphrieses being related in the female line to the Beesleys. The boatman's world was now self-contained and separated from that of the Row, and it is therefore not surprising, though disappointing, that memories of them were so sketchy.

[26] L. T. C. Rolt, *The Inland Waterways of England* (London, 1950), 191.

The history of the dynasties of the Row reaches back over a very long period indeed. What did the old families of the Row know of their history? Were they aware, and in how much detail, of the centuries that lay behind them? What did the Bossoms and Beesleys know, for instance, of their past? The Bossoms' connection with the river goes back to the 17th century, and perhaps, through their connection with the Howse family to John Howse, who was the first man to take out his freedom as a boatman in 1583. The Beesley family can be traced back to the 17th century too, through their connection with the Gardners. Not only were all the 19th-century fishermen of the parish members of these two families, but many of the boatmen had married girls from these families, especially in the early years of the canal.

The oldest family in the Row at present is the Tustins. Mr Aubrey Tustin's father and mother, Aubrey and Florence Tustin, kept the Nag's Head from about 1932 to 1939. They were well-connected to run such a pub, which was, even then, still patronised by boatmen, for Florence Tustin was the daughter of the boatman, Richard Corbey, who had married Betsey Skinner, and she was therefore, as the Skinner family tree shows, a cousin to Joseph Skinner, the last man to run his own boat on the Oxford Canal. Through the Corbeys they were related directly to the Bossoms in the female line, and therefore the family goes back as far as the Bossom family can be traced (see Corbey and Bossom Family Trees). The Tustin family's knowledge of the recent history of the Row was detailed. From them, for instance, I learnt exactly who Abel Beesley's daughters had married, and this was confirmed subsequently by the parish register. They knew that their grandfather had married a Skinner, but had no knowledge of the earlier history of the family, and its connections with the Row. There was no tradition of the centuries-old connection with the river and with boats. The present generation has found employment elsewhere.

There are no known members of the Beesley family left in the Row, but there are still Beesleys on the river. Messrs F. J. and J. H. Beesley, father and son, work as watermen for St Edward's School and live at Godstow.[27] In this family there is a tradition that the family has been connected with the river

---

[27] *St. Edward's School Chronicle*, XVIII (1936), 321.

for over 300 years, but detailed knowledge of the family only reaches back a little further than in the Tustin family. The eldest living member of this family is Mrs Julia Lowe, aunt to Mr F. J. Beesley. Her knowledge of the family stretches back to her grandfather, the fisherman, James Beesley, who died six months before she was born. He had married Elizabeth Hands (see Family Tree 5.4), and she remembered a distant cousin on that side of the family, Thirza Hands. This cousin told her that the Beesley family had come from Woodstock, which was, apparently, inconsistent with the tradition of the family known to her nephew. Yet, though her grandfather had been baptised in St Thomas's parish, the evidence that the family came from Woodstock is correct – so far as it goes. James Beesley's father, who was lessee of tenement 1Aa at the top of Upper Fisher Row in the early 19th century was referred to in one of the leases, in 1824, as Thomas Beesley, fisherman of Blenheim Park' (which is at Woodstock). In this case what appears the less likely and less well-substantiated tradition is nearer the mark. Family memory here, unaided by records, as with the Tustins, only goes back to the grandparents of the oldest member of the family. The families of the Row, whose histories we have traced had only a limited awareness of their past and little of the society of which their great grandparents were part. In this they are in no way exceptional. The variety and the complexity of our history is illumined only partially by memory, and its significance is only half understood in the present.

The community has broken up now, and nearly all the families have left the Row. All have found a new sort of life, and the grinding hardship and the sparse comforts of the Row are a thing of the past. As I listened to memories of life in the parish fifty years ago, and looked around me at the comfortable rooms, bright with paint and redolent of comfort, I was struck by the sharp contrast between living conditions in the past and the present. When did the change come? The answer was always the same. The coming of the motor car brought employment, and it brought a wages revolution which affected workers in other jobs also. The wages of the car industry were related to the national wage-structure, and if other employers wished to attract workers, they had to compete. The centuries of chronic underemployment were ended, even if the car industry might have its ups and downs.

The car industry has all but eliminated the Row, and has been the basis of improved standards of living generally in Oxford, but old people look back with a sigh to the days when the Row was bursting with life and neighbours were bound together by closer ties than they have been able to establish since. Yet most are realists, and have no illusions about the improvement they have seen. One old man summed it up. When he was young, children were often deformed: they were cross-eyed and bandy. 'They were ugly,' he said, 'but now the children are all beautiful.' And he is glad.

The Castle Mill Stream flows gently past the Row, its surface filmed with scum, the Lock choked with leaves, polythene bags, and old sandwiches; bottles bob at the dead end of the canal by Hythe Bridge. The tramps and winos who have a refuge down near the site of Oseney, sun themselves on the towpath. These remain – the transient stream of the parish population has outlasted the stable community.

The Row lived by exploiting the river, and now its trade is ended. The mill is pulled down, the fishermen have gone; the wharves are empty, the boatmen are dead and their children dispersed. The river remains, unused, unkempt, superseded.

Appendices

APPENDIX I: Building a Mill

Almost every parish in England had its own water-mill. In building them artificial channels were dug and rivers diverted, and the geography of the countryside was changed. Yet because most of them were built at a very early period (many are Saxon), the process has almost entirely escaped documentation. What appears to be the building of a new mill will usually be found to be the rebuilding or refurbishing of a mill on an ancient site. A very full account of the process however has been found. It comes from a new country. A Devizes miller who emigrated to New Zealand described the building of a mill there, at Ashburton on the Canterbury Plains during the nineteenth century. The problems he encountered, and the elation of overcoming them come through with equal clarity:[1]

As soon as this important business of settling into our home at Avonbank was satisfactorily disposed of, I sought for profitable employment in my own line by the erection of a flour-mill and the creation of a good water-power in the evidently rising town of Ashburton. After a good deal of careful exploring, I thought that I had discovered that the Ashburton River had, at some far-distant time, taken a different course to that which it now pursued: and that I could, by a rather bold expenditure, and by obtaining the permission of the Colonial Government of New Zealand, the Provincial Government of Canterbury, the Ashburton Road Board, and a large number of land proprietors, procure a valuable water-power, close to the town of Ashburton, in the centre of a large agricultural district. It was not a pleasant task, and it took a long time, to obtain all these permissions, but, as the new river that would thus be directed through some twenty miles of land would injure no one and benefit all, the public bodies gave me all the authority that they could.

It was an unusual thing to be building a water-mill and a large water-wheel on a spot where it was difficult to get enough water to drink, and opinions varied very much as to whether I was seeing further or was a greater fool than the other inhabitants of Ashburton. I sent to Nelson for four carpenters who had more faith in my directions than the residents of Ashburton, and I procured four extraordinarily good working navigators to whom I gave 50 per cent, more than the ordinary wages-which they did not fail to earn.

The timber for the mill was very expensive, as it had to be carted through the often flooded Rakaia River where it was a mile wide. The intake for the water had to be made very secure with many tons of cement, and the water had to be taken across public roads under bridges constructed to the satisfaction of the Ashburton

[1] *Tales of a Pioneer: Episodes in the Life of Mr Alfred Saunders,* edited by his two youngest daughters (Christchurch, New Zealand, 1927, privately printed), 159-62. I am grateful to Mrs Kae Miller for drawing my attention to this book.

Road Board. Near the mill, some high, strong embankments had to be built to give the neces-sary height to the headwater, and some obstructions in the ancient course below the mill had to be cut through to take the water freely away from the waterwheel. After all had proved secure, on Monday, February 17th, 1873, 1 went up with a bar to draw the hatches and try the water down through the ancient course that had possibly had no water running through it since the time that Joshua crossed the Jordan. Although this natural course brought the water only a mile and a half nearer the mill, it wound about so much that it took the water five or six miles and had lots of gullies and back water courses dry, hard, and cracked, after an unusually dry summer-to fill up. To what extent, and for what length of time, the water would be absorbed by this dry ground, 1 could not tell.

When I returned, I found all the men looking out from the mill in the expectation of seeing the water flowing up. They looked surprised and incredulous when I told them not to expect it for at least four days and nights. When this time had passed, and still no water came anywhere near the mill, 1 was overwhelmed with pitying condolences for having spent so much money upon such a fine mill, without knowing whether any water would come to it or not, and the favourite talk of the country round about was the extraordinary act of lunacy that I had committed.

I turned on more water every day, until at last I put nearly the whole river in, but all seemed lost in the old course. The carpenters began to work like men who know that their work is wasted, and would not take the trouble to put their tools out of the way of the no-longer-expected water, so that I had to do it for them. At last the dry and thirsty land was saturated, and the water came creeping on towards the embankment. I went to bed that evening leaving the water-wheel so that it would turn if the water came. At two o'clock next morning, it came up to the mill hatch with a bang, and I heard the joyful sound of the wheel turning. I had an opportunity to see and try everything before anyone else was about. Standing alone in the mill, I imbibed it all. All proved right and tight, and the fall greater than I had ventured to expect.

APPENDIX II. *The Extent of the Free Waters*

The Free Waters

Mag. Bridge thro Millam to the Corner of Deep Martin   Then from the corner where the draw Bridge stands to F. Water stone   from thence to Folly Bridge   Thro Tauntons Arch *all Round* Stump Pool Meadow   Preachers Pool and Bakker head are in dispute   From the corner near Bricknells to Castle Mills & the back Stream to Morrells Engine   All Hogacre Ditch from the Main Stream   Near by Oseney Lock up to Ferry Hinksey & the Hope near Botley to the Boundary Stone   Freemen always fish Botley Ditch & then to the Lasher   there begins Seacourt which continues to Pricketts long Eyott   There begins Ld Abingdons water   There is a stream leaving from Seacourt thro Binsey Bridge called the Dunge all of which is free & likewise on to The Four Streams   Then to Bullstocks Old Bridge Stream   from thence to Hinksey – in dispute   All free from the Four Streams & likewise from High Bridge up to the Free Water Stone on the E. side of Godstow – both Wick Stream is free   Likewise the Back Stream to Medley & a ditch from Port Meadow Stream by Binsey Chuch is likewise Free – all free from Hall's summer House down back stream by Littlegate to Ch.Ch. Meadow.

In 1824 the question of the extent of the city waters was raised before the Council, and the matter was investigated. It was decided to publish the report, and each member of the Council was to receive a copy. If this was ever done, no copy has survived. The description of the waters which has been given below comes from the volume in the City Archives

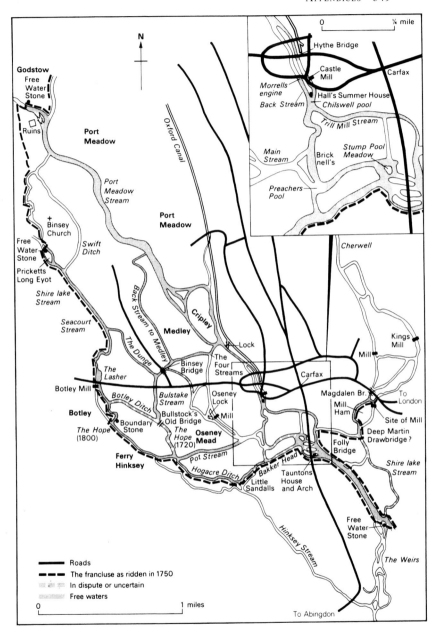

Fig. App. II.1 The free waters of the city of Oxford.

known as 'Alderman Sadlers Collection'.[2] The material in it dates from
the years 1823/4, and was probably written out at the time of the inquiry.
Although the punctuation is non-existent, and some of the names of places
now obsolete, it gives a clear picture of the larger part of the waters

Those parts of the waters about which there is any doubt have been indicated on the map by broken shading. Uncertainties arise from two causes:
firstly, certain stretches of the river are said to be 'in dispute', that is, contemporaries could not pronounce on their ownership. Secondly, though the
writer of this account of the waters knew what he was talking about, the
reader has difficulties. Thus, though the Wick Stream is mentioned from time
to time in documents in the past, its exact location is not known, though
it was somewhere near Binsey Bridge. The name The Hope, or The Hope
River seems to have been used for different streams at Hinksey in the 18th
and 19th centuries, but the description of the Free Waters only makes sense
if the 19th-century stream is referred to, which is not surprising, as this
extent of the waters is a 19th-century document. Nothing at all seems to be
said about the part of the river between Bullstocks Old Bridge and the Pot
Stream. Is it free? There is also difficulty about the piece of water 'from
the corner where the draw Bridge stands to the F. Water stone', for whilst
this describes a stretch of water known as Shire Lake Stream, it is not that
stretch of the Shire Lake which was followed when the Freemen rode the
Franchises of the city,[3] but well beyond it. On the whole the limits of the
Free Waters follow the Franchises, but here the two diverge, and it is difficult
to know what to make of it. Nevertheless, even if these doubtful portions
of the river are ignored, the Free Waters were still very extensive. It seems
absurd that so little has been registered. As so often happens, legislation
intended to con,serve rights has been used to destroy them.

At the time of the Commons Registration Act of 1965, an act which the
freemen of Oxford do not regard as relevant, no statement of the extent of
these fisheries was known, and the Council rejected as insufficient such
evidence as could be gleaned from the Council Acts and other sources by
Mr R. A. J. Earl, the Secretary of the Freemen. In the end only 'the right to
fish from the banks of Port Meadow' was registered, and the freemen have,
rightly, felt that this in no way represented the full extent of the waters.[4]

---

[2] City, E.4.9. I am grateful to Dr Janet Cooper for drawing my attention to this document. The
same volume also contains a second, incomplete account of the extent of the waters, probably
given by Deodratus Eaton.
[3] MS Top. Oxon d. 309, fo. 11.
[4] *The Oxford Freemen*, June 1970; 'Fishing Rights, historical notes compiled by Mr R. A. J. Earl
on behalf of the Freemen', a manuscript in the possession of the Freemen of the City of Oxford.

APPENDIX III: The Leases of Upper Fisher Row

Upper Fisher Row was built on land owned by the city, which, like Christ Church, granted beneficial leases with variable entry fines, usually for forty years. H. E. Salter did not include the leases of Upper Fisher Row or the wharf in his book on city leases, *Oxford City Property*. This seems strange to a modern historian, but clearly editors reflect the preoccupations of their age, and Salter wrote in an age when economic and social history were still not universally studied.

The Ledger Books of the City of Oxford record the City leases until about the middle of the nineteenth century, and later leases were briefly recorded in the printed *Schedules of the Property of the Mayor, Aldermen and Citizens of Oxford*, which appeared at intervals. These show that many leases were still for forty years, some longer.

In the margins of the lease book the amount of the fine and various notes were entered. As some of these proved useful in establishing the sequence of the houses in Upper Fisher Row they have been given below the summary of each lease. Leases are numbered from the North.

TENEMENT 1

City Archives:

D.5.5.fo.401   *8 Sept. 21 Jac. 1. (1623).* To *Thomas Pemerton, boatman*, 'all that their plot or parcell of ground with its appurtenances at the North end of the Tymber wharfe' by High Bridge from the ditch now under the wall there called Rewley wall 4 score feet southward and in breadth from east to west 50 ft. or thereabouts be it more or less 2s. 6d. by equal parts L.D. and Mich., to pay one couple of good fat capons yearly after any tenement had been erected; for term of 40 years; to grind at the Castle Mill.

D.5.6fo.63   *20 Jan. 19 Car. 1, (1644).* To *Thomas Pemerton,boatman*, renewed. Also, to save city and parish harmless from charges arising from servants, tenants and children in the demised premises No subletting without permission.

D.5.6.p.1 75*   *9 May 1655. To William Pemerton*

D.5.6.fo.497 *28 Oct. 24 Car. 11, (1672). To William Pemerton, boatman.* The property was now said to be 106 ft. from the ditch by the wall of Rewley southwards at the east side; at the west side 68 ft.; in breadth from N. to W. at the N. end, 56 ft.; and at the S. end, 64 ft.

D.5.7fo.121   *4 Apr. 34 Car. 11, (1682). To John Curtice, fisherman. Henceforth the property was divided in two parts, 1A and 1B. Part 1A.*

D.5.9.fo.39   *14 Apr. 1699, to Richard Brookins of Oxford, boatman,* their mess. or ten. lately erected by John Curtice, at the North end of the 'Tymber wharfe', bounded N. and W. by the lasher, and on the S. by a ten. of John Cutice in the possession of William Thomas [erased], John Dewy.

*Ledger Book D.5.6 slips from foliation to pagination and back.

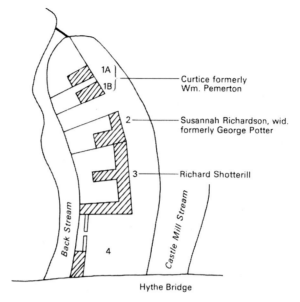

Fig. App. III.1.   Upper Fisher Row, late 17th century, based on Loggan's map of 1675.

Renewed at 17 yrs. for £2; 3 Sept. 1716 to Richard Brookins.

D.5.8.fo.199   *3 Sept. 3 Geo. I (1716) to Richard Brookins the younger of Bablock Hythe* in the parish of Northmoor, victualler; S. John Dewy.

Lse. renewed at 17 yrs. for £2.

D.5.10.p.101   *1 May 1730 to Richard Brookins of Stanton Harcourt, fisherman*; S. Thomas Gardner.

Expired 14 yrs. Fine £3.

D.5.11.fo.32   *1 May 1744 to William Marriner, mealman*, together with half the out house and paring wall; S. Thomas Gardner.

Expired 14 yrs. Fine £3.

D.5.12.fo.157   *25 Nov. 1762 to Richard Spindlowe of the University of Oxford, cook*. It is now in the occupation of William Gardner; S. Rebecca Gardner, widow.

Renewed last to Richard Brookins. Expired 32 yrs. Fine £5. Renewed to Mr Charles Curtis in 1776. Ren. to Mr T. Beesley.

D.5.13.p.249   *22 May 1776 to Charles Curtis, gent of Oxford*; now in occupation of William Gardner. S. Rebecca or her assign. Subject to such trusts as in the last will of Rd. Spindlowe of Oxford, cook, dcd. (PROB 11/961/378)

Chas. Curtis (late Spindlow). Expired 14 yrs. Fine £14 4s. 9d. [in a new hand] now Beesley.

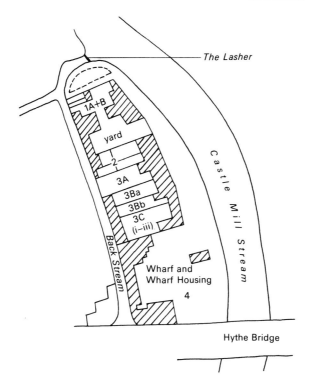

The Lasher

Castle Mill Stream

1A+B

yard

2

3A

3Ba

3Bb

3C
(i–iii)

Back Stream

Wharf and
Wharf Housing

4

Hythe Bridge

Fig. App.III.2 Upper Fisher Row, mid-18th century, based on the map
of J. Taylor, published in 1750.

1 May 1795, to Thomas Beesley, S. Thomas Bossom, fisherman. [Not
in Ledger Book.]

— *Jany. 1800 License to Thomas Beesley* to assign his premises at the
top of Fisher Row to John Flory of Abingdon, fisherman. Beesley's lease
is said to have been made for 1 May, 1795, but there are several blank
pages amongst leases of that date, as if it had not been copied in.

From L.D., 1810, 40 yrs., late Chas. Curtis.

D.5.15.p.357   *1 May 1811, to Thomas Beesley of Oxford, fisherman*; S. another
tenement of John Curtis, fisherman, in occupation of —

This property was now divided again into Tenements 1Aa and 1Ab.

Tenement 1Aa

(See license of 10 May 1818 to Thomas Beesley to sublet 1Ab, a portion
of 1A to Jeremiah Whitehouse, below.)

D.5.16.p.311 *1 May, 1824, to Thomas Beesley the elder of Blenheim Park*, fisherman, a tenement at the N. end of the Timber wharf, lasher N. and W; S. tenements in the occupation of — — and others, the under-tenants of Samuel Steane. The above demised tenement in the occupation of Thomas son of Thomas Beesley, the elder, and lastly leased to Thomas Beesley by indenture of 1 May 1811.
From L.D. 1824 for 40 yrs. Fine £8.

E.5.2.fo.139 *9 March, 1852, to Thomas Beesley, fisherman*, all that their cottage and tenement with appurtenances at the north end of Fisher Row, adjoining The Lasher there now in the occupation of Thomas Beesley, and also all that their piece or parcel of ground called The Ham adjoining at the sound end to the said lasher, situated and being under Rewley Wall, also in the occupation of the said Thomas Beesley, described more particularly in the Plan or ground plot thereof drawn on page eighty of a certain book called the Vellum Book. From 25 March inst. for one yr. and so from year to year until ½ a years notice to quit be given on either side. £5 p.a.

'Provided also and it is hereby declared and agreed by and between the said parties to these presents that the said Lasher called Ruley Lasher is not included in this demise and that the said Thomas Beesley his executors administrators or assigns shall not draw the sluices thereof or meddle with or use the same in any way whatever and that it shall be lawful for any per- sons appointed by the Council of the said City to enter upon the said demised premises at any time for the purpose of drawing or shutting down the said Sluices or for any other purpose connected with the management or repair of the said lasher.'

Tenement 1Ab

D.5.16.p.93 *10 May, 1818, license to Thomas Beesley*, scaled 14 Nov. 1818, to assign all that the said little mess. or ten. lately built by Thomas Curtis and the said half of the said outhouse and the partitioning wall and also all that part of the backside or garden extending 'from the North end of the Stone Wall lately erected' ... all now in the occupation of Jeremiah Whitehouse, be ing part of the premises demised by the said recited indenture of lease to Samuel Steane of Oxford, wharfinger.

D.5.16.p.316 *1 May, 1824, to Samuel Steane, wharfinger*, that little mess. or ten. lately erected and built by Samuel Steane; N. Thos. Beesley jun., S. another ten. built by the said Thomas Hands, fisherman. The tenement was part of certain premises demised to Thomas Beesley by indenture 1 May, 1811.
From L.D. for 40 yrs. Fine £40.

E.5.1.p.367 *25 Sept. 1838, to Samuel Steane*, their ten. built by John Curtis now in the occupation of John Howkins and their three brick tenements erected by Samuel Steane in occupation of

Robt. Coxhead, Abel Beesley and John Coombs, also four other tenements erected by Samuel Steane in occupation of Wid. Beesley, Jas.
Bentley, John Pash, all eight being at the north end of the Timber wharf;
N. Samuel Beesley; S. Thomas Hands. These tens. now demised formerly
leased to Thomas Beesley.
9 Aug. 1844, lic. to assign to John Pike of Oxford, hop-merchant. Fine £45.
2 Aug. 1848, lic. to Hy. Leake of Maidenhead, esq. & John Purdue, High St South-
wark, hop-merchant (the acting executors of the will and codicil of John Pike) to
assign to Rev. Edward Steane of Champion Park, Camberwell, Surrey, D.D.

Tenement 1B
By a lease of 4 Apr., 1682, John Curtice held the first tenement. By 1699
he had built two tenements on the holding, for the first, I A, see above, for
1 B see below.

D.5.9.fo.40 *14 Apl. 1699, to John Dewy, boatmaker*, their little tenement lately
erected by John Curtice, fisherman on part of the ground leased to the
said John Curtice, fisherman, at the north end of the Timber Wharf by
Hythe Bridge together with the little backside or garden lying behind it.
Richard Brookins N.; George Lea or his assigns S.; 40 yrs paying 1s 3d.
at L.D. and Mich., a couple of good fat pullets or 2s. 6d.
Deed of Trust: John Dewy holds it only in trust for such purposes as are
mentioned in the will of Richard Dewy, hempdresser, his late father. (MS.
Wills Oxon 18/5/80)
Renewed at 17 yrs for £2.

D.5.10.p.103 *1 May, 1730, to Thomas Gardiner, Boatman.* Richard Brookins
N.

D.5,11,fo.48 *10 Apr. 1744, to Rebecca Gardner, widow,* Richard Brookins N.

D.5.12.fo.49 *10 May, 1759, to Rebecca Gardner, widow.* N. William Gardner;
S. Edward Crawford.
Expired 14 yrs, Fine £2 10s. Renewed to Christian Gardner and John Sellwood
and Rebecca his wife in 1773.

D.5.13.p.78 *20 Sept., 1773, to Christian Gardner and John Sellwood and Rebecca his wife.* Rebecca is said to be late Rebecca Gardner, spinster.

D.5.15.p.136 *1 May, 1817, to William Bossom.* N. Jeremiah Whitehouse, bargemaster; S. Richard Bossom.
Fine £8 from L.D. 1817. Late Thomas Bossom.

D.5.16.p.15 *31 Aug. 1819, License to William Bossom, bargeman* to alienate to
Thomas Hands of St Thomas's, bargeman.

E.5.1.p.161 *15 Nov., 1815, to Thomas Hands, bargeman.* All those two tene-
ments with the wash-house, fuel house, yard and appurtenances, stream
E. and W., N. John Howkins; S. Thomas Corbey. Now in occupation of
Thomas Hands.
Late Wm. Bossom, from L.D. 183 1. Fine £10.

TENEMENT 2

D.5.6.fo.102   *16 June, 1649, to George Potter, boatmaker*. It is three score feet in breadth, and adjoins Richard Shotterill's newly leased tenement.

D.5.6.fo.331   *1 March, 16 Car. 11 (1664) to Mary Potter, widow.*

D.5.6.fo.439   *23 Sept. 23 Car. 11(1699) to Susanna Richardson, widow*. (She later married George Lea.)

D.5.7.fo.1 85   *3 June 1 Jas. 11 (1685) to Ann and Ralph Richardson, boatman*, their newly erected tenement. (Ralph and Ann-children of George Lea's wife, formerly Widow Richardson,–to sublet to George Lea and his wife for a peppercorn rental. (See *Council Acts* 1666-1701, 172).
Renewed at 16 yrs. Fine £6.

D.5.9.fo.238   *25 Sept. 1702, to William Gardner and Ann his wife*, lease renewed. fo.240 *Deed of Trust of William Gardner*: the 'Low Room' is to be   reserved for the use of Ralph Richardson, brother of the said Ann.

D.5.8.fo.343 *2 Apl. 8 Geo. 1 (1722), to John Nichole of Oxford, butcher*. It is next to a messuage in the possession of William Gardner Jun. It is said to be 70 ft. from North to South. (This seems to be a simple mistake.)
Renewed, 17 yrs. expired, for £6.

D.S.12.fo.171 *4 May, 1763, to John Gardner, boatmaster*, a tenement three score feet from north to south; William Gardner N., the said John Gardner S.
Renewed last to Mr John Nicholls, now wholly expired. Fine £22 1s. 0d.

D.5.14.p.515 20 Aug. 1799, to *William Wakelin, victualler*, on the N.; — on the South, formerly leased to John Gardiner.

D.5.14.p.264 — day of —, 180 — License to William Wakelin to assigned to Thomas Beesley.*

D.5.14.p.565 — — 1800, *license to Thomas Beesley* to assign the lease to James Pyne of Oxford, servant.*

D.5.14.p.415 *1 May 1813, to Stephen Davis*, — — N., and — — S.;
N. Thomas Hands; S. — Beesley. Now in the several occupations
Late Wm. Wakelin. Fine £16.

E.5.1.p.45 *21 Nov., 1827, to the Exorcs. of Stephen Davis, boatbuilder*. N. Thomas Hands; S. — Beesley. Now in the several occupations of Catherine Robinson, George Petty, tailor, John Davis, boatbuilder, and Thomas Corbey, labourer. Formerly leased to John Gardiner, boatmaster. (Stephen Davis's Exorcs. were Martha, wife of William Robinson, College servant, David Williamson Dean, coal-merchant, John Archer, brewer, John Parker, timber-merchant)
Fine £36.
The holding was now subdivided.

* These three licences may or may not have been scaled. The book is badly kept at this time.

Tenement 2A

E.5.2.fo.23 *30 Dec. 1841, to Elizabeth Corbey, of St Thomas's, widow.*
A mess. or tenement with wash-house, stabling, piggeries and yard. N.
James Beesley; S. — — Now in the occupation of Elizabeth Corbey, for-
merly the exorcs. of Stephen Davis. 1*s.* and one fat pullet on 1 Oct., lessee
to insure.
Fine £15.

Tenement 2B

E.5.2.fo.25 *30 Dec. 1841, to Mrs. Catherine Charlton, wid.* Three messuages
with garden, yard and appurtenances. N. Thomas Hands, now Wid. Corbey; S. now or late Samuel Beesley. Now in occupation of Joseph Ashley,
Thomas Wickson and — Capel. Paying yearly 10*s.* in equal portions
29 Sept. and 25 March, and one fat pullet or 1s. 6d.
Fine £25.

TENEMENT 3

D. 5.6. fo. 101 *6 June, 1649, to Richard Shotterill, boatman.* On the N side of
'Highe Bridge, being part of the Timber wharf, containing in breadth from
N.—S. 2 score and ten feet, and lying between the two streams, leading to
the Castle Mills on the East, and from Rewly towards St Thomas' parish
on the west, adjoining ground newly leased to George Potter, boatmaker
from 25 March last past for 40 yrs., 1*s.* p.a., and 2 pullets. To erect a house
within 2 years, and all mounds, banks etc. to be kept up.

D.5.6.fo.306 *11 Aug. 1662 to Richard Shotterill*, that newly erected messuage,
malt-house, backside and garden ground formerly part of the Timber
wharf, adjoining George Potter dcd. This property was now subdivided, a
tenement of 20 ft. wide being reserved to Richard Shotterill's widow, and
leaving behind a tenement 70 ft. from N.-S.

Tenement 3A

D.5.7.fo.84 *18 Oct., 1679, to William Gardner, boatman*, a newly erect ed
messuage, with the backsides and outlets thereto belonging. On the N. side
of the timber wharf near High Bridge, containing 70ft. in breadth 20 ft.
or thereabouts between a mess, and garden in the possession of — Shotterill, widow, on the —, and another tenement in the possession of George
Lea on the —, abutting E. and W. on the stream. Now in the possession of
William Gardner.

D.5.7.fo.331 *1 June, 1695, to William Gardner*, a messuage with Matthew Abell
S. and George Lea N.

D.5.8.fo.112 *7 Jan. 11 Anne (1713) to John Gardner* (William scored out) a tenement between Matthew Abell and William Terrill.

D.5.10.p.43 *1 Aug, 1728, to John Gardner*, Matthew Abel S.; William Terrill N.
Expired 15 yrs ½. £4 10s. 0d.

D.5.11.fo.33. *1 May 1744, to Mary, widow of John Gardiner*; Matthew Abell now or late S.; William Terrill N.

D.5.14.p.23 *1 Apr. 1786, to Richard Crawford.* Stephen Scale S.; — — N. It is now in the possession of the said Richard Crawford.

Late Mary Gardner. A new grant. Fine £44. Now Stephen Davis.

D.5.14.p.631 *24 Sept. 1801. License to assign.* By a lease of 1 Apr.

D.5.15.p.35 *1 June 1802, to Stephen Davis, boatbuilder*, a tenement between Stephen Scale S. and — — N. It is now in the possession of Richard Crawford.

No fine mentioned.

D.5.15.p521 *1 May 1816, Stephen Davis, boatbuilder.* Widow Hands S.; — — N.

Fine £14.

E.5.1.p.119 *25 Nov. 1830, Exorcs. of Stephen Davis.* N. Catharine Robinson; S. James Ward. Now in occupation of Samuel Beesley, bargemaster.

11 July 1839, Lic. to assign to Ann Norgrove, wid.; 10 Aug, 1839, Indenture of Assignment. £235 paid to exorcs. of S. Davis.

Tenement 3B

D.5.7.fo. 158 10 Oct. 1683, to *Phillip Francklin, yeoman and Elizabeth his wife.* (On 24 Oct. 1681 Phillip Fraricklyn married Elizabeth 'Shatril' at St Thomas's.) a messuage and malthouse etc. near Hythe Bridge, now containing 7 0 ft. N.-S., next to William Gardner.

D.5.9.fo.34 *7 Nov. 1698, to Matthew Abell, clerk of Hinton, Berks,* their tenement and malthouse, lately part of a premises and houses let to William Gardner.

D. 5.8. fo.111 *7 Jan. 11 Anne (1713), to Matthew A bell, clerk*, a malt-house next to William Gardner. (William is scored out in the lease of 3A and John substituted.)

This property is now subdivided into three tenements.

The most northern 3Ba was said to be 20 ft. wide at the east end, and 13 ft. 2 ins. at the west end; the second 3Bb was 19 ft. 5 ins. at the east end and 15 ft. at the west end; the third, 3C, was 35 ft. N.-S. at the east end.

Tenement 3Ba

D.5.8.fo.410 *5 July 1727, to Thomas Gardner.* John Gardner N.; Elizabeth Chillingworth S.; formerly amongst those things leased to Matthew Abell.

Renew at 14 yrs. for £2 5s.

D. 5.1 1.p.1 *10 May, 1742, to William Gardner, boatman.* John Gardner, boatman N.; Elizabeth Chillingworth, widow, S.

Fine £2 5s.

D.5.11.fo.389   *10 May, 1756, to William Gardner, boatman.* John Gardner, boatman, N.; Francis Chillingworth S.

D.5.13.p.149   *1 July, 1774, to Christian Gardner, wid. and admin. of the will of William Gardner,* boatman. John Gardner, boatman N.; Francis Chillingworth S.

Fine £3 16s. 0d.

D.5.14.p.109   *24 June, 1788, to Christian Gardner, widow and admin. of the will of William Gardner, boatman,* — — N.; — — S.

D.5.15.p.19   *24 June, 1802, to John Hardaway, bale and hatchet maker,* John Gardner, boatman N.; Francis Chillingworth, formerly Matthew Abell S.

Late Christian Gardner, from Mich. 1801, 40 yrs., Fine £6.

D.5.15.p.487   1 Oct., 1815, to *Anne and Sophia Hardway.* Samuel Beesley, Bargemaster N; Francis Chillingworth S.

This ten. is now in occupation of Wid. Hands and lately leased to John Hardway, Fine £8.

E.5.1.p.213   *29 Nov., 1832, to Sophia Hardway, spinster.* There are two messuages with yards and appurtenances, formerly let as one messuage. Samuel Beesley N.;Thomas Beesley S. Now unoccupied.

Fine £9. 28 Sept., Lic. to Jas. Dolley of Oxford, vict. and exorc. of the will of Sophia Hardway to assign the lease to Richard Smith of the City of Oxford, gent.

Tenement 3Bb

D.5.10.p.2   *1 May 1727, to Elizabeth Chillingworth, widow of Oxford,* a tenement 19 ft. 5 ins. N.-S. in the front; 15 ft. at back, N.-S.; 71 ft. 6 ins. E.-W. on the N. side, 71 ft. 9 ins. on the S. side, W. and E. the two streams. John Gardiner boatman N.;William Hands fisherman or his assigns S., formerly among other things granted to Matthew Abell.

Expired 14 yrs. Fine £2 10s. 0d.

D.5.10.fo.22   *20 June, 1742, to William Collinson of* — John Gardner, boat man N.; William Hands, fisherman S.; formerly among other things granted to Matthew Abell.

Renewed before to Eliz. Chillingworth. Fine £2 12s. 6d.

D.5.12.fo.13   *10 May 1758, to Jane Collison, widow.* William Gardner, boatman, N; Francis Chillingworth S.

D.5.14.p.275   *2 May, 1792, to Moses Keats, carpenter.* — — N.; — — S. Amongst other things granted to Matthew Abell.

Fine £14. Assigned 1 June 1801 to Thos Fletcher, coal-merchant of Abingdon by exorcs. of Moses Keats.

D.5.15.p.136   *1 May, 1804, to Thomas Bossom, bargemaster.* John Gardner N.; Francis Chillingworth S.

D5.15.p.484   *1 May, 1815, to Thomas Bossom, bargemaster.* William Hands N.; Thomas Bossom S.. In occupation of Dashwood Hooper;

Late Moses Keats. Fine £8.

D.5.16.p.166   *1 May 1820, to Thomas Bossom.* Widow Hands N.; Thomas Bossom S.

Now in occup. Dashwood Hooper. Fine £8.

E.5.1.p.275   *2 Dec. 1834, to George Bossom, waterbailiff.* — Quartermain N; Benjamin Bossom S., lately leased to Thomas Bossom.

Tenement 3C

D.5.10.p.194   *1 May, 1732, to William Hands.* All their three messuages or tenements now divided and mounded out and in the several occupation of William Hanns and ?Bossom, widow on the north side of Hythe Bridge. N.S-S at E. end *ca.* 35 ft.; E.-W at S. end ca. 70 ft.

D.5.1 I.fo.74   6 Nov. 1745, to Mary Ayres, widow and assign of Ralph Ayres of the University of Oxford, musician. Three messuages or tenements etc. now or late in the occupation of William Hanns.

Express. 14 years. Fine £4. Sold by Auction to Henry Gardner. New Ise. for 40 yrs.

D.5.14.p.201   *1 Apr., 1786, to Henry Gardner.* One tenement has replaced the three occupied by William Hanns and — Bossom, widow.

Hy. Gardner (late Mary Ayres) A new grant. Fine £81. 0. 0. (in pencil) Licence to the Trustees to assign to Thomas Bossom, bargemaster of Oxford. Lease to be dated 1 June, 1800. Date — 13 June.

D.5.14.p.549   *1 June 1800, to the executors of the will of Edward Tawney, Messrs.* John Parsons, mercer, John Ireland of the University of Oxford, apothecary, and Joshua Cooke, bookseller.

D.5.14.p.551   *13 June 1800. Lic. to assign the Ise. to Thos. Bossom, bargemaster.*

Fine £8.

D.5.15.p.452   *1 Apl. 1814, to Thomas Bossom, bargemaster,* all that their corner tenement lately built by Henry Gardner on the N. side of Hythe Bridge, abutting on a tenement in occupation of Richard Bossom, and in the occupation of Thomas Bossom.

E.5.1.p.67   *26 Nov., 1828, to Thomas Bossom,* their four messuages, formerly one, and called a corner messuage or tenement, with the Boat House, Boat Shed, Pig Sties, Yard and appurts. on the N. side of High Bridge, formerly part of the Timber Wharf, Samuel Lewis N.; the said wharf S.

Fine £40. From L.D., 1828, 40 yrs.

E.5.2.fo.36   *30 Dec. 1842, to Benjamin Bossom of St Thomas's, boatbuilder.* Samuel Lewis N.; the Wharf S. All now in the occupation of Benjamin Bossom and delineated in the Vellum Book at p. 34.

Fine £50. Formerly Thomas Bossom.

TENEMENT 4: The Wharf and the Wharf range of buildings
The wharf range lay on the west side of the wharf, and 3C lay adjacent to
the north end.

The Wharf range

D.5.6.fo.402   *1 Sept., 19 Car. H (166 7), to John Taylor, Tobacco-pipe
maker*, the plot of void or waste ground on the west side of the High
Bridge, being part of the Timber Wharf, containing in length N-S. at
the E. side 119 ft., and on the W. side, 115 ft., and in breadth from E.-W
at the N. end 28 ft., and in breadth from E.-W. at the N. end 28 ft. and
at the south end from the outside of the wall that is now built towards
the river 22½ ft. A lease for 40 yrs., paying 1s. yearly, and to build one
sufficient tenement in the space of three years.

D.5.7.fo. 118   *3 Feb., 1681 to John Taylor*, all that plot of ground with the
messuage or tenement lately erected thereon, the dimensions of the
plot as above.

D.5.9.fo.20   *23 Sept., 1698, to Daniel Prince*, described as above.
This lease was renewed at 16½ yrs. for £4 10s. Renewed 10 March 1713 to
Thomas Winslow.

D.5.8.fo. 119   10 Mar., 1713, to Thos. Winslow, victualler.

The Wharf

D.5.8.fo.261   *1 Apr., 1719, to Matthew Marshall, brewer*, all that their piece
of void or waste ground, lying or being on the N.W. side of High Bridge
called the Wharfe containing in length from N.-S by the side of the river
from the said bridge 130 ft. and in breadth from E.-W. at the south end
thereof — ft. and at the N. end — ft. or thereabouts, except and always
reserved out of this demise at the north end thereof — ft. or thereabout
at the N. end of the sd. piece of waste ground from a tenement now in
the possession of William Hanns towards the said bridge 36 ft. at the
least and also except from the said bridge and Highway leading towards
the messuage or tenement now in the possession of the said Matthew
Marshall from the said tenement all along by the wall extending to the
Brewhouse now in the possession of Matthew Marshall or his assaigns
20 ft. at least by way of a passage. For 40 yrs, paying 5s. and a cple. of
good fat capons or 5s. To set up posts, rails or stones 10 ft. distant to
keep carts and carriages from the said demised premises and to keep
the passage pitched and paved.
This was the first lease and was granted for £5.

The wharf and buildings were let together in the next lease.

D.5.10.p.412   *10 Oct., 1730, to John Webb of Oxford, yeoman*, all
that their tenement, Brewhouse, and strip of ground on the West
side of High Bridge, being part of the Inner Wharf, dimensions
given as before. Also a parcel of waste ground with a stable newly
built on the N.W. side of High Bridge called the Wharf from N-S
by the side of the river from the bridge 130 ft., and from E-W. at

the S. end — ft. and at the N. end — ft. (except reserved from this demise at the north end of — the said piece of waste ground from William Hanns tenement towards the bridge 36 ft. and also from the High Bridge to the tenement now in the possession of John Field from the said tenement all along the wall extending from the Brewhouse now John Field's 24 ft. at least for a passage.

Memo. this lease never passed the seal. This pair of leases were ingross'd but never paid and to be paid before renewed.

Wharf Buildings only:

D.5.11.fo.72   *6 Nov., 1745, to Rev. John Vivers of Sidling St Nicholas, Dorset, clerk, and Dinah his wife,* all the wharf range except the brewhouse, let to — — Fine £15, renewed in 1759 to Mr. Henry Gardner.

D.5.1 1.fo.424   *4 Oct., 175 7, to Henry Gardner, boatman.* Lease of the Wharf, to commence Lady Day, 1759.

D.5.12.fo.71   *7 Nov., 1759, to Henry Gardner, boatmaster.*
Ren'd last to the Rev. Mr. Vivers and his wife and by them assigned to Robt. Phillips, brewer dcd., and by his exorcs. assigned and conveyed to the said Henry Gardner. Expired 14 yrs., Fine £12. 0. 0. Renewed 1774. Leased to Mark and James Morrell, 1807.

D.5.13.p.166   *1 July, 1774, to Henry Gardner, boatman,* the Wharf Buildings.

D.5.13.p.168   *1. July 1774, Wharf to Henry Gardner, boatman.*

D.5.14.p.59   *2 Apl., 1787, Wharf to Henry Gardner.* It now has a warehouse on the N.W. side.

D.5.15.p.146 — of —, 1789, to Sir Richard Tawney, Kt., Alderman, the Wharf Buildings.

Expired 14 yrs. Fine £9.

D.5.14.p.593 *n.d. (1800?) License to the Executors of the will of Edward Tawney* to assign the Wharf Buildings to Messrs. M. and J. Morrell [Unwitnessed and unsigned. This lease occurred in what was a monster lease for seven properties.]

D.5.14.p.608   *2 Apl. 1801, to M. and J. Morrell, the Wharf.*

D.5.15.p.37   *1 July, 1803, to M. and J. Morrell, the Wharf Range.*

Late Sir Richard Tawney, from Mich. 1801 for 40 yrs. Fine £18. This lease not to be renewed again-now belongs to James White, bargemaster. See License entered at p. 56, new ledger.

D.5.16.p.56   *1 Apl. 1814, sealed 13 Nov. 1817.* The wharf was leased to the Morrells by an indenture of 1 July 1803 to hold it from Mich. 1801. They lately had leave to grant it to Thomas Bossom, bargemaster, and he has now occasion to alienate it to James White for the remainder of the 40 yrs.

E.5.2.fo.40   *10 March, 1855, to James Morrell, the younger, brewer,* the wharf and wharf range consisting of a messuage N.W. of Hythe Bridge called the Running Horses and six tenements.

31 yrs. from Midsummer 1842 (no fine) rent £84. New grant. To insure. Ingross'd the compact and left it with Mr. Webb for signature.

E.5.2.fo.125   *1 May, 1859 (unsigned) Mortgage to William Capel of Grove*, in the parish of Painswick, Gloucs. of many tenements and also the Borough Tolls to raise money to build a Reading Room under the Guildhall and also for other projects. It includes the Wharf, and the Wharf range of buildings, consisting of the Running Horses and stable in occupation of William Howkins, the tenements of Thomas Farmer, Daniel Faulkner, Widow Simpson, James Stroudley, Widow Collis. James Beesley N. All at present leased to James Morrell for 31 yrs. from 24 June 1842 at £82 p.a.

*APPENDIX IV: Estimates for the Cost of Working Barges by
bow-haling by men and horses c.1770*

i. Oxford to Mapledurham near Reading (Oxon. RO, Wi/VII/18)

An Account of the Supposed present expenses of a Barge of 110 Tons and a
Lighter of 50 Tons therewith being the mode they are usually navigated from
Oxford to London and back so far as concerns the Expences between Oxford
and Mapledurham.

	£	s.	d.
Downward			
Six Service Men on board from Oxford to Mapledurham 2 days each being 34 Miles at 4s. a Day each for their wages and provisions	2	8	0
N.B. These Mens wages are generally paid by the voyage but they would average as above.			
Upwards			
40 Hirelings or Men to Tow from Mapledurham to Days Lock 17¾ Miles – 2 days at 5s. each for wages only – being the price commonly paid.	10	0	0
Provisions and Beer for said 40 Men at 1s. a day each including 4d. each for one nights quarters	4	0	0
M			
10 Horses from Days Lock to Sutton 6¾ & Carter	2	15	0
40 Men to Cullham 2 miles at 1s. each	2	0	0
40 Hirelings or Towers from Cullham to Oxford as far as towed by men at 2s. 6d. each	5	0	0
6 Horses also used with the men at 5s. each	1	12	0
Hire of Cable at 8 Locks at 3s. 6d. each	1	8	0
6 Service men 4 days from Mapledurham to Oxford at 4s. a day each for wages & prov.[ns]	4	16	0
Tolls of the present Locks and Winches at abt. 1s. 8d. a ton on 160 Tons Greatboat & Lighter	13	6	8
N.B. Some of the Tolls are paid by the Barge – some by the year – and some by each horse passing	47	5	8
	43	10	8

Saving Each Voyage by the improved State and also the
safety, certainty, & dispatch – and if the trade is increased
the savings will be greater.   3   15 0

An Acco[t.] of the probable Expences of a Barge of 110 Tons and a Lighter of 50 Tons navigated from Oxford to Mapledurharn (in the way to London) and back on a supposition that Eight new Pound Locks were erected and a Horse towing path made according to the Improvemen[ts.] below Mapledurham.

<table>
<tr><td></td><td align="center">Downward</td><td>£</td><td>s.</td><td>d.</td></tr>
<tr><td colspan="2">Four Service Men on board from Oxford to
    Mapledurham 2 days at 4d. each a Day</td><td>1</td><td>12</td><td>0</td></tr>
<tr><td></td><td align="center">Upwards</td><td></td><td></td><td></td></tr>
<tr><td colspan="2">10 Horses 34 Miles and Carter at 4d. a horse a Mile
    being the full price of postchaise horses and nearly the
    Average expense of towing in the improved part of the river</td><td>5</td><td>13</td><td>4</td></tr>
<tr><td colspan="2">Or the Horses may be reckon'd by the day 10 horses 2 days
    at 5s. a day each & 3s. a day for the Carter amo[n]. to
    £5 6s. 0d.
    There are a set of as many horses let at Marlow to Tow
    the Barges to the Kennet which is % of the above Distance
    and through 6 pound Locks those are charged £3 6s. 0d.
    so that according to this the Horses wd. come only to
    £4 19s. 0d.</td><td></td><td></td><td></td></tr>
<tr><td colspan="2">Additional or New Tolls to be paid at the 8 New pound
    Locks at 4d. a ton at Each or 2s. 8d. in the whole on
    160 Tons Greatboat and Lighter</td><td>21</td><td>6</td><td>8</td></tr>
<tr><td colspan="2">4 Service Men two days from Mapledurham to Oxford at
    4s. a day each Wages & prov[ns.]</td><td>1</td><td>12</td><td>0</td></tr>
<tr><td colspan="2">Tolls of the Old Locks and Winches as on the other side
    Though it is presumed sev[l]. of the paym[ts]. for the Horses
    towing as at present would cease-and in the improved
    state the Boats would last much longer – and not be liable
    to the Dangers and delays at present</td><td>13</td><td>6</td><td>8</td></tr>
<tr><td colspan="2"></td><td>43</td><td>10</td><td>8</td></tr>
</table>

	£	s.	d.
From Brentford to Twickenham, 25 Men	1	5	0
From thence to Hampton-Court, Average eight Horses	1	5	0
Through Bridge 1s. Carter's Average 3s.	0	4	0
Lord Dyset's 3d. per Horse, Kingston Eyot ditto	0	4	0
From Kingston to Hampton-Court Bridge 6d.	0	4	0
From Ditton to Waybridge, 10 Horses 10 Miles	2	2	0
Carter	0	3	0
Three Horses round Stone's Gut	0	7	0
Carter	0	1	0
At Weybridge Mead Gate	0	0	6
From Weybridge to Windsor, thirteen Horses, twenty Miles	5	5	0
Carter	0	3	0
At Laleham, two Gates, 2d. per Horse, has been 3d.	0	2	2
Mr. Windsor's ld. *hf.* per Horse, at Average	0	1	7hf
Staines 32 Men up Caps, at 9d. about one Mile	1	4	0
Milson's Point 1s. Average at 9d.	0	0	9
At Old Windsor 2s. 6d. per Quarter per Barge, Average	0	1	0
Mr. Aldsworth's Bridge, 3s. per Qr. Average	0	1	2
At Romney 1s. Quarter, ditto	0	0	7
Winch and Block at Windsor 1s. thro' Bridge	0	1	6
From Windsor to Sunning, 45 Men, 30 Miles	15	15	0
Bovney eight Horses to Water Oakley	0	12	0
Carter	0	2	0
At Hammerton Bank, 7 Horses to Boulter's	0	12	0
Carter	0	2	0
Boulter's Lock	0	11	6
Twelve Men to Hedsor, at 2s.	1	4	0
At Turner's Wharf six Horses to Mr. Wildman's	0	8	6
Carter	0	1	6
At Spade Oak eight Horses to Marlow Bucks	0	13	6
Carter	0	1	6
Eight Men up Marlow Bucks, and Lock	0	4	0
Marlow Lock	0	11	6
Temple Lock	0	11	6
Mr. Clayton's Towing Path per Barge	0	1	0
New Lock 9s. 6d. Winch 2s.	0	11	6
Hambledon Lock 10s. Winch 1s. 6d.	0	11	6
Marsh Lock and Winch 10s. Joel's Bucks 1s. 6d.	0	11	6
Cottrell's Lock	0	10	0
Sunning Lock	0	10	0
Forty-five Men, three Nights, at 4d. per Night	2	5	0
Sunning up Blake's eighteen Men	0	18	0
Blake's Lock	1	4	0
Fulling Mill each Time	0	1	0
From Blake's to Reading Wharf 12 Men at 3d.	0	3	0
Provisions for the Voyage up to Reading	10	0	0
Barges Lock Shutters and Water Fetchers and Lock Shutters Fees	2	0	0
	53	13	9hf

AUGUST, 1770

Expences of a Barge, from *Reading* to *London*.	£	s.	d.
Three Men Voyage up and down at £31 10s. each	10	10	0
Two ditto at £31 each	6	0	0
Two ditto at £21 10s. each	5	0	0
Provisions for three Days	1	11	6

	£	s.	d.
Note, Lighting Boats not charged, which I will upon an Average put against the Charges from Sunning to Reading ... Nor Cableage or extra Horse Lines, nor present Freight of each, equal two Tons up and down, which will not be in the improved State.	23	1	6
	76	15	3hf

Expences of a Voyage, from London to Reading and back to London, in the
proposed mended State of the Thames.

	£	s.	d.
Thirteen new Works, including the Turnpikes to the present Locks, at each 1s. 4d. for a Barge of 100 Tons up and down this Fund to keep in Repair	0	17	4
Eight present Locks 2d. for six Tons up and down, the Proprietors to give up their Property	1	1	4
One Penny for six Tons up and down, as a Fund to repair	0	10	8
Four-pence per Horse per Mile, for four Horses for 70 Miles, from Mortlake to Reading	4	13	4
Two-pence per Horse per Mile down	2	6	8
	7	0	0
Allow five Men to a Barge, and each Barge to make 25 Trips a Year, at £21 2s. per Man each Trip, including provisions	10	10	0
This is the certain expence of 100 Tons	19	19	4

To and ditto from London to Reading, Barge Matter not included,
whose Profit at £10 1 per Voyage, 25 Voyages per
Year, £250 per Annum on one Barge..

The above Allowance for the 13 new Works, produce on 200,000 Tons up and down, per Annum, for Repairs for each	66	13	4
The above Allowance to the present Locks Owners each	138	17	9
Ditto to the Commissioners for Repairs to each present Lock per Annum	68	8	10*hf*
And the above Pay for the Horses produce for six Horses and two Men kept at Stages at five Miles each per Day, on the 200,000 Tons, working 300 Days per Year	1	13	4

APPENDIX V. Upper Fisher Row: Census 1841–1871

Summary of family relations of heads of families

1841	1851	1861	1871
Ten. North of Lasher			Thos. Beesley, F & Mary (née Lee) Tenements from The Lasher South
Thos. Beesley, F. Hannah (née Wheeler); Adam, B.	Thos. Beesley, F. & Mary (née Lee); William, F.	Thos. Beesley, F. & Mary (née Lee)	empty
Thos. Beesley, F. & Mary (née Lee)	John Paish, B. & Ann		John Collier, Bam = Ann (née Paish)
Jas. Watson, B & Eliza.	Chas. Brooks, coal labourer & Mary		Mary Ashley wf/o Ed.; d/o Thos. Beesley, F & Mary
Jas. Bentley (ex-B) hawker & Caroline	Wm. Phipps, coal labourer & Mary Ann		
Jane wid./o Wm. Collis Bam., laundress	John Holmes, B. & Priscilla	Benj. Collis, smith = Ann d/o John Howkins, B.	Ann Collis (née Howkins) wife of Benj., laundress
Thos. Beesley, B, s/o Saml. and Ann, = Maria Collier	John Faulkner B and Mary	John Pimm builders carter	Thos. Kersey, maltman, coalheaver
Abel Beesley, F s/o Thos. and Hannah, = Eliz. Culpepper	Ann Humphries, boatman's wife d/o Thos. & Maria Beesley	empty	
empty	Thos. Beesley & Maria (née Collier), mason's lab.	Thos. Beesley & Maria chaffcutter	Wm. Wall, coalheaver & Eliz.
empty	Alfred Woodley coal labourer & Rebecca		

empty	Benj. Collis = Ann d/o John Howkins, B	Hannah Lamsden, B's wife (née Skinner)	Hannah Lamsden wid./o Thos., boatwoman
John Howkins, B = Sarah wid./o John Ashley, B	Jas. Watson, B & Eliz.	Emma Glover, B's wife d/o Jas. Watson, B, dressmkr.	Emily Tolley, boatman's wife d/o John Howkins
	Jas. Beesley, F = Eliz. d/o Thos. Hands, F	Jas. Beesley, F = Eliz. d/o Thos. Hands, F	Jas. Beesley, F = Eliz. d/o Thos. Hands, F
	Chas. Carpenter, B	Joseph Glover, B and Mary; John & Chas. Carpenter B	Wm. Pratt, B and Elizabeth
	Jane Berry, boatman's wife; Emma, boatman's wife, her d.	Chas. Walker = Sarah d/o Thos. & H. Beesley	Chas. Walker, railway porter & Sarah d/o Thos. & H. Beesley
Eliz. Corbey, wid./o Wm. Corbey, coachsmith	Eliz. Corbey, wid.; Mary Howkins, boatman's wife, her d.	Adam Beesley, F. s/o Thos. & Hannah = Caroline	Adam Beesley, F. s/o Thos. & Hannah = Caroline
	Wm. Collis, mason's labourer & Rebecca		
	Robert Cockhead, B & Mary Ann		
	Samuel Mailing (ex. B) = Eliz. d/o Rd. Barton (ex. B), lab.	Samuel Mailing & Eliz. coal labourer	Samuel Mailing & Eliz. coal porter
	Abel Beesley, F, s/o Thos. and Hannah, = Eliza	Abel Beesley, F = Caroline (sic.)	Abel Beesley, W. = Eliza
Samuel Beesley, Bam. & Maria Spindler, his daughter	Ann M. Spindler, wid./o Samuel Beesley; Thos. Hunt, B. & Mary her d.	Ann Spindler, laundress and grandchildren	Ann M. Spindler & Mary Hunt, her d., laundresses

APPENDIX V. Upper Fisher Row: Census 1841–1871, Summary of family relations of heads of families (*cont.*)

1841	1851	1861	1871
Joseph Clements (ex. *B*) labourer, = Sarah	William Shore & Sarah brewer	William Wall coalheaver	
Wm. Sadler, lab. and Anna	George Myers & Hannah coal labourer	Eliza Noke no occupation	John Noble, stonemason & Eliza
	William Wall & Eliz. coal labourer	Hannah Myers, wid. charwoman	
Jas. Crozier, schoolmaster of Floating Chapel & Eliz.	Ann wid./o Chris. Collier d/o Saml. & Ann Beesley, laundress	Ann Collier laundress	
Thos. Taylor (ex *B*) labourer = Edith	John Copson, boatbuilder = Mary	John Copson boatbuilder = Mary	John Copson, boatbuilder = Mary
Benj. Bossom, boatbuilder = Hannah Collier	Benj. Bossom, boatbuilder = Hannah Collier	Thos. J. Sear = Eliz. d/o James Beesley, *F.*	Samuel Beesley, *W.* = Ann d/o Benj. Bossom

The Wharf, Upper Fisher Row

1841	1851	1861	1871
Thos. Luckett, salesman & Sarah	Eliz. Bowell, boatman's wife	Eliz. Bowell, wid./o William laundress, Jane Bond, wid./o *B*, her d.	John Carpenter & Mary Glover, his mother
Eliz. Williams	Joseph Simpson (ex. *B*), coal labourer = Ellen d/o B. Bossom	Samuel Beesley s/o Thos. & Hannah = Ann d/o Benj. Bossom	Ellen Simpson wid./o Joseph, d/o Chas. Bossom
Thos. Hooper, tar clothmaker	Ann Wickson & sister, tailoress		Richard New, *B.* = Mary d/o Joseph & Ellen Simpson
	John Taylor, *B.* = Hannah d/o Wm. Fisher, *B*	John Taylor, *B.* = Hannah d/o Wm. Fisher, *B*	Mary Wheeler, tailoress

Charles Bull, *B.* & Mary	Margaret Holder, wid. Jas. s/o above, *B*.	Caroline Peake, d/o John Howkins, tailoress	Edward Capel & Caroline builders labourer
Charles Bossom, *Bam* & Mary & Chas. Bossom, *Bam*	Nathaniel Rivers, mustard maker	empty	Chas. Carpenter coalheaver
Samuel Beesley, *F.* = Ann d/o Benj. Bossom, boatbuilder	Martha Harris, widow, charwoman	Benj. Bishop, *B.* s/o Wm., *F* = Eliz. d/o Wm. Bowell, *B*	George M. Webb & Ellen discharged soldier
Hester Smith, Hester Price, John Matthews, lab.	Toby Midwinter, *B.* = Maria	Ann M. Johnson seamstress	
Chas. Bowell, shoemaker	Maria Fisher d/o Wm. & Mary Beesley, *Bam*, w'finger, vict.	Ellen Simpson, wid., d/o Chas Bossom, laundress	Mary Curtis d/o Samson Beesley, ferryman's wife
Sarah Worth	George Turner, mustard maker = Lydia	Daniel Faulkner and Caroline, brewer's lab.	Daniel Faulkner and Caroline, brewery stoker
Thomas Farmer, vict., & Ann (née Latham)	Thos. Farmer, vict. and Ann	William Beesley, lab. s/o Thomas = Harriet	William Beesley = Harriet, sculptor's labourer
William Fisher, vict. = Caroline (née Collier), wid./o Wm. Howkins, Running Horses	Wm. Howkins, vict, s/o Wm. & Caroline = Susan, Running Horses	William Howkins, vict. = Susan, Running Horses	William Howkins = Susan, Running Horses

APPENDIX VI

1841 Census, Middle Fisher Row (HO 107/891/11, pp 28-32)

Ten.		Age	Occupation	Place of birth	Relationship etc.	1829 Survey
A	Edward Cox	50	Publican	Y		Thomas Farmer
	Caroline Cox (née Jarvis)	45		N		
	Ann Jarvis &	80		N		
	2 Servants	both 15		Y & N		
B	Sarah Crawford wid. of Edward	75		N	widow of a bargeman	Sarah Crawford
	Jamima Pearson (née Crawford)	35	frockmaker	Y	her daughter	
	Rebecca Crawford	12		Y		
	Sarah Crawford	9		Y		
C	Wm. Neville	84	Carter	Y		William Nevell
	Thos. Cattle	25	Carter	Y	of Islip at marriage; boatman in Psh. Reg.	
	Ann (née Newell)	25		Y	daughter	
	Jane, Thos. and Ed. Cattle	6-2		all Y		
	Richard Edwards	25	Boatman	Y	grandson of W. Beesley	
	Sarah Edwards (née Wickson)	20		Y	d/o Boatman	
	Joseph	5 months		Y		
D	Joseph Lewis	50	Boatman	Y		Joseph Lewis
	Jane (née Beesley)	45		Y	d/o W. Beesley	
	Maria (in 1844 = John Ashley)	17		Y		
	Joseph	15		Y		
	Martha	13		Y		
	Richard Baker	27		Y	[said to be boatman in baptismal reg.]	
	Mary (née Lewis)	25		Y	d/o Jos. Lewis g.d./o W. Beesley	
	Susan	3		Y		
	Ann	11 months		Y		

E	Stephen Judd	40	labourer	Y	In 1843 a boatman	Widow Stewart
	Mary (née Neville	40		Y	See Ten. C	
	Sarah (= Thos. Ashley 1843)	17		Y		
	5 other children	15-10 months		all Y		
	Sarah Judd	84		Y	n.k.	

F	Eliz. Collis	45	Widow [scored out]	Y	Aunt to Esther	John Seymour
	Edward Fisher	25	trunk maker, boatman at marriage	Y	Reln. to Wm. Fisher II n.k.	
	Esther (née Collis)	20		Y	Youngest sister of Eliz. Fisher, wife of William Fisher II, Niece to Eliz. Collis	
	Amelia	2		N		
	Mary	1		N		

G	John Giddins (s/o a farmer)	30	Boatman	Y	1848 m. Jemima Pearson of ten. B (née Crawford)	Stable
	Mary Giddins	40		Y		
	Charles	12		Y		
	George	7		Y		
	Joseph	4		Y		

H	Joseph Glover	40	Boatman	Y	not in parish register at all	John Justice
	Mary Glover	40		Y		
	3 children	12-4		all Y		

I	Chas. Kirtland	45	Boatman	Y		Chas. Curtland
	Eliz. (née Swallow)	40		Y		
	Martha	15		Y		

J	Ann Bowen*	85		N		Thomas Ashley
	Mary Redman*	70		N		
	Thomas Redman	70		Y		
	Ann Ashley	15		N	chdn. of the boatman Thomas Ashley and Mary his wife	
	Joseph Ashley	10		N		
	Phoebe Ashley	4		N		

K	John Bossom	80	Fisherman	Y		Rd. 'Coleby' [Corbey? Kilby?]
	Eliz. Bossom	70		Y		

L	Ann Woodward	30		Y	John & Henry	John Hooper
					Woodward	
					were boatmen	
					in 1840s	
	Ann Justice	30		Y	wid. of John	
					Justice, boatman,	
					see Ten. H & M	
M	Edward Cattle	20		Y	see ten. C	Mrs Justice
	Amelia	20		N		
	Alfred	1		Y		
N	Jas. Gardener	30	labourer	N		
	Mary Ann	35		N		
	Emma	1½		Y		
	John	7 months		Y		
	Mary Rhodes	60		N		
O	John Beesley	45	no occupn. given	Y	son of William	
	Eliz.	40		Y		

* Cf. Kirtlington Parish Register.

2/4/1838 John Redman, full age, bachelor, Boatman of Kidlington, s/o Jeremiah, clothier = Mary Bowen Ashley, full age, sp., servt., of Kidlington, d/o Thomas Ashley, Boatman.

St. Thomas Parish Register.

16/10/43 Ed. Dash, full age, bachelor, Boatman of Hythe Bridge, s/o Robt. Dash, Boatman = Ann Bowen Ashley, full age, sp., of Fisher Row, d/o Thomas Ashley, Boatman.

Bibliography

I. Manuscript Sources

Bodleian Library, Oxford

Dep. a. 16 Oxford Canal Accounts 1772-1800

Add. D. 114 A collection or Original papers relative to the Seige (sic) of Oxford MS D.D. Pprs.
   Dew c. 26 Lease of Wharf, Folly Bridge.

Parish Records: To save space the shelf-mark of individual items is not given.

They may be found in the calendar of deposited records in Duke Humfrey (R. 7.3.11^).

Banbury: baptisms 1813-52; marriages 1837-77

(For earlier registers see J. S. W. Gibson under 'Printed Primary Sources')

South Banbury: baptisms 1853-1967; marriages 1853-1919

Kidlington: baptisms 1790-1812, 1837-1920; marriages 1790-1893

Northmoor: baptisms 1653-1812; marriages 1654-1812

Oxford, St Aldates: baptisms 1678-1889; marriages 1678-1911; burials 1678-1891

— St Barnabas: baptisms 1869-1911; marriages 1870-1926

— St Giles: baptisms 1576-1891; marriages 1599-1890

— St Mary Magdalen: baptisms 1602-1837; marriages 1602-1886; burials 1602-1878

— St Paul: baptisms 1837-1910; marriages 1837-1935

— St Thomas: baptisms 1655-1918; marriages 1667-1923; burials 1667-1900; Church rate book
   1812-37; Church Warden's accounts, 1738-46 and 1746-7; Church accounts of receipts and
   expenditure, 1872-92, 1893-1921; Overseers' accounts, 1738-46 and 1746-7; Overseers' accounts, 1769-70, continued as vestry minutes 1818-38; Poor Rate Books 1731-6, 1736-59,
   1763-9

Shipton-on-Cherwell: baptisms 1873-1964; marriages 1790-1836

MS D.D. Oxford Methodist Circuit c. 9

MS G.A. Oxon 4' (3), Poll Book, 1768 Election

MS Oxf. Dioc. Pprs. c. 28 Archdeaconry Court Depositions, 1665-80

MS Oxf. Dioc. Pprs. c. 91 Bishop's Court, Depositions

MS Oxf. Dioc. Pprs. c. 2171(9) Petititon for License for the Boatmen's Chapel

MS Oxf. Dioe. Pprs. c. 436: Deed of establishment for the Boatmen's Chapel

MS Oxf. Dioc. Pprs. d. 481, Bishop's Transcript, Wolvercote Parish Register, 1840-69

MS Oxf. Dioc. Pprs. d. 553 Visitation Returns, 1738

MS Oxf. Dioc. Pprs. d. 571 Visitation Returns, 1808

MS Oxf. Dioc. Pprs. d. 708, Answers to Visitation Inquiries, 1685

MS Top. Oxon. b. 145, Police Report Book

MS Top. Oxon. c. 22 (formerly Gough MS Oxon 70), Papers concerning Oseney Abbey and
   Christ Church, 1520-1630'

MS Top. Oxon. c. 280, Miscellaneous papers relating to the parliamentary representation of the
   City of Oxford

MS Top. Oxon d. 505, Minn Collection, St Thomas's Parish

MS Twyne-Langbaine 1, Miscellaneous papers including material on the navigation of the Thames

MS Wood D. 5, A. Wood's extracts from early Oxford parish registers

MS Wills Oxon., Wills proved in the Diocesan and Archdeaconry Courts of Oxford 1509-1857

MS Wills Berks., Wills proved in the Court of the Archdeaconry of Berkshire*

MS Wills Peculiars, Wills proved in the Courts of Peculiars of Berkshire, Buckinghamshire, and Oxfordshire

R.6.155b/1-12, Index of Oxford Diocesan Marriage Bonds and Affidavits, 1661-1850: ed. D. M. Barratt and others

R.7.58/1-4, Berkshire and Oxford Archdeaconry Marriage Bonds and Affidavits (Berks. 1616-1846, Oxon. 1634-1849)

R.6.155e/1-9, Oxfordshire Marriage Index, compiled by J. S. W. Gibson (Salt Lake City, 1972)

John Johnson Collection, Sport 13, Box 'Regattas and Rowing'

British Library

Landsdowne Collection 30, fos. 41-4, 48, 51 Thames Navigation

— 41, fo. 43 Thames Navigation

— 44, fos. 117, 118 Thames Navigation

B.L. 357.b.9(77) 'The Case of the Bargemasters and others Navigating in the Rivers of Isis and Thames from Oxford to London.'n.d.

College Archives

Christ Church (Oxford)

    Ch.Ch. MS 1.c.2., The Book of Evidences

    Ch.Ch. MS xii.b.22-31, Disbursement Books

    Ch.Ch. MS xxix.b. 2-6, Oxford City Rents

    Ch.Ch. MS Estates 77-8, estate papers, St Thomas's parish

    Ch.Ch. MS Estates 62, estate papers, Binsey

    Deed Boxes for St Thomas's parish

Corpus Christi College Library (Cambridge)

    MS 128, pp. 393-401, The expenses of Cranmer's imprisonment

Lincoln College

    St Aldate's deeds

    Iffley deeds

    'A register of the Fines of Lincoln College beginning ... 1679'

New College

    No. 12527 A Terrier of Egrove Waters

County Record Offices

Berkshire

    D/EH 09 Papers of J. K. Hedges of Wallingford, member of the Thames Conservancy to 1892

    D/EX 7 5 TI 5 Leases of a fishery at Kennington

    D/ER E 211 Lease of fishery to William Clarke of Clanfield

    D/TC 25 A Minute Book of the Thames Commissioners, Sixth District

    Q/SO 1-3 Berkshire Quarter Session Minute Books, 1703-49

Gloucestershire

    Q/RR1 Register of Barges and Trows ... 1795

    T.S.1 I 0A Letter Book of the Thames and Severn Canal Company

    Parish Registers, Lechlade

    Wills and Inventories, Gloucester Diocese

Oxfordshire

    CH.N.III/ii/14 Expences of a Barge, London to Reading

*Moved to Berkshire Record Office, 1981.

CH.N.IX/i and ii Thames Navigation Account Books
CH.N.X/i/4 Papers concerning Navigation
CH.N.X/iii/7 Papers concerning Navigation Dew IV (d) 3 [provisional number] Register of Inspections of boats, Bicester Sanitary District, 1889-1921
M and G 23/1-2 Marshall and Galpin Collection
MSS D.D. Halls Breweries
Wi VI/iv/1-30 Willoughby Papers
Wi VII/13 Expences of a Barge from Oxford to Mapledurham
Shropshire
    QR305165 Quarter Session Rolls
Staffordshire
    Q11.UB1 Staffordshire Register of Boats and Barges, 1795-7
Warwickshire
    QS 95/4-8 Register of Boats and Barges, 1795-6
    CR 1590/1 Oxford Canal Letter Book, 1791-1800
    DR 225/327 Bedworth Poor Law Papers: Examinations
    DR 225/333 Bedworth Poor Law Papers: Removals
    DR 435/6-9 Foleshill Baptismal Registers 1813-90
    DR 435/15-19, Foleshill Marriage Registers 1813-92
    DR 225/4 Bedworth Baptismal Registers 1813-31
    DR 225/11-12 Bedworth Marriage Registers 1813-53
    DR 256/6-8 Hillmorten Baptisms 1813-92
    DR 256/13-14 Hillmorten Marriage Registers, 1813-1914

City Collections
Coventry City Record Office
    PH/Reg/1/1 Coventry Canal Boat Register 1879-1924
Records Office, The Guildhall, London
    Repertories 22, 86, 88
Oxford City Archives c/o Local History Dept., City Library, Oxford
A.4.1 Council Minute Book, 1559-1607
    A.5.1 The Old White Book
    A.5.2 Skinners Collection
    A.5.3 Apprenticeship Enrolments 1541-9 1, Hanaster (i.e. freemen) enrolments 1520-91
    A.5.5 Council Book, Proceedings, 1528-92
    B.5.4 Council Book G, Proceedings 1788-1813
    B.5.5 Council Book H, Proceedings 1813-32
    C.13.1 and 2 Papers concerning the City and Christ Church, 1543-1761
    D.5.2 Sundry Documents
    D.5.5-16 City Leases
    E.53-2 City Leases
    F.4.9 Apprenticeship enrolments 1697-1717, 1733-4
    F.5.2, F.5.4 Hester's Collection
    L.5.1-6 Apprenticeship enrolments and Hanaster Enrolments, 1591-1837
    N.4.1-6 Licenses to Alehouse keepers and Innholders
    O.3.1 Licenses to Alehouse keepers
    O.2.1-11 Quarter Session Minutes 1687-1807
    P.5.7 Poll Tax, 1667 awaiting cataloguing: Oxford Canal Boat Register, 1879-1925
Local History Dept., City Library, Oxford
    OXFO 797.1 Pamphlets on City Rowing
    Census: 1841-71 for St Thomas's Parish, on Microfilm
        1841 HO 107/891, Box 7
        1851 HO 107/1728, Boxes 7 and 8
        1861 RG 9/895-6, Box 4

1871 RG 10/1440-1, Box 7

Oxford University Archives

    G.G.5 Registrum Curiae Cancellarii Universitatis Oxon., 1545-55

    Hyp.B.1 Attestations, 1566-78, fos. 70-80

    Hyp.B.2136 Chancellor's Court, Wills

    S.E.P. G. 1-13 Papers connected with the navigation of the Thames

    W.P. α 34 Leases of Oseney Mill

    W.P. β 13 Leases of fisheries in the Cherwell

    W.P.P 5(4) Charges of Roger Jones in Connection with barges and waterworks.

Public Record Office

Court of Chancery (C)

    3 Proceedings: Bundle 177; no. 30, *Thomas v. Bodye*

        182/18 *Thomas alias Plummer v. Mounson*

Court of Requests (Req)

    2 Proceedings: 7/109 *W. Howse of Wightham v. Abbot of Oseney and Sir Simon Harcourt*.
    Wages

        74/4 *Samuel Newman v. John Kay and wife*. *Carriage of fish*

        270/37 *John Smith of Oxford v. William Chapman of London*. Transactions involving fish

Exchequer (E)

    179 Kings Remembrancer, Subsidy Rolls

    161/198 Lay Subsidy, 1523

    161/174 Lay Subsidy, 1524

    162/229 Lay Subsidy, 1544

    164/499 Lay Subsidy, 1648

    164/504 Hearth Tax, 1662

    163/514 Hearth Tax, 1665

Probate (PROB)

    11 Wills registered in the Prerogative Court of Canterbury

British Transport Historical Commission

    RAIL 855/106-11 Letters to the Proprietors of the Oxford Canal Navigation, 1797-1805

    RAIL 855/114 Letters to the Proprietors of the Oxford Canal, 1816

Tawney Family Papers

J. J. Tawney, 'Notes on the Tawneys of Oxford', (MS for family circulation, 1974) G. A. Tawney, Family Tree

Wills etc.

Theses

Davies, H. S., 'The Thames Navigation Commission, 1771-1867' (Reading University M.A. Thesis, 1967)

Hammer, junior, Carl I., 'Some Social and Institutional Aspects of Town-Gown Relations in Late Medieval and Tudor Oxford' (Toronto University, Ph.D Thesis, 1973)

Iredale, D. A., 'Canal Settlement: a study of the origin and growth of the canal settlement at Barnton in Cheshire between 1775 and 1845' (Leicester University, Ph.D. Thesis, 1966)

II Published Primary Sources

Acts of the Privy Council

Blome, Richard, The gentlemans recreation (London, 1686)

Bowdler, Dom Hugh, ed., Recusant Rolls 3 and 4 (Catholic Record Society, LXI, 1970)

Burton, John, *The Present State of the Navigation of the Thames considered, by a Commissioner* (Oxford, 1764)

Burton, Robert, *The Anatomy of Melancholy* (Oxford, 1621), Introduction, 'Democritus to the Reader', only

Calendar of Patent Rolls, 1258-1575

Calendar of State Papers Domestic

The Canal Boatman's Magazine (London, 1829-32), the monthly magazine of The Paddington Society for Promoting Christian knowledge among Canal Boatmen and Others

The Church Pastoral-aid Society, Reports and Occasional Papers, 1837-41

Clark, Andrew, ed., *Register of the University of Oxford*, II, pt. 1 (OHS X, 1887)

Cogan, Thomas, *The Haven of Health* (London, 1584)

Coles, Arthur, 'Working the Cut: Reminiscences of a Boatman', interview by Christine Bloxham, *Cake and Cock Horse*, VI (1975)

Collins, John, A Plea for the Bringing in of Irish Cattle and keeping out of Fish (London,1680)

The Diary of Thomas Crosfield, M.A., B.D., ed. F. S. Boas (London, 1935)

The Dictionary of National Biography

Directories: of the Directories listed by E. H. Cordeaux and D. H. Merry in *A Bibliography of Printed Works relating to Oxfordshire* those bearing the following Cordeaux and Merry numbers were used: 1381, 1382, 1383, 1384, 1385, 1388, 1389, 1390, 1391, 1394, 1396. Also the following listed in the same authors' *A Bibliography of printed Works relating to the City of Oxford*: 3009, 3010

Flower, C. T., ed., *Public Works in Medieval Law*, II (Selden Society, XL, 1923)

Gibson, J. S. W., ed., *The Baptismal Register of Banbury, Oxfordshire, III* (Banbury Historical Society, XVI, 1978)

— ed., The Marriage Register of Banbury II, and III (Banbury Historical Society, III and V, 1961, 1963)

The Good man of Paris by a Citizen of Paris, trans. Eileen Power (London, 1928)

Remarks and Collections of Thomas Hearne, ed. C. E. Doble and others (11 vols., OHS, 1886-1918)

Hewlett J. T. J., *Peter Priggins, the College Scout* (3 vols., London, 1841)

Hobson, M. G., ed., *Oxford Council Acts 1666-1701* (OHS, New Series 11, 1939)

- ed., *Oxford Council Acts 1702-1751* (OHS, New Series X, 1954)

- ed., *Oxford CouncilActs 1752-1801* OHS, New Series XV, 1962)

Hobson, M. G., and Salter, H. E., ed., *Oxford Council Acts 1626-1665* (OHS XCV 1932)

House of Lords Journal, LXXIII (1841), Appendix II, *Report of Select Committee on Carrying on goods on Canals ... on Sundays*

Jackson's Oxford Journal

The Itinerary of John Leland in or about the years 1535-1543, ed. L. Toulmin Smith (London, 1907)

Letters and Papers, Foreign and Domestic of the Reign of Henry VIII

Manuscripts of the Corporation of Rye (Historical Manuscripts Commission, XIII, pt.iv, 1892)

The Naval and Military Bible Society, Reports and Proceedings, 1827-31

The New Sailors' Magazine and Naval Chronicle (under various titles) 1827-61

Norden, J., *The Surveyors dialogue* (3rd edn., London, 1618)

Ogle, Octavius, ed., *Royal Letters addressed to Oxford and now existing in the City Archives* (Oxford, 1892)

The Oxford Boatman's Floating Chapel, Reports, 1839-41, 1844, 1849, 1858, 1861-3

Parliamentary Papers

First Series, vol. X, *Reports from Select Committees on the state of the Fisheries*, 1785-1800

First Series, vol. XIV, *Report on the Improvement and Trade of the Thames and Isis Navigation*, 1793

PP. Eng. 1830/viii (380), *Report of the Select Committee on the State of the Coal Trade*

PP. Eng. 1830-1/iii (263), *Report of the Select Committee on Petitions in favour of Parliamentary Reform*

PP. Eng. 1835/xxiii, pt. a (116), *First Report of the Commissioners on Municipal Corporations*

PP. Eng. 1837-8/ix (692), *Report on Church Leases*, 482-8

PP. Eng. 1840/xi (465), *Report on Operation of Municipal Reform Act on Privileges and Property of Freemen*

PP. Eng. 1857, Session 2/viii (170), *Select Committee on the Oxford City Election Petition*

PP. Eng. 1865/xii (399), *Report on Management of the River Thames above Staines*

PP. Eng. 1866/xii (391), *Minutes of Evidence before the Select Committee on the Thames Navigation Bill*

PP. Eng. 1870/M (184), *Return relating to Inland Navigations and Canal Companies*

PP. Eng. 1881 /xliv (C–2856), *Report of the Commissioners into the Existence of Corrupt Practices in the City of Oxford*

PP. Eng. 1884/viii (32 1), *Report on the Thames River Preservation*

PP. Eng. 1.892/xxxvi, Pt. ii (C. 6795-v), *Royal Commission on Labour, Minutes of Evidence: Group B*

PP. Eng. 1906/xxxii (Cd. 3184), *Royal Commission on Canals, First Report Evidence and Appendices*

PP. Eng. 1907/xxxiii, Pt. i (Cd. 3717). Ibid., *Second Report, Evidence and Appendices*

PP. Eng. 1909/xiii (Cd. 4840). Ibid., *Third Report, Evidence and Appendices*

Pyecroft, James, *Oxford Memories* (2 vols., Oxford, 1886)

Rogers, J. E. Thorold, ed., *Oxford City Documents, Financial and Juridicial* 1268-1665 (OHS, XVIII, 1890-1)

Rowing: collections of reports, programmes etc. of City and University Clubs are listed in Cordeaux and Merry's *Bibliography of Oxford*, numbers 2693-718

Salter, H. E., ed., *The Cartulary of Oseney Abbey* (6 vols., OHS, 1929-36)

— *Oxford Council Acts, 1583-1626* (OHS LXXXVII 1927)

— *Properties of the City of Oxfo9d* (OHS LXXXIII, 1962)

— *Snappe's Formulary and other Records* (OHS LXXX, 1923)

— *Surveys and Tokens* (OHS LXXV, 1920)

— *A Survey of Oxford*, ed. W. A. Pantin (2 vols., OHS, 1960-9)

Salter, J. H., and Salter, J. A., *Guide to the Thames* (44th edn., Oxford, n.d.)

Shadwell, L. L., ed., *Enactments in Parliament Concerning Oxford and Cambridge* (4 vols., OHS, 1911-12)

Sills, Joseph, *Report of the State of the Navigation of the River Thames between Radcott-bridge and Abingdon* (London, 1796)

Smith, George Charles, *Birmingham or No Preaching: being a Narrative and Corres- pondence respecting ... the British and Foreign Seamen's and Soldiers' Friend Society* (London, 1828)

Stevenson, Joseph, *Chronichon Monasterii* de Abingdon (2 vols., Rolls Series, 1858)

Talboys, D. A., *The proposed bye-laws* (Oxford, 1838)

Tavener, J., *Certaine Experiments Concerning Fish and Fruites* (London, 1600)

The Terrae Filius Speech as it was Spoken at the Publick Act (London, 1733)

'T. Tims: an autobiographical sketch' (*Oxford Magazine*, XVI (21 May 1896, extra no.) 4-5

Turner, H. W., ed., *Selections from the Records of the City of Oxford 1509-1583* (Oxford, 1880)

The Waterman, the monthly Magazine of the incorporated Seamen and Friend Society, 1909-1915

Wood, Anthony, *Athenae Oxonienses*, ed. P. Bliss (4 vols., 3rd ed., 1813-20)

The Life and Times of Anthony Wood, antiquary of Oxford, 1632-1695, described by Himself, ed. Andrew Clark (5 vols., OHS, 1891-1900)

Woodforde at Oxford 1759-1776, ed. W. N. Hargreaves-Mawdsley (OHS, New Series, XXI, 1969

Young, Arthur, *A General View of the Agriculture of Oxfordshire* (London, 1813 repr. 1969)

III. Published Secondary Sources

Allen, T., and Greenhill, W. A., *Report on the Mortality and Public Health of Oxford during the years 1849, 50* (Ashmolean Society, Oxford, 1854)

Anderson, Michael, *Family Structure in nineteenth century Lancashire* (Cambridge, 1971)

Arensberg, C. M., and Kimball, S. T., *Family and Community in Ireland* (London, 1940)

'Argonaut' E. D. Brickwood, *The Arts of Rowing and Training* (London, 1866)

Arkell, W. J., *Oxford Stone* (London 194-7)

Ashton, T. S., 'Richard Henry Tawney, 1880-1962', *Proc. of the British Academy*, XLVIII (1962)

Barker, Denis, 'The Marketing of Corn in the First Half of the Eighteenth Century: North East Kent', *Agricultural History Review*, XVIII (1970)

Barnes, Greville F., *The Rail and the Rod, or, Tourist Anglers' Guide to Waters and Quarters around London, II, Great Western Railway* (London, 1869)

Barratt, D. M., and Vaisey, D. G., *Oxfordshire, a handbook for students of local history* (Oxford, 1973)

Bassett, Arthur Tilney, *S. Barnabas' Oxford* (London, 1919)

Bede, Cuthbert [Edward Bradley], *The Adventures of Mr Verdant Green* (London, 1853)

Belsten, Kingsley, *The Story of Botley Mill* (Oxford, 19 70)

Belsten, Kingsley, and Compton, Hugh, 'Eynsham Wharf, Oxfordshire', *Journal of the Railway and Canal Historical Society*, XIV (1968)

Bennett, R., and Elton, J., *History of Cornmilling* (4 vols., London and Liverpool, 1898-1904)

Blackstone, W., *Commentaries on the Laws of England* (4 vols., 5th edn., Oxford, 1778)

Bolland, R. R., *Victorians on the Thames* (Tunbridge Wells, 1964)

Booth, Charles, ed., *Labour and Life of the People*, 1 (2 vols., 2nd edn., London, 1889-93)

Bradbrooke, William, 'North Hinksey and the Willis Family', *North Oxfordshire Archaeological Society*, LXXXI (1935)

Bumby, J. G., and Parker, M., *The Navigation of the River Lee, 1190-1790* (Edmonton Hundred Occasional Paper, New Series XXXVI)

Byrne, L. S. R., and Churchill, E. L., *The Eton Book of the River with Some Account of the Evolution of Boat-racing* (Eton, 1935)

Cannon, John, 'The Parliamentary Representation of the City of Oxford 1754-90' *Oxon.*, XXV (1960)

Carew, Thomas, *An Historical Account of the Right of Elections of the Several Counties, Cities and Boroughs of Great Britain* (London, 1755)

Carter, Harry, *Wolvercote Mill* (Oxford Bibliographical Society, New Series, extra publication, 1957)

Chambers, J. D., and Mingay, G. E., *The Agricultural Revolution* (London, 1966)

Cholmondeley-Pennell, H., *Fishing: Pike and other Coarse Fish* (London, 1886)

Clark, Andrew, ed., *Survey of the Antiquities of the City of Oxford, composed in 1661-6 by Anthony Wood* (3 vols., 1889-99)

Clark, G. N., *Open Fields and Inclosure at Marston* (Oxford, 1924)

Clark, Peter, and Slack, Paul, *Crisis and Order in English Towns 1500-1700* (London, 1972)

Coleman, Terry, *The Railway Navvies* (London, 1965)

Compton, Hugh J., *The Oxford Canal* (Newton Abbot, 1976)

Cooper, Janet, 'The Hundred Rolls of the Parish of St Thomas, Oxford', *Oxon.*, XXXVII (1972)

Cordeaux, E. H., and Merry, D. ll., *A Bibliography of printed Works relating to the City of Oxford* (OHS, New Series XXV, 1976)

Cordeaux, E. H., and Merry, D. H., *A Bibliography of Printed Works relating to Oxfordshire* (OHS, New Series XI, 1955)

Cornish, C. J., *The Naturalist on the Thames* (London, 1902)

Cotes, Cecil V., *Two Girls on a Barge* (London, 1891)

Cottle, Basil, *The Penguin Dictionary of Surnames* (Harmondsworth, 1967)

Cox, G. V., *Recollections of Oxford* (London, 1870)

Crozier, Dorothy, 'Kinship and Occupational Succession', *The Sociological Review*, XIII (1965)

Dalby, L. J., *The Wilts & Berks Canal* (Lingfield, Surrey, 1971)

Dannatt, G. H., compiler, *The Oxfordshire Election of 1754: an archive teaching unit* (Oxford, 1970)

Davis, R. H. C., 'The Ford, the River and the City', *Oxon.* XXXVIII (1973)

Davis, F. M., *An Account of the Fishery Gear of England and Wales*, Ministry of Agriculture and Fisheries, Series II, ix 6 (rev. edn., 1927)

de Villiers, E., *Swinford Bridge 1769-1969* (Eynsham, 1969)

The Dictionary of National Biography

Dully, A. J. F., 'The Early History of the Rye Fishing Industry', *Sussex Archaeological Collections*, CVII (1969)

Elton, G. R., *Reform and Renewal (Cambridge*, 1973)

Fasnacht, Ruth, *A History of the City of Oxford* (Oxford, 1954)

Fenby, Charles, *The Other Oxford* (London, 1970)

Firth, R., and Djamour, Judith, *Two Studies of Kinship in London* (London, 1956)

Fisher, F. J.,'The development of the London Food Market 1540-1640' *Economic History Review*, V (1935)

Forbes, R. J., 'Power', *A History of Technology*, II, ed. Charles Singer, E. J. Holmyard, A. R. Hall, and Trevor I. Williams (Oxford, 1956)

Foster, Joseph, *Alumni Oxonienses, The Members of the University of Oxford 1500-1714* (4 vols., Oxford, 1891-2)

Frear, Mary Reno, 'The Election of Great Marlow 1640' *The Journal of Modem History*, XIV (1942)

Gordon, Mrs, *Life and Correspondence of William Buckland* (London, 1894)

Graham, Malcolm, *A Thousand Years of Folly Bridge*, reprod. from typewriting (no place, 1972)

Graham, Rose, 'A Description of Oxford from the Hundred Rolls of Oxfordshire, A.D. 1279', *Collectanea*, 4th Series, edited under the superintendance of the Committee of the Society (OHS XLVII 1906)

Green, John Richard, *Oxford Studies*, ed. Mrs J. R. Green and Miss K. Norgate (London,1901)

Green, J. R., and Roberson, George, *Studies in Oxford History*, ed. C. L. Stainer (OHS XLI, 1901)

Hadfield, Charles, *British Canals* (revised edn., 1859)

— *The Canals of the East Midlands* (Newton Abbot, 1966)

— *The Canals of the West Midlands* (Newton Abbot, 1966)

Hall, Mr and Mrs S. C., *The Book of the Thames* (London, 1959)

Hanson, Harry, *The Canal Boatmen, 1760-1914* (Manchester, 1975)

Hardy, Thomas, *Jude the Obscure* (1895)

Heavisides, M. D. [Matthew Davenport Hill], 'The Staffordshire Collieries' *Knight's Quarterly Magazine*, 1 (1823)

Hickling, C. F., 'Prior More's Fishponds', *Medieval Archaeology*, XV (1971)

Hollingshead, John, 'On the Canal', *Household Words*, XVIII (1858)

Hoskins, W. G., *Local History in England* (2nd edn., London, 1972)

Hoskins, W. C., and Stamp, L. Dudley, *The Common Lands of England and Wales* (London,1963)

Household, Humphrey, *The Thames and Severn Canal* (Newton Abbot, 1969)

Hughes, Diane Owen, 'Urban Growth and Family Structure in Medieval Genoa', *Past and Present*, XLVI (1975)

Jenkins, J. Geraint, *Nets and Coracles* (Newton Abbot, 1974)

Jones Barbara, *The Unsophisticated Arts* (London, 1951)

Keene, M. H., *The Outlaws of Medieval Legend* (London, 1961)

Laithwaite, Michael, 'The Buildings of Burford', *Perspectives in English Urban History*, ed. Alan Everett (London, 1973)

Lambrick, Gabrielle, 'Oxford Colleges and some Country Parishes around Oxford in the early 18th Century', *Oxon.* XXV (1960)

Laslett, Peter, *The World we have lost* (London, 1965)

Laslett, Peter, and Wall, Richard, eds., *Household and Family in Past Time* (Camb paperback edn., 1974)

Lattey, R. T., Parsons, E. J. S., and Phillip, I. C., 'A Contemporary Map of the Defences of Oxford in 1646', *Oxon.* 1 (1936)

Lea, George, *Memoir of the Rev. John Davies, M.A.* (London, 1859)

Lee, F. C., *History and Antiquities of the Church of the Blessed Virgin of Thames* (London, 1883)

Leeds, E. Thurlow, 'Oxford Tradesmen's Tokens', *Surveys and Tokens*, ed. H. E. Salter (OHS LXXV, 1920)

Leslie, George D., *Our River: an artist's life on the River Thames* (London, 1888)

Lewery, A. J., *Narrow Boat Painting* (Newton Abbot, 1974)

Linebaugh, Peter, 'The Tyburn Riot against the Surgeons', *Albion's Fatal Tree*, Douglas Hay, Peter Linebaugh, E. P. Thompson, and others (London, 1975)

Lyte, H. C. Maxwell, *A History of the University of Oxford to 1530* (London, 1886)

Macfarlane, Alan, in collaboration with Sarah Harrison and Charles Jardine, *Reconstructing Historical Communities,* (Cambridge, 1977)

Macleod, Roy M., 'Social Policy and the "Floating Population": the Administration of the Canal Boats Acts 1877-1899' '*Past and Present*, XXXV (1966)

McKenna, Frank, *A Glossary of Railwaymen's Talk* (Oxford, 1970)

Maitland, F. W., *Township and Borough* (Cambridge, 1898, repr. 1964)

Markham, Captain F., *Recollections of a Town Boy at Westminster 1849-1855* (London,1903)

Marshall, Edward, *An Account of the Township of Iffley* (Oxford and London, 1870)

Martin, A. F., and Steel, R. W., eds., *The Oxford Region* (London, 1954)

Mathias, Peter, *The Brewing Industry in England 1700-1830* (Cambridge, 1959)

Miller, Edith, *The History of the Village of Islip* (Oxford, 1930)

Mogey, J. M., *Family and Neighbourhood: Two studies in Oxford* (Oxford, 1956)

Moore, Stuart A., and Moore, Hubert Stuart, *The History and Law of Fisheries* (London, 1903)

Morgan, Blacker, *Historical and Genealogical Memoirs of the Dutton Family of Sherborne in Gloucestershire* (privately printed, 1899)

Morris, R. J., 'The Friars and Paradise: an Essay in the Building History of Oxford, 1801-1861', *Oxon*. XXVI (1971)

Namier, Lewis, *The Structure of Politics at the Accession of George III* (2nd edn., repr. 1975)

Naylor, Leonard G. R., *The Malthouse of Joseph Tomkins* (privately printed, n.d., no place)

Ordnance Survey Gazetteer of Great Britain (Chessington, Surrey, 1953)

Oxford English Dictionary

Pam D. O., *Tudor Enfield: The Maltmen and the Lea Navigation* (Edmonton Hundred Occasional Paper, New Series XVIII, n.d.)

Pantin, W. A., 'Houses of the Oxford Region, I – Fisher Row, Oxford' *Oxon*. XXV (1960)

Pearse, Mark Guy, *Rob Rat-a story of Barge Life* (London, 1878)

Phelps-Brown, E. H., and Sheila V. Hopkins, 'Seven Centuries of the Prices of Consumables compared with Building Prices', *Economica*, XXIII (1955)

Philip, I. G. 'The River Navigation at Oxford during the Civil War and Commonwealth', *Oxon*. 11 (1937)

Phillips, J. A General History of Inland Navigation (4th edn., London, 1803)

Pollard, Graham, 'William of Brailles', Bodician Library Record, V (1954-6)

Pollock, Sir Frederick, and Maitland, F. W., The History of English Law (2nd edn., Cambridge, 1952)

Pressnell, L. S. *Country Banking in the Industrial Revolution* (Oxford, 1964)

Prichard, Mari, and Carpenter, Humphrey, *A Thames Companion* (Oxford, 1975)

Pycroft, James, *Oxford Memories* (2 vols., London, 1886)

Ravensdale, J. R., *Liable to Floods: village landscape on the edge of the fens, A.D. 450-1850* (Cambridge, 1974)

Red Quill [Englefield, James], *The Delightful Life of Pleasure on the Thames* (London, 1912)

Robinson, H. R., 'Life on the Upper Thames', *The Art Journal*, New Series XIIXIII

Robson, R. J., *The Oxfordshire Election of 1754* (London, 1949)

Rogers, J. E., Thorold *A History of Agriculture and Prices in England* (8 vols., Oxford, 1866-1902)

Rolt, L. T. C., *The Inland Waterways of England* (London, 1950)

— *Narrow Boat* (London, 1944)

Rowe, R. P. P., and Pitman, C. M., *Rowing* (London 1898)

Salter, H. E., ed. *A Cartulary of the Hospital of St John the Baptist*, III (OHS LX1X 1916), Appendix V, 329-78

Medieval Oxford (OHS C 1936)

Samuel, Raphael, 'Quarry Roughs', in Raphael Samuel, editor, *Village Life and Labour* (London, 1975)

Sherwood, W. E., *Oxford Rowing* (Oxford, 1900)

— *Oxford Yesterday* (Oxford, 1927)

Sieveking, A. F., 'The Origin and Early History of Locks', *Field*, 10 Apr. 1915

Skempton, A. W., 'Canals and River Navigations before 1750', *History, of Technology III*, ed. Charles Singer (3 vols., Oxford, 1957)

Smiles, Samuel, *Lives of the Engineers* (3 vols., London, 1861-2)

Smith, George, *Canal Adventures of Moonlight* (London, 1881)

- *Our Canal Population: a Cry from the Boat Cabins* (new edn., London, n.d.)

Smyth of Nibley, John, *The Lives of the Berkeleys, Lords of the Honour, Castle and Manor of Berkeley ... with a description of the Hundred of Berkeley and its Inhabitants*, ed. Sir John Maclean (3 vols., Gloucester, 1885)

Spufford, Margaret, Contrasting Communities, *English Villages in the sixteenth and seventeenth centuries* (Cambridge, 1974)

Squires, Thomas W., *In West Oxford* (Oxford, 1928)

Stevenson, W. H., and Salter, H. E., *The Early History of St John's College*, Oxford (OHS, New Series 1, 1939)

Stone, Lawrence, *The Crisis of the Aristocracy 1588-1641* (Oxford, 1965)

— 'The Educational Revolution in England 1560-1640', *Past and Present*, XXVIII (1964)

— ed., 'The Size and Composition of the Oxford Student Body', in *The University in Society*, I ed. Lawrence Stone (London, 1975)

Suncliffe, John, *A Treatise on Canals and Reservoirs* (Rochdale, 1816)

Taunt, Henry W., *A Map of the River Thames* (Oxford, 1872)

Tawney, R. H., *The Agrarian Problem in the Sixteenth Century* (new edn., with introduction by L. Stone, New York, 1967)

Taylor, Audrey M., *Cilletts, Bankers of Banbury and Oxford* (Oxford, 1964)

Thacker, Fred S., *The Thames Highway* (2 vols., 1914-21, London and Kew, repr. 1968)

Thirsk, Joan, ed., *The Agrarian History of England and Wales*, IV (Cambridge, 1967)

Thirsk, Joan, *Economic Policy and Projects* (Oxford, 1978)

'Industries in the Countryside' ed., F. J. Fisher (Cambridge, 1961), *Essays in the Economic and Social History of Tudor and Stuart England*

Thomas, J. Alun, 'The System of Registration and the Development of Party Organisation 1832-70' History, New Series XXXV (1950)

Thompson, E. P., *The Making of the English Working Class* (London, 1963)

Thurston, E. Temple, *The Flower of Gloucester* (London, 1911) Vale, Edmund, By Shank and by Crank (Edinburgh and London, 1924)

Vance, William F., *Sermons: with a Voice from the Mines and Furnaces* (Wolverhampton, n.d.)

Vernon-Harcourt, L. F., *A Treatise on Rivers and Canals* (2 vols., Oxford, 1882)

The Victoria County History of Berkshire

The Victoria County History of Oxfordshire Vince, John, *Discovering Watermills* (Tring, 1970)

Ward, J. R., *The Finance of Canal Building in Eighteenth Century England* (London, 1974)

Ward, W. R., *Georgian Oxford* (Oxford, 1958)

Webb, Sidney and Beatrice, *English Local Government IV, Statutory Authorities for Special Purposes* (London, 1922)

Willan, T. S., *River Navigation in England 1600-1750* (Oxford, 1936, repr. 1964)

Williams, Aidin, *Lechlade* (Cirencester, 1888)

Williams, Charles, *George Mogridge: his Life, Character and Writings* (London, 1856)

Wood, Anthony, *History of the City of Oxford*, ed. Andrew Clark (3 vols., OHS, 1889-1899)

Woodgate, W. B., *Boating* (London, 1889)

Wright, D. G., *Democracy and Reform 1815-1885* London, 1970)

Wrigley, E. A., ed., *An Introduction to English Historical Demography* (London, 1966)

Youings, Joyce, *The Dissolution of the Monasteries* (London, 1957)

Young, M. and Willmott, P. *Family and Kinship in East London* (London, 1957)

Indices

Notes on Indices

An italic page number denotes a family tree, map, or table on that page. A page number followed by n is a reference to a footnote. An asterisk is used to express an uncertainty about identity or attribution.

1. INDEX OF NAMES

Abell, Rev. Mat. 357-8
Abingdon, Lord 275
Alder:
    Chas. (boatman) and Marg. 221
    Ric. (victualler) 289
Alexander, Mr (lawyer) 289
Algar, Earl 37
Angell, Thos. (fisherman) 65, 86
Applebee, John 78
Aris and Taylor (timber merchants,
    bargemasters) 197-8
Ashley:
    family 224, 238-41, 316
    Edw. (boatman, bargemaster) 213;
      and Mary Anne (Beesley) 221, 240,
      368
    Eliz. Rachel 240
    Geo. (boatman, coal-merchant,
      victualler) and Mary (Hooper)
      221, 240
    John 240
    Joseph (boatman) and
      Lydia 221
    Joseph (boatman) and Phoebe 220-1,
      223
    Joseph* 357
    Mary Anne, *see* Darby
    Mary Bowen, *see* Redman
    Samuel Joseph (bargemaster) 240

    Sarah, *see* Howkins
    Thos. (boatman, coal merchant) 213,
      239-40; and Mary (Beesley) 221,
      238, 373
Ashmall, Mrs 33
Astell, Miles 59
Astill, John (tallowchandler) 59
Atwood, Jas. (clothier) 52-3
Austen:
    John (fishmonger) 86n.
    John (mayor) 86n.
Ayres:
    Harry 332
    Mary 164, 360
    Ralph 360 Wm. and John (barge-
      masters) 111, 131

Backester:
    John (labourer) 78, 124
    Rob. (waterman) 78, 101, 124
Bailey, Thos. (boat-owner) 224
Baker, Ric. (boatman) and Mary (Lewis)
    316, 372
Banks, Thos. 125
Barfoot, Joseph (boatman) and Mary 221
Barrett, John 275
Basson:
    Eliz. 268, 221
    Ric. (boatman) 221

385

Bateman, Mr 128
Bayzand, Wm. 60
Beauchamp:
    family 342
    Edw. (victualler) 211
    Edw. (boatman) and Hannah
        (Skinner, Lamsdon) 318
Beckley:
    Jas. (fisherman) 175
    John (fisherman) 174-5
    Thos. 168
    Wm. (fisherman, of Islip) 75, 102
    Wm. (fisherman, of Oxford) 102, 169
Beesley:
    family 226-7, 250-1, 253, 256, 257;
        24, 196, 221-3, 225-7, 255-8, 264,
        271, 286-96, 302, 335-6, 343-4
    v. Bossom 271-3
    A.* 302
    Abel, sen. (fisherman) 252-3, 287,
        291, 296, 355; and Eliz.
        (Culpepper) 258, 368-9
    Adam (boatman, fisherman) 252,
        258, 291, 368-9
    Ann* 287
    Ann, see Collier
    Ann Maria or Maria, see Spindler
    Benj. (boat-owner, victualler, of
        Sutton Stop) 241, 339
    Francis J. (waterman) 344-5
    Geoff. (owner of pleasure boats) 306
    Horace S. J. (owner of pleasure boats)
        306
    Jacob (owner of osier works), 266,
        305-6, 355
    Jane, see Lewis
    Jane Julia, see Lamsden
    Jas., sen. (fisherman) 252, 287, 289,
        345, 357,363*; and Eliz. (Hands)
        258, 369
    Jas., jun. 296
    Jeffrey H. (waterman) 344
    John (cordwainer) 364
    John, son of Wm. 241; and Eliz. 374
    Joseph (fisherman) 252, 256, 287, 291
    Maria, see Collier
    Maria, see Fisher
    Mary, see Ashley
    Mary (Collis), widow of Wm. 198,
        226, 228-9
    Mary, see Edwards

    Mary Anne, see Ashley
    Ric. (fisherman) 252, 256, 287,
        291
    Rob. 114
    S* 302
    Sampson 303
    Samuel (bargeman), brother of Wm.
        196, 252
    Samuel (bargeman), son of Wm.
        238-9, 355-7, 359, 369
    Samuel (fisherman), son of Thos.
        252-3; and Anne (Bossom) 258,
        287, 291, 296-7, 370-1
    Samuel* 272
    Samuel* 296-7
    Sarah 273
    Thos. (bargemaster), brother of Wm
        195-7, 232, 249-53, 255-6, 264-6,
        268, 352-6, 368
    Thos. (fisherman), son of Thos. 47,
        252, 258, 284, 290-1, 352, 354,
        368
    Thos. (boatman, labourer, chaff-
        cutter) 17, 238, 274-5, 368
    wid.* 355
    Wm. (bargemaster, wharfinger,
        victualler), son of John 195-8, 210,
        224-5, 228-9, 232, 238-41, 249,
        252, 256, 264, 268, 287
    Wm., son of Joseph 295
    Wm. (labourer), son of Thos. 253,
        271
Belsyre:
    Alexander, President of St John's 114
    Leonard 85, 114
Bentley, Jas. (ex-boatman) 355; and
    Eliz. 368
Berry:
    Jane (boatman's wife) 246-7, 369
    Thos. (boatman) 247
Bertie, Capt. Peregrine 174
Best:
    Joseph (bargeman) 173
    — 176
Beziles, Mathias de 111
Biddle, Ric. 175
Birley, Rev. T. H. 334
Bishop:
    Benj. (boatman) and Eliz. (Bowell)
        246
    Jeremiah 81, 103, 170, 246

Wm. (fisherman) 371
Wm. (boatman) and Eliz. 221
Blackstone, Wm. 284
Blagrave, family 114
Bley, Ant. 101
Blome, Ric. 69
Bokeland, John 49
Bond, Isaac (boatman) and Jane (Bowell)
    246, 370
Boner, Walt. 76
Bonner alias Pitts:
    family 96; 78, 87, 89, 91, 97-101
    Anne, wife of Hen. 99 (*see also*
        Noble)
    Eliz., *see* Curtice
    Hen. I (fisherman) 98-100
    Hen. II 100
    Joan 78, 97-8
    Mary, *see* Feild
    Mary 100
    Ric. I (fisherman) 99, 124
    Stephen (hempdresser) 99
    Walt. (I) 97
    Walt. (II) (fisherman) 67, 78, 80, 86n.,
        98-102; and Eliz. (Woodley)
        99-100
    Walt. (III) (barber) 100
    Walt. (IV) (tailor) 99
    Wm. (glazier) 98
Booth, Chas. 10, 12
Bossom:
    family, 256, 262-3; 24, 170, 223-4, 232,
        255, 258, 264-5, 267-70, 302, 344
    Mrs (laundress) 312
    Anne, *see* Beesley
    Benj. (boat-builder) 255, 258, 287,
        360, 370
    Chas. 264, and Deborah (Costar) 267
    Chas.* and Mary (House) 267
    Chas. (bargeman) and Mary
        (Ashfield) 371
    Chas. (bargeman) 371
    Christian (Crawford) 169-70
        (*see also under* Thos., *below*)
    Eliz., *see* Corbey
    Fanny 312
    Geo. (water bailiff, police inspector)
        269, 271, 273-6, 282, 287
    John (boatman), brother of Thos. 265;
        and Eliz. 220-1
    John* (*bis*) 269

John* (fisherman) (*bis*) 269
John (water bailiff, Medley) 282-3,
    287, 290
John, jun. Medley 303
Ric. 269, 355, 360
Rob. 267
Thos. (bargemaster) 243, 268, 355,
    359-60, 362; and Christian 264,
    267
Wm.* and Eliz. (Basson) 268
Wm.* and Eliz. (Gunn) 268
Wm.* and Eliz. (Mailing) 221, 268
Wm. (lock-keeper) 282
Wm., son of Thos. 243
    — 273
Bowell:
    Eliz. (wife of Wm., below), 243
        246-7, 370
    Mary 370
    Thos. (maltster) and Anne (Wright
        Broade) 78, 95
    Wm. 246
Bowen, family 240, 373
Bricknell, Thos. (boatman) and Mary
    (Bossom) 221-3
Briggs, Hen. 183
Briscoe, — , highwayman 173
Broade:
    Anne, wid. (Wright, *see* Bowell) 78,
        94-5
    Thos. 94
Broadwater:
    family 70, 98
    John (fisherman) 98
    Swithin (fisherman) 65
Brookings:
    family 168
    Jonathan (fisherman, Stanton
        Harcourt) 168
    Ric. sen. (boatman) 168, 351, 355;
        and Mary (Tawney) 140
    Ric. jun. (victualler, Bablock Hythe)
        168-9, 352
    Ric. (fisherman, Stanton Harcourt)
        352
Brunner, W., Recorder of Oxford 284,
    291, 295, 297
Bryce, — , highwayman 173
Buckland, Wm. (geologist) 199
Bull, Chas. (boatman) and Mary 221, 371
Bulteel, Rev. H. B. 216

Burden, Mrs (Kilby) 330, 333, 342
Burgess, Ric. 297
Burnham, John (boatman) and Elinor 221
Burton, Rob. 127, 216
Buswell, Mr 175

Campion, Edm. 98
Capel:
   — 357
   Edw. (labourer) and Caroline 371
   Wm. (of Grove) 363
Capulets, the 305
Carpenter, Chas. (boatman) 369, 371
Cartwright: Edw. (boatman) and Sarah 236n.
   Maj., T. 8
Cattle, Edw. and family 374
Cecil, Wm., Lord Burleigh 112-13, 116
Chadwell:
   John 174
   Mr 164
Chamberlain, Canon Thos. (vicar of St Thomas's) 217, 311-12
Chapman, Walt. (boatmaster) 138
Chappell, Elianor (Clarke, May) 141, 166
Charles I 127
Chillingworth:
   Eliz. 168, 358-9
   Francis 359
Clarke (Clark):
   Elianor, Helen, see May, Chappell
   Eliz. 79
   Eliz., see Tawney
   Emme (wid.) 141
   John* 159
   John (fisherman, of Garford) 63
   John (dyer) 143-5
   John (boatman, waterman) 78, 95, 141, 144-5
   John and Martha 141, 144-5
   Ric. (bargemaster, of Bray) 144
   Rob. (Quaker) 145
   Stephen 141, 144
   Thos. 141, 144
   Thos. (woodmonger, of London) and Eliz. 144, 147
   Thos. (boatmaster, of Sutton Courtney) 144
   Wm. (bargemaster, of Culham) 141, 144

Clements, Joseph (boatman) and Eliz. 221; and Sarah 370
Cockhead (Coxhead), Rob. (boatman) and Mary Ann 355, 369
Coles, Art. (boatman) 340, 342-3
Collier:
   family 255
   Caroline 239 (see also Howkins)
   Chris. (victualler) and Ann (Beesley) 210, 239
   John (bargemaster) and Ann (Paish) 368
   Maria (widow of Chris.) 240, 370
Collis:
   family 255
   widow 363
   Benj. (smith) and Ann (Howkins) 368, 369
   Eliz. and family 373
   Jane and Wm. (bargeman) 368
   Mary widow of Wm., see Beesley
   Wm. (bargeman) and Jane 368
Cooke (Cook):
   John (fisherman) 93, 126
   John and Ann (Hicks) 93, 124
   Rob. (fisherman) 78, 82, 93, 124
   Thos. Albert (victualler) 2 10
Cooper, John (boatman) and Anne (Leverett) 221
Copson, John (boatbuilder) and Mary 370
Corbey:
   family 244; 243
   Eliz. (Bossom) wife of Thos. 243, 245, 255, 318, 357, 369
   Florence, see Tustin
   Mary, see Howkins
   Ric. (boatman) and Betsey (Skinner) 318, 344
   Thos. (ostler) 243, 355, 356
   Wm. 369
Cordingley, Thos. (boatman) and Eliz. (Collis) 221
Costar, Deborah, see Bossom
Cox:
   family 300
   Lazarus 337
   M. see Massarella
   Olive, see Gibbs
   Thos. Edw. (victualler) 210, 238-9, 372

Cranmer, Archbishop Thos. 57-8, 61, 64
Crawford (Crafford):
    family *165*; 153, 156, 163, 166-70
    Mr* 166
    Mrs* (3) 163-4
    'Beauty', or John* 170
    Christian, *see* Bossom
    Eliz. (victualler, of Abingdon) 170
    Edw. 164, 166, 170, 174
    John (I) (bargeman) and Joan 168-9
    John (II) (bargeman) and Marg.
        (Gardner) 166, 267
    John (III) (boatmaster) and Mary
        (Gardner) 166, 167, 170
    John, son of John (II) 169
    John and Eliz. (of Abingdon) 170
    Joseph* 170
    Rebecca, *see* Finch
    Rebecca, *see* Robinson
    Ric.* (bargeman, victualler) 174, 358
    Sarah and family 330, 372
    Wm.* (bargemaster, of Lechlade)
        170
    Wm., son of John 169
Cripps, Mrs 334
Crozier, Jas. (schoolteacher, Chapel) 370
Culpepper, Eliz., *see* Beesley
Curtice:
    family 96; 100, 102-3
    Chas. (gent.) 103, 352
    John (I) 100
    John (II) (fisherman) 78, 102, 103,
        351, 355; and Eliz. (Bonner alias
        Pitts) 100, 351, 355
    John (III) (fisherman) 78, 102

Darby, Abraham (boatman) and Mary
    Anne (Ashley) 221, 224
Darkin, Isaac (highwayman) 174
Davies:
    — of Burcot (coalmerchant) 113
    John 113
Davis:
    John (boatbuilder) 356
    R. H. C. 110
    Stephen (boatbuilder, 300, 356-8
        waterman)
Day:
    Nic.(miller) 63-6, 68
    Ric. 63
    Rob. (fisherman) 73

Thos. (fisherman) 63, 65
Dean, D. W. (coalmerchant) 356
Derick, John Macduff, architect 216
Desborough, Lord 301, 305
Dewy:
    John (boatbuilder) 351, 352, 355
    Ric. (hempdresser) 355
Dickens, Chas. 6-7
Dix, Wm. (boatman) and Mary (Stuart)
    221, 223
Dodwell:
    family 114
    Phil. 78
Dolley, Jas. (victualler) 359
Dorchester, Secretary 121
Drayton, Wm. 109
Duffin:
    family 137; 136-9
    Alice, *see* Hicks
    Elianor (widow, wharfinger) 138
    Humphrey (boatman) and Ann 138
    Priscilla, *see* Etty
    Ric. (wharfinger) and Joan (Hooper)
        138-9

Earl, R. A. J. 350
Eaton, Hopkins & Co. (coalmerchants)
    203
Edmonds (Edwards), Mrs (canal
    missionary) 214
Edwards, Ric. (boatman) 238; and Mary
    (Beesley) 221, 224, 372
Eeley, — 275
Eldridge, Capt. 296
Elizabeth I 116
Elliot, Capt. (canal missionary) 215
Elliot, Ebenezer 307
Ellis, Will 97
Emony, — ('the Eton Pet') 304
Etty:
    family 137n.
    Ric. (boatman) and Priscilla (Duffin)
        138

Farmer:
    family 316
    Rob. (boatman) 225, 239n.*
    Thos. (victualler) 225, 238, 363;
        and (1) Rachel (Latham) 210; and
        (2) Ann (Latham) 371, 372
Farr, Wm. (fisherman) 126

Faulkner:
    J.J. 288, 335
    John (boatman) and Mary 368
Feild:
    Jas.(boatman) and Mary (Bonner alias
        Pitts) 99, 124
    Thos. 99, 125
    nuper Cook, Wm. (fisherman) 124
Fell, Bishop 114
'Filthy Lucre' 211
Finch:
    Edw. (fisherman) 169
    Thos. and Rebecca (Crawford) 169
Fishe, Thos. 3, 126
Fisher:
    family 222, 316
    Edw. (boatman) and Phoebe (Gibbons)
        321
    Thos. 224
    Wm. (I) (boatman) and Maria
        (Beesley) 221, 223-4
    Wm. (II) (boatman) and Eliz.
        (Collis) 221
    Wm. (victualler) and Caroline
        (Howkins) 210, 228, 238, 371
    Wm. (victualler of Oldbury) and Jane
        225
Flaxney:
    Ralph (mayor, fishmonger, chandler)
        62-5
    Ric. (chandler and fishmonger) 64
Fletcher:
    Mrs 166
    Mary 167
    Thos. (coalmerchant of Abingdon)
        359
Flory, John (fisherman of Abingdon)
    266, 359
Folly:
    John (boatman) 168
    Ric. 168
Ford, Wm. (boatman) and Sarah
    (Matthews) 221
Francis I, of France 112
Francklyn, Phil. 358
Froyle, John 47
Fuller:
    Ric. (felon) 172
    Thos. 34
Furness:
    Marg. (*see* Wodeson) 85

Wm. 85

Gambier, Capt. 215
Gardner:
    family *154-5, 254, 256*; 153-65
    Mrs* 163-4, 166, 168
    Ant. 175
    Eliz., *see* Stevens
    Eliz.*, *see* Mollineaux
    Gideon* (boatman) 160
    Hen. (bargemaster, victualler) 163-4,
        174, 267, 360, 362
    Jas. 374
    John (I) (boatman) 160; and Mary
        (Hawlings) 162-3, 356, 358-9
    John (II) (bargemaster) and Mary (II)
        162-4
    John (III) 163
    John, son of Wm. (III) 161, 356
    Marg., *see* Crawford
    Mary, *see* Crawford
    Rebecca, *see* Sellwood
    Rebecca 162
    Ric. (boatman) 78, 162
    Thos. (boatmaster) 78, 159; and
        Rebecca (Hicks) 160-2, 164, 175,
        352, 355, 358
    Wm. (I) (boatmaster) 78, 95, 159*, 161,
        357, 358; and Marg. (? Pemerton)
        160
    Wm. (II) (boatmaster) and Ann
        (Richardson) 160-1, 355, 356
    Wm. (III) and Ann (Thomas) 161
    Wm. (IV) (boatman) and Christian
        (Wells) 162, 164, 355, 358-9
Gibbons:
    family *320*; 223-4, 342-3
    Daniel (boatman) 318-19, 321
    Fanny (*see* Humphries) 321, 343
    Joseph (boatman) and Charlotte
        (Rogers) 321
    Leonard (boatman) 321
    Phoebe*, *see* Fisher
    Samuel (boatman) and Mary (Smith)
        220-3
    Sophia, *see* Seymour
    Wm. (boatman, victualler, china
        merchant) and Martha 221
Gibbs, Olive (Cox) 336
Giddins, John (boatman) and family 373
Giles, Wm. (boatman, victualler) and

Joan (Hooper) 139
Gillett & Tawney (bankers) 152-3
Glover, Joseph (boatman) and Mary
    369-70, 373
Goode, Ric. 91
Gough, Mr (lawyer) 297
Grain, — (bargemaster) 192
Grant:
    Edw. 79
    Jas. (boatman) and Louisa 221
Graves, Rob. 75, 102
Green, J. R. 175
Griffin, Rog. 101
Gunn, Eliz. (*see* Bossom) 268
Gunter, Ric. (mayor, fishmonger, brewer)
    59, 62

Hadfield, Chas. 304
Hall:
    family 146
    Mr and Mrs S. C. 4
    Wm. 79
Hambridge, family 342-3
Hand alias St Peter, Peter (boatman) 201
Hands:
    Eliz., *see* Beesley
    Thirza 345
    Thos. (bargemaster, fisherman) 258,
        355-6, 369
    Thos. (boatman) and Hannah 221
    wid. 357-9
    Wm. (fisherman) 142, 359-60, 362
    Wm.* and Grace (Tawney) 140
Harcourt:
    Earl 173, 175
    Mr 295
Hardway:
    Ann 359
    John 359
    Sophia 359
Hart:
    John and Eliz. (Tawney) 141
    John (fisherman) 141
    Joseph 141
    Ric. (fisherman) 175
Hawkins, Hubert (wharfinger) and
    Florence (Beesley) 336
Hawlings, Mary, *see* Gardner
Hearne, Thos. 3, 73, 83, 128, 158
Heavisides, M. D., *see* Hill, Matthew
    Davenport

Henry VIII 9, 35, 112
Hester, G. P. (town clerk) 283, 288-91, 295
Hickis, John (fisherman) 89
Hickman:
    David 213
    Wm. Ashley (victualler) and Martha
        (Pacey) 213
Hicks:
    family *88*; 82, 89-95
    Ann, *see* Cooke
    Anne, widow of Thos. 92-3
    Denis or Dionysius (fisherman) 53,
        63, 65, 76-8, 86, 89, 115
    Hen. (waterman) (*see also* Hicks alias
        Pitts) 93, 100
    Isabell, *see* Whistler
    Joseph* (mason) 161
    Katharine* 100
    Marg., *see* Wright
    Mary* 94
    Rebecca*, *see* Gardner
    Thos. (fisherman) 78, 90-3, 124, 161
    Wm. 90
Hicks alias Pitts, Hen. (waterman) and
    family 137-8
Higgins, Ralph (boatman) and Esther 221
Higginson, John (boatman) and Anne 221
Hill, Matthew Davenport 6-8, 13
Hoby, Mr 171
Holland, Ward & Co. (coalmerchants) 203
Hollingshead, John 5, 9, 200, 207
Holmes, John (boatman) and Priscilla 368
Hooper:
    John (boatman) and Eliz. 220-1, 223,
        374*
    Joane *see* Duffin
    Thos. (boatman) and Eliz. 221
Hopkins, Samuel (coalmerchant) 215-16
Hoskins, W. G. 285
House (Howse):
    Adam (miller) 124
    Geo. (boatman) 159
    John (boatman) 116, 123-5
    Thos. (boatman) 159
    Wm. (fisherman) 124
Howkins:
    family *236*; 4, 239
    Caroline, widow of Wm. (boatman),
        (victualler) (Collier, *see* Fisher)
        210, 221, 239, 243, 245, 255, 371
    John (boatman) 239, 243; and Sarah

(Ashley) 221, 369
John (victualler) 210
John (boatman) and Mary (Corbey)
  243, 245, 318, 354-5
Wm. (boatman) 221, 255
Wm. (victualler) 210, 239, 363; and
  Susan 311
Humphries:
  family 340-3
  Ann (Beesley) 243, 245, 368
  Rob. 245, 341n.
  Samuel (boatman) and Fanny
    (Gibbons) 245, 321, 340-1n.
  Wm. (boatman) 340n.
  Wm. (boatman) and Mary Ann
    (Humphries) 340n.
Hunt:
  Sheriff 287
  Thos. (boatman) and Mary (Spindler)
    369
Hutchinson:
  Ralph and Mary (Wodeson) 87
  Thos. 87

Inge, Dean 333
Irish, Ald. Edm. 64
Irving, Edw. 215

Jacobson, Dr 313-14
James:
  Geo. (boatman) 342-3
  Jack (boatman) 337, 339-42
Jarrett, family (boat-builders of
  Abingdon) 147-8
Jessopp, Wm. (engineer) 119
Jessoppe, Jas. (millwright), son of Thos.
  118-19
Johnson, Benj. (fisherman) 174
Jones:
  Rev. John (Tegid) (vicar of
    St Thomas's) 217
  May (Beesley) 336
Joules, Francis (canal carrier) 192
Joy, W. (antiquarian) 281
Judd, Stephen (boatman) and Ann 223, 373
Justice:
  Mrs 374
  Ann 374
  John (boatman) and Ann 220-1, 223,
    373-4
  Ric. (lock-keeper) 117

Keats, Moses 359
Kempster, Chris. (stonemason) 131
Kendall, Ant. (fellmonger) 146-7
Kensall:
  John (boatman) 145-6
  Martha and Wm. 145
Kenwright, Martha 145
King:
  Edw. (parish clerk) 34
  Rob., Bishop of Oxford 97
Kirtland Chas. (boatman) and family 373

Lamsden:
  family 340-3
  Hannah, see Skinner, Beauchamp
  Joseph 342
  Stephen (boatman) and Jane Julia
    (Beesley) 258, 318
Lant, Bartholomew 64
Laslett, Peter 11, 34
Latham:
  Ann, see Farmer
  Francis (victualler) 210
  Rachel, see Farmer
Lea, Geo. (boatman) and Susannah
  (Richardson) 161, 355-7
Lee, Mary, see (Beesley)
Leland, John 52
Leonardo da Vinci 112
Leverett, Rob. (boatman) and Mary
  (Mires) 221
Levi, Lawrence 208
Lewis:
  family 316
  Joseph (boatman) and Jane (Beesley)
    221, 223-4, 238, 372
  Mary Ann, see Ashley
  Ric. (boatman of Stoke) 224
  Sam. (boatman) 360; and Mary
    (Curtis) 221
  Wm. and Mary Anne (Bossom) 287
Lincoln, Bishop of 48
Linebaugh, Peter 172
Lipscombe, Wm. 290
Lloyd:
  Ann 119
  Griffith 114, 118
Loader.
  Deborah 79
  Mary, see Treacher
  Thos. (brewer) 79, 145, 150

Lockhart, J. I. 79
Lovelock, family (shopkeepers to canal
    boatmen) 339
Lowe, Mrs J. (Beesley) 333, 335, 345
Luckett, — 303-4
Luker, Ann (victualler) 211

Macfarlane, Alan 12-13
MacLean, Donald (M.P. for Oxford) 278
Mailing:
    Eliz. (Bossom) 268
    Sam. (boatman) and Eliz. (Barton) 369
Maley, Mr (lawyer) 284
Mallynson, Thos. 85
Manning, Serjeant 289, 295
Marlborough, Duke of 174, 187
Marriner, Wm. 352
Marshall:
    Matt. (brewer) 361
    Wm. (boatman) and Ann 221
Massarella, Mrs M. (Cox) 332-4
Mathews:
    Francis (pamphleteer) 184
    John (boatman) and Sarah (Hands)
    221
Mathias, Peter 146, 149
Maxwell alias Redman, John (boatman)
    201
May, Elianor, see Clarke, Chappell
Mayhew, Hen. 7, 208
Messer:
    Gilbert le 111
    Walter le 111
Midwinter, Toby (boatman) and Maria
    371,
Mogridge, Geo. (Jeremy Jaunt) 5-7, 199
Mollineaux (Molyners):
    family 256; 67-8
    Mrs 166
    Adam (labourer) and Eliz. (Gardner)
    166, 196
    Jane or Ann 196
    John (lock-keeper) 117
    John 174-5
Monmouth, Duke of 171
Montagues, the 305
Morrell:
    family 152-3, 329
    Jas. (brewer) and Jane (Wharton,
        granddaughter of Rob. Tawney)
        150

Jas. jun. (brewer) 362-3
    M. and J. 362
Mounson, Rob. 97n., 115; and Joan
    (Wodeson) 85-6
Myzzell, Ric. 174

Namier, Sir Lewis 24
Naylor, L. G. R. 149
Neville:
    — 223-4
    Sampson (boat-owner) 224
    Wm. (carter) and family 372
New, Ric. (boatman) and Mary 370
Newman:
    Cardinal 216
    Rob. 275
    Wm. 274-5
Nicholls (Nichols, Nicholes):
    John (butcher) 161, 356
    Wm., sen. (yeoman) 160
    Wm., jun. 160
Noble, John (of Denton Court) and Anne
    (Bonner alias Pitts) 99
Norgrove, Ann 358
Nuffield, Lord 326

Oili:
    Rob. de (I) 2
    Rob. de (II) 38, 43, 326
Orum, Nic. (fishmonger) 66
Owen, Dr Geo. (physician) 51, 97
Owen (Owens):
    John (weir-keeper) 63-4, 117
    Thos. 63
Owens alias Stour, Thos. 201

Pacey:
    Jas. (victualler) 213
    Martha, see Hickman
Painter, Nic. (fellmonger) 126
Paish:
    Ann (boatman's wife) 221, 368
    John (boatman) 221, 355, 368
Parker, John 356
Parsons, John 360
Payne:
    Jas. 168
    Wm. 95
Peake, Serjeant 272
Pebody, Eliz. (Lewis) 287
Peirse (Pers, Perse):
    John 64

John, Archbishop of York 68
Thos. 68
Pemberton (Pemerton):
    family 102-3, 125
    Alice 159
    Chas. (bargeman) 159
    Marg. 159-60
    Thos. (boatman) 124, 126, 168, 351
    Walt. 124
    Wm. (boatman) 159
Petty, Geo. 356
Perry, Ric. 228
Philip, I. G. 127
Phillips, Alf. Hen. (victualler) 210
Phipkin, Mr 325
Pickering alias Shiner, Wm. (boatman) 201
Pike, John 355
Pitts:
    family 98
    Art. (I) 98
    Art. (II) 98
    Marg. 98, 117
    Phillip 98
    Walt. 53, 76
    alias Bonner, Joane 78
    alias Hicks, family (see also Hicks) 137, 138
Polley, Thos. 203
Pope, Alexander 2
Potter:
    family 159
    Ald. 128
    Geo. 161, 356-7
    Mary 356
Powell, Edm. 97
Pratt, Wm. (boatman) and Mary 369
Preedy (Priddy), Jas. (boatman) and Ann (Bridgewater) 221
Price:
    family 225
    Edw. (bargeman) 159
    John (boatman) and Hannah (Ioins) 221, 224
    Ric. 228
    Thos. (boatowner, of Shirleywich) 224
    Wm. and Rachel (Farmer) 224
Prickett:
    family 145
    Marg. 152

Prince, Dan. 361
Purdue John 355
Pusey, E. B. 216-17, 313
Pye, John (mayor, fishmonger) 59, 62

Queen Mother, the 44, 49

Radbourne, Wm. (boatman) and Mary or Frances 221
Redman, John (victualler) 210; and Mary (Ashley) 239, 241
Richardson:
    Ann (see Gardner) 161, 356
    Ralph 161, 356
    Susannah (boat builder's (see also Lea) 161, 356
Roberts, John (bargeman) 159
Roberson, — 274
Robinson (Robynson):
    Mr 166
    Cath. 356, 358
    Edm. 53
    Eliz. 144
    Francis (plumber) 78, 82
    Ric. 91-2
    Rob. (plumber) 78, 82
    Wm.* (bargeman) 159
    Wm. and Rebecca Crawford 166
    Wm. (college servant) and Martha 356
Rogers:
    Charlotte see Gibbons
    J. E. T. 109-10
Rolt, L. T. C. 343
Rose, Francis (fisherman) 78
Round, family (coalmerchants, boatmen) 224
Rowe, Mr 117
Rudge, family (fisherman) 102
Russell, Lord John 277, 279, 282

Sadler, Ald. 282, 288
St Thomas à Becket 35
Salter, H. E. 43, 110, 351
Samuel, Raphael 331
Saunders, Alfred 3478
Saxton, Wm. 275
Sclavonians, King of the 281
Seale, Stephen 358
Sellwood, John 174-5; and Rebecca (Gardner) 355
Seymour, John (boatman) and Sophia

(Gibbons) 221-3, 321
Shepherd, Joseph (boatman) and
    Christian 221
Sherwood:
    Mr (brewer's agent) 311
    W. E. 304-5, 329
Shillingworth, family (*see also* Chilling-
    worth) 163-4
Simpson:
    wid. 363
    Jas. 228
    Joseph 225; and Ellen (Bossom)
        228, 370
Sjoberg, Gideon 10
Skinner:
    family *317*; 318, 342
    Abel (boatman) 318, 321
    Betsey, *see* Gibbons
    Harriet, *see* Gibbons
    Hannah, *see* Lamsden, Beauchamp
    Joseph (boatman) 344
    Samuel (boatman, labourer) 318
Smith:
    Geo. (publicist, of Coalville) 314-16
    Geo. Chas. (missionary to seamen
        and boatmen) 214-15, 217-18
    John, Esq. 58
    Ric. 359
    Thos. (fisherman and boatman) 124-5
    Sir Thos. 112
Spencer, Lord Rob. 174
Spindelow (Spindlove):
    Edw. (fisherman) 79, 95, 103
    Ric. (cook) 103, 352
    Thos. (fisherman) 79, 95, 103
Spindler:
    family 241
    F. G. 242
    Mary, *see* Hunt
    Samuel (boatman, victualler) 210,
        241
    T. H. (victualler) 210, 242
    Wm. (boatman, bargeman) and Anne
        or Anne Maria (Beesley) 221, 241,
        252, 369
Stacey, Francis (agent of the Waterworks,
    Folly Bridge) 157
Stamp, L. Dudley 285
Steane:
    Rev. Edw. 355
    Samuel 252, 266

Thos. 354-5
Stevens:
    Eliz. 95, 160, 166
    Hen. 160, 162
Stewart (Stuart), wid. 223-4, 373
Stone, Jonius 118
Stow, John 11
Strange, Nic. (fisherman, boatman) 124
Streak, Chas. (boatman) and Avis 221
Stroudley, Jas. (cabinet-maker) 303-4,
    363
Stumpe, Wm. 52

Talboys, D. A. 282
Tappenden, Mr (hoyman) 128
Target, Harry 53
Tawney:
    family *142-3*; 139-53
    Rev. Bradnam 149
    C. H. 152
    Edw. (bargemaster), son of Edw.
        144-5
    Edw. (boatmaster), son of Nic., and
        Eliz. *see also* Clarke) 143
    Edw. (brewer, mayor), son of Ric. 79,
        149, 151-2
    Eliz., daughter of Rob. 145
    Eliz., *see* Hart
    Grace, *see* Hands
    Hen., son of Edw. (bargemaster)
        144-5; and Amey (Jarrett) 147- 8
    Hen. (banker), son of Ric., canal
        agent 152
    Hen., son of Rob., and Eliz.
        (Treacher) 151
    Joan (Brookings) 140
    John (currier) 139
    John, son of Edw. 141
    Marg. *see* Prickett
    R. H. (historian) 152
    Ric. (bargemaster, brewer, mayor) son
        of Edw. 144-5, 148-50
    Sir Ric. (brewer, mayor) 149, 151,
        329
    Ric. (canal agent) 152-3
    Rob. (bargemaster), son of Edw. 144,
        145, 148; and Jane (Tawney) 149-50
    Rob. (watchmaker), son of Rob. 152
    Wm.* 125, 142
    Wm. (I) (weelmaker) 139
    Wm. (II) (boatmaster) 139

Wm. (III) (boatmaster) 164
Taunt, H. W. (photographer, author) 305
Taunton, Daniel 79
Taylor:
  John (maltster, bargemaster, of E.
    Anglia) 149
  John (water poet) 184
  John (tobacco-pipe maker) 361
  John (boatman) and Hannah (Fisher)
    370
  Thos. (boatman) and Edith 221, 370
Terrill (Tirrell):
  Hen. 95
  John 95
  Jone (Backester) 95
  Marie 95
  Nic. 160
  Wm. (fisherman) 78, 95, 160
  Wm., son of Wm. 95
  Wm.* 161, 357
Thacker, Fred. S. 110, 123
Thame, Lord William of 113
Thomas alias Plummer, Wm. (plumber)
  85-6n., 97
Tolley, Emily (Howkins), (boatman's
  wife) 369
Tomkins family of Abingdon (maltsters,
  bargemasters, bankers) 149; 149-50
Towseye, Thos. 53
Treacher:
  Eliz., see Tawney
  John (mayor, brewer), 148; and Mary
    (Loader) 79, 150
  Sir John (mayor, brewer) 79, 151
  Rev. Thos. 117
Tromp, Von, of the Upper Thames, see
  Eldridge, Capt.
Tubb, John 275
Tustin:
  family 333
  A. 345
  Aubrey 344
  Florence 344
Tysdale, Thos. (lock-keeper) 117

Venables, Wm. (waterbailiff) 295
Vivers, Rev. John and Dinah 362
Vluuius (fisherman) 43

Wakelin, Wm. (victualler) 356
Walker:
  Edm. 175

Thos. (town clerk) 150
Walter, John 124
Ward:
  family (coalmerchants) 203
  Geo. 290
  Hen. (coalmerchant) 216, 232
  J. R. 188
  Wm. (coalmerchant) 216, 222, 232,
    322-4
Watson:
  Jas. (boatman) and Eliz. 368-9
  Joseph (boatman) and Susannah 221
Webb:
  H. L. 335
  John 361
West, Thos. (merchant, barge-owner) 113
Westwood, Isaac (boatman) and Marg.
  221
Wetherell, Sir Chas. 278
Wharton, Jane, see Morrell
Whistler:
  Humphrey (baker, mayor) and Isabell
    (Hicks) 93-4
  Ralph 93
White, Jas. (timber merchant, barge-owner)
  268-9, 362; and Mary Bossom) 268
Whitehouse, Jeremiah 353-5
Whiteley, Thos. 47-9
Whitelock, Bulstrode 171
Wickson, Thos. (victualler) 357
Widdowes, Thos. (hempdresser) 99
Wilkinson:
  Kath. 59
  Wm. (apprentice-fishmonger) 59
Willan, T. S. 9
William son of Andrew (ship-owner)
  108
Williams:
  Sir John (see also Thame, Lord
    Williams of) 52, 97
  Ric. (waterbailiff) 64-5
  Ald. (waterbailiff) 65
Willis:
  family 114-15
  Francis, Pres. St John's 87; and Kath.
    (Wodeson) 115
  John (chapter clerk) 114
  Thos. (physician) 114
Wilson, Ric. (brewer) 78
Winkle, Thos. (smith) 61
Winslow, Thos. (victualler) 361

Wodeson:
   family *84*; 83-7, 89
   Alexander 85-6
   Joane, *see* Mounson
   John 86-7, 126; and Marg. (Furness)
      85
   Mary, *see* Hutchinson
   Nic. 83-7; and Kath. (*see also* Willis)
      86-7
   Thos. 85-7
Wolsey, Thos. 51
Wood, Ant. 3
Woodforde, Jas. 3, 149, 174
Woodley:
   Eliz., *see* Bonner alias Pitts
   Wm. 99n.
Woodward, Ann 374
Woolly, Rob. 113
Wren, Chris. 131

Wright:
   Ald., *see* Wm., below
   John (tailor) and (1) Marg. (Hicks)
      78, 94; and (2) Anne (*see* Broade
      and Bowell) 94
   Lady 172
   Martin (mayor) 94
   Wm. (mayor, Recorder) 91-2, 171-2
Wrigley, E. A. 12, 16-18
Wyatt:
   Messrs., bargemasters, Folly Bridge 192
   Wm. (waterbailiff) 290

Yeatman, Mark (stonemason) 246
Yonge (Young, Younge):
   Mic. 59
   Ric. (rippier) 59, 61
   Rob. (fishmonger) 58
   Thos. 59

2. GENERAL INDEX

Abingdon 29, 35, 48, 52, 100, 108, 113,
      116, 121, 129, 130-1, 138-9, 170,
      172, 189, 192, 230, 294, 297, 321
   lock, 117
Adventures of Mr. Verdant Green 211
advertisements 187
Agas, Ralph, map by 30, 41, 50, 54, 76
alienation 206, 214, 301, 313-14, 340-1
allotments 270
amateurs, rowing 300
American War of Independence 185
Amiens, Peace of 198
anatomists 172-4
angling 288-9, 335
apprenticeships:
   fishermens' 56, 63, 65
   weelers and net knitters' 65
Artificers, Statute of 148

Ashburton, N.Z. 347
Aston, nr. Bampton 111
Atherstone 185-6
Aynho 187

Bablock Hythe 116, 167-8
Back Stream *45*; 41, 42, 48, 295
Badcock, Benj., survey of 222-3 269,
      372-4
Bagley Woods 33, 332
bailiffs 61, 63-5
Bampton 105, 111
Banbury 186
   Fair 340
   New Bank 152
bankruptcies 197-8, 265-6, 268
baptisms 167, 324
   multiple 341

barbers 71, 93, 100, 335
bargeman 2, 14-15, 23, 105, 123-4,
    170-6, 219, 259-61, 306
  and associated trades 15, 145-9
  and work 129-35, 145-6
  and family 23, 136, 138-9, 153, 156
    (*see also* boatmen, family)
barges 105n., 130, 188-9, 195 (*see also*
    boats)
Bear Key, London 128
Beaumont St. 1
bedells 61, 83-7
Bell's Sporting Life 304
Berkshire 107
  county boundary 33, 275
Binsey 38, 124-5, 149, 151, 284
Birmingham 223-4
Black Country 13n., 205-6, 218, 225
Black Death 2, 36
Blenheim Park 268, 354
boat 105n.
  boatmasters 150 (*see also* bargemen
    and barges)
Boat and Barge Registers 219, 224
Boat Races 299, 301
boats and barges:
  Competition 241
  King's Arms 144
  Pattern 197
  Sovereign 144
  William & Mary 197
Bodleian Library 10-11
Boffins, bakers 338
Bookbinders Bridge 42, 48
Botley 32, 42
  causeway 179
Boveney 135
bow-halers, boat-halers, hirelings, towers
    108, 135-6, 167-8, 364
Braunston 192, 194, 209
Bray 144
Brentford 192
Brewers (*see also* Morrell and Hall
    families)
  Morrells 48-9
  Swan 146
bribery 24, 175-6
bridges, London 299
Broadway 269
bucks 68
Bullstake, Bullstock Stream 45, 54n., 111,

    158, 189-90
Burcot 73, 113, 117, 120
Burford 131
buses 327
bye-employment 69-70, 331

C. & A. Modes 129
Cambridge 98
canals (*see also under the names of
    particular canals*)
  boatmen *219, 221, 233*; 5-9, 15,
    199-205, 219, 231-4, 275, 308-9,
    314-15, 341
  boats 199-205, 321-4, 338
  Boats' Act 315-16
  boatwomen 202, 235-7, 242-7
  chapels 9, 214-18, 232, 313, 324
  communities, villages (*see also*
    Thrupp, Jericho, Braunston) *319,
    342*; 9, 200-2, 235, 242-3, 245,
    259, 261, 306, 322
  decoration 5, 199-200, 307
  development *184*; 183-95
  investment 187-9, 194, 307-8
  origins *223*; 218-30, 238
  wharf, Oxford 182, 195-6, 199, 326
  work 202-6, 247
Cardinal College 51
Carfax 107
cars 33, 326-7, 345-6
Cassington 113
Castle, Oxford *56*; 41, 43, 199, 328
  moat of 126, 180
  Mill *41, 45*; 31, 37-47, 49-51, 53,
    115, 326, 328
  stream 1, 41-2, 44-8, 182, 346
Catholic Apostolic Church 215-16
Catte St. 11
causal connections 228
Caversham 113, 192
Census 9, 18, 229-33, 243-53, 331,
    368-74
chamberlains 61, 64
chandlers 59, 62, 65-6
Chandos clause 277
charters, ancient 286, 297
Cherwell River 29, 61
Chipping Norton 130, 173
Chipstead 60
choir boys 334
cholera 214

Christ Church 51, 127
    leases *78-9*; 9, 52-4, 76-82, 87, 89,
        91, 126, 141, 144, 162, 330, 351
Church, the 25, 310-13
Church Pastoral Aid Society 217
Cirencester 61
City, *see* Oxford
Civil War 73, 127
Clarendon Press 304
Clayworth 34
cleanliness 334, 341
clergy, work patterns of 206
cloth-making 36, 52
coal 186-7, 190
    merchants 203-4, 207-8, 266, 337
coastal trade 191-2
College Servants, the 304
collieries (*see also* Atherstone, Park
    End) 185-6, 206
commons (*see also* Port Meadow) 62,
    281-5, 289, 291
Cooper's Marmalade Factory 333
copyhold 77
corn 190, 230, 266
cost-bearer 133-4
Cotswolds 235
Coventry Canal 181, 184-7
Cowmede 63
Cricklade 46, 118
Crimean War 313
Cripley 91-2, 94
Crowley & Co., canal carriers 203, 231
Culham 113, 135-6, 139, 144, 321

disenfranchisement 282, 287
Dissolution 9, 51-2, 75
Domesday Book 43
Dorchester 230
'down the water' 302
Duke's Cut 187, 316
Dutton's Holdings 91, 99

Edgehill 127
elections 4, 19, 24, 171, 331
employment 195, 331-4
Enslow Bridge 187
Eton 298
evangelicals 215
executions 172-4, 328
Exeter College 174
Eynsham 211, 316

Falcon, the 304
family 22-6, 70-1, 76, 129-30, 156, 159,
    166-7, 235-6, 242-58, 260-1,
    264-5, 318
    reconstitution 12, 17-18, 268
farmers 66-7, 70-1
fasting 55, 57-8, 73, 102
fee-farm 36-7
Ferry Hinksey 29, 48
feud 24, 258, 264-5, 269-73, 286-7,
    302-4
Fifield 124, 143
fish 57-8, 261
fisheries (*see also* Free Waters)
    leases of 64-7, 70, 87, 91, 110
    private 293, 295, 297
fishermen 2, 9-10, 22-3, 61-104, 115,
    123-4, 129-30, 132, 136, 159, 161,
    249-59, 261, 264, 266, 269, 273,
    288, 302, 305, 334-5, 346
    associated trades 67-8, 71
    work and bye-employments of 69-70
Fisher Row *159, 181-2, 234, 264*; 1-5,
    18-20, 24-5, 39-40, 42, 53, 68, 76,
    105, 107, 112, 159, 181-2, 234,
    264, 302
    Lower *78*; 79-104, 124-5, 141, 145,
        148, 151-2, 160, 162, 213, 222,
        229, 231-2, 269-705 273,
        325-7, 330-1
    Middle *212*; 125-6, 159, 166-7, 179,
        196-8, 211, 213, 222-3, 229, 232,
        234, 236, 238-41, 248, 273, 316,
        325-7, 330-1, 372-4
    Upper *253, 254, 352, 353*; 125-8,
        140, 159-60, 164, 166-7, 197-8,
        211, 213, 222-3, 231-2, 234, 236,
        245, 252-8, 266, 268-9, 273, 305,
        326, 330-1, 351-63, 368-71
    wharf 3, 85-7, 105, 110-11,
        115-16, 123, 127, 157-8, 163,
        361-3, 370-1
fishmongers (*see also* chandlers) 56-66, 86n.
fish ponds 101
Flam, the (*see* Ham, the) 335
Foleshill 181, 241, 321
Folly Bridge Wharf 105, 107, 110,
    122-3, 127-9, 134, 139, 157-9, 298,
    301, 306-7
Foreign Waters 61, 64
Fradley 185

Framilode 188
franchise, the 19, 260, 276, 279
Franchises, riding the 280-1
freemen:
    foreign 67, 72, 102
    rights of (*see also* franchise,
        Free Waters, Port Meadow) 62-4,
        270, 272-3, 278-9, 281, 283-52,
        297
Free Waters: *349*; 62, 266, 269, 279-83,
    288-91, 293, 296-7, 248-50
    bye-laws 57, 69, 279, 281-2, 287-93,
    295, 296
        contraventions of 273, 283, 286-7,
        289-90, 295-8
Friars' Wharf 215
Frome, River 184
funerals 300, 312

Gainsborough 192
goal 199, 276
Gas Works, the 304
George III 189
Gloucester 9, 52, 60
Gloucester College 31
Gloucester Green 327
Godstow 61, 64, 103, 170, 280-1, 303
Goring 93
Grand Junction Canal 192, 194, 203, 321
Grandpont (*see also* Folly Bridge) 107
Great Western Railway 230, 288, 306
Grimbly Hughes, grocer 338

halers, *see* bow-halers
Hall's Brewery 211, 329
Ham, the (*see also* Flam, the) 266-7,
    272-3, 254
Hannington, the 304
Harecastle 192
Harwich 24
Hastings 60
Headington Quarry 331
Hedsor 135
Hell's Angels 200
hemp-dressing 71
Henley 109, 113, 301-2
Heyford 130, 187
Hinkseys, the 124 (*see also* Ferry Hinksey)
hirelings, *see* bow-halers
Hogacre Ditch 28
horsemills 45, 48
horse stations 203

houseboats 305
housekeeping 334
Hundred Rolls 38
Hythe Bridge 3, 42, 182
    Street *212*; 42, 213, 222-3, 326
    Wharf 83, 85, 87, 105, 110-11,
        115-16, 125, 157-8, 361-3, 370-1

identification, problems of (*see also*
    names, nicknames) 267-8
Iffley 73, 98, 99
impressment, press-gangs 175-6, 204
Industrial Revolution 179, 194-5
infant mortality 264
Inglesham 181
inventories:
    Bibles 91, 146
    boats 71, 92, 86, 97n., 99 (*bis*), 101,
        125
    glass 90-1
    sheets 91-2, 101

Jericho 32, 309
Jesus College 172
Jews 36
Jude the Obscure 195
Junctions, Canal: *see* Abingdon,
    Braunston, Fradley, Inglesham, Long-
    ford, Napton, Oxford, Preston, Brook,
    Reading, Swindon, Wilden Ferry
Juxon Street Wharf 326

Kempsford 189
Kennington 117
Kidlington 239-40, 316, 332
King & Co. 324
King Henry VIII College 51
Kyndelweir *45*; 48

labour exchange 332
Lake District 235
Lambard's Land 110
Lasher, The *45*; 41-2, 47. 50, 53-4, 68,
    102-3, 126, 169, 197, 266, 270, 326
Lea, navigation of the 113n.
Lechlade 134, 143, 170, 184, 246
leeches 71
Lent, *see* fasting
Lincoln College 128, 294
lobster pots 333
Lock, The 41-50, 53, 68, 76, 81-2, 85,
    97, 102, 126, 181, 269, 346
locks (*see also* The Lasher, The Lock,

weirs) 41, 45; 41-51, 67-8, 120
Abingdon 117, 192
Benson 192
Caversham 113, 192
Culham 139
Day's 135
flash 132-3, 202
Iffley 117
Isis (Louse) 182
Louse, see Isis
Medley 270, 282
Nuneham Courteney 117
Oseney 45; 43, 52
pound (turnpikes) 106, 120, 122-3,
  132-4
Rewley 41, 45; 42-4, 47, 49-50, 53
Sandford 117
Wallingford 192
Whitchurch 192
Loggan, David, map of 3; 42, 50
London 58-60, 105, 117, 128, 144, 181,
  183, 188-9, 192, 194, 197, 293
London and Western Canal 192
Longford 9, 186, 321
Long Wittenham 63

Magdalen Bridge 61
Maidenhead 116
Manchester 192
Mapledurham 134-5
Marlow 135, 171-2
Marriage 224-5, 229, 235, 238, 310, 319,
  340-1
matriculands, 72; 72-3
matrilineal relationships 235, 255, 264
matrilocal households 235-6, 242-3,
  245-9, 252
Mayor of Oxford, see Oxford, Mayor of
Medley 124, 190, 264
Meedlemelle 109
Meeting House, Presbyterian 147
Melksham 239
Mercia 29
Mersey 185
Merton 36, 110
Midi, Canal du 112
Mileways Act 151
millers 67-8, 71, 75, 132-3, 202, 270
mills (see also weirs, and under the names
  of mills) 41; 40-1,107-8, 347-8
soke of 37

missions, see under canal boatmen and
  seamen's missions
Morrell's Brewery 48, 329-30
Morris Motors, the 304
Mothercare 129
motor car, the 325, 345-6
Municipal Corporations' Act 271, 277-8,
  281, 286, 291, 297
Murston 128

names, unambiguous (see also nicknames;
  identification, problems of) 16
Napton 186
Naval and Military Bible Society 215
naval ship-building 128
navvies 200, 231, 312, 313
Neptune, the 304
net knitters 63, 65
nets 68-9, 71, 92, 101, 267, 290, 292, 295
Newbridge 130
Newgate 151
New Road 42
nicknames (see also names, unambiguous;
  identification, problems of) 13-14,
  200-1
Nimesfield 60
Nonconformity 145-7, 153
Northern Ireland 265
Northmoor 102, 140, 167-8, 170
North Wilts. Canal 190
Nuffield College 182, 326
'Number Ones' 203-4
Nuneham Courtney 117
Nurser Bros., boatbuilders 323

occupational communities 2, 9-13
occupation and family, see family
occupations, inherited 18, 22, 24
  changing status of 67-8, 71, 83
Oseney Abbey 1, 2, 9, 31, 35, 38-40,
  43-54, 59, 76, 80-1, 85, 124, 126,
  346
  Mill 45; 38-9, 43-4, 49-53, 133
  Stream 158, 190
  Town 33
osiers, osier works 70, 266, 332-3, 335
outrides 337
Oxford 1, 4, 9, 11, 20, 29, 35-8, 44, 46-7,
  50-1, 55-61, 72-3, 92, 105, 107-15,
  121-2, 127-9, 136, 153, 163, 168,
  170-6, 181-2, 194-5, 203, 215, 230,

260-1, 274, 276-8, 283-6, 310, 341
Canal Boat Register 322
Cathedral 51
Council 116-18, 270-3, 276, 278-81,
   288-9, 294, 297
   leases 126, 351-63
   City Quarter Session 170, 175
   Mayor of 271, 279-81, 295
     v. Thos. Beesley, 291
   Survey of 163, 166
Oxford Boat Co. 197
Oxford-Burcot Commission (for their
   wharf see Folly Bridge Wharf)
   120-1, 123-4, 128, 138, 171
Oxford Canal 151-2, 179, 181-92, 194-7,
   203-4, 218, 229-31, 241, 261, 306,
   316, 321-3, 326, 346
   northern section 194

Pacey's Bridge 42, 180-1, 213, 325
Pangbourne 240
parishes, Oxford City 32
   St Aldates (see also Folly Bridge,
     Grandpont) 123, 161
   St Barnabas 32, 216, 309
   St Ebbe 1, 30, 195, 215-16, 277
   St Frideswide 32
   St Giles 30
   St Mary Magdalen 30, 213
   St Nicholas (see also St Thomas) 35
   St Paul 32, 309
   St Peter le Bailey 30
   St Thomas 1, 32-5, 51, 75-6, 105,
     123-4, 127, 161, 168-9, 179-83,
     194-5, 216-17, 222, 231-2, 298-9,
     302, 308-9, 311-12, 327
     registers of 140, 216-17, 219-22,
      232-3, 298-9, 309-10, 318-19,
      324, 340-1
Park End:
   Colliery 213
   Street 42, 213
   Wharf 213, 240
paupers 276
pawnships 209
Peasants' Revolt 49, 288
Phil and Jim, the 304
Pickfords, canal carriers 200, 203, 225, 231
pleasure boating 298-306, 336
police 279, 294, 296, 329
poll tax 76

Pompeii 233
Pontypool 240
poor, setting on work 51-3
poor-rate 147
population, St Thomas's parish (see also
   hundred rolls, subsidies, poll tax,
   census Oxford parishes, registers of
   St Thomas's) 193; 36, 72-3, 126,
   194-5
   of its boatmen 219, 231-5
Port Meadow (see also commons, Free
   Waters) 32, 35, 61, 70,125, 182,
   270-1, 273, 278-81, 283-5
   Stream 296
Potteries, the 192
Preachers Brothers, Prior of the 89
Presbyterian Meeting House, see
   Meeting House, Presbyterian
Preston 23, 194-5
Preston Brook 9, 185
primogeniture 71, 249
'Prinses Weres' 61
publicans 175, 210-11, 213, 224-5
public houses 210; 201, 206-13, 225 9,
   236, 238-42
   functions of 207-8
   Anchor 139
   Boat Inn, Oldbury 225, 228
   Engine & Tender 230
   Fishes (see also Nag's Head) 196-7,
     210
   George & Dragon 213
   Greyhound, Longford 241
   Hollybush 181
   Nag's Head (see also Fishes,
     Navigation House) 210; 210-11,
     224-5, 238-42
   Navigation End 213, 240
   Navigation House (see also Nag's
     Head) 241
   Packet 211, 318
   Plough, Wolvercote 275
   Racers, Race Horses, Running Horses
     210; 210-13, 238-9, 241, 269, 326,
     371
   Swan, Pangbourne 240
   Turk's Head 210, 329
   Welsh Pony 211
pugilism 288
Punch 305
punt-racing 302-5, 336

Quaking Bridge 42

Radcot 111 , 143
    Bridge 105, 120, 131
railways 179, 207, 215, 229-31, 261,
        292, 298, 300, 305-7, 322, 325
    Buckinghamshire 207n., 231
    Great Western 230-1, 288, 306
    London & Northwestern 231
    stations, Oxford 1, 10, 207n., 230-1,
        327
ratting 211
Reading 108-9, 294, 297, 366-7
Reform Bill, the Great 276, 283
regattas 299, 310-2, 304
Rewley Abbey 1, 31, 35, 39, 45-6, 49, 51,
        54, 85, 110
    Abbot of 50
    leases 87, 91
    wall 39, 52-3, 85, 266-7
    watergate 39
Richmond 135
riots 20, 171, 201
rippiers 60-1
robbery 225
rowing 298-302, 304
    clubs, see Clarendon Press, College
        Servants, Falcon, Gas Works, Han-
        nington, Morris Motors, Nepture,
        Phil and Jim, Y.M.C.A.
Royal Oxford Hotel 181
rushes 284, 335
Rye 60

Sabbatarianism 215
sailors 215
St Aldate Street 107
St Frideswide's Monastery 51
St George in the Castle 31, 37
St John's College 83-4, 87, 115, 294
St Katharine's House 87
St Monday 205-6
St Saviour's, Leeds 216
St Scholastica's Day 36
St Thomas's (see also Oxford parishes)
    churchyard 174
    High Street 39, 42, 83, 231, 329
    school 217
Salisbury, diocese of 107
salt, carriage of 199, 218
Sandford 63, 73

Sapperton Tunnel 189
Scottish Church, Regent's Square 215
Seamen and Boatmen's Friend Society 311
seamen's missions 214-15
Settlement, Law of 236n.
Severn, River 185
shanties 135
Sheriff: of Oxford, the 279, 281, 286, 288,
        290, 295-6
    of Nottingham, the 286
Shire Lake (see county boundary)
Smiths, John, the superabundance of 16
Sonning 135
sources 15
Southampton 121
Staffordshire & Worcester Canal 185
Staffordshire boatmen 192
Staffordshire terriers 211
Staines 293-4
Stamford 52
Stanton Harcourt 99, 352
stone, carriage of 111
Stourbridge Fair 59
Stroud 188
Stroudwater Canal 187-8
subsidies, lay 75-6
Sunday working 206, 214-16, 232
Sutton Courteney 113, 117
Swan's Nest 42, 82
Swindon 230
Swinford Ferry 179

Terrae Filius 172
Thames, River 106 (see also Oxford-
    Burcot Commission)
    Commission, Commissioners 123,
        151, 189, 292-4
    Conservancy 293-6, 298
    course of 29-30, 107-8, 157-9,
        189-90
    navigation of 2, 35-6, 73, 108-12,
        118-20, 123, 183, 189-90, 219,
        294-5
    trade of 109-11, 113-14, 147, 153,
        159, 190-2, 196, 320-1, 240, 301
    Upper (above Oxford) 105-8, 111-12,
        119-20, 189-90, 192, 213
    villages of 111, 173
    Thames & Severn Canal 181, 183,
        187-91, 195, 261, 293
        Carrying Company 191, 195-7

Three Men in a Boat 305
Thrupp 181, 316, 318
timber, carriage of 113, 116
Times, The 315
tolls, London 117-18
'Tom and Jerry' 211
Tom Brown at Oxford 300
Tommy Shop Bridge 208n.
Tom-Rags 337
Tooley's boat-yard 343
Tories 173-4, 277
Towcester 321
towing paths 120, 134
Tractarianism 216-18, 310-11
trade, internal (*see also* Thames, trade
    of) 20, 190, 301
Trent, River 185
Trent & Mersey Canal 185-7, 192
trips 134-5, 208, 228, 364-8
truck 208-9
Tyne, River 190
Tyrrell's, butcher 338

universities 300
University, Oxford (*see also* individual
    colleges) 72; 29, 36-7, 59, 60-1,
    247, 331-5, 73, 83, 118, 120, 128,
    195, 300
    vice-chancellor of 170-1
'up the water' 302

values, industrial and pre-industrial 24-5,
    260-1

Wallingford 108-9, 113
Walton 64
war, its repercussions 73, 185-6, 191-2,
    220, 265-6, 269
Warham Bank (*see also* weir-ham, weirs)
    56; 40-3, 46-7, 53, 83, 126

Warwickshire boatmen 192
Waterbailiff, High or Thames 61-2, 65,
    69, 295
Waterbailiff(s), Waterbaileyship 61, 5,
    270, 273, 282, 287, 289, 293-6
Water Lane, Richmond 136
watermen 253, 298, 300
Water Oakley 135
Waters, Free, *see* Free Waters
Waters Foreign, *see* Foreign Waters
Waterways Museum, Stoke Bruern 342
Waterworks, Folly Bridge 157-8
weather 127, 131-2, 182, 205, 294, 323
weels, weelers, weelmakers 14, 47, 65, 68,
    139
weir-ham 2, 40, 54
weirs (*see also* locks) 42-4, 67, 108, 111,
    117, 120, 132
Welshmen, Oxford 97n., 172
Westminster School 298
wharves, *see under individual names*
Whigs 24, 172-5
Whitchurch 93, 189, 192
Whitehouse & Son, canal carriers 225
wife-sales 182-3
Wilden Ferry 185
wild-fowling 70
Wilts & Berks Canal 230, 240, 306
Windsor 135
wives 167 (*see also* canal boatwomen)
Woodstock 345
Worcester 9, 60
Worcester College 1, 31
work 14-15, 66-73, 129-36, 202-6, 247,
    331-5, 284
Wolvercote 38, 63, 68, 108, 187, 274-5,
    284
Wytham Woods 33, 124-5

Y.M.C.A., the 304